The
People
of the
Book

Drama,
Fellowship,
& Religion

The
People
of the
Book

Samuel C. Heilman
with a new preface by the author

Transaction Publishers
New Brunswick (U.S.A.) and London (U.K.)

Second printing 2002
New material this edition copyright © 2002 by Transaction Publishers,
New Brunswick, New Jersey. Originally published in 1983 by The University of Chicago Press.

This book is printed on acid-free paper that meets the American National Standard for Permanence of Paper for Printed Library Materials.

Library of Congress Catalog Number: 00-064813
ISBN: 0-7658-0747-5 (paper)
Printed in the United States of America

Library of Congress Cataloging-in-Publication Data

Heilman, Samuel C.
    The people of the book : drama, fellowship, and religion / Samuel
C. Heilman ; with a new preface by the author.
        p.cm.
Originally published: Chicago : University of Chicago Press, c1983.
With new pref.
Includes bibliographical references (p.) and index.
ISBN 0-7658-0747-5 (pbk.: alk. paper)
    1. Orthodox Judaism—United States. 2. Jewish religious education of adults—United States. 3. Talmud—Study and teaching (Continuing education)—United States. 4. Talmud Torah (Judaism)
I. Title.

BM205 .H43 2000
296.6'8—dc21

00-064813

*To my Mother and Father
Lucia and Henry Heilman
and my four sons
Adam, Uriel, Avram, and Jonah
If I inquire into my Jewishness, I do so because of them*

The Torah is acquired by: study, attentive listening, ordered speech, sentimental understanding, awe, reverence, humility, joy, purity, attendance on scholars, fellowship, discussion with students, sitting patiently with Scripture and Mishna, moderation in business, moderation in worldly pursuits, moderation in pleasure, moderation in sleep, moderation in conversation, moderation in merriment, patience, kindheartedness, faith in its wisdom, acceptance, knowing one's place . . . , asking and answering, listening and adding to one's knowledge, learning in order to teach and in order to practice . . .

Tractate, Avot 6:6

CONTENTS

ACKNOWLEDGMENTS

There are a number of institutions and individuals whom I would like to thank for their help during the preparation and writing of this book. Queens College of the City University of New York, my home base, provided me with the necessary time and support services to complete my work. While I was in Israel, the Hebrew University of Jerusalem graciously took me in as a visiting professor and treated me as well or better than they would anyone on their regular faculty, and I thank them for it. The especially warm reception I received from the Department of Sociology and Social Anthropology there and their wonderful administrative assistant, Sabina, was likewise deeply appreciated.

For their financial assistance for a project that less imaginative institutions might never have funded, I thank the Memorial Foundation for Jewish Culture, the Research Foundation of the City University of New York, the American Council of Learned Societies, and especially the National Endowment for the Humanities which gave me three separate awards that made up the blood and tissue of my finances during much of the time I worked on this book.

There were many people, friends and scholars—true people of the book— who read all or part of the chapters of this book. I have not always incorporated their advice, but I always appreciated their support and interest. They are Steven M. Cohen, Shlomo Deshen, Joshua Fishman, Renée C. Fox, Erving Goffman,

Barbara Kirshenblatt-Gimblett, Dean Savage, Lauren Seiler, and Eviatar Zerubavel. Carol Diament, absorbed as she was in the completion of her doctoral dissertation, graciously took time to help me trace Jewish literary sources.

For their help in the preparation of the manuscript, I wish to thank especially the women of the Word Processing Division at Queens College; my student assistant Teri Neufeld and my administrative aides Elaine Silver and Claire Semel who saw to many of the last tedious details.

To the people in the various study groups I observed, who opened their circles, books, and minds to my project and to me, I owe a most profound thanks. I hope they will view the results with understanding.

Finally, I give special thanks to my sons—Adam, Uriel, and Avram—who were patient with a father who often left them in order to study Talmud and who sometimes stayed locked in his study typing instead of playing with or reading to them. To my wife Ellin, who not only encouraged me to start studying Jewish texts again but kept me writing and tolerated my long hours in the study circle or at the typewriter, who read every word of this book more times than either I or she care to mention, I owe my deepest thanks.

PREFACE TO THE
TRANSACTION EDITION

Almost twenty years ago, when I began the field work that led to the book contained between these covers, I was animated by one central question: what was it about the ritualized Jewish study of ancient sacred texts—and in particular, Talmud—that had managed to attract and hold, not only previous, but current generations of Jews who spent many hours of their lives laboring over these pages? It was a question that grew out of both my previous sociological and anthropological research into synagogue life as well as out of my personal experience as a Jew. Both of these convinced me that only an understanding of the inner life of those who pursued this sort of study as an avocation, as a part of their lives, would provide an answer. I believed then, as I do still today, that the best way to gain access to this inner life was by means of participant-observation, or what the filmmaker, François Truffaut, once called "verification through life." So that is what I did. I joined such study groups and pursued the ritualized study of Talmud—*lernen*—as did those whose inner lives I sought to enter and motivations I wished to comprehend. What follows here is a thick ethnographic description of what I found.

It is in the nature of thick description, as Clifford Geertz tells us, not only to provide the details of what happens, but also to be "interpretive," to focus those interpretations on "the flow of social discourse," and to capture and articulate what is actually "said" or expressed so that the description "perusable" by others.[1] Accordingly, much of what follows here is both detailed and interpretive, concerned more with what goes on socially in the course of the ritualized study than with the substance of the texts themselves. Some have argued that in thus focussing my attention, I may have missed the essence of the appeal: the subject of the Talmud itself. Simply stated, these critics suggest that the uncomplicated answer to my question would have been that Talmud, like so much else that is part of the sacred Jewish canon that is often called simply "Torah," is inherently attractive. But, such an answer, I believe, begs the question. Torah, and no less the Talmud, have been understood differently by each of those who have over the generations reviewed it, as the commentaries which have become appended to these texts make obvious. Moreover, while it may be that the texts themselves are in and of themselves fascinating and engaging, this at best accounts for those who have pursued Jewish study as a vocation. For those who do it as appendage to their lives, however, for whom it is an avocation, for whom it has become a part of their personal inner life and not simply the framework for full time occupation, the attraction is more complicated and comprehended more fully via the more subtle perspectives of social anthropology and the tools of ethnographic description. These allow us to understand how different generations of Jews have been able to discover in the circumstances of *lernen* something that is socially meaningful and personally engaging. My book tries to explain the how, and in that to also provide the why, of ritualized avocational Jewish study. I do this—to borrow once again from Geertz—by drawing "large conclusions from small, but very densely textured, facts; to support broad assertions about the role of culture in the construction of collective life by engaging them exactly with complex specifics."[2] This book takes the reader into the minutia of a class debate, the little dramas of puzzling redundancies, failures to understand a small piece of text, the course of a digression, and even into the language switching, cadence and inflection of participants' word play—all in order to explore and explain what is this time-honored occupation with Talmud. In a sense, this book is talmudic, for the Talmud itself draws large conclusions from small, but very densely textured facts or narratives.

At the time this book was written, the kind of Talmud study circles I described were, for the most part, found in the precincts of Orthodox Jewry, a parochial backwater in the contemporary Jewish stream, and even here there were only a minority who engaged in it. Since that time, there has been a kind of explosion of interest in avocational Talmud study. The growth of the *daf yomi* movement, a program of coordinated daily study of a single folio of the Babylonian Talmud throughout the world, has been remarkable. Celebrations of the completion of the seven-and-a-half year cycle within which all the volumes are studied have drawn tens of thousands in America, Israel, and Europe.

Moreover, when I undertook this study, the participants in such study circles were overwhelmingly Orthodox Jewish men. But in the years since, the population so engaged has broadened. A simple search on the Internet reveals countless Talmud study groups associated with Jews of all denominations, linked to synagogues of all types or federations and Jewish community centers, and even some that meet independently in office complexes. Consider the following, reported in *The Los Angeles Times*: "A dozen Jewish lawyers and judges this week completed a 2 1/2-year-long tractate of Talmud, meeting in monthly sessions to study ethical lessons contained in Pirkei Avot, or'Ethics of the Fathers.'" This was an event that "grew out of a lunchtime Talmudic group that met at the Rutan & Tucker law firm in Costa Mesa...."[3] Or, consider the report in *The New York Times* that recounts the experience of at least fifty non-Orthodox Jews who studied Talmud in Manhattan conference rooms and suburban living rooms, and who found that such study provided them with more than simple instruction. In the words of one participant, Aaron Priest, a literary agent: "I can walk out of my office with so many problems. By the time the class is over, I've forgotten all about them."[4] Or another story from the American Midwest: "Downtown Columbus, [Ohio] a place to work, shop and be entertained, is becoming a place to study religious documents, pray and talk about how religion and the workplace can be reconciled. Once a month in a Downtown law firm, Rabbi Gary Huber of Congregation Beth Tikvah, a Reform synagogue, meets with 15 people to study the Talmud, sacred Jewish writings.

"'We have been doing this since the fall. The group consists of professional people who work in offices clustered in the Downtown area. We have stockbrokers, accountants, attorneys. We have a variety of other professional people, too,'the rabbi said.'We study the ancient texts but also have a lot of discussion. We have looked at theology and interpersonal relationships. It represents a spiritual break. I think it is meeting a deep need when you are in pressures or stresses of the workday.'"

These are just three reports. Yet whether on the East coast or the West, or in between, and wherever else Jews are found, such Talmud study groups are to be found in growing number. Whatever I discovered in my original study, one wonders if today's new study groups have likewise encountered these attractions or whether there are new fascinations that tie them to this activity.

While my book describes a group that contained women in it ultimately falling apart, in the years since, the experience of *lernen* has increasingly become part of the Jewish woman's life. Many of today's Jewish women are passionate about the study of Torah, Mishna and even the intricacies of Gemara—the heart of Talmud—which were once thought suitable exclusively for the province of male minds. Six thousand of them appeared at New York's celebration of the completion of the *daf yomi* cycle. Many young women now meet regularly in a wide variety of schools and communities to share such study experiences—albeit often around Jewish texts other than the Talmud. According to a report in the *Jerusalem Post,* "the past fifteen years have seen the number of advanced Jewish-study institutes for Orthodox women in Israel—called *midrashot*—shoot up from less than a handful to more than a dozen, with many more already on their way."[5] Reports of women's study circles abound.[6] And a number of books have explored aspects of them.[7]

Whether these increasing encounters by both the non-Orthodox and women with ritualized, avocational Jewish study represent a cognate or contrary experience from that of the men I have described here is a matter for the contemporary reader to decide. Yet, one hopes that the ideas and approaches suggested in this volume will still inform our understanding of the ways in which the inner life and the social circumstances within which Jewish study occurs become meaningful parts of the experience.

Beyond that, this book will, I believe, still speak to those who are searching for a way to observe how the ethnographer can move from a consideration of externals to the revelation of how inner life is affected. Even for those readers who are not particularly interested in the specific question of avocational Talmud study, this book still provides a model of how the social anthropologist and ethnographer looks at behavior and can use it to point beyond itself to larger cultural and social issues. As my late teacher and mentor, Erving Goffman, showed all of us in his many books, we can learn a great deal about the fundamental character of interaction by exploring its details. While he was fond of using illustrations from a wide array of often exotic situations to demonstrate this point, I have used a particular community and type of setting to do some of the same.

Samuel C. Heilman

Notes

1. Clifford Geertz, "Thick Description: Toward an Interpretive Theory of Culture," in *The Interpretation of Cultures* (New York: basic Books, 1973), pp. 20-21.
2. "Thick Description," p. 28.
3. March 27, 1999
4. October 12, 1997, Sunday, Late Edition—Final, Section 14WC; Page 1; Column 3; Westchester Weekly Desk
5. *The Jerusalem Post*, April 2, 1999, Friday, FEATURES; Pg. 3B, "No more Yentls," by Calev Ben-David
6. See for example, "Suburbanization of Orthodox Jews," by Elsa Brenner *The New York Times*, April 6, 1997, Sunday, Late Edition—Final, Section 13WC; Page 1; Column 5; Westchester Weekly Desk.
7. See for example, Debra Kaufman, *Rachel's Daughters* (New Brunswick: Rutgers University Press, 1991) and Maurie Sacks, *Active Voices: Women in Jewish Culture* (Chicago: University of Illinois, 1995) and Tamar El Or, *Be Pessach Haba: Nashim ve Oryanot baTzionot Hadatit.* (Tel Aviv:Am Oved.1999.)

The People of
the Book

1
LOOKING INTO "LERNEN" AN INTRODUCTION INTO THE TALMUD STUDY CIRCLE

If I ask myself whether I ever had what one might call an Erlebnis *[a living experience] in my relationship to things Jewish, I can give only one answer: it was the thrill I experienced on a Sunday in April 1913 when [my rabbi] Bleichrode taught me to read the first page of the Talmud in the original, and later that same day the exegesis by Rashi, the greatest of all Jewish commentators, of the first verses of Genesis. It was my first traditional and direct encounter, not with the Bible, but with Jewish substance in tradition.*

GERSHOM SCHOLEM, "Jewish Awakening,"
in *From Berlin to Jerusalem*

This is a book about Orthodox Jews, all of whom live in the modern world and some of whom also consider themselves to be part of it. It is not, however, about all Orthodox Jews but rather about those who regularly spend some of their free time engaged in the traditional Jewish practice of *lernen*, the eternal review and ritualized study of sacred Jewish texts. These are people who return again and again to the pages of the Bible or the prophets, the Psalms or to codebooks of Jewish law, to mystical tracts or to the Talmud. Long after the world detailed in the pages of this literature has faded in the memory of most of their kin and when *lernen* has ceased to be the sole legitimate activity for the Jewish male or a primary source of escape from the vagaries of everyday life, these Jews remain attached to their texts. They are, indeed, the "People of the Book."

Although Judaism has for generations derived its identity and justification from its books—the book or scroll, more than the picture or statue, became the preferred emblem of the diaspora Jew—the influences of the outside world, the exigencies of physical survival, and the imperatives of involvement in modern civil society have over the years turned Jews away from the traditional house of study. *Lernen*, a spiritual meditation on and lifelong review of Jewish books, became exchanged for learning, an intellectual acquisition of all knowledge, and for earning, economic and material survival.

Those who saw themselves as defenders of the faith and anchored to the ways of the past, Jews who by the late nineteenth and early twentieth centuries came to be called Orthodox, did not wholeheartedly take part in this exchange. They kept on *lernen* in their free time, even as some of them became more and more engaged in other pursuits.

To be sure there were those, particularly in Ashkenaz, the European Jewish community in which the idea of *lernen* bloomed and was celebrated, who took up Jewish study as a career. These were men—they were always men, for Jewish study was traditionally considered beyond the realm of the possible or permissible for women—who entered the yeshiva or academy of higher Jewish learning and sought to become virtuosi of the texts.

Among them, those who excelled would become rabbis, adjudicators or *poskim*, and scholars—the elite of the Jewish world in the days before emancipation. Always a minority, such men whose entire life was spent in the pages of the sacred texts did

1

not so much meditate upon or review the pages as they did probe, analyze, and work through the texts to make them fit into a legal framework for Jewish life. But if the Torah, the corpus of law and lore whose source was believed to be God, was for the men of the yeshiva a field to be systematically explored, for the rank and file, the everyday Jews, it was a field in which to wander in love and in leisure. For these laymen the Torah was a "tree of life" to be held onto with the heart as much as the mind.

I first became interested in the people who still pursued *lernen* not as a vocation in the yeshiva but as an avocation in their homes, synagogue study halls, or social clubs during the years I was preparing my study of modern Orthodox synagogue life. My observations in that part of the synagogue which was the house of study made me realize that there were still people for whom *lernen* was not only a félt religious obligation but also appealing and engaging. These were for the most part men who *lernt* in the after-hours of their lives. On evenings, weekends, Sabbaths, or holy days, when different people might be otherwise engaged, these Jews would assemble together and with a teacher—commonly a rabbi—occupy themselves with the holy books of their people. I wondered why.

From early on I realized that, for many of the Jews I was observing, this experience was more than simply the assimilation of knowledge. For one thing, many of those I watched had been *lernen* for years but seemed still to be unable to review the texts on their own or recall very much of the content in front of them. For another, even those who had *lernt* a lot and displayed an erudite familiarity with the texts took apparent great pleasure in repeating what they had already studied rather than looking for the new and the as-yet-unknown. The best *lernen*, it seemed, was the sort which reiterated what everyone already knew. The best questions to ask were those the texts themselves asked; and the best if not the only true answers were those already written on the pages open before one. Finally, while the members of the study circles I observed ostensibly gathered in the house of study to get the wisdom of Judaism from the books into their minds, they often spent more time in class getting their feelings about Judaism off their chests. Clearly much more than learning or the accumulation of information about Jewish texts was going on. I wanted to find out what that something more was.

Following the publication of my *Synagogue Life,* in which I had tentatively described the house of study and its activities as an extension of the synagogue and the rituals of worship, I went back to the study circle for a more exacting look. I knew in general what I wanted to find out: why people come to *lern,* particularly in an age when such ritualized review of sacred texts seems hopelessly out of tune with contemporary normative behavior; what actually happens during *lernen* and how it may be perceived; and, finally, how it is that this activity is commonly carried out with a regular circle of others more often than alone. By answering these questions I hoped I would as well come to understand something more about those Jews who, like generations of their forebears, continue to identify and recognize themselves as people of the book. In this, I believed I might penetrate one of the essential themes of Jewish existence.

There are, as I have already suggested, various sorts of Jewish study circles. Although I shall in a subsequent chapter offer a brief history of them, for now it is enough to note that what manifestly differentiates them—at least at first analysis—is the book around whose study a circle is formed. There are Bible study circles, circles for studying Jewish codes or reviewing mystical tracts. There are groups organized to retell legends or explore Jewish ethics. And there are fellows who gather together to recite the Psalms. Among Ashkenazic Jewry, however, the most important and by now the most common is the Talmud study circle. Since the Talmud contains in it citations of Scripture, laws, legend, rabbinic discussions, and commentary, review of it can be said to subsume the activities of all other study circles. Indeed, to properly make one's way through the pages of the Talmud, a student is often required to take from his shelf his Bible, a codex of Jewish law, a Psalter, writings of the prophets, volumes of posttalmudic commentaries, and even a prayer book. Often, especially in the yeshiva, the common practice during *lernen* is to place one's volume of Talmud atop a *shtender* or lectern under which is stored a small library of supportive texts. Literally and symbolically, then, the Talmud rests upon and above the entire corpus of sacred Jewish literature.[1] Similarly, the student and teacher of Talmud sit at the top of the hierarchy of *lernen.*

There are in fact two Talmuds: the so-called Jerusalem and the Babylonian. Both contain elaborations of the Mishna, the codification of basic Jewish law, which after generations of oral trans-

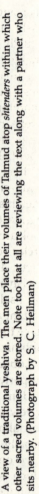

A view of a traditional yeshiva. The men place their volumes of Talmud atop *shtenders* within which other sacred volumes are stored. Note too that all are reviewing the text along with a partner who sits nearby. (Photograph by S. C. Heilman)

mission was redacted and arranged around the second century. The Jerusalem Talmud consists of the interpretations and elaborations, the so-called completion (*gemore*)* of the Mishna, as developed in the Jewish scholarly academies of the land of Israel. It was long neglected and became superseded by the far longer and more detailed Babylonian Talmud (B.T.). Containing nearly six thousand folios or double pages divided into thirty-nine tractates or volumes, the Babylonian Talmud is a series of abbreviated, almost telegraphic notes of oral discussions that the sages held about the meaning of the Mishna. Its *gemore* deals both with matters of law (*halakha*) and with lore (*aggada*). Being a record of oral debate and discussion among the sages, it is often neither concise nor systematic in its treatment of subjects. The *gemore* will often be found to move without warning from one subject to another, sometimes breaking in with narratives in the midst of legal disputation. It follows question upon question along lines of reason quite difficult to follow for those uninitiated in its style. Moreover, because the text is written in a combination of Aramaic, Hebrew, and an admixture of Greek and other loan words, its language is often difficult to understand. To add to all of this, the standard text of the Talmud is neither punctuated nor vocalized and thus hard to read. What may, for example, seem at first glance to be a statement may turn out to be either a rhetorical question or a genuine one. Similarly, two identical statements that may appear to the uninformed to be echoes of one another can in fact be properly understood as a question and answer: "The table is *covered?*" "The table *is* covered." Intonation and inflection—indeed a kind of cantillation—are often necessary for penetrating the meaning of the text.

The Babylonian Talmud, the one to which I shall refer throughout the rest of this book, was developed sometime between the third and fifth centuries (after its Jerusalem counterpart) in the great academies of Jewish study in Babylonia. It was and remains the great monument of the Jewish people's survival in exile. Separated from their land and holy places, the Jews rebuilt their identity as a people through the structure of their law and lore. In Babylonia, perhaps more than anywhere before, the People of Israel were transformed into the People of the Book. And that book was the Talmud.

*The word *gemore* is here written in an orthography which suggests the more common Yiddish pronunciation of the term.

One could hardly expect that a literary work of such vast dimensions as the Talmud would be preserved in an authoritative version in all its details. There are therefore a number of variant readings of the text, and commentators throughout the ages have tried to determine which one was most accurate, true to the oral tradition. Until the first printing of the Talmud in the late fifteenth and early sixteenth centuries, most versions were in handwritten manuscripts with a resultant plethora of variations. Ironically, the first complete Talmud was printed by a Christian, Daniel Bomberg, in Venice between 1520 and 1523. This edition determined the external form of the Talmud for all time, including the pagination which always begins with page two, the inclusion of Rashi's commentary—the work of the great Jewish exegete of fifteenth-century Europe—on the inner margin and the commentaries of the Tosafists, his disciples and kin, on the outer margin. Finally, it was this edition that set the format in which the Mishna is given first and the *gemore* following. A typical page, therefore, looks like the one shown below.

Ashkenazic or European Jews emphasize the study of Talmud. On the other hand, the Sephardic or Mediterranean Jews, while fully accepting the legal authority and religious importance of the Talmud, did not develop a tradition of reviewing it. Rather they were more prone to emphasize the review and recitation of the Zohar and other mystical tracts or to recite the Psalms as part of their ritualized study. This process they came to call "*iyun*."[2] *Iyun* connotes a kind of meditation in which recitation of the sacred texts may be sufficient for the fulfillment of the imperative to study.

Lernen, the Ashkenazic sort of study, however, requires something else. Its process can be divided into four primary steps or moves: recitation, translation, explanation, and discussion. Briefly, the first of these consists of an oral reading of the text, usually by one person who is cued or echoed by the others who are with him. Commonly in a study circle, the rabbi is the one who recites. He is called the *Rav* or the *Magid Shiur*, the narrator of the class. In many circles recitations come close to chant, a sing-song or *gemore-nign*—as insiders refer to it—whose rising and falling cadences help disambiguate the text. The tune which helps to vo-

A page from the Babylonian Talmud. Note the framing commentaries surrounding the core text which is in bold print. (Photograph by S. C. Heilman)

calize and punctuate the page resonates with many of the cadences of Yiddish, a language which at one time became closely associated with Talmud study among Ashkenazic Jews. Indeed, the word *"lernen"* is itself Yiddish.

Translation, the second step, became especially necessary when Jews no longer were fluent in the primary languages of the Tal-

mud, but it was always part of the necessary expansion of the
sketchy text. While the translation languages for Talmud study
have changed from place to place and generation to generation
according to the vernacular of the students, Yiddish and Hebrew
as well as Aramaic have remained embedded in the language of
lernen in ways I shall later make clear.

Explanation, the third move, is the effort to briefly clarify the
meanings and implications of what has been recited. During explanation, *lerners* identify questions and refine answers. They
organize a text, determining where one subject or *inyan* ends and
another begins. They frame matters, detailing what the Talmud
is trying or has tried to do. Finally, they provide short glosses or
footnotes to what they have just recited.

Discussion, the last move, allows for the broadest possible consideration of the text. Mirroring the give-and-take of the sages
quoted in the Talmud, the *lerners* refer to parallels in other sacred
Jewish literature, review supporting commentaries and related
codices of Jewish law, evaluate the significance of what they have
read and debate its conclusions, digress to tell stories or ask and
answer questions sometimes only remotely related to the issues
on the page before them, and in general stretch the boundaries
of what may properly be considered *lernen*. In short, during discussion the text often becomes, as I shall later demonstrate, a
*pre*text for conversation about a variety of things. The students'
concerns and words merge with the issues and language of the
Talmud they review. This is the ultimate step of the process, the
point at which life and *lernen* become one.

SIX CIRCLES: FROM AMERICA TO JERUSALEM

There were many reasons for the decision to focus my attentions
specifically on the Talmud study circle. First was the already cited
fact that Talmud stands at the pinnacle of all *lernen* and literally
as well as symbolically subsumes other kinds of Jewish study: to
look at talmudic review is to see a little of other types of ritual
study as well. Second, the relatively consistent and standard
moves of the process offer instrumental advantages. Observations
can be organized easily around the four basic moves, and various
study circles thus can be compared more easily. Third, Talmud

lernen is one of the most common forms of avocational study in the contemporary Orthodox Jewish environment, the locus of my observations. What was once effectively limited to the elite scholars and rabbis has, in a decimated Jewish world after Auschwitz and in the face of the threats of assimilation, become open to all those who would participate. While there are various levels of study—some groups demanding a greater background in Talmud than others, some being more contemporary in their orientations than others, and so on—in principle, any Jew who today wants to join a *shiur* (class in Talmud) will not be categorically shut out. This advantage of access was also useful.

As a Jew having a familiarity with and closeness to Orthodoxy, I had little difficulty in finding and joining such circles. Throughout my life I, like other Orthodox Jews, had been exposed to the various Talmud study groups that distinguished the communities in which I lived. Wherever an Orthodox synagogue had succeeded in establishing itself, a Talmud study circle was sure to be found somewhere nearby. Where the Orthodox community was dense, supporting a number of synagogues, it would also foster the rise of several such circles. Where, on the contrary, it was sparse, there might be only one, closely aligned with the synagogue. In most places, however, the imperative to study sacred books—Torah—was as strongly felt as the need to worship. Indeed, the two were often seen as stemming from the same religious spring. As the Talmud itself puts it: "In the place of study, there one should pray."

Embracing the native-as-stranger approach in which one turns an eye on the familiar as if it were novel and strange, taking nothing for granted while at the same time making use of the subtle understanding that only an insider can have, I began to examine study groups that I would join. My approach was that of the participant-observer, one who learns by watching while doing. This method, which I had successfully used in my examination of Orthodox synagogue life could—I continued to believe—best allow me to fathom the meaning of *lernen*. Not only would I be able to see action as an insider, but I would also be able to look into myself and my feelings to discover something of its subjective aspects. If there was joy or pain, excitement or tension, triumph or boredom to be felt during *lernen*, I would only discover it by doing it myself.

During the course of my Jewish education I had never excelled in Talmud nor had I ever felt any great fondness for it. I was, however, always curious about what so many of the people I knew saw in and felt for it and why Orthodox custom and Jewish tradition placed such a heavy emphasis on it. The Jew in me knew what was supposed to draw people to Talmud: it was the "glory" of Judaism, the "source of all wisdom." The social anthropologist in me, however, needed different answers.

At first I believed that I could follow the pattern of my synagogue study. I would simply select one typical study circle, join it, and draw my conclusions from a comprehensive series of observations. I had already collected much material from my observations in "Dudley Meadows," where the synagogue I had described in my first book was located. While some of my notes from there were useful as background, I soon realized that they were nowhere nearly sufficient; *lernen* had during those earlier observations been of only marginal interest to me. Searching about for another place to study since I had left Dudley Meadows, I came upon a community I shall call "Smotra."* Although most of what needs to be known about Smotra will come out in my description of *lernen* there, a few preliminary words are in order.

In many ways Smotra is similar to Dudley Meadows. Like the latter, it is an essentially suburban community within easy commuting distance of a large metropolis. In both places, Orthodox Jews are in the minority vis-à-vis the general American population and the local Jewish one. In both places, the kind of Orthodoxy practiced is modernist in character. That is, the people consider themselves at once steadfastly committed to the beliefs and practices of Orthodox Judaism while remaining attached to many of the values and ideals of the world outside their Jewish environment. They believe they can be both parochial and cosmopolitan at once, good Jews and good Americans, anchored to the timeless traditions of their faith and adaptable to the changing demands of the secular world.

At the time of observations there were two Orthodox synagogues in Smotra but essentially one Orthodox community. The older of the two, Knesseth Jacob, is the oldest synagogue in Smo-

*This and all other names used hereafter to refer to people and places I observed are pseudonyms.

tra and the county. Founded in the days when the city had not yet become a suburb but was simply a resort town, it remains nominally Orthodox in its liturgical format and is led by a rabbi, Solomon Gafny, who places himself firmly within the boundaries of traditional Judaism. Few of the synagogue members, however, remain similarly committed. In many cases they have retained ties to the synagogue either because their families have always belonged, because the building is close to their homes, or, as is the case among many, because they feel a warmth for and spiritual attachment to the rabbi.

The second synagogue, Ahavat Israel, about three miles away, contains a little more than fifty families, the overwhelming majority of whom come from an Orthodox background and are generally observant. It is younger, with nearly three-quarters of its members having children of elementary school age. Most of those children attend a nearby Orthodox day school or yeshiva. The adults are for the most part college educated, and more than half the men have advanced professional training as do many of the women. By all measures, these Jews have achieved conventionally successful careers in American society and have become part of that world. There are doctors, lawyers, businessmen, storekeepers, and college professors. Their children are as likely—or perhaps more likely—to attend an Ivy League or state college as the more parochial Yeshiva University.

Between the two congregations there is one Talmud study circle. Originally formed as a result of some of the lay members of Ahavat Israel joining with some of their counterparts from Knesseth Jacob and asking Rabbi Gafny for leadership and instruction, the group began at first to meet in various members' homes. Ostensibly meant to symbolize the communal rather than synagogal nature of the circle, this practice lasted for only a year, after which the group decided to meet in the library of Knesseth Jacob. In this way, the men argued, the entire community would feel free to attend. Holding classes in private homes, some had believed, might prevent newcomers from joining in the *lernen* because they either might feel uncomfortable in the home of someone they did not know or have difficulty in finding the class on any given occasion.

The shift in location did result for a time in some additions to the group. In the end, however, the circle never grew larger than fifteen men and sometimes shrunk to as few as seven or eight.

Still, held in the library, the class achieved perhaps a closer identification with the books which lined its shelves. The setting somehow seemed more appropriate to the task of *lernen*. I had joined
the circle at Knesseth Jacob first as a participant, answering the
call of ages of faith and the promptings of my wife who believed
it to be my religious duty to *lern*. By the beginning of the second
year, however, my research plans became crystallized and I also
became an observer. I decided to bring a tape recorder to class—
something I had failed to do in Dudley Meadows—in order to
collect a comprehensive oral record of all the goings-on. The tape
recorder was already a recognized feature of the setting since one
member of the group whose background in Talmud had been
weak had begun taping each session, ostensibly to review the
material covered at home. My tape recorder was a bit more suspect
since everyone knew I had already written a study of a synagogue
of which I had been a member. The idea of my observing them as
a social anthropologist was initially greeted with some ambivalence. On the one hand, people were flattered by the idea that
I might see their behavior as sufficiently significant to spend my
time thinking and writing about it. On the other, not everyone
was certain that what I would see and later describe was what
they would want shown to the world at large. In time, they
learned to ignore the machine and my research interests.

"Just make sure that no one will be able to identify me," the
rabbi once said when I told of progress in my writing. He however
never prohibited me from going forward with my observations,
even after I had shown him some of my written descriptions and
analysis. Indeed he, perhaps more than anyone else among those
I have included in this book, served as a sounding board for my
ideas and conclusions.

After another year and a half, I began to put together my notes
on what I was seeing and hearing. The extraordinarily comprehensive record of talk I had gathered, together with my supporting field notes always written upon my return home from the
circle, made me focus upon speaking. I became struck by the
participants' play with words. I listened to them switch from
Hebrew and Aramaic in the text to English and to Yiddish. I
discovered the extent to which one language might interfere with
another. People whose speech outside of class was in perfect
American English during class sounded like immigrants from
Europe. Their syntax became fractured; their cadences were

marked with the distinctive rise-fall of Yiddish and *gemore-nign.*
I began to see patterns in the shifting. These patterns disclosed
a great deal about the people, their feelings for the books they
reviewed, and the character of their Jewishness in general.
Through their speaking, I believed I could make out the duality
of their lives as modern Americans and traditional Orthodox Jews.

I wondered if what I was seeing and hearing was an artifact of
my setting: Did all *lerners* in every circle reveal the preoccupations
of their minds as they reviewed the sacred Talmud texts? Was
social and cultural reality bound to show through *lernen,* or was
this particular to the settings I had chosen to observe?

To answer these questions I looked for a time at other American
Talmud study circles. Wherever I went I found echoes of what I
had already heard in Smotra and Dudley Meadows. Moreover,
moving from study circle to study circle in America was a time-
consuming process since most were aligned with some local community, and an accurate picture of each required a greater cultural
competence and participation in the life of that community than
I could gain in the time I had. Finally, I remained uncertain of my
capacity to see new things in America.

It was a curious dilemma. On the one hand, I had discovered
nuances of *lernen* I had never thought about or seen before, a
kind of speech play new to me. At the same time, my subjective
involvement convinced me that more went on in the circle than
this kind of play with sounds and words—but I could not see it
very clearly. Every new observation led me back to something I
had already deciphered. I needed to go elsewhere.

There were many reasons for my choosing to go to Jerusalem,
not the least of which was my deeply felt conviction that it represented the spiritual center of the Jewish people. I wanted to see
how this former center of a Temple cult had been transformed by
the People of the Book. To be sure, from as early as the fifteenth
century organized study circles, started in great measure by the
mystical Kabbalists, had been reported in Jerusalem. But I wanted
to see the contemporary scene and circle.

Jerusalem and Israel represented at once a different cultural
milieu from the one I had been observing and yet were still Jewish
enough to offer some continuity for me. The Hebrew vernacular,
in which I was fluent, might nevertheless force me to look beyond
words. For all my familiarity with Hebrew, I realized right away
that I would not be able to follow the subtle speech shifts in Israel

in the same way that I had been able to in my native America. This, I hoped, would lead me to fresh insights and discoveries which would not only enlighten me about *lernen* in Jerusalem but reflect back on what I had seen in Smotra and elsewhere in America. In the end, while I discovered real differences between the circles in America and those in Jerusalem, I found important and undeniable similarities.

Armed with a sabbatical year that provided time for fieldwork and grants that helped in my financial support, I went to Jerusalem. As had been the case in America, I was still primarily interested in the after-hours, avocational study circles where Talmud is pursued without career motives and not as a matter of formal curriculum but as an extension of everyday life.

In Jerusalem such circles abounded. With its dozens of synagogues, in each of which could be found at least one and often several classes in Talmud, its social clubs and home study groups, this city provided me with an embarrassment of riches beyond my wildest dreams. I felt a bit like a child in a candy store, not knowing where to turn first. Should I go to those apparently exotic sections of the city inhabited by the so-called *eda haredit* (pious community), where men in black hats and frockcoats with faces rimmed by earlocks and beards studied Talmud as their forebears in Europe had for generations? Or, in deference to my personal proclivities and background, should I try to join circles composed of the modern Orthodox where I would feel most at home? Perhaps a random selection would be best, with my simply entering a synagogue around the time of the evening prayers and waiting for the inevitable class to begin. In the end, I chose all three approaches and also sought out others.

For several weeks, I went everywhere I could, spoke to any Jew who would talk to me about where I could find a circle to join, and rapidly became overwhelmed. There was just too much to see and join. I remember often walking to or from one Talmud class and being able to hear the distinctive recitation and conversation of another through an open window or doorway I passed. Men carrying large volumes of Talmud would pass me on the street, on their way to or from some class; and it was all I could do to stop myself from following them or asking where it was they went and if I could join.

In Jerusalem the synagogue is not the only center of religious or even communal life as is the case in America and other diaspora

Jewish settlements. While many of the members of a particular study circle might worship in the same synagogue, it is not uncommon for people to pray in one place and with one group and *lern* with another somewhere else. The circle creates its own boundaries and life. This was an enormous advantage for me since I could join a circle without having simultaneously to move into a specific neighborhood or community. Here I could enter study groups in ways that had never been possible for me in the context of American Jewish life.

Still, as I have said, my wealth of sites was burdening me with more information than I could assimilate. Deciding that I had to cut down the number of groups I joined, I started to select from those I had already participated in and which had accepted me and my tape recorder. While I occasionally visited different groups after my selections had been completed, the five Jerusalem circles which I settled on and the one in Smotra served as the core of my field research.

Although study circles remain in principle open to all Jewish comers, I soon realized that every group was surrounded by some barrier or at least threshold over which one needed to pass in order to be fully inside. In America being a member of the synagogue community was often enough. In Jerusalem, the requirements were a bit more subtle. Gradually I discovered that one had to become separated from the general community and became morally incorporated into the *khavruse* or fellowship of *lerners*. I shall have something to say about this process in a later chapter. For now, I simply point out that continuing presence at circle meetings and active participation in the discussions of *lernen* are the sine qua non of moral belonging.

This belonging, moreover, requires one at least temporarily to share the group's sense of what is significant and important—a common cultural viewpoint and social reality. Members must be ready to become interested in the same things during the class, or at least recast their own concerns into an expressive form that arouses the interest of the group. Often this means presenting everything as a gloss on the Talmud. They must likewise be willing to be bound up by the particular rules of discourse indigenous to the circle. They must share an ethos and world view, and they must feel spiritually in tune so that during class one person's religious sensibilities are not dissonant with another's. Once this kind of association and fellowship is established, it is very hard to dissolve. Joining a circle was perhaps easier than leaving one, as I discovered when I tried to disengage from some.

From my first contacts with the people who formed the circles I joined, I tried to explain the duality of my role as participant-observer, to clarify the fact that I was there to study them as well as to be with them. Most of those to whom I explained this, however, chose to view me simply as a Jew interested in their kind of *lernen*. Perhaps the moral demands of fellowship militated against their acceptance of the notion that I could keep myself in some way distant from the group's common task and charm. Maybe they felt an ideological and religious need to support the idea that the only legitimate purpose for anyone joining their *lernen* was the fulfillment of what they perceived to be the divinely inspired obligation to study Torah. Whatever its source, this attitude made my penetration into the center of the circle much easier. It also made my leaving more painful.

The five groups into which I settled represented a spectrum of types. On the one extreme was the group meeting in the Kahal Reyim synagogue. I had come to this group on the recommendation of a Hasidic rabbi whom I had met in the Jewish quarter of the Old City, the ancient walled section of Jerusalem. He told me that at Kahal Reyim I would find one of the most fertile places of *lernen* since the synagogue was a veritable maze of chambers, each of which had its set of worshippers and classes. Indeed, I found one or another room of the synagogue almost always full, with the voices of talmudic review or prayer coming from every corner. The group into which I entered, in part because I had turned to the right instead of the left upon walking in the door, assembled each evening after the conclusion of the evening prayers and was composed of men for whom the contemporary world was something to escape from and the precincts of tradition were a welcome haven. Carried on in Yiddish, the class dealt primarily with those tractates which detailed the long-abandoned practices of Temple sacrifice. For the hour or so they met each evening, the *lerners* at Kahal Reyim would revel in the images and ideas of the ancient past, leaving twentieth-century Israel and their workday lives outside. To be sure, these were not men who obsessively or schizophrenically cut themselves off from their temporal surroundings. They knew very well where they were and remained aware of the times in which they lived; and occasionally they even added a gloss or joke about contemporary life, commenting on matters ranging from the sorry state of the Israeli economy to the search for alternative sources of energy. But these references to the contemporary world were disturbances, reminders of mundane reality rather than celebrations of it, and the group never lingered on these topics as would their more modern counterparts in other circles.

Led by Rabbi Moses, a religious functionary of the *eda haredit* and overseer of ritual baths, the group was made up in the main of men from the working class. There were some shopkeepers, but there were also peddlers, factory workers, and pensioners. Yet in spite of their relatively low station in the world outside the class, during it they displayed all the majesty, erudition, and competence of talmudists. They knew the texts they reviewed almost by heart, and hardly a line would be recited without someone in addition to Rabbi Moses displaying a flash of recognition or offering some scholarly gloss.

My competence in Yiddish was not sufficient to allow me to follow every turn of phrase or syntactic nuance during class as I had at Smotra. But, with this line of sight cut off, I began to see other aspects of *lernen* I had never before seen. What they were I shall describe in subsequent chapters. Suffice it to say here that I became aware, more than ever before, of the social dimensions of *lernen*, of the role which fellowship plays in what happens. These men came together to review Talmud, but they also came together simply in order to share one another's company and repeat the familiar lines of a book they loved in common. I was younger than all of those in the class and clearly from another cultural milieu, yet the men accepted me and soon got used to my presence. As for my tape recorder, it charmed them to think I was immortalizing them since they remained certain I would never erase the "holy words of Torah." After their initial curiosity and amusement that I should find them and their *lernen* anthropologically interesting, they soon looked upon me as just another element of the circle; and I got the impression that their classes were not carried on for my benefit but for theirs.

Twice a week after leaving Kahal Reyim in the early evening, I made my way to a larger synagogue in another neighborhood. At Beit Rachel, as this place was called, I joined a group of nine men who with their teacher, Rabbi Horowitz, a man who during the day taught in a religious high school, regularly reviewed the Talmud. The circle which was composed of a tailor, factory fore-

man, a part-time window dresser, a small-time contractor, a school
teacher, a bookkeeper, and several pensioners, was one of several
that met in the synagogue. Not all of those in the circle worshipped at Beit Rachel, but all lived in its neighborhood. The
classes were carried on in the Hebrew vernacular, but frequently
the men would revert to Yiddish, a language they all spoke
fluently. As men in their fifties, sixties, and seventies, they could
still identify with a time when Yiddish was the sound of the
Jewish people. In contrast to those at Kahal Reyim, these *lerners*
usually did not chant their recitations. Sometimes, however, they
could fall into a sing-song that, like their Yiddish, echoed the
sound of more traditionalist circles.

The neighborhood in which Beit Rachel stood was more affluent
than the one near Kahal Reyim. Still, it was not the best part of
town, and the synagogue had been largely forsaken by the young
in favor of other more recently organized congregations. Those
who still worshipped at Beit Rachel were older than the congre-
gants of other synagogues nearby; they were the ones who felt
a loyalty to the institution in which they had spent most of their
lives.

In a corner of the large sanctuary which could hold perhaps
five hundred worshippers, I found a small bulletin board announcing the times of various Talmud classes. Of the several I
attended in the early weeks of my fieldwork, one was sufficiently
different from the Kahal Reyim group to offer an appealing variety
of observations. I have already mentioned the differences in recitational style. There were other distinctions as well. Unlike the
Kahal Reyim group that almost never exceeded its regular hour
of study, the men of Beit Rachel went at their *lernen* at a far more
leisurely pace. Often they would linger over their books for close
to two hours, during which they might lapse into gossip or folktales, debate heatedly some nuance of the text or discuss a related
matter. They would come early, before their teacher arrived, and
spend the time *shmoosn*, engaged in the easy conversation in
which what is said is less important than the fact that one person
speaks and another listens and neither is alone. As at Kahal Reyim
the matter of fellowship was of special importance to the men of
this circle, and I often came away from a session of *lernen* with
the sense that afterward the men were closer to one another and
to the world of the page than they had been upon entering. The
warmth they expressed toward one another they also showed to

me so that, when it came time for me to pare down the number of groups in which I would participate, I felt it impossible to abandon this one. They chose me even more than I chose them. They asked after my absences, welcomed me enthusiastically when I returned, and in general made me feel that if I were to leave I would transgress some hidden but unmistakable prohibition. I later began to discern the bonds which held me close to these men, but of that I shall have more to say in what follows.

With regard to matters of contemporary life these men were well informed, and they never hesitated to bring the outside world into their *lernen.* For them what happened outside did not disturb the Talmud; it reaffirmed its relevance and its power as a living document. To be able to tie together the ageless work of wisdom that they recited with the timely events of life through which they passed was one of the goals of their *lernen.* It was as if these men often read the newspaper through the prism of their study circle.

On Tuesdays, I followed my daily page at Kahal Reyim with a trip to Mekadshey Torah, a synagogue in a one-room wooden shack at the end of an alley off one of the main streets of the city. There, in what had once been a British officers' hut during the period of the mandate in Palestine, sometimes as many as fifteen men sat around three tables and listened to Rabbi Rotenbush lead them in a weekly class in Talmud. The founder and factotum of the synagogue, the man whom everyone referred to as the "*gabbai,*" or officer in charge of the conduct of public prayers, dispensing ritual tasks and other honors, had several years earlier approached the rabbi, the teacher assigned by the Ministry of Religion to oversee the needs of religious instruction in the neighborhood, and asked him to help in the formation of a *shiur* or class in Talmud. Taking up the task himself, Rabbi Rotenbush had led the group through their first tractate and was near its end when I began my observations.

I had come to Mekadshey Torah at the recommendation of a friend who told me of the great pride he and others in the circle had in their class. Here too I discovered myself swept up in the atmosphere of camaraderie, and when it came time to choose circles to leave I found I could not depart from this group without seeming to deny the others their pride.

Although the rabbi did the reciting and most of the explaining and translating—I discovered that even where the people who study Talmud speak Hebrew, they still translate the text into terms

they can understand—it was often the students who determined
the pace and direction of the *lernen*. Here, more than anywhere
else, I found the men eager to digress from the matters on the
page. Some would ask the teacher riddles, the answers to which
were verses from Scripture or Talmud. Others would engage him
in casuistic debate, jockeying for position as top student in the
class. Still others would occasionally embark on paths of philosophic or spiritual reflection, using the Talmud as a stimulus for
far-reaching considerations of all that was Jewish. They would
explore the boundaries of the religiously permissible, seeking to
discover how a Jew ought to behave and what he should believe.
Indeed, when later in the year a man more tightly anchored to
consideration of the specific text began increasingly to dominate
discussion and hold the group to a single-minded concern with
the subjects on the page, several of the senior members signaled
their displeasure with his conduct, warning him not to be too
gripped by the particular argument in the Talmud but to look
through it to "more fundamental" matters. What thus distinguished the men of Mekadshey Torah from the other circles was
the boldness with which they revealed and reveled in their preoccupations during the Talmudic review.

A number of men in the circle did not worship at Mekadshey
Torah. Nevertheless, here as in the other places, it was the synagogue that gave the group its name and which in a sense har-
bored its identity (although, to be sure, some referred more
precisely to "Rabbi Rotenbush's *shiur* at Mekadshey Torah"). Certainly it was the synagogue that gave the group its *lernen* table,
the "altar" on which they would serve their God through talmudic
review.

More and more, I was beginning to recognize the dialectical
character of the rabbi's role. On the one hand, he was, within the
framework of the *shiur*, the formal leader, source of ultimate authority about the text and matters Jewish, the ratifier of all remarks
and arbiter of all controversies. Yet he was also, like any other
participant in the circle, subject to the effects of collective life.
Much of his behavior was a reflection of and reaction to what
went on in the group.

The best way to observe this synthetic nature of the teacher is
to watch one rabbi in different circles. About two months after
I had joined Mekadshey Torah the opportunity to do precisely
that occurred. One evening one of the younger members of the

circle, a man with whom I had spent many hours in conversation and who had provided me with keen insights into his *lernen* experiences, told me that on Sunday evenings this same Rabbi Rotenbush met with a small group of "fellows our age" to study Talmud in his home. The circle, he assured me, was significantly different from the one on Tuesdays; the level of study was "more intensive," the tractate reviewed "harder," and the evening far "more stimulating." Above all else, he warned me, the rabbi was "a completely different person."

I had already become quite impressed with the rabbi. He was at once warm and authoritative, close to his students and yet expressing a certain distance through which he maintained their respect for him. He had managed to combine his vocation and avocation in the course of *lernen:* on the one hand he had taken up the job of leading the Mekadshey Torah men as an official duty, but on the other, as I shall detail later, had also allowed himself to become socially and emotionally caught up with them. I wondered how he would seem in a different group and setting.

The next Tuesday after class I asked his permission to join the Sunday circle.

"Your comments in class indicate a clear interest in *lernen*," he replied. "I shall be happy to have you join us."

The answer was more than permission; it was a signal of what was to come for it implied that only those with a "clear interest," a seriousness about Talmud study, could participate and that my actions at Mekadshey Torah had so marked me. For perhaps the first time I began to realize that there were a great many layers of meaning in every word spoken or action taken during a class. While I had been trying simply to appear involved at Mekadshey Torah, I was in fact performing—categorizing myself—and being evaluated as a *lerner*.

The circle I encountered at the rabbi's apartment was in sharp contrast to what I had seen at Mekadshey Torah. Here the informality of the setting made itself felt in an intimacy among the members greater than any I had yet observed. The students were treated like members of the family (indeed two were, being the rabbi's brothers-in-law). We were called by nicknames and joked with the rabbi in ways that would not have been dared at Mekadshey Torah. He sat in shirtsleeves rather than in frock coat, as was his habit in the synagogue. And he was not averse to telling stories about the Ministry of Religion where he worked or about

the "great rabbis" with whom he came in contact. Yet in the face
of this intimacy and informality the group was rigorous in its
review of the Talmud. The class resonated much of the yeshiva
experience through which each of its members had passed. There
was the tension of examination during which the teacher would
ask someone to review the Talmud's arguments and provide some
scholarly erudition. There were strong efforts at one-upmanship
as each student tried to outdo his fellow in explaining the text.
There were moments of crisis during which students sometimes
challenged the teacher's intellectual authority and explanation of
a text. All of these were the sorts of actions I had not seen at
Mekadshey Torah and only fleetingly sensed at Kahal Reyim.

Sitting around the rabbi's dining room table, surrounded by
the holy books which lined the walls of his apartment, the experience of *lernen* became, however, more and more an echo of
the time-worn Jewish practice of the father *farhern* (interrogating)
his sons. In that give-and-take, traditionally the way in which
father and son would relate to each other through the medium
of the holy book, far more can be demanded and allowed. There
was intimacy and authority, confidence and anxiety, closeness
and competition.

The circle was composed of young men in their thirties. Two
were shopkeepers, two bank employees, one an electrician, one
an accountant, another a graduate student in criminology, and
the last was a craftsman who made cases for Torah scrolls. Here,
as in the other circles, identity in the outside world entered only
obliquely into the activities of *lernen*. Instead, the men distinguished themselves through their performances in class and in
their relationships within the circle. There was a top student, a
questioner, one slow to understand, and so on. Here in the circle
the rules of order and social status had less to do with income
and occupation and more to do with Talmudic recitation and discussion.

In all the circles I had joined I had discovered ties among those
who reviewed Talmud together. From America to Jerusalem, the
notion of fellowship as an abiding characteristic of *lernen* impressed itself upon my observations. Here was an association
which allowed the camaraderie of adolescent peer groups to continue in later life. Indeed, it often seemed to me that the *lerners*
looked forward more to being in one another's company than to
going through the complex and frequently dense texts. They

would often spend as much as a third of their time together in preliminary and then postliminary conversation. As much and sometimes more than the formal study, these conversations served to stimulate a collective consciousness and weave social bonds.

I wondered if *lernen* could be carried on without these sorts of collective ties. I wanted therefore to discover and observe what may best be termed an "anonymous study group." In theory this would be a collection of individuals who knew or cared little if anything at all about one another and who join in a group purely for instrumental reasons. This circle would be analogous to the "anonymous *minyan*,"[3] the quorum of ten or more adult Jewish males formed purely to allow unrelated individuals to fulfill their felt religious obligation to pray with other Jews. Commonly occurring in public places like bus depots, airports, synagogues in shopping districts, and other similar places where anonymous crowds gather, these assemblies are from the point of view of religious doctrine defined as congregations but in point of social fact fail to lift the individual out of his solitariness. In such gatherings, each worshipper remains essentially alien to and untouched by the others. The services are distinguished by an absence of conversation, either before, during, or after the prayers—something foreign to communal synagogue life.[4] Worshippers do not linger in one another's company for even a moment longer than required by the liturgy and commonly make their ways for the exits even as they recite the concluding "amen."

An anonymous study group would arise out of the same sort of needs and have many of the same characteristics. It would be an assembly of people who felt an obligation to study Talmud but who needed an instructor. The class would remain essentially instructional and lack most if not all of the social qualities of established study circles. Teacher would hardly know student nor would the latter feel any ties to one another. Discourse would be formal and limited. Neither conflict nor sociability—both signs of the human ties I had come to expect within the circle—would be manifest. At the end of the class, everyone would disperse quickly and quietly, as if nothing that bound them together remained.

At the Jerusalem Social Club I found just such a class. As a civic institution the club provided a class in Talmud as part of its general program of cultural activities. Once a week a few people who apparently had no other opportunity to review Talmud gathered here, while in other rooms groups met to learn judo or macrame. Under the tutelage of Asher Auerbach, a retired rabbi from Ireland, the group spent an hour with their books. This was the first place where I found women regularly in attendance.[5] Closed out of most other Talmud circles, they had come to this public place to review the texts along with the few men who were also there.

The group impressed me with its silence. When people talked, they addressed their remarks to the rabbi and seldom if ever to one another. There were few questions, hardly any echoes of recitation, few debates and controversy. The only digressions that occurred were those which the teacher included as part of his discussion of the text, but they were less conversations than extended monologues. Before the class began its formal study, everyone sat in stony silence. And when the rabbi closed his book and ended the proceedings, the few people who were there quietly filed out of the room. It was all a shadow of what I had participated in and experienced at the other study circles.

Gradually, the group disintegrated and the *lernen*, such as it was, wound down until only the rabbi and I were left. But what was a failure for the rabbi and the group was instructive for me. It made clearer to me what the necessary ingredients for a vital and successful circle were.

At the club there was no sense of fellowship. In the other circles, such collective feelings fairly hung on each word and were embedded in every action. If there were intellectual, religious, or ritual needs that brought people to the club, these were not sufficient to serve as a source of support for the group. While the teacher was competent as a Talmud scholar, he failed to organize the collective life of the gathering. In the club there was silence and distance, while in the other circles there was noise and drama, involvement and engagement, both with the text and with the people who pursued it.

SIX ANGLES OF VISION

Out of these six circles—Smotra, Kahal Reyim, Beit Rachel, Mekadshey Torah, Rabbi Rotenbush's home study group, and the Jerusalem Social Club—came my sense of what it means to *lern*. Each circle provided me with its own angle of vision until I realized that there was no single reality to *lernen*, no one way to tell the whole story. The reasons that people had for coming to the circle, the meaning of what they did there, were as varied as the number of circles themselves. It was not so much that each circle was totally different from another—to be sure, there were differences among them, but there were also important similarities—but that each circle made me see something about these people of the book that I had not seen before. Once I saw that something, I could often discern it in a number of the circles.

In the end, therefore, I decided that there was no one portrait or analysis that could be presented that would give any kind of comprehensive picture of what I had found. Rather, I had to tell my story from a series of perspectives.

My observations had suggested six angles of vision of *lernen*. For one, I saw the *shiur* as a drama, a performance during which the *lerners* became swept up in their action and set into motion their entire creative apparatus. The drama was by no means simple. It was of four types. One was a social drama during which the relationships among the participants and between them and the act of study was played out. A second was a cultural performance during which the people through their talmudic review at once enacted, exhibited, and discovered the meaning of being a Jew. A third was an interactional drama or game during which the participants played at *lernen* as if it were a game with stylized moves and prefigured reactions. And the fourth was speech play during which members got caught up in the words they spoke and the languages they used for communicating.

But *lernen* was more than drama and play. It was also an experience of fellowship and community. While some people might go to a pub, others to a bowling alley, and still others would play cards in order to share one another's company, these People of the Book came into a study circle for much the same reason. Instead of getting together over a beer or game of gin, they got together over and through a page of Talmud.

Finally, on top of all this, there were people who joined in talmudic review because they felt a religious obligation to do so. For them *lernen* was a form of worship, an act of homage to their God, nation, history, and faith.

In each of the following chapters, I have tried to emphasize one of these perspectives. None of them alone presents the entire picture for they are each but a single point of view. The various angles of my vision are not always mutually exclusive—life is never that neat—and the attentive reader will find elements of one perspective present in another. Together these sometimes overlapping and parallactic points of view are meant to give a full sense of what *lernen* is; I therefore tell the story anew six times.

There are a number of ways to read this book. The most obvious of going from beginning to end will give one something of what I have been able to conclude. Each chapter is, however, also meant to stand on its own in combination with this introduction. Thus those who wish only to get a sense of what *lernen* is all about may read only one more chapter or read the following in any order they choose.

There are some chapters which tend to be analytic and relatively technical—the one on *lernen* as interactional drama, and the one on word or speech play and the language of *lernen* in particular. Other chapters tend toward the essay in style and content. The selective reader may choose to skip some and focus upon others. Each will give him a self-contained view of the phenomenon.

Finally, in spite or perhaps because of the fractured nature of my presentation, I have added a closing chapter which provides an unencumbered descriptive account of three circles' celebration of the *siyum*, the momentous completion of a volume of Talmud when group life seems most intense. This chapter is offered as an opportunity for those who have struggled through the preceding analytic chapters to try their own hand at analysis. But it is there as well for the reader who simply wants a nontechnical and relatively uncluttered view into the circle.

In sum, the book tries by way of deduction, generalization, extrapolation, supposition, intuition, imagination, and observation to draw large conclusions about culture, society, and religion from small but very densely textured facts. It aims to decipher the unapparent import of actions and words in order to understand and explain study circle life and the People of the Book.

One last word in the way of introduction. A book such as this one may attract a variety of readers. There will be some who are curious about the People of the Book, who know little or nothing about them. These are in many ways the easiest readers to satisfy for, if my text is clear and my ideas reasonable, they need only persevere and they will get through with little difficulty.

Others will come to these pages because they are themselves People of the Book, participants in study circles like the ones I am describing, who want to look at themselves through my eyes. I trust they will find things in here that resonate authentically with their own experiences. I have no doubt that they will also find ideas that seem foreign and strange. My hope is that I can get such people to see old things in new ways. To those who would object that they never understood matters as I have and therefore I must be completely wrong or at least exaggerating the significance of what I have found, I would simply echo the comments of Durkheim: "Which of us knows all the words of the language he speaks and the entire signification of each?"[6] To be a participant is not always to see things as an observer. To be both is perhaps to be marginal but also to have a clearer line of sight than those who look at matters completely from inside.

With these warnings in mind, let us enter the world of talmud study circles.

2
SOCIAL DRAMA

There are those who . . . come to life only when they feel themselves actors upon a stage, . . . act fearlessly only in situations which in some way are formalized for them, see life as a kind of play in which they and others are assigned certain lines which they must speak.

ISAIAH BERLIN, *Personal Impressions*

It is evening, the after-hours of what may have been a long workday. Perhaps the night air is cold or rain falls, making it unpleasant to go outside. Maybe there is work to be done at home or time to be spent with one's family. There are countless reasons why men should choose not to take themselves out and spend an hour or two with a small circle of others engaged in the study of a nearly two-thousand-year-old text of Talmud written in a language which no one any longer speaks and dealing with topics that often appear quite unrelated to the times in which the students live. Yet they come, stay, and return, sometimes every evening, sometimes several times or at least once a week for years.

To discover some explanations for this behavior one needs to know what it is the men do once the circle has been formed, once the study, or *lernen* as it is called, begins. No single explanation will suffice. The text is multivocal, its subjects and styles of presentation various. Like most social situations, the public activity of *lernen* is characterized by a multiplicity of involvements and motives, both formal and informal. Finally, the behavior of the participants is multifarious and its meaning, depending on the strip of activity one chooses to observe and one's analytic perspective, polysemic.

As a start perhaps, the class or *shiur*, as it is most often called by the participants, may be considered as a drama and the members of the study circle as both dramatis personae and audience.[1] Thus begins an understanding of what, in the contemporary cases I have observed, both draws people to and holds them in the Talmud study circle.

The capacity of drama "to attract [and] to excite" attention, to "set in motion [the] whole creative apparatus," to take in and possess both actors and audience is perhaps as old as human consciousness.[2]

For everyone concerned, involvement in a drama with its acts, agents, scenes, performances, and ends replaces reality with a socially reconstructed world.[3] Not altogether unlike ritual or symbolization, drama (which is but another incarnation of these other two) makes "visible, audible, and tangible beliefs, ideas, values, sentiments and psychological dispositions that cannot [otherwise] directly be perceived."[4]

It may "depict moods and ideas, instincts even, of so private and yet so public a nature that no other aspect of civilized life seems as revelatory or explanatory."[5] At the same time it expresses

29

all these, however, it may reaffirm and thus reinforce them. In dramas, people acquire their faith as they express and portray it.

Demonstrating that the Talmud *shiur* is a drama, that *lernen* is composed of acts and performances, that the circle of students is made up of both agents and audience, that there are ways of perceiving action in terms of scenes, and that there is a dramatic inevitability about the development of the action will go a long way toward deciphering the phenomenon. Of course I, like others before me who have used the metaphor of drama as an explanatory device, am aware of its inadequacies. It cannot hope to answer all the questions, and I shall therefore in subsequent chapters use other concepts—principally the notions of fellowship and the role of religion in everyday life—to help in unraveling the meaning that the Talmud study circle has for its members. For now, however, I shall begin with drama.

In the interpretation of real life, "drama" can and has been usefully considered in four forms: (1) social drama, (2) cultural drama (sometimes called cultural performance), (3) interaction (often referred to as the games people play or impression management), and (4) speech or word play. Each of these organize the understanding of human behavior in the general terms of drama, but each emphasizes a different aspect of it, a variant level of meaning in the play. I shall begin with "social drama."

In essence the idea of social drama emerges from the assumption that social situations create their own tacit order, which insiders more or less sense and which they try to protect. Any subversion of this order not only calls into play redressive action, it also makes clear what the taken-for granted arrangements existing beforehand were and how much was at stake in them.

In the social science literature, Victor Turner is perhaps foremost among those who have made use of the concept to explain human behavior. For him social drama, with its definite beginning and line of development, mirrors staged drama. Both are public episodes initiated by some breach in normative order that demands repair or at least response. The latter constitutes the plot line of the drama. People, both as actors and audience, are engaged by the drama because, simply stated, they want to learn how things will turn out. For Turner[6] social dramas typically have four main phases or scenes accessible to observation: (1) the breach of a norm and the irruption of tension associated with it; (2) the resultant mounting crisis; (3) consequent redressive action; and (4) either a reintegration, with the breach repaired, or a legitimation of irreparable schism. Throughout the episode, "fundamental aspects of society, normally overlaid by the customs and habits of daily intercourse," are brought into prominence.[7] Accordingly, to discover what is normally important in a particular social situation, one might usefully observe moments of drama during which norms are breached. One might add that the more important the norm breached is to the persons involved, the higher the drama, the more it attracts and holds the attention of the involved.

During the Talmud *shiur*, moments of high social drama occur, and when they do they make the experience of *lernen* extraordinarily engaging for the participants and profoundly revealing for the observer. An analysis of two cases will illuminate the drama. I shall call the first "The Puzzling Redundancy" and the second "Dissenting Opinions."

THE CASE OF THE PUZZLING REDUNDANCY

To perceive the drama in the following case one needs first to understand the perspective and social situation of the dramatis personae, the members of the study circle. Without this, one cannot perceive a breach of norm nor feel the consequent tension. On the contrary, what seems important and dramatic to the insiders might appear trivial or even meaningless to the uninformed observer. Accordingly, a first task is to ethnographically delineate the situation of the study circle and its members.

Once a week on Sunday evening between seven and ten Orthodox men (sometimes more and sometimes fewer) in their thirties and early forties would assemble around a table in the Jerusalem home of their teacher, Rabbi Rotenbush, to study Talmud. Rabbi Rotenbush, employed by the state rabbinate and serving as the neighborhood clergyman, ministers to the religious needs of those living in the region and also offers a number of Talmud classes in various locations in what might be called his "parish." As a public figure in daily touch with the lay community, he is not insulated from the strains his students experience in trying to bring their religion into line with their modern lives. Unlike the yeshiva rabbi who, protected by the splendid isolation of the talmudic academy, can remain a purist and ideological conservative in his religious outlook, Rabbi Rotenbush—in spite of his strictly Orthodox proclivities—has had to come to terms

with the this-worldliness of his parishoners and students. If this
has not resulted in his totally embracing modernity, it has at least
made him aware and more tolerant of its demands.

As modern Orthodox Jews, his students in this circle are men
who are traditional and pious, committed to the faith of their
fathers as well as to an observance of the laws of Judaism, while
simultaneously wedded to the timely, rationalized, contemporary
world in which tradition and piety are out of place. In their Orthodox incarnation, they view the Talmud as a sacred text, part
of the corpus of Torah, which is the product of a sacred tradition
initiated by divine revelation; in the spirit of rationality, they also
conceive of it as a document of laws and debates to be rationally
comprehended. As Orthodox believers, however, they are unwilling to supplant faith with reason as might the more thor-
oughly contemporary man nor reason with faith as might the
more strictly Orthodox.

For them the Talmud is not simply another book. It is the epit-
ome of Torah, a human translation of God's oral law, a monument
of their religion and culture, a symbol of their historical identity
as the people of the book.[8] Each *inyan* (topic), *sugia* (talmudic
discussion unit), and *memra* (statement of an idea) is approached
by the faithful with a confidence in its inherent significance. To
suggest that the page is filled with superfluities, redundancies,
or hopelessly opaque remarks is to admit to a hollowness in the
monument, an emptiness in the heart of the symbol, and a confusion about the word of God. It is also to call into question the
group's manifest purpose in gathering together: If they cannot
together understand the Talmud, why then get together to review
it? While some students may be ready to overlook the implications
of acknowledging the meaninglessness of the text or their inability
to comprehend it, finding other reasons for *lernen*, these men
around Rabbi Rotenbush's table are, by and large, not. For them
the norm is—at least *a fortiori*—that each line of the Talmud can
be shown to make sense; the Torah is both sacred and instructive.
"The holy *gemore* must be completely understood," as one of them
put it.

Lest one doubt the urgency of this belief, one need simply note
what happened in this circle once when one of the students responded to an explanation of a particular *sugia* by commenting,
"Oh I see, reason has nothing to do with this." The comment
may have been preliminary to his admitting that he was ready

nevertheless to accept the Talmud's argument as an article of faith. But even before his words had died away, he was met by a chorus of explanations from the teacher and the others which provided him with the "reason" for the law.

The strength of the norm of finding meaning in the words of the Talmud is such that any *sugia* or *memra* has the potential to test one's faith in the reason of the text. Any inability to comprehend may spark a crisis for the modern Orthodox rational believer. Accordingly, the possibilities for crisis and drama are high as the men review the complex discussions on the page that lies open before them.

Opening Scene

Seated around the table in Rabbi Rotenbush's library, the students follow along as their teacher recites, translates, explains, and comments upon the text. It is a usual Sunday evening, the close of the first full workday of the Israeli week. Everyone is a bit tired. The hot Turkish coffee that Yisrael, one of the students, serves near the end of the class hour is not yet on the table, and so attention occasionally flags. We are studying *Yoma*, the tractate dealing primarily with the myriad procedures surrounding the Day of Atonement (Yom Kippur) as it was celebrated in the days of the Holy Temple in Jerusalem. The *inyan* which has taken up our attention for the last several weeks concerns the sacrifices that the high priest carried out on that day. We have already learned about the number of goats he was to slaughter and of the scape-goat he was to send out toward the wilderness of Judea. We have reviewed the order of his sacrifices and know which ones he brought while robed in white and which he carried out while dressed in his golden garments. Each detail has been discussed until the procedures, which no one around the table has ever seen (the ceremonial having been discontinued some two thousand years earlier), seem totally familiar, and we talk about them as if we had witnessed the event dozens of times.

Rabbi Rotenbush (hereafter called the "Rav" as his students refer to him) as always presents the Talmud as a sacred document that must be respected, even revered, and only afterward comprehended. The slightest flippant remark or joke about something on the page (a means by which his modernist students try at times to distance themselves from what may too obviously clash with their contemporaneity) is met with reactions in which he

stresses the sanctity of the text and calls the men back to the faith:
"This is the holy Torah you are talking about"; or "You are speaking of the words of the Rambam [a major exegete and codifier],
the 'Eagle,' the holy among holies who comprehends all mysteries."

Throughout the *shiur*, the students do not sit silently like an
audience at a lecture but instead take turns at speaking. They
echo the Rav's recitations, cue his reading, amplify his remarks,
ask questions, provide glosses on something he or another student has said, and generally keep their involvement active. Each
sugia and *memra* offers an opportunity to demonstrate not only
their involvement but the depth of their commitment to the text
and the task of studying it. The depth of this commitment, however, will be tested by the crisis about to occur.

The Breach of the Norm

The discussion revolves around the order of the High Priest's
activities on Yom Kippur. Some matters, we learn, must be done
in the "Holy of Holies," the inner sanctum of the Temple; others
are carried on in the sanctuary, the outer chamber. Through the
statements of various rabbis, the Talmud describes the consequences of possible errors in the ceremony. The description is
complex, and after several readings of the text the Rav in chorus
with the students has boiled the complexities down to a series of
steps. We have learned to describe each step and the consequences of an error at any one.

With our comprehension so schematized, we now reach the
statement of "Ulla," one of the voices in the text. Ulla, we read,
notes that the entire discussion of error in the ceremonial concerns
itself only "with events taking place in the sanctuary." Again we
review the entire *sugia*, assimilating Ulla's remark into our
schema. As the Rav speaks, the students fill in the blanks in his
presentation, cue him on the steps, and gloss his explanations
with brief insights of their own.

Satisfied from this display that they have comprehended the
discussion in the Talmud, the Rav now recites the next and last
line of the *sugia*: "Therefore Rabbi Afays said, 'We are dealing
only with events taking place in the sanctuary.' "[9]

Yitzhak, one of the students who has been echoing the Rav
throughout the review of the *sugia*, suddenly falls silent. A moment later the Rav does too. How can it be that Rabbi Afays says

precisely what Ulla himself has just explained? Yitzhak asks the question, and this time the Rav echoes *him:* "What has Rabbi Afays added?"

Is it possible that he is simply redundant, that his contribution to the *sugia* is essentially meaningless?

In the evaluative terms of this study circle, this is not a "good" question. Judging from what may be observed in the class, a "good question" is one which exhibits a curiosity about matters which the Talmud chooses to explain. Earlier, for example, Moshe, one of the students, asked something to which the Rav reacted with, "Very good; look, look, the answer to your question will just now be taken up by the *gemore* [Talmud]." To ask a question that forces one to plunge more deeply into the page, that indicates one is thinking along the same lines as the Talmud, is to be "very good." This sort of question does not create any crisis at all but demonstrates, on the contrary, that all is right with the world: what you want to know is what you need to know. The question assists in the affirmation of the significance and logic of the text.

The question about Rabbi Afays's contribution to the argument, however, does not generate further reading in the text. His comment, after all, ends the *sugia.* Rather, the question forces us to read *into* the text, to probe its significance. To be sure, a penetration of Rabbi Afays's meaning will add to the integrity of the text. Before that significance is uncovered, however, the question stands as a challenge and casts doubt upon the logical right of certain words to exist. It breaches the norm—accepted in this study circle—that nothing in the Talmud is meaningless.

Reacting to the question, the Rav repeats it and rereads Rabbi Afays's statement. This he does several times, slowing his recitational tempo, following each repetition with long pauses. It almost sounds as if, through an incantational and deliberate repetition of the question and quotation, the logic that connects them could be revealed. There is, to be sure, no conscious effort here to resort to such mystical practices but rather a kind of fiction being played out. (This is not to gainsay the traditional association between the recitation of the text, even its singing, and some mystical sense of comprehension. The notion that "the Talmud has its own sweet melody, and when the lerner has the correct sound, one hears more than words" is firmly rooted in the folk beliefs of traditional Jewish students of Talmud.)[10] As long as one keeps reading the text and asking the same question, it is as if time stops and the problem has not succeeded in overwhelming the *lernen*. Once one stops completely, one admits to being stumped and the *lernen*, a process requiring a constant hum of recitation and explanation, breaks down. So the Rav goes on for a while, sounding a bit like a record running down.

His change of pace, repetitions, and silences, however, all signal the students that something has gone wrong. Yitzhak's question has opened a gaping hole in the logic of the page, and the group cannot continue until it has been filled. Others rush to help.

At first the reactions are simply those of a team that, seeing its captain in trouble, comes to his aid out of a sense of "reciprocal dependence and reciprocal familiarity."[11] To the extent that the *shiur* may be understood as a public performance, our efforts to help the Rav pass over this gap in his understanding can be understood in much the same way that audiences or other members of the cast are often willing to overlook an actor's flubbing his lines. There is a bias which favors continuation, even if it means that something opaque must be left that way.

Additionally, like members of any face-to-face group, we are expected to "sustain a standard of considerateness," and to go "to certain lengths to save the feelings and the face of others present . . . willingly and spontaneously because of emotional identification with the others and with their feelings."[12] If one of us were stuck, he would want help in getting out of the predicament. The greater prestige of the Rav—a scholar among laymen—makes us display even greater considerateness toward him in his pedagogic predicament.[13]

The efforts to help take the form of simplistic, one-line explanations that do little more than restate Rabbi Afays's comment in other words. These quasi-explanations are offered to bridge the silence—to keep the talk going—and not really to fill it with firm logic and comprehension.

To be sure, there may be some students who consider these half-answers as sufficient, who wish to use them not to support the team struggle to get through the text or to save the Rav's face but instead to suggest their own superiority and intelligence. As earlier noted, the student is always in search of ways to demonstrate his competence, ability to understand the teacher, and involvement.[14] What better way to do so than to help the faltering teacher out with an explanation?

Whatever the reasons generating the student responses, the Rav refuses to accept them. To each answer offered, he presents an objection (something easily done since the explanations are not really thought out or complete). In addition to the change of pace, the repetitions and the silences, these objections serve to heighten the drama. His voice rises, its cadences transparent in their meaning:[15] we have reached the breach; there are no easy solutions. If he, the Rav, is puzzled, the problem is not to be easily overcome by a quick student gloss.

"One moment," he cries out. The students' repetitions cease, their explanations die down. A time out has, as it were, been called. This is a liminal break, a moment outside the boundaries of *lernen*, "betwixt and between" the question and the answer. We wait, suspended in our puzzlement. Clearly a breakdown in the train of *lernen* has occurred.

As if to underscore the liminality of the occasion, the Rav shifts suddenly into Yiddish—a language not normally used in this circle—and asks, *"Vus ligt er tsu"* (What has he [Rabbi Afays] added)? While this is not the place to dwell on the matter of language shift, something more properly belonging to the later consideration of word play and the language of *lernen*, it is important to explain how this use of Yiddish emphasizes the crisis atmosphere. Surely it is not accidental nor does it occur because the Rav thinks the students failed to understand the same question when it was phrased in their native Hebrew. Rather, the Yiddish cry, coming as it does as the actuality of the breach is confronted, is a "heart-word," an unmistakable reference to a consciousness in which all layers of civilization and its pretenses have been peeled away until the mother-tongue (*"mama-loshn,"* as Yiddish was often called) and its primordial ethnic consciousness is laid bare at last.[16] It is not that these students are Yiddish speakers, but rather that they come from an Ashkenazic, European tradition in which Yiddish represents the inner language of simple truth and genuine ethnicity. For generations of their forebears "Jewishness" was *"Yiddishkeyt."* To ask in Yiddish what Rabbi Afays has added is as if to say, "Hold on a minute, all pretenses aside, let us be honest with one another, what has been added here?"

The Rav has by now totally appropriated Yitzhak's question. He has heightened the drama, drawn it out by underscoring our mutual inability to comprehend the text logically. The more puzzling the *memra*, the greater the sense of crisis, the greater will

be the Rav's accomplishment should he succeed in resolving the
matter. By emphasizing *his* perplexity, the Rav grabs our attention
and intensifies the drama. Will he or won't he solve the puzzle?
We are held by our curiosity.

Indeed, he has done this before. It is a common procedure for
the experienced Talmud teacher to manufacture an apparent puzzle in order to hold the attention of his students, and then once
he has it to miraculously resolve everything in a sparkling display
of logic and erudition.

Suddenly lowering his voice and letting the tension slip away,
the Rav tries out an answer on us: we have simply failed to realize
that Rabbi Afays, although using Ulla's words, is referring to
something discussed in an earlier part of the *inyan*. The solution
is simple; the text exquisitely logical. There has been no real breach
in the norm that the entire Talmud is meaningful; the crisis that
never was has been resolved.

The Mounting Crisis

Silence. The recapitulations, glosses, and comments by which the
students normally signal their acceptance of an explanation are
missing. Apparently, they are not yet persuaded that the crisis
has been resolved.

Yitzhak is the first to break the silence. Outlining his objections
to the solution, he finds himself quickly joined by several other
students who offer their own amplifications of his arguments.
The resistance appears to catch the Rav off guard. At first somewhat distractedly but with mounting attentiveness, he responds
to the objections and reviews his answer. His voice begins once
again to grow tentative, his tempo slower. At last he admits to
a flaw in his solution. On the heels of this admission, he reverts
to Yiddish and in its words bares the puzzlement he feels. In
tremulous voice and rising pitch, he calls out, while pointing to
Yitzhak, *"Er ot dokh rekht"* (He is after all correct). Repeating and
affirming the propriety of Yitzhak's argument in Yiddish, the Rav
seems to have dropped all pretenses of having reached a solution.
The crisis of meaning mounts.

Until now the focus of attention has been on the crisis of meaning which headlines this episode. A second more obviously social
drama has however been joined to it. The Rav's inability to penetrate the meaning of Rabbi Afays's *memra* has breached the
group's normative expectation about his capacity to always ex-

plain the Talmud to them. By resisting his solution and plunging him and the group back into puzzlement, the students have implicitly undermined the basis of their teacher's supreme authority. In part, "the 'ganging-up' of group members in some sort of hostile attack on the assigned group leader" and their consequent independence of him is a common feature of small group interaction.[17] But the revolt which denies the Rav success also throws the students into even further tension and crisis. As each one tries to supplant the teacher and provide his own solution to the puzzle, he is confronted with the objections of his fellow students and the teacher. The anarchy that results not only fails to solve the crisis of meaning which began all of this, it also raises doubts about the capacity of the study circle to remain intact. Their inability to assist one another in the *lernen* and their subtle criticism of one another serve as challenges to the men's sense of fellowship which normally unites them.

As the crisis mounts, the Rav in fact further intensifies it at all three levels. His admitted puzzlement underscores the problem of meaning and the vacuum in leadership. Now he begins to ask each student for his "*pshat*," his explanatory reading of the text. While manifestly seeking understanding, he not only shifts responsibility for explanation to us and locks up our attention, he also sets each student up for attack by the others. By asking us for answers, he necessarily intensifies the anarchy and sets the stage for his own return to dominance. By the time we are through with one another and convinced that none of us is able to solve the problem of meaning, we shall be ready to reinstate the Rav and accept his answer.

To be sure, he is taking a risk. It is possible that one of the students will arrive at an answer that satisfies everyone and will thereby emerge as a new leader. The risk is, however, slight. Not only do the students not have the Rav's talmudic skills but they are not nearly as erudite. Moreover, the social consequences of having a student outshine the teacher threaten group order and would perhaps presage new alignments—something few would welcome. Accordingly, the chance that one will arrive at a solution that the Rav cannot either deny or at least amplify so that he will have the last word is very slim. In short, the cards are stacked against the success of the revolt.

All this is not to say that the Rav is cynically or strategically manipulating the situation consciously. His moves are in great measure the result of long experience and second nature. He no longer has to figure out how to handle himself in situations like this one; it is all disposed of unwittingly and automatically.

By now, we have all become in *propria persona* implicated in the drama. Increasingly there are long silences filled with intensive rereadings of the page. Bodies begin to sway back and forth; the general tension in the room is palpable. No one would dare close the book or walk away. We are hooked.

Speaking more and more in Yiddish—outside the normal boundaries of the class, as it were—the Rav sustains the atmosphere of crisis and tension. In a voice resonating urgency, he calls out, *"sken dokh nisht zayn,"* it cannot be, Yitzhak; it cannot be that your objection is right.*

---

*In his novels *The Chosen* and *The Promise*, Chaim Potok captures an element of this tension and crisis. Consider the following extracts from the former book:

Because Sunday Talmud classes at Hirsch ended at one in the afternoon, the period of preparation ran from nine to a few minutes before eleven, and the shiur ran from eleven to one. The next morning Rav Kalman called on me again. I saw my classmates exchange grim looks. I began to read. He let me read and explain for a long time. All the while he paced back and forth, smoking. Then he stopped me on a passage I had struggled with during the period of preparation and still did not clearly understand.

I started to give him one of the commentaries on the passage. He stopped me again.

"I did not ask you for the Maharsha, Malter. What do the words mean? Explain the words. Can you explain the words?"

I tried to put the words together as best I could; they did not hang together properly; there was clearly something wrong with the text.

On this occasion, Malter, the modern student, holds back his reservations about the significance of the text, aware that an assertion of its wrongness would enrage his Orthodox teacher and mark him as a heretic. On another occasion, his final examination for ordination, however, he does not:

In a very quiet voice, Rav Kalman asked me if I thought I could add anything to our understanding of the passage. I told him it seemed to me that the text was very difficult to understand. I did not say it was wrong; I said it was very difficult to understand. . . .

The Dean stopped nodding and opened his eyes very wide. Rav Gershenson did not move. The smile froze a little on his face.

I emended the text.

There was a long silence in the room. I could feel the silence. It was electric with sudden tension.

The decision taken by Malter to emend the text is not one likely to occur in Rabbi Rotenbush's study circle, although the possibility hovers menacingly just beyond the realm of piety. Feelings of intimacy and fellowship, to say nothing of religious tradition which discourages such manipulations of "holy writ," forestall such a breach of norm and irruption of tension. But the possibility remains a kind

Redressive Action

"In order to limit the spread of crisis," Turner reports he has found "certain adjustive and redressive 'mechanisms,' . . . informal or formal, institutionalized or ad hoc, are swiftly brought into operation by leading or structurally representative members of the social system."[18]

Following a long silence in which the students have put on displays of concentrated thinking (intense looks, sotto voce chantings of the text, inspired swaying), precisely this sort of redressive effort occurs. As if having reconsidered, Yitzhak, tacit leader of the revolt and the one who asked the question that threw the class into crisis, is the first to speak. "It can't be" that his objection is correct. Casuistically, in the time-honored method of *pilpul*—the talmudic argument in which one tries to demonstrate that even opposites can be brought into harmony—he retreats from his objection and offers essentially the same answer the Rav produced earlier. Why?

There are several explanations possible. First, as Slater—following Freud's more classic statement in *Totem and Taboo*—notes, revolts are commonly followed by "identification with the overthrown leader."[19]

Appropriating the Rav's answer as his own is one way in which Yitzhak, representing the students who have joined in his objections, can accomplish this. Second, the revolt has effectively failed since until now no one has been able to come up with a better answer than the Rav's. Instead the circle has fallen into an anarchy where there is no leader and no answer. As already suggested, their modern Orthodoxy commits these men to a rational faith that is intolerant of continuing puzzlement about the meaning of the Talmud. Moreover, as members of a tightly bound study circle, these men normally share a profound concern for one another as well as a dedication to the common goal of *lernen*. For both reasons they do not welcome the present situation. Life was easier when all were subordinate to the Rav, accepting his explanations and at peace with one another.

In social drama, "people have to take sides in terms of deeply entrenched moral imperatives and constraints, often against their

---

of unspoken threat which further adds to the drama of faith and reason herein being played out (*The Chosen* [New York: Simon & Schuster, 1966], pp. 134 and 343; see also *The Promise* [New York: Knopf, 1969]).

own personal preferences."[20] Whatever his personal inclinations, Yitzhak's moral obligation to the study circle requires him to redress the crisis he has generated. Twisting and turning his argument, he becomes even more insistent that his objection was wrong than he was when he earlier contended it was right. Raising his voice, rushing his words, he offers a rebuttal to his own argument. In favor of the study circle and the Rav, he turns against himself. The group listens silently, manifestly to follow his argument but at a deeper level gripped by the drama of the encounter and watching Yitzhak's tortuous retreat.

Breaking in, the Rav begins his climb back to his position of supremacy. He, and not Yitzhak, will offer a rebuttal. There is no vindictiveness in his voice or manner; he like the rest of us is bound in fellowship with all those around the table. But he will nevertheless not abandon his position of leadership and authority now that it is clear that we have left the way open for his return.

As he did when the crisis first broke out and before Yitzhak's objection plunged us into protracted puzzlement, the Rav reviews the problem with the text. He restates Yitzhak's objection. The process is repeated over and over as he addresses each one of us in turn, until the whole circle has been touched. With each restatement, the problem is refined and made more manageable. Finally, the Rav reaches Meir, the man on his right.

"Yitzhak, it's not at all difficult," the Rav calls out as he finishes reviewing the issue for Meir and glances back into the page open before him.

It is, however, no longer Yitzhak who reacts on behalf of all of us.[21] Beaten back by his "act of contrition," he is silent, and instead Meir becomes the voice of the students. He parries with the Rav over the explanation, offers glosses, and forces refinements of the solution. Each of us is now addressed by name as the teacher hammers out his answer; each of us must be symbolically reenlisted as a student. Only Meir replies.

Perhaps trying to exercise a new position as the leading student voice, Meir appears ready to rekindle the revolt. He offers an alternative solution to the questions: Rabbi Afays is simply agreeing with Ulla, hence the repetition. But even as he argues his point of view, Meir finds no great swell of support for it as did Yitzhak earlier. One or two half-spoken encouragements are voiced by several students, but none of these is attended to by the Rav who, with the victory over Yitzhak and his revolt behind him, refuses again to be turned away from his explanation.

Now, in the face of the Rav's relentless declamations, Meir capitulates. In a curious "fractured utterance,"[22] he begins what sounds at first like an objection, a plaintive remark, but ends in what is unquestionably an echo of the teacher's explanation. With this last rebellion broken, the Rav can begin the process of reintegration, a process in which both the meaning of the text and social relations among the members of the circle and himself are brought back into continuity with what existed before the breach.

Unlike the therapy group which Slater describes or the primal horde in Freud's allegory of origins, the members of the Talmud study circle are confronted not only by a leader but also by a rabbi and instructor. While perhaps willing to revolt against the leader, their religious and intellectual commitment to study militates against their overthrowing the teacher. After all, no amount of identification with the overthrown Rav will help the others arrive at an understanding of an opaque text. This latter need, supported by the students' Orthodox Jewish reverence for rabbis, necessarily limits all revolts—just as it has done in the present case.

Reintegration

Hearing Meir come around to his point of view, the Rav calls out: "*Ot a zoy, Oh*," a Yiddish exclamation that denotes roughly, "Oh that's it!" Here is a call indicating a heartfelt embrace of the errant student by his teacher. Here, accordingly, begins the reintegration.

Before this continues, however, we are provided with a "cooling-off" period, time during which we are given a chance to recuperate from the heat of the crisis but during which we still remain linked to the subject. Occasionally cooling off takes the form of periods of silence during which members of the circle peruse the text, presumably putting it in order in their minds. Sometimes it is filled with the telling of a parable or a story that is digressive but not altogether unrelated to the *inyan*. This time the cooling-off period is filled by a review of the Rashi commentary on the lines just discussed. Reading from the column on the inside margin of the page, the Rav swiftly recites the glosses and amplifications which Rashi has added. The reading is part of the mandatory, formal process of *lernen*. Often the object of reverence and sometimes the center of attention or controversy, Rashi's commentary is in the present context anticlimactic. While the Rav reads through it in an unanimated style and rapid monotone, the others have an opportunity to collect their thoughts and come to terms with the solution and realize the crisis has passed.

"*Moyredik*" (Formidable), says Moshe in the heart language of Yiddish when the Rashi has been concluded. It is clear to all of us that he is referring to something other than the glosses we have just read through in the commentary. Not only has the effort to get through the text been "formidable," the social drama surrounding it has been too.

"What?" asks the Rav, as if wanting us all to hear this evaluation and tacit affirmation of the authority of his solution.

"*Moyredik*," the student repeats.

"*Moyredik*," agrees the Rav, smiling broadly, allowing all the implications of the term to resonate throughout the room.

Quickly, various other students display and echo their comprehension and acceptance of the answer. Some repeat key words; others ask for brief clarifying points, implying these are all they miss for a full assimilation of the matter. The reintegration process is now fully under way; the performances perfectly crafted to suit the occasion.

Yitzhak now begins the final phase of the process. Taking up his question again, he summarizes his understanding of the Rav's reply. Gone are his objections. Instead he offers a long but faithful reiteration of the solution, allowing the Rav to guide him here and there over some of the rough spots in his comprehension. The rest of the students listen silently to what seems to become the apodictic version of the *sugia*, the one in which the student and teacher, rebel and Rav, for the last time play out their interchange.

In a sense this replaying of the question and answer is a central element of the reintegration for it presents a version of the episode in which there is no crisis or breach of norm. Everything that has gone on for nearly an hour before has been in preparation for reaching this point in which the asking of the question and offering of the answer could go on smoothly and without tension. Moreover, not only does this replaying weave the text together into a logical whole, it also reknits the social fabric of the circle. In the accord between student and teacher, the rest of us are implicated as well. Instead of the veiled aggression in which each of us tried to deny the solution of the others to the troublesome *sugia*, there is unity in our acceptance of the Rav's answer.

It is important to recognize here that there may be a difference between a student's comprehension of the text and his understanding of how it must be explained. The former requires an intellectual apperception while the latter needs a social competence and performing ability. The participant in the ritual *lernen* must learn how to express the "right answer," the authoritative one, as if it were his own, as if he comprehended it totally. Ideally his intellectual and social needs coincide such that the way he is supposed to comprehend it is the way he does. But if this is not the case, the *lernen* in the Orthodox Jewish circle requires him to exercise an intellectual and moral discipline in which the traditional answer is made to appear more than sufficient. This is his special responsibility as an Orthodox Jew. It is sometimes the case that this responsibility restricts his powers of reasoning. This matter will be returned to in subsequent chapters.

To be sure, all students do not all simultaneously succeed in getting the answer straight. A few continue to express some confusion. They are, however, helped by the others who already understand how to explain the matter. Thus, instead of criticism directed at one another there is fellowship and assistance as everyone gets into line. This does not mean that aggression has evaporated. On the contrary, one might argue that helping a fellow understand tacitly demonstrates one's own superior capacity and is in fact a sublimated form of one-upmanship.[23] But in this form the net result of the action is group unification rather than anarchic disintegration.

The rush to demonstrate comprehension takes up our attentions during this last phase of the social drama. Thus even though the climax of the crisis has passed, there is no real dropping off of involvement in the *lernen*.

I remain now as the last man who still has not fully understood how to state the Rav's answer. Expressing my lingering confusion and consequent dissatisfaction with the explanation (I have really been too occupied observing the events as a sociologist to have followed the arguments as a Talmud student, although I do not admit this in class), I ask for yet one more restatement. By now, I find myself confronted by a unified set of responses from students and teacher. My puzzlement cannot be disregarded because I am a member of the circle and as such must be reintegrated.

Should I fail to reach an understanding I might be dismissed as one incapable of *lernen*. This sort of judgment would, if supported by a continuing inability to catch on, ultimately lead to my exclusion from the circle. I would not necessarily be asked to leave, but my questions and comments would no longer be treated with any sort of seriousness and I would be treated like a child, a nonperson, a junior member at best. As an insider I am aware of this risk. Accordingly, insofar as I wish to remain a member of the circle, I have a vested interest in coming around to the generally accepted understanding of the *sugia*. In this I am like all the others, and generally like most members of small face-to-face groups, ready to bend under group pressure.

In spite of all the pressures militating against an unyielding puzzlement—the desire of the group to complete its reintegration and my personal wish not to be excluded from the circle—my inability to understand still seems to arouse some tension. The possibility always exists that I could undermine the solution and the harmony it has brought about by some penetrating criticism, some discovery of a "fatal flaw" in the answer, which would undermine the team performance. Dramatically, of course, such a replay of the entire crisis near the end of a play would hardly be countenanced, but this is not a stage play, after all; it is real life with all its vagaries and possibilities. My challenge is thus immediately taken up, the tension of it softened by joking.

Using the coffee cups and ashtrays on the table, the Rav reviews the entire *sugia* for me, beginning with the ashtrays which he tells me will stand for the goats and the white cups for the cows that the priest must slaughter on Yom Kippur.

"No, the white cups should be the goats," someone calls out, and we all laugh. This is not going to be allowed to arouse tension again. The message is clear; the crisis must be over. We are united again, joking, bantering, ready to go on to another *inyan*.

As the Rav reviews the discussion with his cups and ashtrays, I begin to call out a few key words in my display of understanding. Gradually others do so even before I do. Identifying with me, they are taking no chances that this retelling of the *sugia* will get bogged down in incomprehension. At the same time, the boundary between the group and me disappears. As Meir could answer when someone else was addressed, so now others answer for me.

The Rav completes his explanation by phrasing it as a question; the answer will complete the *inyan*. I provide it.

"That's right," he answers me in English and, with a flourish, closes his book. We all laugh. It is past nine o'clock, our normal time of adjournment, but the time has passed quickly; no one has looked at his watch. Caught up in the drama of events, no one indicated any interest in stopping before everything was resolved.

Overlapping Dramas: A Summary

As earlier noted, there are really two dramas embedded in this single episode. The first, essentially an ideological one, centers around the crisis stimulated by the group's sudden inability to discover the reason they have come to believe in and expect from the Talmud. The consequent irruption of tension is a result of the incongruity between a belief in reason, to which as contemporary men these Orthodox Jews have attached great moral significance, and the perceived reality of a possibly redundant, meaningless text. Before this drama is concluded, however, a second and related one develops. With the Rav, whose authority as teacher is nominally supreme, unable to provide an immediately acceptable explanation for the opaque passage, his position of dominance is undermined. The normal feelings of resentment fostered by the students' institutionalized position of inferiority are no longer held in check; they too try to provide explanations, to usurp the role of teacher-leader. In the process they not only assault the Rav's assertions of authority but also one another by criticizing one another's attempts at explanation. The result is an anarchy and disintegration of the social order of the circle. This is far more obviously a social drama.

Ultimately, however, the felt obligation to continue *lernen*, dependent as it is upon competent instruction, limits the group's willingness to mount a full-fledged revolt. Within this frame, the circle is able to repair any damage to their ties of fellowship; the acceptance of the Rav's authority is what protects the students from freely attacking one another. The denouement of this social drama in turn sets the stage for the resolution of the text's meaning. Thus, the very same answer which was rejected early on is now acceptable in the interests of continued *lernen*. *Lernen* thus not only gives the group members a definition of their situation, it also serves as a protective framework in which their circle remains intact. Having joined together for the purposes of Talmud study, they are prevented from breaking apart by it as well.

Social dramas, however, as Turner notes, do not always end like this one—with a restoration. Some close with a legitimization of schism.[24] In the Talmud study circle, schism need not always lead to disintegration of the group. The following case illustrates this point nicely.

THE CASE OF DISSENTING OPINIONS

The study circle at Kahal Reyim quite often found itself faced with dissenting opinions on the proper interpretation of the passages of Talmud under review. Each evening, from Sunday through Thursday, in one of the many rooms that make up the Kahal Reyim synagogue, a group of eight to ten men would assemble around two of the tables at the back of what served as both sanctuary and study hall. On the heels of the regular evening prayers, this circle would review a folio of Talmud under the nominal leadership of "Rav Moses."

The procedures surrounding the prayers and the *lernen*, which for sixty years had without interruption preceded and followed them, were patterned to the point of ritual. Two clocks hung on the wall; one told the time, and the other was always set so that at the precise moment of sunset it would read twelve o'clock. When this second clock reached 12:45, the evening prayers would begin. Heralded by a thump of the *gabbai*'s hand against a table, the preliminaries to the prayers would begin. Those who had been engaged in study during the interval since the afternoon prayers now closed their books and moved to put them away, while those obligated to recite the memorial *kaddish* prayer did so as is customary at the conclusion of study. Others, taking prayer books in hand, headed for their regular seats or niches and readied themselves for the opening words of the liturgy. Those who had not been in the room beforehand came into the *besmedresh* (sanctuary-study hall) exactly on cue.

At the close of the service, as most of the assembled men shuffled out, Rav Moses's Talmud *shiur* would begin. Those who were members but not present at the prayers appeared, as if they had been waiting somewhere in the wings. In fact some had, coming from other rooms and other classes or services. While several men moved together the two tables on which we would study, another turned off the lights in the unused parts of the room. Others arranged the benches, polished by sixty years of trouser bottoms.

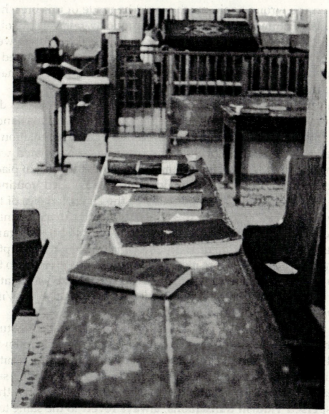

A study table in the back of a synagogue similar to the one at Kahal Reyim. Note the well-worn tomes of Talmud which have not yet been reshelved. (Photograph by S. C. Heilman)

The remaining men distributed the volumes of Talmud, which were kept on a special shelf in our corner. In the half-darkness of the evening, an intimate atmosphere was being created by these repeated, ritual-like activities. With the preliminaries accomplished, each member moved to his regular seat. So permanent were these that, even if an entire row of people were missing save one who sat at the far end of the bench, the remaining man would nevertheless sit at his regular spot.

Each man had his own favorite copy of the text which he insisted on using each time. If someone sat in the wrong place or

received the wrong book, much would be made of this breach of
norm, but commonly the tension was quickly relieved by jokes
and displays of mock anger during which all the wrongs were
redressed. In a sense, these minor breaches of norm resulted in
minor social dramas, preliminary sketches preceding the major
event: the *shiur*.

With the opening of the books, there was a simultaneous distribution of snuff. Each man took a pinch and held it in his hands,
the stimulation of the mind to be preceded by this stimulation of
the senses; the sharing of time and ideas to be associated with
the sharing of the physical pleasures. Everything was set in place.

Entwined in ritualized behaviors and established routines,
lernen at Kahal Reyim takes on many of the characteristics of the
prayer which precedes it. In this, the emphasis is on maintaining
an unimpeded train of spoken words: to recite (chant) text, translate, explain, and comment all in one concise and uninterrupted
cadence. Just as prayers are mouthed without interruption, so too
lernen is chanted without disturbances. The call repeated after
even the smallest digression or briefest pause is always, "*Viter,
di gemore*" (Onward, [in] the Talmud).

In the time-honored procedure of European Talmud study
which serves as a model for this circle: "Each phrase is followed
by a long, often free Yiddish translation. To maintain the unit of
so complex a structure, melody is used in such a way that subordinate clauses of the same hypotactic level, together with their
interspersed Yiddish translations, always revert to the same tone
level, which does not return to the tonic of the scale until the
main clause with its translation have been completed."[25]

The chant, or *gemore-nign*, is what identifies the ritual character
of the *shiur*. Anything which stops the tune, and all the continuity
it represents, is immediately perceived by the insiders as something unusual, a potentially dramatic moment, and it engages
their "sensory attention."[26]

To be sure, in addition to expecting an uninterrupted ritual
chanting of their text, the members of the Kahal Reyim study
circle, like those at Rabbi Rotenbush's house, look upon the text
as "apodictic truth," a truth that is absolute: "It is so because it
is said that it is so."[27]

Anything that casts doubt on what is "said" accordingly also
breaches the normative expectations. Thus something that at once
disturbs the train of words that make up the *nign* (chant) of *lernen*,

while also raising questions about what the Talmud has to say, can at Kahal Reyim be expected to generate an irruption of tension and consequent crisis. Consider the following.

Itzik's Objection

As usual, the Rav has been chanting his way through the page, interspersing text with translation, explanation, and brief commentary in an unbroken thread of sound. As he nears the end of the *sugia*, his voice is lowered and inflected with appropriate cadences; and all those who have been saving a question or comment ready themselves to speak. The experienced insider knows the etiquette of interruption and that a challenge is best mounted now.

In the *sugia*, the closing point declares, according to the teacher, that the law in question is scriptural rather than rabbinic. The distinction is a common one and refers to the two kinds of laws governing the Orthodox Jew's religious life: those whose authority derives from the interpretation of Scriptures, and those instituted by the rabbis as a legal buffer ensuring the observances of scriptural law. In principle, the former are considered significantly more binding than rabbinic laws, and accordingly the sanctions surrounding them are more stringent. In legal terms, it is therefore quite important to determine whether or not something presented by the Talmud as law is scriptural or rabbinic in origin.

Having heard the Rav announce that the law in question is scriptural, Itzik, the *gabbai*, announces that there is another interpretation which suggests the law is rabbinic. Commonly, when questions or such comments arise, Rav Moses handles them as if they were expected. Often without missing a beat, he will assimilate his answer into the thread of what he has been saying. In this way the student's question or gloss will be transformed into a part of the *lernen* without undermining the Rav's legitimacy as teacher. Rather than generating a crisis, the student's remark will then act to plunge us all further into the page; it would not breach the norm of *"viter, di gemore."* Indeed, these comments become, as I shall later argue, cultural performances which "express and reinforce as well as teach [social and religious] . . . norms and promote social cohesion—all in a complex way."[28]

This time, however, the Rav is apparently unprepared to handle Itzik's objection. He simply stops short and asks, "Huh?" His surprise startles the group, for we are suddenly seeing the norm—

that he will handle comments and keep the train of *lernen* un-impeded—broken.

Itzik repeats his comment. As *gabbai*—a term by which he is often addressed—as well as a leader of another study circle meeting earlier in the evening, Itzik considers himself something more than a simple student. Indeed, on some occasions when the Rav is absent, Itzik is the one who leads our circle in a review (in the absence of the regular teacher, the group never covers new material). Trying often to distinguish himself as the premier student, one whose scholarship rivals the teacher's, Itzik seizes this opportunity to demonstrate his erudition and thereby usurp, at least within the boundaries of this *sugia*, the role of teacher. The sudden opportunity created by the Rav's unpreparedness is not, however, to be grasped without a struggle. Nor is the struggle only with the Rav, whose position is the object of the quest. Another character, Mendel, one of the students, mounts a challenge.

Like Itzik, Mendel is a teacher in another study circle. In the early evening, before the prayers which precede this class, Mendel leads a group in one of the other rooms at Kahal Reyim in the study of codes. Some of his students there are his peers here. To compensate, perhaps, for this dual role, Mendel takes a very active role in this *shiur*. Throughout the Rav's chant, he echoes and sometimes—if he is fast enough—cues him. This "signal of togetherness" serves to identify Mendel as one who is not so much studying under the Rav's tutelage as one who is, along with him, reviewing matters they both know.[29]

Itzik's challenge to the Rav's closing remark, which Mendel had echoed, is thus seen by the latter as a challenge to him too. And if the Rav is not prepared to argue the point with Itzik, Mendel is; for in successfully doing so he—and not his rival—will come out as the man who shines in the eyes of the rest of us. In the interstices of the chant and before the Rav has a chance to collect his thoughts, Mendel asks Itzik what sort of alternative interpretation there is. The question will force Itzik to do more than simply assert that he knows another way of viewing the text; it will force him to display his reasoning and competence. In his demand for details, Mendel is putting Itzik on the spot and taking leadership away from Rav Moses.

Sensing the mounting tension, the Rav moves to head off the conflict. His position, like that of any established authority, is dependent upon social order and consensus. While he might gain additional insight into the text out of this confrontation, he indicates by his action that he is more interested in going on with his reading and chant. He would, as it were, de-dramatize the incident.

"*Yo*," he says, an offhanded "yes" which serves to downplay the importance of this discussion between Mendel and Itzik.

And what of the rest of the students? On the one hand, our attention is held by the breach of norm and the irruption of tension over the interpretation of the text and between Itzik and Mendel. On the other hand, the rivalry brought to the surface in this exchange points up a potential line of fracture within the group, one that could ultimately force each of us to choose between one or another opinion and its champions. Only with the Rav back in position of unchallenged dominance will the circle again be characterized by the relative equality and comradeship that we have come to expect. So, caught between the interest in the drama and a desire for stability and the continued fellowship of *lernen*, the rest of us remain silently attentive. When the Rav says, "*Yo!*" the rest of us look back into our books, ready to follow his lead into the page.

Mendel, in a spirit of mounting crisis, refuses to let matters rest. He demands, not in anger as much as in a voice of determination, "I want to ask; I can ask him what the other explanation is."

The Rav stops. He cannot contain the crisis by acting as if it does not exist. His reading is once again halted.

Itzik answers, but in the midst of his explanation he finds himself interrupted by the Rav who tries to diminish the tension that has become palpable in the room. The Rav puns on one of Itzik's words. Perhaps laughter will enable us to move on from this crisis. But the effort fails as Mendel and Itzik move more deeply into their debate, arguing the various fine points of the *sugia*. Their discussion is telegraphic, its language the specialized argot of *lernen*. Only the erudite, those *literally versed* (in the purest sense of these words) in the language of the Talmud and the Scriptures, can follow the debate. To the illiterate, the uninformed—in Jewish terms the *am-ha-arets* (boor)—the conversation between these men, like the text itself, remains opaque and inaccessible. In a sense one might suggest that, in addition to challenging one another, Itzik and Mendel in the way they articulate their argument are also actively distinguishing themselves from those of us who cannot understand them. They are scholars in debate, reserving for themselves their secret language of discourse.[30]

Thus far, the episode has all the makings of a social drama. It begins with a series of normative breaches. First, the *lernen* and its special chant are held up. Second, the Rav is caught unprepared as his interpretation is challenged. Third, the comradeship or at least submerged rivalry among some of the students is replaced by confrontation. On the heels of the breach is a mounting tension, made manifest in the Rav's inability to defuse the situation with his pun or his effort to read further in the text. The redressive action that one expects to follow now will aim to revitalize comradeship or at least lead to the resubmersion of rivalries, replace the Rav in a position of leadership, and finally get the chant of *lernen* started again.

The Tertius Gaudens

The concept of the *"tertius gaudens"* (the third who enjoys advantage from the conflict between two), a concept advanced by Georg Simmel to explain an important dynamism of human interaction, may be helpful in understanding the redressive action here. In outlining the idea of the *tertius*, Simmel suggests that there are two forms in which it can occur. In the first place:

> The advantage of the *tertius* may result from the fact that the remaining two hold each other in check, and he can make a gain which one of the two would otherwise deny him. The discord here only effectuates a paralyzation of forces which, if they could, would strike against him.
>
> Meanwhile, a second form appears when the *tertius* gains an advantage only because action by one of the two conflicting parties brings it about for its own purposes—the *tertius* does not need to take the initiative. A case in point are the benefits and promotions which a party bestows upon him only in order to offend its adversary.[31]

The episode in question here offers both possibilities for the Rav. Because there are only two conceivable points of view on interpreting the *sugia*—either it is based on scriptural or rabbinic law—and the Rav has supported the former, it is necessarily the case that, in the debate between Mendel and Itzik, Mendel while challenging his comrade for supremacy is also arguing for the Rav's interpretation. To "offend his adversary," Itzik, Mendel necessarily helps set the stage for the Rav's return by supporting his explanation.

With the situation thus structured, the Rav now makes use of the fact that Mendel and Itzik seem to be arguing themselves to a stand-off, and he moves to tip the balance in his favor, presumably expecting to rise thereby to his position status quo ante.

"Rashi," he says, citing the towering authority on the Talmud whose commentary, as yet unrecited, lies before us on the open page, "says it's a scriptural law."

In a daring act of erudition, Itzik for the first time reads us the text of another commentary. Faced with this argument, Mendel champions the first commentary. Rashi, he contends, has responded to this alternative explanation and has dismissed it. Now the debate centers around the interpretation of Rashi's comments.

While Mendel continues his increasingly strident argument, the Rav tries a different approach. Rather tenderly, and in sharp contrast to Mendel, the Rav asks: *"Vus darft er zokh shver makhn"* (Why does he make it difficult for himself)?

Both the timing and the ambiguity of the question are exquisitely tailored to the occasion. The timing is right because as all of us can see—and the question seems to be addressed to Itzik but asked of all of us—the debate between Mendel and Itzik is no nearer resolution now than it was at first. Both champion revered commentaries and therefore legitimate opinions. They have reached a stand-off, and some new way out of the situation is necessary if the group is not to be forced to choose sides and become divided.

The wording of the question is also right. *"Shver,"* the key word in the sentence, means "difficult." Manifestly, the Rav has asked why Itzik has had to choose the difficult (i.e., more complex) interpretation rather than the simple one (*poshut pshat*). The normal procedure in the Kahal Reyim circle is to interpret according to *poshut pshat*, this parsimonious approach being best fitted to cover the most material with the least difficulty. The Rav's inquiry, however, is not only about Itzik's interpretive approach: it also implicitly refers to his social situation. It is as if he were asking: Why make it "difficult" for yourself by being in the minority, by being unable to agree with us and going against the accepted pattern? The ambiguity of the words, as well as the contrast in their sound to the high-pitched cadences and plaintive cry of Mendel's challenge, elicit a calm compromise.

As if to make sure that Itzik understands that, should he choose to continue his argument he will face continued counterinterpretations, the Rav suggests that an alternative reading of Itzik's commentary is possible. Summarizing such a reading, the Rav concludes, "It is just as I said."

"M'ken a zoy zugn und a zoy zugn" (one can say thus and [one can say] otherwise), Itzik replies. As there are two commentators who seem to disagree, so there may be two dissenting opinions among the members of the circle. Neither is dominant. With this effort to legitimate schism, Itzik has found a way to make matters less "difficult." No longer insisting on the ultimacy of the interpretation he has supported, he nevertheless refuses to totally capitulate.

"This is also the *pshat"* (simple explanation), he adds, emphasizing his continuity with the established norms of our *lernen.*

With this compromise, Itzik has left an opening for Mendel as well.

"Good, good," Mendel answers, willing to settle for this sort of stabilized division.

The drama completed, the Rav acts to provide a cooling down of any lingering tensions and also to reconfirm his position as the one who conducts the *shiur.* Beginning with a phrase associated with the handing down of a rabbinic judgment—*"Ikh halt as"* (I hold [maintain] that)—he concludes, ". . . nothing will happen; he *can* say this." This mock judgment and fractured phrase which seems to affirm the acceptability of Itzik's compromise elicits a relieved laughter from all of those assembled around the tables. What sounded at first as if it would become a divisive verdict has concluded amiably. Dissent has been legitimated without undermining our continued *lernen* and without opening an unbridgeable rift in the circle. To be sure, the teacher's tolerance of a muted dissent is as much a reflection of his perception of the desires of the group as the result of his own magnanimity. Were he to be an unyielding authority, he would risk his position of esteemed dominance. Having legitimated and thereby defused and de-dramatized the dissent, the Rav recites the words of the next *inyan;* the crisis has passed.

The Metaphor of Social Drama

Caught up in the flux of activity, the participants in the Talmud circle are unlikely to look upon what they do as dramatic or to sense that they are dramatis personae. Asked to explain what they do and what draws them together, most will simply say *"lernen."* Even as someone seeking to be a careful observer, I did not—precisely because I was also a participant—conceive these two episodes and others like them immediately as social dramas. Only later, as I analytically reviewed my tapes and notes did I begin to see how this metaphor of social drama would enable me to discover the direction and development of something which in the heat of the action I sensed only intuitively and vaguely. With the concept of social drama to demarcate the lines of behavior, I could begin to perceive norms, tension, rivalries, loyalties, social positions and roles, conflict and consensus, and strategic interactions. Rav Moses may have been quite unaware that he was acting out the role of *tertius gaudens,* and Rav Rotenbush likewise may not have consciously realized that he produced and encouraged conflict among those challenging his authority, thereby dividing and conquering them.

The metaphor of social drama, however, reveals the beginning, development, and dénouement of the happening. That is, it frames the episode and renders it "isolable and minutely describable," and thereby subject to analytic comprehension.[32] An essentially unknown and uncomprehended social activity becomes by way of a metaphor illuminated and comprehensible. As Robert Nisbet put it: "Metaphor is, at its simplest, a way of proceeding from the known to the unknown. It is a way of cognition in which the identifying qualities of one thing are transferred . . . to some other thing that is, by remoteness or complexity, unknown to us."[33] To be sure, any "metaphor selects, emphasizes, suppresses, and organizes features of the principal subject by implying statements about it that normally apply to the subsidiary subject," and in thus trying to make phenomena appear "clearer than nature presents them" runs the risk of taking what cannot be put into the metaphor's framework as having a "kind of pseudo-existence as a phenomenon."[34] At the same time, however, it informs in ways that go beyond what is available to the senses. That the members of the study circle do not necessarily define themselves as involved in drama in no way detracts from the capacity of the concept of drama to explain their behavior.

The two episodes described here, different in plot but similar insofar as they underscore the degree to which social relations enter into *lernen*, are by no means the only examples of social drama in the study circle; they are however representative of what at times holds the attention and engages the consciousness of those who come together in the study circle.

What of the other moments, the times when there are apparently no social dramas occurring? Is there something else that occupies the consciousness of the participants? Is there something else about *lernen* that attracts the members of the circle, makes them stay involved, and moves them to return again the next time? I believe the concept of "cultural performance" provides an answer, and I shall now turn to it.

3
CULTURAL PERFORMANCE

"We are, in sum, incomplete or unfinished animals who complete or finish ourselves through culture—and not through culture in general but through highly particular forms of it. . . ."

CLIFFORD GEERTZ, *The Interpretation of Cultures*

"By lernen, *so to speak, one becomes a complete person. . . ."*

MAX GRUNWALD, "Das 'Lernen' "

Joining in *lernen* with a circle of one's fellows (at least among those who pursue it as an avocation) is something more than simply an intellectual acquisition of the information in the text. It is also as a public performance during which the participants make use of their culture to correct or complete themselves. Precisely because "it is through culture patterns . . . that man makes sense of the events through which he lives," and through *lernen* that some Jews make sense of their culture patterns, the two may be related.[1]

Attending a *shiur* (class) in the intimate atmosphere of the study circle may be understood as a "kind of sentimental education," during which what one "learns is what his culture's ethos and his private sensibility (or, anyway, certain aspects of them) look like when spelled out externally in a collective text."[2] As they recite and reiterate talmudic controversies, review and react to the text's logic, use its terminology, perceive the world through its perspectives, collectively reaffirm the legitimacy of its laws and authenticity of its narratives, and accept the necessity of its theological limitations, the *lerners*—at least within the boundaries of their class—form and discover their temperament and their culture's temper at the same time.

Listening to himself and his fellows bring to life the voice of the Talmud and its associated commentaries, the major cultural monument of this People of the Book, the participant not only learns what the texts have to say; he also has a chance *to say it himself, to reenact and react to it.* Like the page before him, he may engage in debates, ask questions, tell stories, or digress with his fellows along a not always direct path of associations that nevertheless remain linked to the Talmud. By so doing, he publicly reflects, communicates, perpetuates and develops the pattern of meanings and inherited conceptions that define traditional Jewish culture. In this sense, *lernen* may be termed a *cultural performance.*

For the members of a circle, these cultural performances are, as I shall try to show, enactments, materializations, and realizations of, among other things, Jewish folkways and the religious perspectives of the tradition as expressed through the Talmud and its associated sacred texts. They are "not only models of what they believe, but also modes *for* the believing of it. In these plastic dramas men attain their faith as they portray it."[3] The recitation, translation, explanation, and discussion of the text along with digression induce and reflect a set of moods and morals—an ethos—and define a picture of the way things are understood to be—a world view—both of which are anchored in the symbols and meanings of the Talmud. The sacred text—and the insights which emerge during its explication and discussion—become in effect transpositions of one another. *Lernen*, the framework in which this goes on, thus evokes and at the same time embodies the religious sensibilities and cosmic order of the text and by implication the traditional Jewish world.

This performance, moreover, represents "not only the point at which the dispositional and conceptual aspects of religious life converge for the believer, but also the point at which the interaction between them can be most readily examined by the detached observer."[4] (This incidentally provides yet another rationale for the examination of the Talmud study circle by students of culture.) There appear to be two main trends of these sorts of cultural performance: "traditioning," and "contemporization." Traditioning allows the participants to slip into the framework of meaning—the ethos and world view—of the Talmud, become inhabitants of its temporal realm and subject to its rules of order and logic. Here a group of twentieth-century men seem to sit in the first-century academies of Babylonia or at least the primordial yeshivas of Europe and look at the world—past, present, and future—through their windows. If not always a total transformation of consciousness, this kind of performance nevertheless gives the students and teacher another world in which to live. Here, for example, legends come to life; miracles are treated as facts; debates about the order of sacrifices at the Holy Temple are matters of pressing urgency; and verses of Scripture become the building blocks of reason. This is a turning of oneself from the present-day world to the ways of the Talmud.

The ethos of traditioning is, simply put, that there is no experience or idea in the Talmud so archaic or remote that it cannot be imagined or understood by the contemporary Jew. The traditioning *lerner* chants the Talmud in the time-honored cadences of the yeshiva and, as he tries to do with similar incantations of prayer, takes on the ethos and world view of those who in previous generations likewise intoned or studied those words. The past, his source of ultimate legitimacy, becomes "reversible and recoverable, a sort of mythical present that is periodically reintegrated" into current existence by means of *lernen*.[5] The traditioning *lerner* thereby temporally enlarges his world. Not only can he choose to be part of his contemporary milieu, he can also during *lernen* become an intellectual and moral contemporary (although not necessarily an "equal") of the Talmud which he believes "corrects" or "completes" what seems to him the more shallow and imperfect reality of the present. This is the great advantage he may feel he has over those who cannot or do not *lern* as he does and who are therefore trapped within the narrow confines of their own lives and time.

To be sure, there are those who may choose to abandon completely the present-day world in favor of the one in the Talmud. This plunge into the past may be termed "radical traditioning." For those who espouse this sort of *lernen*, there is nothing real except what the Talmud describes and defines. It does not correct or complete but rather replaces the situation in which they find themselves. Indeed, the way they *lern* is often also the way they live, comfortably ensconced in the embrace of an eternal yesterday.

If, as Santayana has argued, "another world to live in—whether we expect to ever pass wholly over into it or no—is what we mean by having a religion," then the disposition of the traditioning *lerner* (including the radicals) may be properly understood as "religious."[6] He displays a willingness to be shaped by the world, the ideas, and the morals of the ancient sacred texts.

The second direction in which cultural performance may go during *lernen* involves an imaginative reach back into the world of the Talmud during which the old words and ideas are swept forward into the contemporary social and psychological cosmos of the *lerner*. Here the past becomes embedded in, completed, or corrected by the present, just as in traditioning the opposite is the case. The modern world becomes the cultural context within which the Talmud can be intelligibly discussed and understood. This kind of *lernen* performance may be termed "contemporization."[7] "It is the process by which old meanings are ascribed to new elements or by which new values change the cultural significance of the old forms" and is another means of integration of what would otherwise appear as archaic into a receiving culture.[8] Here, "the past is reinterpreted to conform to the present reality, with the tendency to retroject into the past various elements that were subjectively unavailable at the time."[9]

Historically among Jews contemporization has had two or possibly three overlapping stages. In the first, where contemporization and traditioning merged, the Orthodox defenders of the faith integrated new ideas "into the context of traditional thinking," and thereby the "new elements forfeited their original revolutionary character and were neutralized," as Jacob Katz has pointed out.[10] By definition, nothing accepted as part of the tradition was considered genuinely new. With regard to the Talmud, this meant the book had to be considered complete as it stood. Later, the boundaries and character of the tradition became shredded and challenged by an infusion of more and more of the realities of modernity with its undeniable novelties. The tradition and its proponents were thus forced into open ideological struggle with the new; and often the result was a compromise: a reduced authority for tradition along with a restrained modernity. In the study of Talmud this meant that one admitted that on certain contemporary matters the text was silent, while on other matters what it said could not be taken seriously without some reinterpretation. Thus, for example a contemporizer of this sort would suggest that the Talmud seemed to say nothing about a contemporary issue such as the propriety of women drivers or that its discussion of medical remedies had to be understood allegorically or as folk medicine. Still, one retained a faith in the text and dared not dismiss it completely, for *perhaps* with sufficient understanding it could be found to provide more guidance than might be immediately apparent from the contemporary perspective.[11]

Finally, in the last stage, contemporary values invaded and at times overwhelmed tradition. In the process, the legitimacy of that tradition—in our case the Talmud text—became entirely dependent upon its capacity to become integrated with the new concepts, values, and ideas. Talmudic dicta and views at odds with modern ideas and ideals were considered irrelevant and trivial, if not altogether despised. This last type of unrestrained contemporization—call it "radical contemporization"—was by and large never accepted among even the most modern of Orthodox Jews as an appropriate way of *lernen* because the culture which it affirmed and expressed was more modern and secular than Jewish. Nevertheless, radical contemporization, although *uncelebrated and often truncated* in practice, occasionally displays itself on certain occasions among the modern Orthodox—particularly where the text of the Talmud deals with miracle tales and cures that the contemporary student is hard put to accept. Commonly, however, even the most modern among the Orthodox would prefer to leave their doubts unspoken and disattended.

Generally, contemporization is possible because the text and Judaism, while concerned with details and even the minutiae of everyday life, like all great books and religions in general is made up of what Victor Turner has graphically called a "forest of symbols."[12] In many cases a single symbol may stand for many things and be understood from a variety of perspectives. What in one age might have been concreteness becomes a metaphor in the light of another. What was a fact clearly recalled in one generation may in another become an item of parable.

Contemporization and traditioning are thus interpretive performances which are fundamentally syncretistic in character. The world as experienced and the one which the Talmud describes become fused and in the process of *lernen* "turn out to be the same world."[13] Panchronism and anachronism paradoxically become the central principles of order.

Throughout Jewish history there were those whose approach to the Talmud as to all matters Jewish was traditioning. This way "did not call for an adjustment to the spirit of the [present] time" but rather "endeavored to preserve in the changed time a maximum of culture elements of earlier days."[14] In this approach to *lernen*, "one is not afraid of repetition, one is not in search of originality; it is impossible to improve upon eminent men of former days."[15] The Talmud, like all holy writ, is comprehended as "a source of prefigurations," an already written script which generations of *lerners* patiently and ritually play out again and again.[16] The excitement in such study is to uncover for oneself the old truths. The challenge is to be able to find the ancient paths of logic which one's forebears hacked out in the overgrowth of oral laws and received traditions and to feel as if one is oneself the pioneer. The traditioning *lerner* is by no means simply mimicking or mouthing the words of the past. There are people who study that way, but their actions do not qualify as genuine traditioning any more than an empty mechanized speaking of the words of liturgy qualifies as intentioned and devotional prayer. The traditioning *lerner* is dramatically possessed by the text and its world; yet to him its words and reasoning seem to be his own.

On the other hand, contemporizers are swept up by the belief that current situations can and should exert an influence on the Talmud (and tradition). "Insights can be salvaged, but they must be recast and paraphrased," in the words of one champion of this point of view.[17] "In each and every generation," writes another, "we have had our exegetes who have been able to take a core, reinterpret it, and maintain its authenticity through *change* and thereby through *contemporary relevance*."[18] In brief, "one delved deeply into the Talmud; one read into it all contemporary problems: problems of dietary laws of today, of family relations of today, in general how to be Jews today."[19]

PREFIGURATION: REPLAYING THE TEXT

Begin with a simple phenomenon: prefiguration, a situation in which the *lerners* play out a text with which they are all familiar but which they still feel they must review. In general, because most of the classes I attended were filled with people who had studied Talmud for years, it was safe to assume that often a particular text under consideration was familiar to the participants. Signs of previous knowledge often revealed themselves in the students' ability to refer to arguments occurring later in the text or in comments which assumed a greater knowledge of the whole than a first reading could normally be expected to provide.

Certainly the rabbi more often than not had already studied the page through which he now led others. Indeed, an unspoken assumption on the part of all was that *he* knew the tractate being reviewed intimately. Each teacher had his own way of displaying erudition. For one it might simply be an announcement that he had taught or *reviewed* the text elsewhere. Rav Rotenbush often did this, detailing his other teaching experiences. Other teachers would indicate their familiarity with the text by reacting to the words they read with gestural or verbal signs of recognition. Rav Horowitz, for example, would often repeat the words of a *sugia* (topic under study) several times as he pondered its meaning and then suddenly respond with an "aha!" or "now I remember," which would preface his explanation. Rav Moses on the other hand needed few such verbal qualifiers to signal his familiarity with the text; he simply reviewed it with a quick pace and style that served to convince all of us in the class that he was an old master of the page.

Rav Auerbach had a unique way of showing his familiarity with the text. Alongside of his book he kept a typed manuscript of his own commentary on what we were studying. Repeatedly referring to this sheaf of papers and often reading to us from it, he left no room for doubt that his *lernen* was in fact a replaying of study that he had done before.

Yet while familiarity with the content is a distinct advantage in reaching some sort of understanding of the page, such previous experience never seems to obviate the need for further study. The notion that once having learned something one need never review or replay it is foreign to the concept of *lernen*, particularly as traditioned cultural performance.

Perhaps the clearest instance of prefiguration occurs when a group reviews a piece of Talmud that the same circle has itself already studied. Here the central question becomes how familiarity with the text is handled. The following case provides some answers.

Monday and Wednesday evenings a little after eight in the evening in a small room, the *besmedresh*, of the Beit Rachel Synagogue in Jerusalem, for slightly more than an hour each session, six or seven men would sit around a large table and be guided through the text by their teacher, Rav Horowitz, who sat at the head. Commonly the students arrived before their teacher. They would sit or repair to corners of the room to talk, smoke, and subtly reaffirm their fellowship. The class would not begin formally until the Rav walked in, opened the book, and began to recite or explain the Talmud.

Accustomed to waiting for the rabbi, the men had ample time to review the text and catch up on anything they might have missed or misunderstood or even to look ahead in the page. Usually, only Reb[20] Moshe, a small man with a scraggly white beard, earlocks, and the serious demeanor of a scholar, would spend the time perusing the page of the open Talmud before him. While others might occasionally make a show of reviewing the text by opening to the proper page, they normally looked away from their books and used this time for activities more social in character.

On one particular evening in December, after a long period of waiting for their teacher, the men agreed—after some debate about his likely activities during the day—that he would not appear to lead them that night. In most instances when the Rav could not make it to class he sent a replacement—usually one of his sons who, as students in a yeshiva, were at least from the point of learning more than equal to taking on his voluntary role. This, however, was not such an occasion.

Looking to one another, the men at the urging of Zusya, one of the circle's most vocal members, turned to Reb Moshe to lead them in *lernen*. He readily accepted but suggested that, instead of proceeding further in the text, they review a page they had recently studied. The others nodded in agreement: "When the Rav comes, we'll move on in the *gemore*," as one man put it. Here then was a clear case of prefiguration.

The first point to note in this replaying is the role that chanting filled. Talmudic chant, cadence, or intonational contour often indicate the capacity to comprehend a text. Although this is not the place to enlarge upon the entire matter of intonation and *lernen*—something to be done later—certain points should be noted here.

In general, the unpunctuated, emaciated, almost telegraphic text of the Talmud and its related commentaries on the page is subject to systematic patterns of intonation, which help to make its meaning clear. Commonly, "exaggerated pitch contrasts are used to restore syntactic colorfulness" to the page.[21] A most common pattern consists of intoning a dramatized transition. A question followed by an answer often has the sound of a rise (the question) and gradual fall (the answer). Stress, when added to this rise-fall pattern, also can dramatize the force of the question and answer related a fortiori arguments.[22]

To be sure, rise-fall patterns, whether partial or elongated chant figures, and intonational contours in general can be interpreted clearly only when the context is known. In prefigured texts, where familiarity with the passages can be assumed, this of course is possible. Indeed, the more familiar the text, the more likely is one to find meaningful chant figures used by the *lerners*.

Finally, "the chant figures, or analogs of these figures . . . are easily transferred by scholars from the reading of the Talmud to oral discussion about it."[23] Thus are spoken commentaries and oral discussion vocally integrated with holy writ.

Normally, the Beit Rachel circle did not chant the Talmud as consistently as, for example, the Kahal Reyim group did. Rather, while they sometimes inserted rise-fall cadences into their recitations (echoes of the chant traditionally utilized in the yeshivas where familiar texts are repeated again and again), they would commonly speak the text, often hardly distinguishing it intonationally from the conversational sound of their explanations and discussions. Now, however, Reb Moshe led off with a marked chant. We knew the text well enough to sing it.

In a cultural performance, chanting also can be used, perhaps even more importantly, as a vehicle for engaging oneself with the world of the text. The Talmud and its commentaries, the written version of oral law and debate, can in a sense be most dramatically entered by reciting its phrases in the cadences which its logic and reason seem to demand. An emphatic, even somewhat stylized and exaggerated chanting thus may be taken as a sort of expressive repetition, a return to oral debate, in which the meaning of the unpunctuated and unvocalized text is disambiguated and declaimed. Questions sound like questions; and statements, rhetorical remarks, or exclamations become unmistakable. Of course the sound is not necessarily the cadence of the original speakers who are being quoted in the text. Rather, the voice is one filtered through the academies of learning of European Orthodoxy. But that plaintive sound, so intertwined with the cadences of Yiddish has for Ashkenazic Jews, come to represent the authentic sound of the academy of learning—be it in Babylonia or Vilna. Still, as Max Weinreich suggests, "we cannot preclude the possibility that the Gemara chant also dates from pre-Ashkenazic times."[24]

To be sure, chanting also can be conventionalized so as to become merely a formal display. In this case, the reader may paradoxically mask his lack of Talmudic comprehension with a layer of regularized sing-song. He uses the steady rise-fall of his recitation as a vehicle for managing the impression of a full-fledged entry into the meaning of the text while in fact avoiding it. Careful listening to this regular cadence reveals its semantic impression, its empty formality. This sort of chanting, quite common among those whose primary interest is getting through (but not into) a page of Talmud, is to be distinguished from *lernen* as cultural performance.

In general, the men at Beit Rachel eschewed this sort of chanting. If they used chant at all, they tried to do so precisely, allowing each intonational contour to express their comprehension. Thus, when Reb Moshe early on intoned a phrase of the text so as to make it sound like a question (ending his reading with a partial rise of pitch as if signaling a transition to a forthcoming answer), he was quickly corrected by Zusya who rechanted the phrase to make it sound right like the statement it was meant to be.

After chanting through a passage of the Rashi commentary, the men of Beit Rachel continued with a relatively simple sort of elaboration: they recast the text as a dialogue in which they articulated implicit questions and then recited Rashi's words as if he were one of them. Moshe began with a summary gloss of what the Talmud, dealing with the subject of ritual immersion, had just concluded.[25]

MOSHE: So he is required to immerse his entire body.
ZUSYA: Why? "Because he has become impurified in his body——"
MOSHE: "Because he has become impurified in his body, and the entire body requires immersion . . ."

Here, Zusya, rather than simply listening in silence to Moshe's comments, expressively joins them to Rashi's text. "Why?" he asks. That is, why is "he required to immerse his entire body?" "Because," and now Zusya answers the question simply by reading further on in the commentary. Taking on the voice of Rashi, as it were, he expressively repeats, "He has become impurified in his body." Moshe then follows the vocal cue of Zusya/Rashi and continues the dialogue. The oral remarks and written texts become part of a single script and performance. The page is thus penetrated symbolically and logically. The spoken drama in the class embraces Rashi.

In a series of increasingly expressive readings, each of the speakers tries to outdo the other in bringing to life Rashi's words. They, in a sense, compete to play the part of Rashi. When Moshe uses only a slight inflection, Zusya uses an even more dramatized one, and Yosef, a third participant, tries an even more noticeable, elongated rise and fall in his speech. The recitation of the text no longer sounds like a formalistic rereading of the page but has all the vocal qualities of an animated discussion whose words come directly from the speakers' imagination.*

The vocalization served as an additional layer of meaning the group was able to add to their text. Singing the material through,

*During a similar episode at Smotra, Rav Gafny, referring to a question that one of the students, Sidney, had asked in a prefiguration of Rashi, commented, "Now we're getting to Sidney's and Rashi's question." "Sidney gets top billing over Rashi?" another student asked incredulously. "Sure, here Sidney is first to get into the *gemore*," the Rav answered. We all, however, knew Rashi was culturally preeminent.

they publicly tested and demonstrated their capacity to comprehend, expressively repeat and reverberate with at least some of its original meaning. In the process, they became unequivocally engrossed in their *lernen*. Then, satisfied that they could be sufficiently in tune with the Talmud to chant it, they moved on to a second approach to a prefigured text: elaboration.

Elaboration builds upon a familiarity with the text. Because the Talmud *is* a telegraphic record of remarks and commentary, filled with cryptic passages packed with meaning that must be carefully decoded with elaborating glosses during the *lernen*, it cannot always be comprehensively reviewed at first reading. In the beginning, progress is often marked by stops and starts, bursts of interpretation during which a sense of continuity may be lost. Reviewing a page for a second, third, fourth, or hundredth time, the *lerners* become sufficiently at ease with its meaning to more fully elaborate it. Each repetition is thus seen as a deeper plunge into the world of its words and ideas. The elaborations need not necessarily add novellae to the text. Rather, they may simply expand "what is said" into "what is talked about," filling in the sketchiness of the page with explanatory glosses, framing remarks, and evaluative summaries.[26]

Talmud study allows for a broad range of elaborations: beginning, as we have seen, with a turning of abbreviated phrases into complete sentences through the recasting of a text into a series of dialogues and debates by making explicit the implicit questions, reactive remarks, and responses; and finally to critical explanations of and discussions about what the Talmud may have had in mind, upon what principles it is basing its argument or even a characterization of the role a portion of text plays in the larger discussion. All elaborations, however, invoke the students' familiarity with the text and context of the page in question. Prefigured *lernen*, with all these elaborations waiting to be played out, thus takes on the qualities of prepared cultural performance whose purpose is not so much to provide the *lerners* with information (although it may do so) but to provide them with an opportunity to fully play out the process of study. In reviewing and elaborating a prefigured text, the *lerners* moreover hear themselves exemplifying talmudic logic and thinking. In the process, they cannot help but be culturally shaped by these patterns of thought and belief as they express them.

In a sense, a prefigured text and its elaboration provide a relatively simple means of playing out the role of a traditionally
cultural and knowledgeable Jew. Accordingly, it retains its appeal
for all those who wish to evoke this image either for their own
benefit or for others. Rather than being a boring exercise in repetition, prefigured *lernen* is instead an opportunity to structure
and exhibit competence and belongingness to the world of the
Talmud.[27]

Reviewing a prefigured text, everyone knew "where" the page
had to take him, and the object now was to make it lead the group
to the prefigured point of understanding via proper phrasing and
correct cadence. The drama was in making everything come out
sounding right. During all of this one could witness the otherwise
curious spectacle of "students" helping their "teacher" teach
them something everyone already knew.

People cannot animatedly *re*cite words of the Talmud—as the
participants in the study circle often do—without *re*animating
themselves culturally in the process.[28] To be sure, the plunge into
the page may be a cynical staging of scholarship, but it may just
as likely be a genuine immersion in what is being reviewed. The
men replay Talmud as a means of speaking about matters of their
Judaism, which they would not or could not say in ordinary language but which nonetheless touch something essential in the
Jewish core. That is why they can become engaged by repetitions:
saying the old truths once again is a crucial step toward their
reaffirmation. In this sort of cultural drama, "the workings of the
inner mind that created the past and breathed in its very atmosphere emerge clear and true."[29] When the texts are thus replayed,
"they tell the story of the . . . past that transcends time . . . they
inhabit the ruins with meaning and motive, with living yet dead
people."[30] Rashi may be dead; the speakers in the Talmud and
their world long ago left in ruins, but in this revitalized elaboration
of a prefigured text, all are brought back to life through *lernen*.

This is not to say that the participants are fully cognizant of
what it is they are doing. "As a participant," Constantin Stanislavski once pointed out, "you cannot see yourself, but . . . you react
with your inner nature to what is going on [in a drama] as truly
as in real life."[31] The dramatic rereading of the prefigured text
simply takes imaginative possession of the readers.

Lernen in this sense is not homologous with "learning" the
Talmud. The latter acquisition of knowledge is a mental activity

in which what was opaque or completely unknown becomes, over time and through effort, intellectually apperceived. There are no guarantees that everyone who *lerns* Talmud will also be able to assimilate, in their entire complexity, its lessons. This fact accounts in part for the fact that a number of scholars and rabbis have historically sought to limit Talmud study to the most intellectually gifted.[32] They realized that without such prohibitions people might go through the motions of study and thereby transform it to something less purely cerebral. In the yeshiva, where Talmud is studied as a vocation, these restrictions are still to an extent in effect. In the avocational study circle, where all comers are generally now welcome, this is not always the case.

For the avocational *lerner*, the aim is often less intellectual. In the public setting of the study circle these men aim to demonstrate devotion to the text and the world it represents and not necessarily always to fully comprehend it.[33] This sort of *lernen* becomes a way of keeping in touch with the tradition, a way of saying something from it in a formal way and along patterned lines.[34] The repetition of paradigmatic ideas and sayings of Jewish tradition come closer to cultic ritual than pedagogic instruction. When, time after time, a person *lerns* this way, he participates in a patterned process of alignment with the traditional culture of the Talmud. He engages in what, in contradistinction to that which Max Gluckman[35] once termed a "ritual of rebellion," may be called a "ritual of conformity."

These distinctions were suggested to me, perhaps most clearly, in the same Beit Rachel class that I have been describing. Time after time, Reb Moshe summed up what had been reviewed and then framed what was about to come next. Sometimes he went beyond simple framing but turned instead to a full explanation of what the Talmud was about to say, revealing the essential features of the upcoming *inyan*. As already noted, none of us saw in his action anything that obviated the need to *lern* what we had by now already learned, fixed in our minds. The two processes were obviously distinct. We were therefore not surprised to hear, on the heels of his explanation, Moshe's call: "Now we shall *lern* this."

Those who might not be altogether certain of the nuances of meaning in this piece of Talmud, who might be unable to chant it precisely, could still participate in the process of *lernen*. An echoed remark, a canonical intonation, a knowing nod or some other gestural signal aligned one comfortably with the informed

others. By the end, even the relative ignoramous could feel fulfilled with a sense that he had participated in a culturally meaningful activity: he had orally devoted himself to a review of the
tradition, ideas, and statements of the Talmud and through it to
his Judaism.

In a sort of choric repetition, the participants symbolized both
their togetherness and their attachment to text.[36] Oftentimes a
student cued Reb Moshe, while on other occasions he echoed
him. And sometimes the speaking of all was simultaneous, taking
on the sound of a yeshiva study hall with its rumble of independent chants of Talmud. Yet within this clamor of voices there
seemed a clear sense of precisely what needed to be said and a
conviction that it had to be spoken.

Throughout, the men of Beit Rachel seemed to accept the page
in its own terms. When they stopped to recap or reconsider the
talmudic discussion, they focused on a literal interpretation of the
words rather than a reinterpretation generated by the needs of
contemporary culture. If there were conflicts between their contemporary consciousness and what they were *lernen*, these failed
to appear during this particular class; the men did not seem to
search for nor did they point out modern parallels to what they
were studying. They did not present the Talmud so as to put it
into harmony with life outside the classroom. Instead, they traditioned: the universe of ritual immersions, purities, and impuri-
ties with which the text concerned itself became "another world
to live in" for the hour or so of class time.

MOVING BEYOND THE TEXT

Cultural performances do not always or even necessarily occur
during the structured recitation, translation, and analysis of the
text. Often they take the form of digressive discussions within
the *shiur*, during which participants publicly make sense of, reflect, and develop their lives as Orthodox Jews. As has long been
realized by the experienced *lerner*, "Jewish study is most creative
when it is a study of, *and digression from*, a text. It then has a
beginning and a continuity, and becomes a means of giving new
life to the text itself."[37]

Normally beginning as a reaction to the text or some comment
made in response to it, the digression is an elaborated conversation betwixt and between the structured textual review. During

it, the roles of teacher and student may become suspended as all the participants freely engage in a conversation that may draw more on their capacity to be sociable and reveal personal experiences or common understandings of life than on their comprehension of the particular piece of Talmud which may have generated the discussion. The normal relationships of super- or subordination which structured *lernen* support give way to a spirit of equality and comradeship. In essence, a digression is a liminal period, a kind of time-out from formal study and structured relationships. That is not to say that the participants forget who they are. They know that some are more scholarly—elders, if you will—and others less so—juniors. However, "in liminality extreme authority of elders over juniors often coexists with scenes and episodes indicative of the utmost behavioral freedom and speculative license."[38] The rabbi and student, talmudic scholar and simple Jew, master and novice can join together in a free-wheeling digression in which everyone can have something to say. During this time, a sense of "undifferentiated, equalitarian, direct, nonrational" intimacy emerges, while structured ties of study fade into unconsciousness.[39]

In this atmosphere of conversation and camaraderie, where the obstacle presented by a necessary comprehension of a complex Talmud text disappears, there are often revelations about what each of the participants understands to be the demands of his life as a Jew. Here the men are willing to admit to behavior and attitudes that deviate from the formal requirements of their Orthodox Judaism. Here they express what they consider to be the basic practical requirements and what can be neglected or at least overlooked. In the process, each person learns what passes for Judaism among his peers, the cultural limits to the range of human behavior. Here the sorts of concerns that might otherwise not be discussed easily—let alone revealed—become a natural part of the conversation. Some examples are in order.

Religious Intentions

One of the abiding concerns in the religiocultural life of Orthodox Jews is the matter of religious intention and devotion. *Kavannah*, the indigenous Hebrew term for this attitude, is the degree to which people tune their "human actions to an envisaged cosmic order."[40] Although it is a spiritual requirement associated with the fulfillment of all religious obligations, its achievement is by no means easy. Nevertheless, observant Jews often try to give the impression that they are carrying out their religious life with *kavannah*, that they are spiritually in tune. In prayer this means a display of worshipful fervor; during the celebration of ritual, it requires a deliberate involvement in the minutiae of the observances. In effect, *kavannah* demands a sincerity in one's religious motives and engagement. Since motive remains, however, an internal matter—sometimes displayable but seldom confirmable by the other—its sincerity can remain one of the hidden matters of religious life.

Because of its doctrinal importance in Orthodox Jewish life, *kavannah* nevertheless is a matter of public, cultic concern. The group wants—indeed, needs—to know whether the faithful are succeeding in their efforts to live up to the spiritual demands of the religion. This ethereal matter is, however, not one that can be easily addressed or expressed in the absence of some supporting framework. The digressive discussions during the *shiur* provide such a framework.

Return once again to Beit Rachel. The episode begins with Moshe reciting a line of text in which the talmudic authority Reb Nachman is quoted. Describing what he considers excessive religious practice, Reb Nachman asserts, "Anyone who performs a ritual ablution on his hands in order to eat fruits is among the 'religiously' arrogant."[41] The statement, so bold in its claim, catches the interest of the listeners and stimulates discussion. Beginning immediately on the heels of Moshe's denotative explanation and Zusya's slightly altered translation, the digression unfolds.

"But washing them is permitted," Yosef notes, adding the gloss that the rabbinic dictum does not preclude people from the observance of basic cleanliness.

This remark could, as many do, simply pass without further comment; or, as in this case, serve as a bridge to continued discussion. A great deal depends on the reactions of the others. If the comment touches others' concerns or if they feel a need to actively engage in the talk of *lernen*, digressions break out. Glosses, which break the train of recitation, translation, and explanation, structurally set the stage for further excursions. Once away from the text, the group can expand its possibilities for talk.

Zusya responds. So do several others. Some focus on the term "arrogant," others on the rituals surrounding the eating of fruits.

A kind of conversational free-for-all seems to take place almost immediately.

Wondering aloud whether or not Reb Nachman's characterization of those performing ritually superfluous ablutions is extreme, a number of men analyze the meaning of *"gass ruakh"* arrogant. They explore the boundaries of religious ritual. Yosef uses the occasion not only to extend the probe but also to display his scholarly credentials by eruditely citing a parallel use of the term in another context. The reference is to a talmudic discussion of the number of times one is required to bow during the *amida*, the core prayer of the Jewish service. The custom, he notes, is to bow four times at specific intervals. Nevertheless, he continues, there are those who exceed this number whom the Talmud considers to be *"gass ruakh."*

In this manner of explanation and commentary, Yosef makes use of the time-honored methodology of the Talmud student. This "student was not content with comprehending a given text but, through comparing it with other passages in the Talmud, sought to deduce certain general principles and new formulations."[42] Repetition and parallelism, the use of analogies and concomitant citations, however, mirror the pattern of discussion in the text itself. By expressing himself as he does, Yosef demonstrates—without necessarily being aware of it—the model-for-model-of dimension of *lernen* as cultural drama. He interprets *and* perpetuates the pattern of talmudic thinking. And all the while he reaffirms the general principle that members of the study circle are expected to be knowledgeable in matters of Jewish law, custom, and Talmud.

The men explore further the meaning of *"gass ruakh."* During a fugue-like series of comments, each man offers his understanding of the notion of religious arrogance.

"Shtoltz," says Zusya, evoking the familiarity of the Yiddish expression. "Haughty. He wants to show that he . . ."

"A shvitzer," Zalman adds in a more colloquial Yiddish. "He wants to show that . . ."

"He's beyond the law," I suggest.

"And that's excessive," Yosef concludes. "Not all of us know what to do during our prayers but that [repeated bowing] is excessive, arrogant."

Having himself raised the matter of prayer, Yosef, as the Talmud often does, allows himself to continue along this tangent.

"Hence, if someone did not direct his devotions during his prayers [i.e., lacked *kavannah*], he would be expected to repeat his prayers. But they [the rabbis] decided not to require a repetition because we are never devotedly intense in our prayers. We cannot direct our devotions."

Here is a cultural revelation, an opportunity to present one man's understanding of an element of his religion. Although starting out to exemplify a case on which the rabbis discourage excessive displays of piety, Yosef has ended by offering an insight into the religious possibilities inherent in the human character. His insight is, to be sure, implanted in his knowledge of the rabbis' judgments. He tries to find his own way to their view of the world. But his emphatic assertion gives the impression of being a personal statement, "of making public what is private or making social what is personal."[43]

This performance does not pass unnoticed. Rather, it makes possible a wider cultural drama during which the others also reaffirm the wisdom of the Talmud as their own.

"It's certain," Zusya adds, "that someone who didn't direct his devotions and therefore repeated his prayers would on the second time also fail to achieve *kavannah*."

Embedded in this comment is Zusya's similar personal conviction about human capacities for devotion. Restating and thereby reaffirming the rabbis' judgment, that prayers lacking proper devotion need not be repeated, Zusya, like Yosef, tacitly stamps the wisdom of the Talmud into his own frame of thinking.

"Precisely," Yosef replies, as the rest of us laugh in our own public confirmation of this "truth" about the general weakness we share in our capacity to pray with *kavannah*. Subtly but unmistakably, the conversation is moving from a repetition of the traditional Jewish position on *kavannah* to a public common agreement about its social and psychological accuracy.

In the spirit of fellowship fostered by this common coming to terms with the view of the Talmud, Zusya offers a personal revelation: "I recall that I once forgot to recite '*Yaleh ve yovo*,'[44] but remembered my omission when I had ended my prayers. I prayed a second time—and forgot to say it again!" he admits, laughing.

In an atmosphere of intimacy, assured that he was not marking himself as a lesser Jew than the rest of us, Zusya allowed himself this public revelation. His personal experience was put in the service of the tradition, demonstrating that with regard to devotion and concentration in prayer the Talmud was right.

To be sure, for the insider to the world of Orthodox prayer, this revelation is nothing new; there is no shocking confession here. There is, however, a reconfirmation that, among practicing Orthodox Jews, the situation of *kavannah* in prayers remains as it has been since at least the times of the Talmud's decision. Then as now, devotion, concentration, intention, and intensity has been hard to maintain even among the putatively pious.

"What then?" asks Zusya. Should he have repeated his prayers yet a third time? The ensuing discussion provides opportunities to ask questions which help complete one's practical knowledge about the day-to-day carrying out of prayer. This sort of inquiry into the nuances of law and custom may be generally characterized as a collective effort to clarify the demands of one's culture. For the Orthodox Jew, this often means finding out what the *halakha*, the set of instructions which in the final analysis shapes his social behavior as Jew, requires.

As each man recites the answers to this question that he has learned, the shape of the religious demands upon all of them begins to emerge more and more clearly. Over time and through a series of such digressions, the men of the study circle will, in a sense, *reenact the Jewish receiving of the law* as they acquire a cultural competence, which they can and will continue to demonstrate in their life and *lernen*.

The lines of conversation are jumbled. Men talk all at once when their enthusiasm rises. In the liminal atmosphere of the digression, all men are equal in their right to ask and answer. Whatever one knows can be freely offered for the group's consideration. This animates the discussion of law and brings life to the performance.

From pure considerations of the law, the men move on to recommendations of how best to live up to it. In reply to Zusya's public inquiry about how to handle repeated forgettings during prayer, Yosef suggests one must read all prayers from the prayer book and thus nothing will be forgotten.

"I pray from the book," Hannan admits, "and I still forget."

"But the 'Gra' [Elijah, the *Gaon* (Genius) of Vilna and a major rabbinic leader of the eighteenth century] said that one must always pray from a book, as *he* did," Yosef concludes. "Seeing the letters adds to one's wisdom."

This last remark may be read as a metaphor for the relationship between the Talmud and digressions from it. The sight of the text, the context of *lernen*, stimulate the talk that completes its wisdom.

Cultural Expressions and Impressions

During the course of study and often during digressions, participants in the study circle find an opportunity to express what they have learned about the wisdom of Jewish life and tradition. These expressions embody rabbinic dicta, folk sayings, or even the common knowledge shared among Jewish insiders about the patterns of their culture. Although not always endowed with the same sense of sanctity or honor as a direct quotation from the text being studied, these declarations—like Yosef's comment that "seeing the letters adds to one's wisdom"—command and receive respect because they are perceived as emerging out of the sacred literature and tradition. As the *lerners* express their cultural wisdom, so they impress it more decisively upon the group and themselves. There are other examples.

A few days after the Beit Rachel class I have been describing, the teacher, Rav Horowitz, returned and once again took up the folio of Talmud that we had reviewed in his absence. Like us, he repeated its comments about the ablution and ritual immersion of hands. In measured and deliberate statements he explained why hands were likely to be perceived as ritually impure.

"A man uses his hands for all sorts of things, and with them he touches every part of his body. He touches places which perspire. So the rabbis created [a hierarchy of] degrees [of impurity]. Thus, if hands are what is called 'polluted,' that is, the hands are soiled, one should not eat anything—neither ordinary, nor consecrated, nor dedicated offerings, and so on.[45] But when a man comes to eat a sacrifice, it is not enough that he makes an ablution over his hands, rather it is incumbent upon him to ritually immerse his hands [in purified water]."

Although as will be recalled, these ablutions had already been discussed previously by the group, in cultural performances like this one old plots are easily played out again. This time, however, the digression develops in another direction. Yosef speaks first, noting that touching one's sweaty face does not require any subsequent watery purifications. Such perspiration is special, he tells us, since the word of God in Genesis informs us: "In the sweat of thy face shalt thou eat bread."

"Yes," the Rav replies. "With facial perspiration, it is something else. All perspiration is dangerous, from the point of view of health. All, that is, except the sweat of the face, for it is said: 'In the sweat of thy face shalt thou eat bread.' So it is written. Even though you sweat on your face, you can eat bread [without first washing your hands]."

Several things have happened during this discussion. First, a situation has been generated that displays the dialogic and collective process of *lernen*: teacher teaches, students respond; teacher ratifies response. This pattern will be elucidated in greater depth later.

Second, through the double recitation of a biblical verse and its elaboration, a traditional Jewish understanding has been recalled and revivified. What was in its original incarnation a declaration of divine retribution for Adam's act of primal heresy has been recited as an organizing principle of ritual cleanliness. Repeating what is essentially a rabbinic interpretation from memory, the men have made it come from out of themselves. To speak rabbinic words of wisdom as if they were one's own and to share in their authority is in effect to make them one's own. We read; we learn; we assimilate; we express, we discuss; and finally we reabsorb and have impressed upon us the lessons of our traditional culture as we listen to ourselves giving them. That is the essence of the cultural performance.

The activity is not sterile. The men who thus reenact (express again) the wisdom of their fathers cannot help but add something of their own practical wisdom to it.

Mumbling what sounds at first like a working through of the principle he has just heard, Simcha reasons, " 'In the sweat of thy face,' so if you don't work, you won't sweat. . . . And if you don't sweat, you won't eat."

"If you don't sweat, you'll eat mud," the Rav concludes, parodying the verse with the practical understanding that Simcha's reasoning conjures up for all of us. "What you mean to say is that if the other sweats . . . ," the Rav ends, leaving it to us to work out the logical consequences.

During the liminal interval of digression, the members of the study circle freely and unhesitatingly complete the rabbis' wisdom with their own. The thinking of the past is made to provide a framework of meaning for contemporary wisdom. In turn, today's light is shed upon yesterday's rabbinic commentary. The effect is mutual and the sayings of the rabbis, set aside from life in the pages of the Talmud, are once again reconnected to life.

INTERSUBJECTIVITY AND MORAL ORDER

Implicit in any cultural performance is the assumption that the participants share a world of meaning. This may be termed their "intersubjectivity."[46] Each individual knows there is an ongoing correspondence between his personal experience, understanding, and expression of Jewish life and that of others in his circle. Intersubjectivity allows a great deal to remain tacitly expressed during cultural performances; references may be and often are made to common culture by means of dicta half-spoken yet fully understood. The apparently obscure becomes effectively obvious. All this makes communication and concerted action within the group possible.

Intersubjectivity, however, is not a condition of cultural life that remains intact automatically. It needs occasional reawakening and revitalization. In part it requires common experiences and a shared sense of moral order with a great population of others. It also necessitates public demonstrations—however recondite from the point of view of outsiders—during which group members rediscover and acknowledge both their capacity to communicate easily as well as what and how much they have in common. *Lernen* allows this sort of revitalization of intersubjectivity to occur. Consider the following illustration.

About to continue reading from and explaining the Talmud to the men at Mekadshey Torah, Rav Rotenbush decides to begin with an explanation of the principle elucidated in what the group is about to review. The focus, he tells us, will be on the issue of precedence in religious practices. The matter, a question of primary versus secondary religious obligations, is of major importance in Jewish life. It concerns the cultural effort to reflect perceived sacred order in human action.

"You have two obligations before you," he begins. "One obligation occurs more frequently, the other less. You must [in such a situation] fix the established. In other words, what is more frequent, which is more established, you shall do first. And this is true with many things."

"*You* have," "before *you*," "*you* must," "*You* shall do." In short order the participants, as observant Jews, are presented with the preconceptions and imperatives of their moral universe. Regardless of their individual histories, all the participants are implicated in the world of practice and precedent that the Rav describes and are presumed to yield to the legitimacy of its religious and cultural demands. Among these is the one highlighted in this example: to fix the established, to do first that which is most frequent in Jewish sacred order.

That stage is now set for a litany of references to ritual practices in which the more frequently performed precede the less. But each of these practices, although invoked and vitalized in the discussion, does not need to be fully described. Instead, as the teacher and students run through them, they make telegraphic— what to the outsider might seem cryptic—references to the normative practices and accepted order. These are, however, sufficient for the insider. Indeed, it is precisely the participants' capacity to quickly pass over the details of these practices and the taken-for-granted acceptance of their legitimacy that revitalizes their intersubjectivity and reaffirms religiocultural order.

The Rav continues speaking: "For example, in the 'Beit Yosef' [a codex of Jewish law][47] it is written that one must put on *tzitzit* [fringes] before *tefilin* [phylacteries]. Why *tzitzit* before *tefilin*? Because . . ."

Here several students, as if to indicate that they are on his wavelength, start to give an answer and end up echoing their teacher. ". . . *tzitzit* are customary day and night and *tefilin* only during the day. *Tzitzit* are [therefore] called 'frequent.' "

There is no need here for the Rav to tell us why he has cited the Beit Yosef codex (or even what it is) for we all know its authoritative claims within the world of Orthodox Jewry. There is no need, furthermore, for him to elaborate the ritual practices he has cited. We know all these things, and he knows we do because we all share an intersubjective universe. He can take for granted— as do we all—that those within the circle are, as Orthodox Jews, fully cognizant of (and probably personally feel) the religious obligation to wear *tzitzit* as part of their clothing all day and evening and that they will don *tefilin* each weekday morning as part of their prayer ritual. Indeed he can even assume—and our echoing of him underscores this—that we are familiar with the customary pattern of behavior which calls upon the worshipper to put on *tzitzit* before *tefilin*.

The same sort of assumptions and evidence of our common culture manifest themselves in subsequent references to practices surrounding the festival of Sukkot, during which observant Jews sit in temporary booth-like dwellings to commemorate the passage through the Sinai when they lived in such dwellings for forty years.

"For example," the Rav continues, "the blessing '*shehekhiyanu*' with the blessing for Sukkot, there is a matter like this one. What goes before what." Frequent and infrequent. We decide. . . ."

Again the students chime in with their teacher to offer the answer, even before he does. Now as before, the Rav is simply voicing something all the others in the circle already know but which they use this occasion for restating-recelebrating, if you will.

References become progressively more condensed. A word or two is sufficient to refer to complex practices and to recall even more complicated articulations of them in the Talmud and other venerable texts. Yet esoteric and compressed as all this may sound to the uninformed outsider, it is enough for this group of natives to Orthodox Jewish culture to plunge them cognitively into a world of tradition where the imperatives of ritual life echo and reecho. Like familiar stories of time-worn memories recollected among old acquaintances, very little can call up a great deal.

As if realizing that his voice and words are resonant with the cultural memories of the tribe, the Rav notes: "I have spoken briefly and elliptically but with particular intention."

It is an extraordinarily discerning observation of the situation in which he has participated. In essence, the Rav is telling the rest of us that while he has spoken in an abbreviated way, we have—as our reactions confirm—understood his full intention. Everything that needed to be said has been spoken and all that was implicit consciously received.

Seeing that we share so much in common in our comprehension of what these rituals mean in the life of the Orthodox Jew, we are engulfed by a feeling of closeness. Talk breaks out again and again—always telegraphic yet always understood. It is as if we all were stimulated by our ability to communicate so efficiently about Jewish life that we become moved to keep the channels open. Put in terms of cultural drama, one might say that one good cultural performance fosters another.

The men accordingly extend their digression and exercise their intersubjectivity with a question about one of the examples the Rav used in his explanation of normative religious practice. Again the model-for-model-of aspects of *lernen* may be witnessed. What is the difference, one man asks, between the obligations of wearing *tefilin* and *tzitzit*? The question is not rejected as irrelevant to the present discussion. In a cultural drama, discussion that allows the players to express their religious curiosity and sensibilities is inherently appropriate.

The Rav therefore responds to the cue and elaborates a reply: "In the *gemore*, it is written that *tefilin* is an obligation upon the man himself. *You* are to go and hear the *shofar* [ram's horn], to don *tefilin* and so forth. *Tzitzit*—this is an obligation for the garment. That is to say, *you* are not obligated to have them but your garment *is* obligated. With *tefilin*, *you* must do it. *You* must hear the sound of the *shofar*. *You* take the *lulav* [palm branch]. *You* pray. *You* read from the Torah."

In short order and condensed form, the Rav again calls up a series of parallel religious obligations in the life of the observant Jew. The commandment to wear phylacteries during one's prayers, to hear the sound of the ram's horn blown on Rosh Hashana, to possess and wave the palm branch on the holy day of Sukkot, to pray regularly and to listen to the words of the Torah when they are chanted in the synagogue are all invoked. In the process, the listeners are once again reminded of some of the claims made upon all of them as observant Jews. The men nod in tacit affirmation of these shared obligations and the intersubjective world they imply.

"It is a *mitzva* [religious obligation]," the Rav continues, "to buy [a garment with] four corners in order to give it *tzitzit*,[48] a *mitzva* to buy it [because, as the passage in the Scripture mandating *tzitzit* points out] 'when you will look upon it [i.e., the fringe] you will remember to follow all the commandments of the Lord.' You will remember the preceding verse where it is written: 'And you will not go after the desires of your heart and eyes which lead you astray.' "

The Rav's quotation is familiar to his audience. As he knows, they recite it daily in their prayers. Now once again they hear it spoken and thereby recall the world it resonates. They are reminded of precisely how the sight of their *tzitzit* is meant to raise their religious consciousness.

Questions which provide the pretext for a full-blown expression of religious and cultural order need not be monumental in themselves. Rav Gafny, the leader of the study circle in Smotra, once pointed out that "sometimes a question is not especially good but it gains its worth by the answer it stimulates." In this case, the simple question which asks for the distinction between the obligations of *tefilin* and *tzitzit* leads to just such an answer. It provides an opportunity for Rav Rotenbush to draw the distinction between personal, primary religious obligations and secondary ones attached to one's possession. It allows him to remind us all of the psychologic implicit in the scriptural verses which combine the commandment to tie ritually knotted fringes to four-cornered garments with moral dictates. Finally, it offers a chance to connect religious behavior to a bit of homily:

"You wish to be restrained from sin. The *gemore* tells us of a particular man who put on *tzitzit* and was thereby saved from catastrophe. The *tzitzit* are the medallions of [survival during] the Six Day War, the War of Independence. A man wears his *tzitzit* on the outside [of his garments] and it serves as a sign and a token that in an external and internal way [he can declare]: 'I am a Jew and a believer.' "

In the atmosphere of intersubjectivity, even such homiletic glosses can remain telegraphic. As the Rav recites bits of tales and verses, others join in re-citing key words, glossing parallel tales with which they are familiar! A soldier left his unit to put on his *tzitzit* or perform some other religious act and returned to find the entire battalion wiped out by a mortar attack. His religion "saved" him.

Such invocations of well-known stories, quotations of familiar verses, explanations reviewing the logic behind Scripture, practice, and moral order constitute the essence of high cultural drama. Their expression leaves an impression upon the performers. Not only have the members of the study circle publicly reviewed and interpreted elements of their Judaism, they have in effect also amplified their sense of intersubjectivity and reaffirmed their union under a common moral order. The world they can talk about in this way is the one they can share.

CUING, ECHOING, AND AMPLIFYING

In her commentary to the autobiography of a Papago Indian woman, Ruth Underhill[49] quotes her description of the tribe's reaction to her father's narration of a story resonant with cultural memories: "When my father finished a sentence, we would all say the last word after him."

By echoing the words of the narrator, the listeners became participants in the storytelling. They did so, at least in part, because they shared a common culture and a feeling of intersubjectivity with the speaker and with the world as presented in the story. They were swept up by him and it.

In our case, the same effects can be discerned. As Rav Rotenbush offered his explanation, his listeners looked for ways to demonstrate to themselves and others that they were alive to the meaning of the text and what he was adding to it. Echoing or cuing him, speaking his words a beat behind or ahead of him were ways this was accomplished. In this as in other similar cultural performances, whether one speaks slightly after or before the narrator is far less important than whether or not one speaks at all. The latter is what indicates an active involvement.

In what sounded at times like simultaneous speaking, the students proceeded to verbally surround almost every phrase their Rav spoke. They created an aural atmosphere of heightened involvement. The pace quickened, the volume increased. Responding to their interjections, the Rav at one point called out enthusiastically, "*Yo', avadeh,*" Yiddish for "Yeah, certainly." This supportive interchange intensified and encouraged the involvement of the others.

The participants did not however limit themselves to cues and echoes. They responded, as already noted, with glosses, comments, questions, and even brief digressions. As if reverberating with what they heard around them, they made references to similar arguments elsewhere in the Talmud, worked out analogous principles of logic for other religious obligations, began elliptical narrations of other tales which underscored the saving grace of religious behavior. Each of these performances progressively engaged the speakers with one another, the topics in question, the Talmud or Scripture, and finally their culture.

In the final analysis, the process described here is the same as that which Durkheim long ago characterized as essential to the vitality of collective life. To him it was clear that at the root of the enthusiasm that people generated for common behavior and values was a celebration of the sensations of collective sentiment and consciousness—culture. These feelings could be perceived only "by fixing themselves upon external objects."[50]

In our case, the Talmud and its associated discussion constitute such an external object, such a representation of culture. As each participant becomes caught up in his public declamation of Talmud, Scripture, and commentary, "the sentiments provoked by his words come back to him, but enlarged and amplified, and to this degree they strengthen his own sentiments."[51] In this, one discovers an essential attraction *lernen* has for those who feel attached to the world of the Talmud. In the course of the cultural performance, an increase of collective force overflows the boundaries of the page and text.

THE PAST IN THE PRESENT

As noted at the outset, one trend of cultural performances during *lernen* is to extend the relevance of the text and through it elements of Jewish culture to contemporary existence. Precisely how this is done is now the focus of consideration. As before, analysis of a particular episode of *lernen* is perhaps the easiest way to consider the issue.

The class is once again the one at Mekadshey Torah, the leader Rav Rotenbush. The subject of the Talmud concerns the specific Torah readings chanted in the synagogue on the four special Sabbaths preceding Passover. The first of these, "Parashat Shekalim," describes the annual Israelite contribution of a "shekel" (the unit of currency) from each household to the priestly treasure. Having made its way through a first reading and explanation of the details of this, the group now moves on to a more complex elaboration of the matter.

"We have not yet clarified," the Rav notes, setting the stage for an exercise in contemporization, "what significance the reading of Parashat Shekalim has today." He continues: "According to what we have just said, this reading was done even during the time the Holy Temple existed [i.e., before it was destroyed and its associated practices for the most part ceased]. [We understand this to be so] since the reason that we read this portion [of the Torah] during the [Jewish] month of Adar is in order that people will remember to bring new [i.e., additional] money by the [Jewish] month of Nisan [which comes next]. For on *Rosh Hodesh* [i.e., the first day of the month] Nisan, it is necessary to bring new money for the sacrifices [around which the festival of Passover beginning on the fifteenth of the month is focused]. That is, we

are speaking [in Parashat Shekalim] about [the relationship be-
tween] sacrifices and money; meaning that [even] during the time
of the Holy Temple [i.e., when sacrifices were still brought at
Passover] they also read the reading of Parashat Shekalim. Is this
clear?"

A few men nod while others grunt their assent. One man signals his comprehension by trying to offer his own explanation of
the practice, but the Rav quickly cuts him off and goes on.

"Now. Now. Why do we read this *today?*"

The emphasis on "today" is unmistakable. He pauses, as if to
let the question sink once again into our consciousness.

"Is it not so that today we also read Parashat Shekalim? Why?
What is going on here [i.e., why read something whose ostensible
purpose was to remind people to bring funds for sacrifices when
today those sacrifices are no longer carried out]?"

The repetition of the question heightens the sense of urgency
and summons our attention. It creates "a dramatic crisis . . . , a
turning point, a moment of unpredictability and emergence."[52]
The crisis concerns more than simply the matter of Parashat
Shekalim. The questions, while focusing on that subject, point
beyond themselves and recall the essential challenges of maintaining Jewish culture in the contemporary world. Namely, can
one discover the significance, appropriateness, and legitimacy of
the apparently archaic and anachronistic within the domains of
the present? Can one continue to fulfill the demands of Jewish
tradition and ritual without lapsing into irrelevance? These are
matters which already preoccupy the members of this circle, and
the occupations of the Talmud class—more suitably than many
others—lend themselves to the expression of these preoccupations.[53]

The crisis is not really new to us; we just act as if it is. Judging
from the cuing and echoing accompanying the Rav's subsequent
answer, at least some of the students know why we read Parashat
Shekalim today. And all of us have at one time or another found
explanations for maintaining the traditions of Jewish culture in
the modern world. What is happening here is a public working
through of this preoccupation. The crisis is being reenacted dramatically and perhaps even obsessively replayed to allow for yet
another reaffirmation that the way of the Talmud is the guide for
the patterns of Jewish culture. Accordingly, it is no surprise to
find that a resolution of the crisis leads back into the text—first

to the Talmud and then the *Mishna Brura*, one of the classic commentaries on its code. These refrains to the holy books will once
again explain Scripture while providing a script for its evocation.

"We have to see," the Rav announces as he turns back the pages
of the Talmud until he has reached the beginning of the section
we have been reviewing. He directs our eyes to the Rashi commentary in the Talmud. We cannot see except through the pages
before us; they are our mind's eyes.

"In a moment we shall see [as well] in the *Mishna Brura* what
is happening." The wider reality, the legally codified framework
for experience is, for the Orthodox Jew, to be found in this holy
book. We shall have to go beyond the Talmud in our hands for
the full playing out of this drama.

As a last reminder that this is no small matter, the teacher adds,
"There is something very interesting here." What is "very inter-

The Rav (on the right) directs the group's eyes to the text, while one of the
students at his side echoes his recitation. (Photograph by S. Binstock)

esting" is not simply a matter to engage our intellect. Rather the vitality of our interest is nourished by our attachment to the culture of Orthodoxy and our consequent desire to resolve all dilemmas we discover in it. Because we are who we are, "there is something very interesting here." Were we not committed to the ways of the books before us, there would be nothing "very interesting here."[54]

Reading along with the Rav, we find now that Rashi, that quintessential talmudic commentator, explains the historical reasons for reading Parashat Shekalim in a manner identical with the one the Rav has extemporaneously offered. Not only does this underscore the Rav's acumen and provide another opportunity to stamp in the information on our consciousness, it also supplies a crucial nexus between what appears to be the free exposition of ideas and a hallowed text. In *lernen*, to find that an idea developed in discussion—the model *of* Jewish culture—is contained in the text—the model *for* Jewish culture—is to legitimate it. Recall that, for the traditional, the ideas that matter most are those already sanctioned and set by the text, that is, by the tradition. If Rashi (or any other hallowed text) is found to say what I say, my words are the worthy and important words of a scholar. The group's inquiry into the need for reading Parashat Shekalim today may now be perceived as a direct reaction to its comprehension of Rashi's commentary. It does not spring from some unsanctioned curiosity; it remains properly within the boundaries of the exploration of the Talmud.

Again the Rav repeats his question, this time in its proper place, on the heels of Rashi's remarks.

"Now what do we read [Parashat Shekalim for] today, in these times?" The question can be abbreviated; its asking is simply an obligatory part of the drama but no longer a question so much as now a cue for the answer.

"In remembrance of the Holy Temple!"

This sudden exclamation is greeted with silence. Not yet assimilated, it floats freely into consciousness. We do not yet know if this is to be a final answer or simply an incorrect hypothesis like so many the Talmud offers before providing the ultimate resolution. Accordingly, we cannot be sure the crisis is over and the drama resolved. In *lernen* as a cultural performance what matters is not the individual's satisfaction but rather the extent to which the demands of the talmudic reasoning have been met. We need to find out if this answer is acceptable to the demands of the tradition; we await its legitimation.

To be sure, it is common practice within the culture of Orthodoxy to explain the present as a memorial to past glories. This will be a sufficient answer as soon as we have seen precisely how this is the case with Parashat Shekalim.

Clarifying the answer, the Rav continues, with the cuing and echoing of Shlomo, one of the students: "It is that we pay for the cows [to be sacrificed] with our lips."

To read the portion of the Torah which recounts the preparations for the Passover sacrifice is "to pay for the cows," to make those preparations "with our lips." To a People of the Book for whom the words of prayers and study have come to take the place of the daily sacrifices at the Temple, as is the case with Jewish liturgy, the notion that words can and do take the place of action is quite conceivable: for them talking *is* doing, as the very exercise of *lernen* attests.

"We cannot bring the [actual] shekel, so [instead] we read the portion [which describes its bringing]."

The men catch on. The reading is to be understood as a symbolic ritual act, a vehicle for the reliving of an important experience in Jewish history. If so, they too can suggest alternative symbolic interpretations. Beginning with the basic premise that the past must be found meaningful in the present and following the temper of their teacher's thesis, four of the men almost simultaneously suggest their own rationales. The opportunity to engage in the intellectual pyrotechnics of traditioning and contemporization is avidly pursued.

One man notes that not only can one understand the repetition of ancient readings as memorials to a glorious past but one can also project into the tradition praiseworthy practices of the present. "For this reason," he asserts, making his own interpretive leap, "many people [today] go to the *Kotel* [i.e., the remaining Western Wall of the Temple] on the days before a holy day."*

*During the period of the Temple, the custom was to make a pilgrimage to it on holy days on which occasion sacrifices were obligatorily offered. With the destruction of the Temple and subsequent exile both the obligation of sacrifice and the custom of pilgrimage ceased. In the modern period, and especially since the unification of Jerusalem in 1967, the pilgrimage has gradually become revivified. It is this last fact to which the speaker above refers.

Past and present are joined in this sort of dramatic improvisation. For several minutes in a flurry of discussion, the men transform themselves from being mere observers of their teacher's acts of interpretation to becoming his equals. Proposing his own resolution or commentary to the questions which have occupied the group, each man attaches himself to cultural drama of the discussion. Excitement is high as we stretch the limits of the text and our personal experience, as we shift back and forth from the words we have read to an inner elaboration of ideas.[55]

Anchoring this free expression, the Rav calls out over the voices of his students and intones the words of the tradition: "The *Mishna Brura* writes," he begins. Once again extemporaneous explanation is to be supported by a text. The essence of the *Mishna Brura* interpretation of the contemporary practice of reading Parashat Shekalim lies in its comment that today we "pay for the cows with our lips." The line of course by now has a familiar ring for us, performed and echoed as if it were a poetic refrain framing our discourses.

"So," the Rav recapitulates, lifting his eyes from the page and stilling our voices, "this is a remembrance of the giving [of money for the cows to be sacrificed] during the time of the Holy Temple."

Once again the men break into discussion, trying now to publicly associate their earlier comments with what must now be accepted as the final and authoritative answer. Each man repeats the points by way of which he entered the discussion but in a manner which allows them to be integrated into the argument of *Mishna Brura*. Throughout one overhears legitimating quotations from Scripture, citations of ritual practices and Jewish customs, or confessions of religious sensibility—in short, many of the things which define the character of religiocultural life. These are distributed into the flow of conversation and implicitly reaffirmed not only as part of sacred order but of the taken-for-granted world. Moreover, as they express their Judaism, so do the men attain it. Hearing themselves declaim the ways of Judaism, they can persuade themselves to follow them. Exegesis becomes praxis and leads toward belief.

To many of the explanations he chooses to ratify, the Rav reacts with: "Momentarily we shall see this [point made] in the Rashi [commentary]," or "That will be taken up later by the *gemore*," or "The commentators [of our holy books] say this [too]." As each man discovers his idea tied to the sacred canon, he likewise becomes tied to it and through it to the people for whom it is sacred. In *lernen* these spoken commitments are strengthened. "Study is great in importance, for it is study that brings one to doing," writes the Talmud (B.T. *Kedushin* 40b).

One might wonder perhaps how the men can be culturally energized, dramatically engaged, or at all satisfied by the answer that the Rav and his sources have offered. After all, there are no monumental turnings of reason, no surprise endings to capture one's attention here. The explanation that Parashat Shekalim is read in order to memorialize the Holy Temple and the activities associated with it may even strike one as weak or forced. For those accustomed to hearing the Temple invoked to explain all sorts of Jewish practices—as these men are—the explanation may also seem overused or hackneyed. But as their obvious engagement indicates, it is not.

To understand this fact one must realize that this circle of men is not peopled by those seeking answers that will convert them to the way of the Talmud or the culture it resonates. Rather they are the already converted and are instead once again rediscovering that way of the book; they begin from its presuppositions. While doctrinally subscribing to the notion that study leads to, indeed *is* a form of doing, they likewise assume that—in the words of the same Talmud—"praxis precedes study." Accordingly, the essence of their cultural performance is "to wait for the surprise which, when it comes, turns out not to be a surprise at all, but a natural path.[56]

CULTURAL TIES

To learn that "everyone asks that question," or "people always think that," or even to realize that others in the class are reasoning along the same path is, like finding one's ideas established within the sacred texts, another way to demonstrate the ties between personal and collective sentiment. This sort of discovery stands at the center of cultural drama. Consider the following example.

The circle this time is once again the one at Beit Rachel. The topic of discourse concerns the Menorah, the candelabrum which was one of the most sacred objects at the Temple in Jerusalem. During most of the class, the group has been discussing the "miracles" associated with the Temple as enumerated in the Talmud. Each man is given several opportunities to reiterate talmudic arguments, engage in religious debates, tell stories and react to them.

Near the end of this class, the group falls into a discussion about the "essential miracle" of the Menorah: its perpetual light. Although the actuality of the miracle is beyond question in this context, there is something to be puzzled through all the same: how did the light manifest itself? The past must be clearly discerned by the faithful.

This group does not normally review the commentaries of the Tosafot, whose critical remarks appear, as will be recalled, on the outside margin of each page of Talmud. This time, however, the Rav takes us through one of the commentaries in order to resolve an apparent contradiction in the traditions surrounding the lighting of the Menorah. On the one hand, we have learned that the priests daily rekindled the Menorah, this being one of their essential ritual tasks. On the other, we have learned of the miracle of its apparently perpetual light. The Tosafot, the Rav informs us, will solve the problem. In it we find that according to one scholar the western-most flame on the Menorah alone burnt constantly. When the priests came each day to kindle the lights, therefore, it was from this flame that they drew their fire. So there could be both a rite of rekindling *and* perpetual light.

To be sure, as the group makes its way through the Tosafot, there is an aspect of cultural performance that is really an act of omission. By their failure to express doubts about the possibility of "miracles" at the Temple, the men display a public commitment to the Talmud's description of sacred order. The absence of any challenges to this basic "truth" constitutes the shaping silence in the drama. Yet what their silence establishes dramatically—that miracles happened—their comments will expand in similar fashion.

Methodically, the Rav re-views the "miracle." He tells us— in effect, he verbally shows us: "The western candle of the Menorah burned twenty-four hours. And when they [the priests] came n the evening to light the Menorah, they would light from it, from this candle. That is to say, there was not a moment that the Menorah did not have a candle burning. All the [other] candles went out, but the western candle remained. In the evening, he [the priest] took fire from the western candle and lit the new candles. Afterward he put out the western candle, but by then there was already fire on the other candles. And why did they act thus? In order that it [the light] be perpetual."

As he opens and closes his eyes slowly while reviewing these details, the Rav appears swept away by his description, as if he imagined himself at the Temple watching all of this being reenacted. When his eyes are closed, he seems to be straining to see the details; and when they are opened, they twinkle with excitement. His rising voice and repetition of the details underscore his involvement in what he is saying. The other men are likewise carried away by his enthusiasm, and when he has finished they break into a reverberating discussion about the details.

"And when did he light the western candle?" asks Zusya above the murmuring of the others. He too wants to see clearly into his Jewish past.

"Right after the others. This was one of the miracles of the Temple. He gave the same measure of oil to each" [but the western candle still lasted longer], the Rav replies without missing a beat. He sounds as certain of the facts of this ancient ritual as if he had done it, or at least watched it many times himself. The source for his knowledge?

"Rashi says this in [his commentary to] the verse [in Scripture]." Zusya's question has already been asked and answered in the text.

Quoting the verse and its commentary by heart, again with his eyes closed, the Rav goes on to describe for us precisely where the Menorah stood, marking its placement with his hands on the large book open in front of him. Through and on the book our vision becomes clearer. We watch those hands and listen to this description and observe the invisible objects of faith once again become visible.

Surely neither he nor any of us in that room pretend to have seen the Temple or any of its sacred objects and rites. Yet through our *lernen* and by means of our faith in what we have read in the holy books, we act out and establish a cultural and religious memory so that we too can close our eyes and open them to what went on at the Temple.

Now comes another question, this one trying to tie the facts of the "miracle" with what we all know about Jewish life. One of the men, Nahum, asks: "If this was so [i.e., that the western candle burned miraculously longer than its supply of oil could account for], then what——"

And the Rav cuts in to complete the question, "is the miracle of Chanukah? Everyone asks that question." In the intersubjective atmosphere of the circle, it is not unusual to find individuals thinking along the same lines, able to complete one another's thoughts and sentences.

With its lighting of eight candles for eight days, the festival of Chanukah commemorates the Maccabees' discovery of a small cruse of oil with which they were able to rekindle the Menorah and thereby rededicate the Temple after regaining control over it from the infidels. This oil, although sufficient for only one day, burned for eight until new oil could be provided. Thus was the Menorah again constantly lighted.

The question asked is, to repeat, one that "everyone asks." Who is "everyone"? It is of course everyone who has made his way through the Scripture, commentaries, and Talmud, and who is familiar with the ways of Jewish life and its festivals. These are scholars and rabbis and generations of students who have been in like circles of study, people who care to explore Jewish tradition. And "everyone" is also the Rav and all of us who are *lernen* now. Through his question, the inquirer—as his Rav assures him—has tied himself both to the great chain of interpreters and to his people—to everyone who asks this question. He has put himself into a world of Jewish culture. To be sure, all Jews are not implicated here. But the ones who are are those immersed in Jewish texts and practices in the cultural milieu of the Talmud. And for *lerners*, the ones for whom interpretation is an end in itself, these people count most.

There will be an answer to this question. While crucial to the act of interpretation and providing closure to the episode, the answer is however not the climax of the cultural drama. That came with the question in which the boundaries of collective sentiment were clearly marked. During that moment, with a willingness to be shaped by the logic of the Talmud, the questioner was provided with "another world to live in" where "everyone asks" *his* question.

SENTIMENTAL EDUCATION

As noted at the beginning of this chapter, *lernen* may be understood as a sort of sentimental education during which the participants, in the course of their review of the sacred texts, rediscover and express the fundamental character or spirit of their culture along with their responses to it. In the process, they define their picture of their world or make sense of the events through which they and their forebears have lived. This publicly acted-out education, the result of an ongoing stream of talk, stamps into the men's consciousness the traditional patterns of Jewish life associated with the way of the Talmud. Its truths become theirs.

This process can perhaps best be illustrated and explained by outlining and analyzing an episode during which such sentimental education occurs. In the following case, part of the class at Beit Rachel which I have just been discussing above, one can trace a path from review of the text through theology, folklore, Jewish history, humor, speculation about Jewish destiny, and back again to a review of the text. In the course of all this, the dispositional and conceptual aspects of Jewish religiocultural life converge. The drama of their convergence is what keeps all the participants intensively engaged in the *lernen*.

The circle has reached the next to last page of the tractate they have been studying for nearly a year. Approaching this benchmark of progress (the end or *siyum* is a matter of great celebration and stocktaking), there seems to be a kind of slowing down of the pace and a willingness to broaden even more than usual the scope of the *lernen*. Freer in their lines of digression, more expansive in their analysis of the text, the men enhance the inherent cultural drama of their approach to study.

Reviewing the Talmud, the Rav reads aloud the lines describing the ritual immersions required for the sacred vessels in the Holy Temple. The placement, dimensions, constitution, and functions of each item are reviewed in an erudite series of quotations from Scripture and Talmud. Through this traditioning review, the *lerners* are once again transported from their small room at the back of the synagogue into the magnificent sanctuary of the Temple which now exists only in their cultural imagination.

One by one the items are discussed. First the Menorah attracts our attention. Next comes the Shulkhan, the table on which the shewbread was placed. Quoting from another tractate, the Rav reminds us—and from the cuing and echoing which accompany his words it is clear that this *is* a reminder for many—that there were various opinions about exactly how the shewbread, whose replacement was mandated once a week on the Sabbath, was removed from the Shulkhan. The view of the talmudist Rabbi

Yehuda, we are told, was that one priest would draw the bread toward him while at the same time another would place a new bread in its place so that the table would not be without its full complement of bread even for a moment.

"As it is written," the Rav concludes, citing Scripture, "the shewbread before me always."

The second opinion, we learn, the view of the rest of the rabbis, asserted that the old bread was removed in the morning and the new bread replaced in the afternoon. Even though the verse in the Torah says "always," this is interpreted to mean that the bread will "always" be offered to God rather than being perpetually on the table.

Here then is the straightforward teaching of a lesson from the Talmud. Scripture is quoted, traditions invoked, and information transmitted. And now comes a moment of crisis, a turning point, the resolution of which will prove to be the essence of the forthcoming cultural drama.

"Did no one remember how it was actually done?" asks Shmuel, one of the men. How, he wishes to know, can something which must be accepted by the faithful as a matter of fact—the sacred order of ritual in the Holy Temple—be a matter of talmudic debate? More than simply a point of information, this question is an implicit call for a theological guidance. It resonates the student's doubts about the legitimacy of rabbinic debate and the facticity of ritual. It displays the strain between his private sensibility and that of the text. His *lernen* will allow him to act out both these doubts and their resolution. It will also offer the others present a chance to guide him or to vicariously work through their parallel doubts.

As if sensing the implications of the question, the Rav responds by reasserting the ties by which the inquirer is tied to the circle of students and through it to the way of the Talmud. He aims to offset any feelings of alienation which may be aroused by the question. Finally, he reveals himself by offering in his answer an explanation of how he, who also had uncertainties, has come to terms with this dilemma.

"Ah!" he replies. "This is a controversy; this is a general question. Yes. Yes, absolutely right. This is a very nice question, but when we studied . . . before we studied this, we studied [the tractate] *Yoma* and found the same sort of question: Is there no one who remembers [the way things were actually done at the Holy Temple]?"

The student is told that the question is a common one, even the subject of a talmudic debate. The doubts it resonates are thus neither heretical nor inappropriate since even the Talmud has inquired about these matters. The curiosity is "absolutely right," the question "very nice." Thus relinked to the culture of the faithful, the student whose feelings of alienation are presumably now held in check may be led along the talmudic pathways of reason back to a reaffirmation of his belonging to its world.

"In truth," the Rav points out, in spite of the fact that some of those who debated these matters of ritual in the pages of the Talmud were alive during the Temple period and might therefore have witnessed the events in question, "they did not remember exactly. Why? Because anything one does not take the pains to remember, one does not remember."

The rabbis are human. Like all human beings they are subject to lapses of memory. There is an implicit psychological continuity posited between us and the rabbis. This kind of connection is, of course, a support for traditioning or contemporization.

Like many Orthodox Jews who have come to believe that matters of sacred ritual are beyond forgetting and the rabbis of the Talmud are superior beings, the student is not easily persuaded by this answer.

"Something as important as this?" he asks with obvious skepticism.

Taken momentarily aback, the teacher begins to stammer, but then he draws on his own experience to convince his student. If he, teacher, rabbi, and guide, can reveal that he, whose faith and commitment to the ways of the Talmud are beyond question, could also forget matters of sacred ritual, perhaps the student will be convinced. Contemporizing, the Rav invokes his experiences in detail. As he does so, we see him again working through, reenacting his doubts and their resolution.

"I, I, I . . . once when I was in the yeshiva [and I, in the same quandary as you are now, asked this same question] someone offered me an analogy [in reply]:

" 'How many years have you studied in the yeshiva?' he asked me.

" 'Seven,' I said.

" 'When they take the Torah [scroll] out of the Holy Ark [during the prayers], do the *Roshey Yeshivot* [principals] kiss the Torah [as is customary]? Does this one approach it, does the other?'

"These were questions [the answers to which] I did not remember.

" 'What's this, you don't remember? For seven years you have prayed there [in the yeshiva]. Each day you are there [and you must surely witness the removal of the scrolls from the ark] and observe the *Roshey Yeshivot.*'

" 'I did not take the pains to remember. Now that you have asked me, I shall pay attention in the future.' The interpretation of these words is clear."

Hardly had the Rav finished this story when he could hear objections rising from his listeners. Over their half-spoken protests he continued, however, without pause, "Thus did someone explain these matters to me. To be sure, he also offered me a parable, a very famous story."

Personal revelations are not enough. Or, perhaps having played out his own doubts, the Rav has legitimated the expression of his students' doubts. He can no longer easily allay them. They look for guidance as they play out their objections. Without allowing these to develop into an epidemic of alienation from the ways of the Talmud, the Rav tries to reassert both the initiative and the atmosphere of intimacy and fellowship within which *lernen* is most at home and in which the tendency to settle crises is most pronounced. A folktale, a people's story is used to charm us. It is a well-known tale that reiterates the theme that it is eminently human to forget even the most familiar details of life.

As the teacher reviews the story, smiles pass across the faces of his listeners. We know the story but, used to reviewing the familiar as if it were fresh and new, we let him recite it without interruption.

In this version, the story is about a grandson and grandfather who have come together for a talk. The former, looking at the older man's long beard, asks, "Grandfather, when you sleep at night is your beard underneath or on top of your blanket?"

Replying that he honestly does not know, never having taken pains to remember the matter, the grandfather promises to pay special attention this night and to report in the morning on the results. During the night he tries to put the beard underneath the covers but finding that uncomfortable puts it on top. That too is not right and so he switches again. So it goes throughout the night.

In the morning when his grandson asked for the answer, the grandfather replied, "I still do not know."

"Why?"

"Because last night I did not sleep."

"Why?"

"Because of your question."

By now the students were laughing loudly. All signs of alienation were gone and camaraderie had returned to the circle. The Rav, cued and echoed by various men throughout his narrative, leaned back and visibly relaxed. He had charmed us. The discomfort with the Talmud was now no longer the generating force of intragroup relations. Now in this atmosphere of intimacy there was a greater likelihood that we could play out an answer to the question harmoniously.

The Rav now concluded his story: "So he said, 'Leave me alone, let me continue on as I have until now, without knowing.'

"So what does this story teach us," he concluded rhetorically. "That matters which a person does not pay special attention to he will not remember."

The grandfather's comment at the end of the story has a quality of *double entendre*. For many persons of faith, among whom the Rav and his students wish to be counted, there is often a desire to respond to those whose questions delve too deeply into the contradictions of belief with: "Leave me alone, let me continue on as I have until now, without knowing." This is the other side of the earlier reaction: "Absolutely right, a very nice question." Here is a display of the ambivalence embedded within the ethos of Orthodox Jewish culture and private sensibility. These men are at once eager to explore their beliefs along the pathways of the Talmud—"absolutely right, a very nice question"—and reluctant to look too carefully at the taken-for-granted patterns of their belief—"let me continue on as I have until now, without knowing."

Having brought the group back together and at least hinted at the psychological and social complexities of their situation in the performance thus far, the Rav goes on, almost compulsively: "There is a better answer, one my uncle once told me."

Again he turns to his own experience, now when we are all committed to one another and open to a solution more so than before. The smiles on the faces are still there, a few chuckles still resonate the closeness established through the story.

Apparently, the Rav too had been unsatisfied with the previous answers for he obviously had asked the question more than once. Having taken us with him through the first answers, he takes us to the last out of which he, and now we, will come away with a sense of being corrected and completed.

"All the controversies in the *gemore* were based not upon what the High Priest actually used to do. [Instead they were based upon] how we, according to [an interpretation of] Scripture, see [i.e., understand] what the High Priest was *supposed* to do."

This is a fundamental cultural truth. For these Jews, interpretation is primary. In the Talmud and the pharasaic tradition from which it emerges, nothing is freed from the need of interpretation and reinterpretation. Even historical facts cannot be assimilated without interpretation. Rather, such facts are stimuli for the hermeneutic process. Just as people may witness events in real life without knowing what they have seen until after they have received an informed interpretation of the events, so too sacred order requires interpretive explanation. This is something not easily expressed. In the context of *lernen*, however, this cultural truth is expressible.

Responding to the Rav's invocation of this ethos of interpretation, a student asks for elaboration, repetition of this central truth, as it were.

Playing it again, the teacher replies, "If they were to ask me what the High Priest *ought* to do, I would say thus [according to the interpretations of the Talmud]."

"And today?" asks Zusya. While one man, Shmuel, may have been asking most of the questions, this interjection from another indicates that we all share in the curiosity. The working through of the patterns of our belief, the sentimental education, is a joint performance. All the members of the circle, speakers and listeners, are implicated in the action.

"Today," the Rav answers, "if the High Priest would not act according to the interpretations of the *gemore*, I [following in its ways] would have to ask him why and [what] his [textual] source [of authority for his actions was]."

Traditioning, we have turned the High Priest into a contemporary presence, not simply a figure of history. "Today," when there is in fact no longer a Holy Temple or High Priest, *we* talk

about what that High Priest must do in that Holy Temple. We see
it and him clearly. Time is conquered within the framework of the
cultural performance.

In what is perhaps the clearest expression of the cultural pri-
macy of interpretation, the teacher now invokes the medieval
exegete, philosopher, and codifier: Maimonides (sometimes called
by his acronym, Rambam). Maimonides will serve as the symbol
of resolution; his interpretations will exemplify how it is we must
come to terms with the ways of the Talmud and its logic. He is
the scholar who, having walked the way of the Talmud, has come
to represent its most reasonable interpreter. A panchronistic master of "creative synthesis," who "responded to the challenge of
the intellectual situation of his time and found the classical for-
mulation of its problems," Maimonides epitomizes the way to come
to terms with our question.[57] Through his "extraordinary Talmudic scholarship," he succeeded in giving the process of *lernen*
(although it was not called that in his time) "a completely new
form."[58] In his *Mishneh Torah* ("Repetition of the Law"), the vast
material arising out of the discussions of the Talmud is exhaus-
tively summarized and organized according to a plan worked out
to its smallest details.[59] Ultimately, this code came to serve as the
basis for many later compilations of Jewish law. It came to represent a more ordered version of the sacred text and—certainly
in this study circle—among the clearest paths into and out of the
Talmud.

"In the *gemore* there are controversies, and in the [commentary
of the] Rambam there are judgments. And when the Holy Temple
will be built, they will have to do what is written in the Rambam.
And that is based upon the controversies [i.e., debates] in the
gemore. Should then a High Priest arise, during the [messianic]
resurrection of the dead, and say . . ."

Now cuing the Rav, Shmuel, the student who originally asked
the question, actually completes the words of this High Priest:
". . . 'I saw it done differently.' "

The student is in effect acting out the scene created during the
lernen. He puts himself into the position of the High Priest who
saw how things were done at the original Temple but is now
seeing something different. He speaks his words and prepares
to be instructed by the Talmud via Maimonides and the Rav. In
this way, his question will at last be answered and his faith re-

paired. In the public performances of *lernen*, moreover, we are all able to watch him attain his faith as he portrays it.

Drawing on our tacit acceptance of this future's reality, the Rav continues: "We shall then say to the High Priest, 'In your time they determined the law one way, and in our time we determine it otherwise.' "

Here at last is a resolution both to the question and the drama. It is a celebration of the dominion of the Talmud and its interpretative power over history, both past and future. To accept this sort of answer, as the men clearly do, is to accept the theological limitations of the text while reaffirming its logic.

It is also to play out one of the central themes of Jewish cultural development. In the many histories of the Jewish people much is often made of how they underwent a profound metamorphosis. With the destruction of their Holy Temple, dissolution of the priestly order, and their exile from their homeland, the Jews ceased being a cult organized around rites practiced in Jerusalem. In time, they became instead the interpreters and keepers of a sacred tradition, a People of the Book.[60] That change, however, did not completely obliterate the cultic past but rather reinterpreted it symbolically. The memories of the cultic past remained important—"symbols which are tenaciously adhered to can hardly be dismissed as altogether meaningless"—but increasingly they became subordinate to the reasoning of those whose debates about and interpretations of the tradition would become the Talmud and its commentaries.[61]

For the Jews, who in their literature often refer to themselves as a "nation of priests," the Temple and its associated activities may be seen as symbolizing the consecration of that peoplehood. To rediscover, as the men in this episode of *lernen* have, that the facts of Temple order are subject to reinterpretation by the Talmud and its commentaries is to arouse in microcosm much of the cultural trauma associated with the change from Temple cult to interpretive People of the Book.

In the performance described here and others like it, this cultural trauma, long since stamped into the collective unconscious of the traditional Jew, can be observed being played out and worked through again. In the plastic drama of *lernen*, however, the individual "expresses it in *action*," the action of his discussion. "He reproduces it not in his memory," that clearly would be impossible, "but in his behavior; he *repeats* it, without of course knowing that he is repeating it."[62] To be sure, the dimensions of the drama are far less monumental and the actors not necessarily aware of the forces underlying it. "Actual conduct," as Max Weber once noted, "is carried on in the large part of its manifestation in semiconsciousness or unconsciousness of its intended meaning."[63] Yet an analytic view of the proceedings cannot help but uncover the lines of cultural change between the lines of dialogue.

"I hope," one student remarks from within the structure of this talmudic reasoning, "that there will not be two Holy Temples."

"No, no," his teacher answers from within that same world. "There will be submission according to the majority [opinion]. That, indeed, is not a cause for worry." To him the future is as clear as the past, writ large on the pages of the text. The way of the Talmud—majority opinion among scholars determines the way things are—will be the way of the future just as it is understood to be the way of the past. Indeed, among those who inhabit the Orthodox Jewish universe guided by sacred texts and Jewish law—as these men do—the interpretations of the Talmud and its commentaries are precisely what make the future foreseeable. They "provide a blueprint or template in terms of which processes external to themselves can be given a definite form."[64] They shape the religious and cultural future.*

The Rav's comments are a model *of* the faith which the material he has cited is the model *for*. His performance thus serves as a paradigm for his students. For him as for them, *lernen* is the way to bridge texts with cultural past, present, and future. That is the dynamic of its drama.

REPLAYING THE PAST

By definition, traditioning *lerners* refuse to live solely within the confines of the historical present. Rather, they feel a need to move periodically into a Jewish cultural past which serves as a paradigm for their Jewish present. Through their talmudic review and as-

---

*I do not here or throughout these pages mean to suggest that the way of the Talmud as expressed during *lernen* is the model for *all* Jewish religiocultural behavior. For those who celebrate the link between themselves and the sacred texts while bonding themselves ideologically to every jot and tittle of the *halakha* (normally those who call themselves "Orthodox" but not necessarily limited to them), it, however, remains the model par excellence, as the second epigraph at the opening of this chapter indicates. The members of the study circles I have observed are overwhelmingly within this group.

sociated discussion, they jointly reactualize the past and reeducate themselves. In the supportive social framework of the study circle and traditional cultural performance, the contemporary anxieties of anachronism disappear, replaced by an appreciation of the way things were back then. In a kind of group compact, the *lerners* tacitly agree to turn their eyes toward the past. Consider the following case.

The circle meeting at Rav Rotenbush's house has been reviewing the Talmud's description of the ancient ceremonies associated with Yom Kippur, the day of atonement, as it was celebrated during the era of the Holy Temple. This archetypical moment stands at the origins of our discussion. Among the most important rituals of the day was the dispatch of the scapegoat. This animal, whose death was meant to atone for the sins of the entire nation in an act of symbolic renunciation, was to be taken by a single designated man—the so-called *Ish Iti*—into the Judean wilderness where its end would come.

At first glance, this ceremony—no longer practiced—may be perceived simply as an archaic rite, out of tune with the contemporary understanding of atonement. Today's fasting, confession, religious stocktaking, and expressions of repentence and spiritual renewal seem qualitatively different from this ritual. That is not to say that it could not be contemporized, recast as a metaphor for the sort of atonement familiar to today's Jew. Indeed, those moderns who search for the significance of ancient practices in the current celebration of Yom Kippur are often engaged in just these sorts of symbolic transformations. Our previous consideration of the reading of Parashat Shekalim may serve as an example.

In the present case, however, Rav Rotenbush and his circle are not interested in transforming the meaning of the scapegoat ritual into a metaphor for today's kind of atonement. They simply want to visualize it, understand it in its own terms, as the men at Beit Rachel strained to see the Menorah.

"What was it like?" one man asks, in a sense for all of us.

Here is a signal for the Rav to launch us on a sentimental journey into the past. Alternating between Hebrew, with which he speaks to our intellect, and Yiddish, with which he arouses our Jewish spirit, he begins.

"Imagine," he says, calling our attention to the *Ish Iti*, "this man went, a bit broken-hearted—I believe the rabbis tell us that the man who took the scapegoat would die during the year [ahead]. In any event, *look, look* what it says here!" The Rav dramatically points to the text. His fingers rap on the open page with each emphatic cadence. What is interesting is what *we see:* "It is crowded. Everyone is standing at the Holy Temple. There's fire *there*. The High Priest, dressed in his raiment, is passing between the fire [on the various alters]. All are wearing white. The world is trembling.

"And what are the wise of Jerusalem doing? Do you know? These precious few, these clear-minded souls of Jerusalem, are going to escort this poor man who goes alone [out into the wilderness with the scapegoat]. They go to escort him! *Give a look!* This is also a *mitzva* [i.e., righteous act].

"They're standing there among all those who are happy [over the imminent atonement for their sins]. Everyone is chanting, and the High Priest is carrying on his service [at the Temple altar], and everyone is praying. [But these precious few decide] 'We shall go and escort the *Ish Iti.*' "

This description, its tone theatrical, stresses our capacity to see and experience the events. We look first at "what it says here" in the Talmud, which itself is quoting and interpreting Scripture. Through that "we see," as the Rav turns our attention to various scenes in the drama of that day. And as we "give a look" at the picture these words present, we are transported back to the place from which the *Ish Iti* leaves for the wilderness. We are able to "imagine."

To be sure, the description is filled with ellipses, drawing more on our sympathy with what happened than on our actual capacity to visualize the events. The trembling, the atmosphere of awe and intimacy that the Rav implicitly associates with our own emotional experiences of Yom Kippur are placed imaginatively into the domain of the past. The present is put into the service of the past.

Having passed into that past, the members of the circle "look" around to publicly and jointly explore it. One by one they make their moves. "Where did all the animals come from?" asks one man, as if like one present at the Temple he was suddenly made aware of the practical problems of carrying out sacrifices. Various answers are offered, some from the Rav and some from the others. "Why did two priests do what technically one alone could accomplish?" asks a second man. "What happens if these goats die prematurely?" asks a third. A fourth man tries to recap the actual order of the ritual procedures. Together, they are there in Jerusalem on Yom Kippur past.

Surrounded by the past, with its distinctive conceptions of the world, the men take on its distinctive mental dispositions. What before they remained unconscious of now grabs and holds their attention and interest.

Comparing the men's questions and comments with those in the Talmud, one cannot help but be struck by the similarity in logic and order and their self-imposed limitations on inquiry. Like the rabbis in the pages before them, the *lerners* appear to immerse themselves in and accept the legitimacy of the past while trying primarily to acquire a clarity about it. They do not simply read through the arguments but play them (or at least their analogues) out, as if they were the rabbis themselves. In this near mimicry, they transform their *lernen* into a cultural performance. They not only "see" the Temple rites; they see them as did the rabbis of the Talmud.

CONCLUSION

Throughout this chapter, a special kind of *lernen* has been described: a cultural performance, a kind of dramatic re-presentation and public reaffirmation of specific Jewish ideas and images whose source, either directly or indirectly, is the Talmud. Through this sort of *lernen*, a person discovers that he is not walled up in his little life and its accidental environment but a part of a wider social and cultural reality. Both the process and product of such *lernen* provide "the structures of meaning through which men give shape to their experiences," and channel "the drive to make sense out of experience, to give it form and order. . . ."[65] The result of all this, as I have several times pointed out, may be not so much a scholarly education as a sentimental one, an infusion of cultural ethos and worldview. In the cultural performance of *lernen*, men follow prefigured paths where they express and act out Jewish beliefs and ideas suggested in or by the texts they review. They digress with their fellows and in an intersubjective way cue, echo, and amplify the tradition in new ways while exploring the contemporary in light of the tradition. They reach out and bond themselves to the people in and of the books they study; and as they vitalize the text, they revitalize those ties, making sense of their Judaism. Indeed, to paraphrase the Hebrew poet and essayist Ahad Ha-Am, more than the religious Jews have maintained the practice of *lernen*, the practice of *lernen* has maintained the religion of these Jews.

4
INTERACTIONAL DRAMA: "LERNEN" AS PLAY

For recreation one goes not to the tavern, but to the House of Study.

ABRAHAM JOSHUA HESCHEL, "The Eastern European Era
in Jewish History"

By now it should be clear that regular, avocational *lernen* within a circle of one's fellows can "represent many different things in different contexts or at different levels of understanding"[1] and that it can engage those who carry it on in a variety of ways. Yet, another aspect of its appeal and meaning for those who normally participate in it is its capacity to allow for human interplay. This may be called *interactional drama*.

To be sure, the concept of interaction is a broad one, including in it formal mutual relations and informal ones, face-to-face and indirect contacts, and expressive or affectively neutral interchanges—to name but a few of the more prominent possibilities. The kind of interaction associated with *lernen*, however, consists of essentially small-group, expressive, face-to-face relations. These may either be "unfocused," loosely organized relations and communications that "result solely by virtue of persons being in one another's presence," or they may be "focused," encounters during which "people effectively agree to sustain for a time a single focus of cognitive and visual attention."[2]

The *shiur*, the formal framework of *lernen*, which I shall refer to more analytically as the "game" or "central performance," is predominantly a focused interaction. Since, however, "more is involved in the games people play than the rules and boundaries by which they play them," other concerns occasionally effectively blur the focus of the class.[3] These nevertheless remain part of the *lernen* "spectacle" within which the *shiur* game takes place. By "spectacle," I mean all the activities that normally accompany formal study, many of which are not always focused. Sometimes the spectacle of *lernen* becomes a kind of three-ring circus in which a variety of focused and unfocused interactions go on, all of which hold the participants together and align their involvement in the occasion.

Why call the interaction occurring during *lernen* "drama"? For an answer one needs to recall the essentials of participation in the Talmud study circle. To recapitulate, regularly a small group of familiars assembles for the manifest purpose of reciting, translating, explaining, and discussing a portion of the Talmud. A teacher or guide, here called the "Rav," normally leads the group; but active participation and spontaneous involvement from everyone present is an expected part of the game. During the *lernen* a world of words, somehow anchored to the text, is socially constructed. Within this world, the talk is variously keyed or patterned around expressive readings of the page, translation and explanation, conversational exchange, amplifying questions and answers, echoing and cuing, and language switching (between the language of the text and the vernacular of the *lerners*).[4] Some of the talk is conventionalized speech, either tied formally to the text and its explication or anchored in the social exigencies of relations in public. At other times, the talk seems freer, a reflection of the warp and woof of social and cultural life, a part of the spectacle. In this second sort of conversation, "what talkers undertake to do is not to provide information to a recipient but to present dramas to an audience."[5]

As during conversation generally so too during the interactional drama of *lernen*, when "an individual appears in person before his familiars and joins with them in talk," talk about anything, including the Talmud, "what he does is to present a one-man show. He animates."[6] He shows off himself, his knowledge, his involvement in and alignment with what is going on, the extent of his connectedness with the group, their culture, religion and tradition, his capacity to respond to and stimulate others, his social status and ability to conform to its associated roles. In short, he displays his capacity to play by the rules and in the roles of the occasion.

He does not, however, act alone for, as in any show, the presence of others—potential audience or fellow players—ensures a continuity of drama. In *lernen* as in other interactional performance, "the action of any one character is inter-dependent in a massive, not merely incidental, way upon the action of the other characters."[7] If one man is animated, so are the others; and likewise, the animation of the others stimulates him even more. It turns out, as *lerners* themselves sometimes put it, that "one good word deserves another," or that a good performance calls forth at the very least a display of "appreciation of a show put on."[8] Whatever the nature of the interchanges, it is their presence in the context of *lernen* that may be termed "interactional drama."

If it seems that there is too much of talk in all of this, remember, as Robert Bales in his research on small groups has demonstrated, "social interaction is made up largely of the talking that people do when they are together."[9] In the Talmud study circle, the animation of talk among fellows is the matrix within which the interaction occurs. In previous chapters the focus has been on the content which overlays the interaction. Now, however, attention will be directed to the process of animation, the rules of interaction which have their own logic and like any game have their own drama. Only within the context of *lernen* can some of these interactions occur. Only here do they make sense and set in motion the creative apparatus, holding the performers' attention and assuring their involvement.

THE CONDITIONS FOR INTERACTION

Under which conditions can interaction take place? In his analysis of the phenomenon, Don Handelman suggests three minimal qualifications: (*a*) a willingness among persons present to engage in focused activity, (*b*) a topic of interaction, and (*c*) the allocation and activation of speaker-hearer roles in conversational activity or doer-observer roles in nonverbal interaction.[10] By the terms of this general definition of the grounds on which interaction may take place, *lernen* can be seen as ideally suited to the purpose. Each component may be considered in turn.

A Willingness among Persons Present to Engage in Focused Activity

Perhaps the first presupposition of the study circle is that those assembled are by definition gathering specifically to review a portion of the Talmud. Although, as has already been suggested, there may be a host of latent reasons that members of the circle have for attending the *shiur* and engaging in *lernen*, none of these can legitimately supersede the manifest aim of Talmud study. Even, as shall later be shown, those celebrations of the completion of a tractate—the *siyum*—where the emphasis is on festivities, a ritual feast, camaraderie, and other normally more marginal activities, a general openness, if not loyalty, to the superordinate claim of study as the predominant focus of activity exists.[11] Thus on no occasion of *lernen* would a regular participant consider it appropriate to attend a *shiur* and openly declare his unwillingness to study a text and instead demand that the entire time together be spent in unfocused, free activity. Recall a situation described in the previous chapter when the Rav at Beit Rachel failed to appear. Instead of simply passing the time in a continuation of the free conversation that had gone on during the period of waiting, those assembled felt the need to spend some time in formal focused talmudic review.

This is not to say that any given player may not come to a *shiur* with the hopes of minimizing if not altogether doing away with this formal study. He may play the study game distractedly, spend the time sleeping (as a number often do), or become lost in thought or whispered conversation with a neighbor. He may even try to bring about a general flooding out of the other performers by encouraging a plethora of digressions and conversations ranging freely away from the Talmud. Such efforts to get himself or others out of play, however, require either their collusion or tacit agreement, a fairly fluid definition of the situation (freer than a class normally allows), or at the very least that involvement shifting remain carefully camouflaged.

Generally, the accepted requirements of *lernen* thus demand minimally a display of openness to study and its associated focused discussions. This claim on the attention and involvement of those present, generated in part by the demands of commingling, fellowship, and felt religious obligation to study, supports a fairly tight definition of the situation. Through their conformity to its demands, the members of the study circle, as I have earlier suggested, come "together in some sort of intersubjective, mental world."[12]

The willingness of those present to play the game of study can perhaps be most simply discovered in the ease with which the transition from the opening banter of unfocused activity to a concentration upon the text is accomplished. Sometimes a simple silence dramatically turns the participants' eyes toward the page and leads to a recitation of it. At other moments subtle shifts in the Rav's voice: a raising or lowering of volume, a slowing down of pace, or a change in timbre and tone are sufficient. Out of the mumble of conversations which normally precede the formal beginning of the *shiur*, a quiet "Nu?" (So?) is often enough to pierce the consciousness of all those present and focus their attention on the Talmud.

The openness to study is so much assumed in the encounter that the students themselves may even feel moved to interrupt their own free and flowing involvements with a call to order. Someone may spontaneously call out the page and line where study left off last time, thereby indicating his readiness to get into play. Domino-like, similar displays of readiness pass through the group. Some students echo this announcement; others may open the book and turn the folios or glide their fingers across the lines of print in a public display of focusing. Still others may begin reciting the opening words of the Talmud in a stage whisper, as if cuing the Rav whose recitation normally marks the formal beginning of the study performance. Others may clap the table for attention, a conventional device sometimes used as well for calling people to prayer. In brief, because talmudic review is the formal raison d'être for the gathering and because each person present has a stake in it, anyone and everyone in the circle has the right to call for such a beginning; and no genuine insider (i.e., one who knows how to properly handle himself in the encounter) would challenge the legitimacy of that sort of summons.

During one extended period of preliminaries, when the members of the Beit Rachel were apparently deeply involved in a series of nontalmudic conversations, all it took was a call of *"rabotey!"* (gentlemen!), a dramatic pause in place of a reply to a lingering conversation, and then the Rav's request for "us to take a little break from all this and *lern*," to have the entire group immediately look into their books.

A Topic of Interaction

Although in theory any focused activity could serve to systematically organize interaction, in these study circles—as just indicated— only Talmud can legitimately do so. While one of the most

All the men of the study circle sit focusing their eyes and attention on their books. The intimate atmosphere of the study circle is apparent. (Photograph by S. Binstock)

obvious ways this is accomplished is through the public recitation, translation, explanation, and discussion of the text, there are other more subtle ways for getting the group to settle on the Talmud as a topic of interaction. The first is undoubtedly the physical presence of the books, the tractates of study. Normally large and imposing volumes, they lie on the tables around which the participants sit from almost the earliest moments of their gathering and cannot be easily ignored. Either brought along by each participant or withdrawn from the shelves in the study room, the volumes of Talmud proclaim the ultimate topic of interaction and serve as a visual cue for the subsequent activity. With arms resting on the books, fingers playing along the edges of the page or binding, the men around the tables signal some level of awareness of the Talmud's presence.

The opening of the books may be properly perceived as a symbolic opening of the study game. Once opened, the books serve to anchor most ensuing activity in the framework of talmudic review.[13] Everything that happens in the face of these open volumes will be defined as keyed to the *lernen*, part of the game. This is not to say that there will be no digressions. As already noted, there normally are. Carried on across the open page, however, they are understood to be endowed with an aura of respectability and importance radiating from the Talmud. They become what members of the circle sometimes refer to generally as "*divrey Torah*," words of Torah which are keys to comprehending the primary matter of the Talmud. They are social and intellectual transformations of it, which are all the while anchored in its dominating presence and derive their legitimate claims on involvement from it.

Some of the same conversations carried on outside the brackets of the *shiur* (or more figuratively outside the margins of the Talmud page) would conceivably not qualify as *divrey Torah* but would rather be perceived as *devorim betalim*, profane or at least irrelevant to sanctified *lernen*. A narrative from one's personal experience, a description of some technical procedure, an examination of some news event can, in the context of the class, all be keyed to the Talmud, used to illustrate or explain its logic. On another occasion, however, they could be viewed as matters altogether dissonant to the tenor of *lernen*. The skilled player knows how to properly key the meaning of his remarks so that even the most farfetched matters can appear to be *divrey Torah*. Part of the drama of the game, however, consists of properly keying one's words.

Occasionally there are disagreements over what properly constitutes *divrey Torah*. Here the Rav, as ultimate arbiter, plays a crucial role. Thus, for example, during the preliminaries of a Mekadshey Torah class, the men focused on the topic of women's responsibilities and prerogatives in Jewish law. Some of the men wanted very much to pursue this topic in the *shiur* while others, those tending toward a more traditioned view, argued that this discussion was a "waste of time," keeping the circle from *lernen divrey Torah*. Seeking a solution that would not open this breach in the group any further, the Rav agreed the topic was important but deserved its own separate occasion for study. Leaving his Talmud closed while he spoke, he silently underscored his position as tending toward the traditioned.

In another case, during the final moments of a class, a similar situation arose. A discussion of the Smotra neighborhood, originally emanating from a point raised in the Talmud but in the final analysis turning attention very far from it, resulted in Rav Gafny, leader of the Knesseth Jacob circle, closing his Talmud. The others followed suit. Clearly, in the perception of this group, this discussion had taken them outside the realm of the Talmud and could not any longer qualify as *divrey Torah*. Coming at the closing minutes of the hour, the matter could be handled by the simple gesture of closing the book. When what he considered to be undeniably irrelevant topics were raised in the middle of the class, the Rav, like others in his position in other circles, would sometimes cut off discussion with the comment, "We'll talk about that later," or "Listen, we're going to have to close the *gemore*, if we keep on talking about this." Indeed, the entire question of what can legitimately be anchored to the predominant activity of study, what topics are keyed to the *lernen* and what denotes something completely different is one that will have to be considered more specifically below. What can simply be said here is that the matter is a fundamental concern within interactional drama, and performers are always on guard for those occasions when something is out of place, miscued, irrelevant, or improperly defined as anchored to the *lernen*. This is one of the abiding dramatic tensions during interaction.

The Allocation and Activation of Roles

Formally there appear to be only two distinct roles in the interactional drama of *lernen:* student and Rav. Normally the latter
most often is speaker and doer while the student is hearer and
observer. In an active *shiur*, especially during the sometimes liminal moments of digression and debate, these positions are sometimes switched. There are, to be sure, those would argue—
somewhat ideologically—that since every Jew (including the Rav)
is always likely to learn something new from a review of the text,
there is only one formal role—*"lerner"*; and in it the player is
sometimes active and sometimes passive. Still, few would deny
the formal distinction between those who lead and guide the
group and the *shiur*, those whose word is final, authority dominant, scholarship putatively superior; and those who are followers, subordinate in a number of ways.

If, however, consideration is given to the actual performance,
the expressive dimension of behavior occurring during *lernen*, a
far larger number of role possibilities appear.[14] Although such
performance-generated roles emerge out of the dynamics of interaction, they tend through their repetition to become sufficiently
crystallized so as to be considered part of the institutionalized
character of *lernen*.

Thus, every circle will have its "top student," the one who—
after the Rav—speaks most often, cues frequently, and whose
success in comprehending the text is often displayed by his instructive questions (which prefigure the Talmud's own) or rati-
fying remarks. He is the one to whom the Rav often looks for a
reaction to his explanations, making the class sometimes appear
as dialogue between the two. He is the one who is tacitly given
greatest license, after the Rav, to direct debate or respond to a
student question. Whereas other students may find their comments greeted with something less than undivided attention, the
top student, like the Rav, can often lay claim to the silent consideration of his colleagues.

Circles will also have a number of others who repeatedly present themselves and thereby establish a situational role identity
as, for example, riddlers, digressors, contemporizers, or erudite
citers of parallel texts and the all-important lines of Scripture.
There are those whose displays of knowledge make them the
group authorities on one or another topic. Sometimes a person's

role outside of class will become relevant to some subject under discussion and on these occasions will become part of his role in the central performance of *lernen*. Thus, when the discussion is about medicine, the doctors or druggists in the group will be called on to ratify or inform a discussion. When the subject is vaguely connected with matters of building and land, contractors or even lawyers may be endowed with a role as task specialist. Matters of business are handled by the shopkeepers or bookkeepers. Discussions about parenting are informed by the men's experiences as fathers, and so on.

Even those who for the most part remain silent during class are endowed with a special situational role. Swept into the interaction precisely because of their silence, these people are often turned into the all-important audience. Often the last ones to be addressed, their replies to the question, "Do you understand?" may determine whether or not a matter is completely understood and the group moves forward in the text, onward to another *inyan*, or whether there is a need to recapitulate. A proficient auditor, one who understands the tacit rules of the *lernen* game, must know when to answer affirmatively and when to ask for a review. He must remain conscious of his role as a kind of group barometer. When the subject is obviously complex and it is likely others are still puzzled, when the group seems poised to enter a discussion which only a recapitulation will make possible, the auditor must say he is still confused. When, however, everyone appears to understand matters and is ready to move on, teetering on the brink of tedium with the current topic, he must know how to display a comprehension. An echo, a restatement of the last point in brief but telling words may be enough. To be sure, if the fellow really does not understand and wants to, he may ask for review regardless of the others' displayed desires. In this, however, he is no longer primarily oriented to the interactional drama but has rather stepped outside of its boundaries for his own ego-oriented interests. In interactional drama, "involvement is an interlocking obligation," and ego interests are often irrelevant.[15] The demands of sustaining the game and maintaining its dramatic tension (to say nothing of fellowship or being a good sport) require one sometimes to sacrifice comprehension. The auditor learns how to be a nondisruptive hearer and observer. This is a serious task in which he becomes a specialist.

In Smotra, for example, a player still puzzled by a piece of Talmud after its apparently final review might publicly disattend his puzzlement with a comment like: "Well, I suppose I'll have to look this *sugia* over again." His willingness to restrain himself is quietly accepted. Indeed those who failed to dampen their curiosity in time were often cued by the Rav to go over the text by themselves for then they "would understand things better."

In addition to these individually allocated roles, there may be mutually supportive pairs, various expressive interactional performances during which two people commonly play out the same or similar sets of behaviors. Thus, one may often discover two students who seek always to outdo one another in the asking of questions or the giving of answers. Competitors for the attention of the Rav and through him the group, the two may be vying for the part of top student. Via their competition, they not only support their own interaction but also may serve to stimulate like activity among others in the group or else generate spontaneous involvement from others who may join the contest, at least for a time.

Other such pairs can be discovered. "While one person becomes a specialist in advancing ideas another is apt to be developing a specialization on the reactive side."[16] These sorts of supportive pairs define crystallized interactive configurations, which are repeated in almost all *lernen* encounters. The cuer-echoer, Rav-top student, riddler-respondent, narrator-auditor, or seat partners who through their propinquity normally engage in whispered byplays together are prominent examples.

From what has been presented thus far, the specific ground or basis for interaction during *lernen* should be established. The character of that interaction as well as the lines of its drama must now be more carefully considered. For this an additional bit of conceptualization is necessary first.

PRIMARY FRAMEWORK AND KEY

Two concepts will prove helpful in advancing the analysis of the interactional drama taking place during *lernen*. Borrowing from Goffman, I refer to "primary framework" and "key." The first of these may be briefly defined as a fundamental characterization or "original interpretation" of an event, a thing or activity.[17] Often a reflection of the culture of the perceiver, a primary framework appears, through the prism of that culture, to be the only frame of reference which can provide one with a genuine definition of the situation, a true view of the way things really are, and what is "really or actually or literally occurring."[18]

This socially or culturally projected frame of reference is, however, not the only or even final perception of events, things, or activities. Rather, "keys" or transformations exist. These are the conventions by which a given event, thing, or activity, "one already meaningful in terms of some primary framework is transformed into something patterned on this activity [event or thing] but seen by the participants to be something quite else."[19] The process of transformation is called "keying." Put somewhat differently, a key is an interpretation of an interpretation, an alteration of a perception, a transformation of meaning, a redefinition, or a reframing of one's references.

In a sense, these concepts may be considered theoretical elaborations of the notion, already characterized as an assumption of interactional drama in the study circle, that "one good word deserves another." That is to say, one word—the recitation of the Talmud, for example—constitutes the primary framework, while another—a translation—is a key of the first (keeping in mind that a translation, as already noted, is more than a set of word-by-word equivalencies). During the course of *lernen*, keyings in turn lead to further keyings. Translations are transformed into explanations; explanations into discussions, discussions into series of questions and answers, these into digressions, and so on to echoes and cues that bring one back to the text. Each "word"* thus has the capacity to reframe the participants' perception of what is going on, of what *lernen* in effect is all about. To those not informed about the process, the keyings may appear the primary framework and vice versa. The outsider may, for example, look upon a gloss as text while perceiving text as mere illustration of an explanation. Each word, however, is a kind of rescripting of the drama or rewriting of the text; the interchange of words a refocusing of the interactive focus.

*In the course of *lernen*, the Yiddish expression *"vort"* is often used to refer to a disquisition that has all the makings of a full-blown reinterpretation of a matter under discussion, a reframing as it were. Literally, however, "vort" means "word." Hence one good word—*vort*—from the Talmud or one of its commentators deserves another.

There is another way to perceive all this. The Talmud, as already noted, is a gloss. One might call it a transformation or key to the comprehension of the primary matter of Scripture. As biblical exegesis, it reinterprets narratives, redefines imperatives, and reorders chronology. But the Talmud itself is subject to reframing. Both literally and in effect, the page is framed by commentaries: Rashi on the inside margin, his successors the Tosafists on the outside.[20] These commentators provide an interpretive key to the interpretations of the Talmud, force one to comprehend it in a new way. What appears to be one meaning when read in the Talmud turns out sometimes to be something quite different when perceived through the commentary of Rashi, whose interpretations are themselves subject to reframing by the Tosafists. They in turn may be reframed by later commentaries which have been added to the outer margins of the page. They are keyings of the earlier exegeses and through them the central text. So it goes; the volume is filled with glosses upon glosses, each providing another key to the Talmud and through it to the even more basic primary matter of Scripture. With each new edition of the Talmud, the publishers may add more commentaries or new appendices—new keys.[21]

Finally, beyond all the printed commentaries, outside the margins of the page, as it were, stand the *lerners* themselves. They too reframe the page and all that is on it; they too represent a rekeying of the primary matter. Passing through layer upon layer of interpretation (the most skilled pass through all or most of the commentaries, the moderately skilled through only the major ones, and the simple students only through Rashi and an occasional Tosafist), they bring themselves, their ethos and world view to bear upon the subject and animate the whole. Reviewing the page, they take their cues in part from what comes before them. As the folio of Talmud is characterized by commentary, replies, responsa, questioning, debate, information exchange, digression, narrative, and repeated recountings, so the *shiur* is marked by keys of all of these. The performers comment, debate, question, reply, tell stories, exchange information about matters of Jewish life and law as well as personal adventure and of course digress. Yet what the class appears to reflect, it often reframes. The conversations during *lernen* are always something different from the written page, patterned by it but not exactly the same. Hence, in each *shiur*, even a review of the same passages of Talmud is different from what appears in the text being reviewed.

So complicated does the process—the *lernen* game— become that without a tape recording by means of which a transcript of the proceedings could be put together, one would have trouble determining where the written page leaves off and oral commentary and reframing begins. Where the vernacular is Hebrew, close to the language of the text, this becomes even more difficult since speakers often use words and phrases from the Talmud which are embedded in the natural conversational stream. In the American cases, language shifts help somewhat in distinguishing boundaries, but even here (as I will later demonstrate) the heavy dosage of quotation and superposed language makes it difficult to know what is primary and what keyed. A remark from a *lerner* may emerge directly from within a quotation and thus key the quoted material so that it is perceived as part of another statement. That is, the animation of talk usurps words of text until it is not clear in the absence of painstaking analysis whether the *lerner* is reciting, translating, explaining, discussing, echoing, or in some other way transforming the written text. An example will be helpful here.

LERNEN MOVES

Before proceeding with an example, however, it will be useful to review and expand upon the four basic "moves" of the *lernen* game. As already noted, these are: recitation, translation, explanation, and discussion. All four do not necessarily occur in any given episode or performance; and as already noted, sometimes the shift from one to another is gradual or layered, resulting in ambiguities during the transition. For purposes of analysis, however, these four moves may be considered the general organizing structure of the game's interaction.

Recitation denotes most simply the oral reading of the text. By "text" is meant anything printed in the volume of Talmud under study, including not only the central words of the Mishna and *gemore* which make up its figurative and literal core but also those of Rashi, the Tosafists, and other printed commentaries on the margins and in the back of the book. The recitation may be chanted in the traditional sing-song cadences that rise and fall along lines which I shall later describe in detail. It may consist of a rapid, almost matter-of-fact mumble, sounding a bit like the murmur of prayer. Finally, as living sacred texts often are, it may also be declaimed theatrically like a premeditated utterance. To be sure, as a vocal animation of a written, unvocalized, and unpunctuated text, the recitation can become a kind of interpretation. What one person recites as a statement another may perform as irony and a third as question. Thus recitation, in its effort to disambiguate the page, may reframe its primary meaning. However, since the text is itself a somewhat cryptic set of notes of a one-time live dialogue in the academies of Babylonia and Palestine, one might argue that for all intents and purposes, the recitation during a *shiur* constitutes a primary move. It is primary in two senses: first, because it begins the process of *lernen*, providing the original interpretation of the text; and second, because it structures or at least anchors the subsequent thought and talk which further interprets and reinterprets it.[22]

Translation is the first of the transformations or what, after Bellack and others,[23] may be called "reacting moves," units of speech or action which serve to modify or evaluate what has been previously said.[24] Although translation is commonly conceived as the substitution of words in one language for their equivalents in another, it is in fact a significantly more complex process. While this is not the place to launch a lengthy discussion of translation, it is necessary to point out, following Eugene Nida,[25] that the process of translation involves analysis and restructuring in which one world of ideas is exchanged for another. The transference from one conceptual domain may be mapped this way:

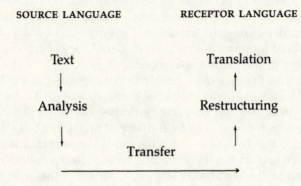

SOURCE LANGUAGE   RECEPTOR LANGUAGE

Text   Translation

Analysis   Restructuring

Transfer

In certain cases this process may appear to leave meaning unchanged. In others, a transformation or keying may be judged to have taken place. Those persons who are fluent in both languages and familiar with the cultural and social perspectives associated with them are often most sensitive to the keying. In any event, translation must be understood as some part of alteration of the primary matter.

Explanation is also a reacting move. In simple terms, explanation is an additional means of modifying the primary matter of the text. It clarifies and aims to remove all misapprehensions. It is, of course, in the final analysis an interpretation which may or may not be accepted. The explanation, like other keyings, may seek to "inhibit original meanings" by replacing them with new ones.[26]

Explanations may be thought of as taking two forms. The most common and simple is the brief "gloss," the one- or two-word lamination to the text that reconstitutes the meaning of what is there. A second and more complex explanation reveals the thrust and motive behind the words. This form of explanation may be termed an "explication" insofar as it unfolds or opens up meaning in a way that a gloss does not. Explication is that form of explanation that leads most easily to discussion. While manifestly trying to remain loyal to the text and indeed not seeking to transform it, explanations latently key it because they suggest that what at first reading might have appeared to mean one thing, after explication or gloss turns out to be another.

The resolution of these apparent differences as well as the evaluation and extrapolation of explanations is what is termed here *discussion*. Discussions can transform the text into a pretext for the consideration of something else: a point of law, a matter of theology, an exploration of Jewish ethics, a narrative, a personal revelation, a test or demonstration of faith. Recall the episodes described in the previous chapters and the discussions which transformed *lernen* into a social drama or cultural performance. The discussion thus has the capacity to key the primary matter of the text in a most radical way, to fracture its perspective and reorient its meaning. When one engages in discussion, one literally shakes to pieces the text under review, hence the potential of discussions to evolve into questions, debates, and digressions.

In the interactional drama of *lernen*, it is also necessary to distinguish among utterances, turns, and moves. The first of these denotes the entire locution or run of words spoken during a turn, the latter being "an opportunity to hold the floor," a chance to perform.[27] Taking a turn at talk means having the right to claim the attention of those in attendance. Utterances and turns may be divided into moves which may be defined as "any full stretch of talk or . . . its substitutes which has a distinctive unitary bearing on . . . circumstances in which the participants find themselves."[28] Moves are normally made during one's turn, but it is not uncommon to find persons interrupting, moving out of turn. During *lernen* recitations, translations, explanations, and discussions are moves, types of utterances occuring during a turn at talk. Cues, echoes, certain glosses, and other byplays are moves which while part of the interactional drama of *lernen* may occur out of turn. Any given performer may make all or some of the moves. Every full-fledged *shiur* will almost certainly require all to be played at some time or another.

There are as well other episoding conventions which mark the beginning of a turn or indicate that another move is being or has just been made.[29] These include vocal inflections, rhythmic adjustments, volume modulations, and other gestural signs such as looking up from or down to the page, leaning forward or back from the table, relaxing one's body or stiffening it,[30] swaying, and "the classical 'talmudic' gesture of analytic incision (fist clenched, thumb outstretched, describing a scooping motion in the air as if digging out an idea), clinching the sentence [or, more precisely, the move] with a table-pounding movement."[31]

In sum, the interactional drama of *lernen* in part may be said to consist of the deft shifting among a circle of performers from turn to turn and move to move. The activity is so fluid that, as indicated, one may not always be able to follow the shifts without an exact transcript of the play. For the insider, the practiced performer, the movement is of course second nature. He knows how to do it, even if he is not always aware or fully informed about what it is he is doing. Here then is an example:

The episode is drawn from a *shiur* in the Mekadshey Torah circle. Rav Rotenbush begins his turn and in this instance the *shiur* with a recitation of the opening words of the evening's text. The subject deals with the disposition of objects associated with the carrying out of religious activity. The Talmud normally divides these into two types: *tashmishey mitsvah*, implements used for the execution of religious duties, and *tashmishey kedusha*, items themselves endowed with sanctity. The former, the text seems to suggest, may be thrown out when they are worn out, while the latter must be stored. Rav Rotenbush speaks:[32]

I.	R:	1–	TANU RABANAN [these are words being read from the Talmud]
	R:	2–	"The wise [our rabbis] have taught" [spoken translation]
	Y:	3–	(Folio 26, side b.) [spoken sotto voce][33]
	R:	4–	TASHMISHEY MITZVA NIZRAKIN, TASHMISHEY KEDUSHA NIGNAZIN [*tashmishey mitzva* are thrown out; *tashmishey kedusha* are stored].
	S:	5–	hmmm aha
	R:	6–	What are "TASHMISHEY MITZVA"; what are "TASHMISHEY MITZVA?" and what are "TASHMISHEY KEDUSHA?"
A & S:		7–	"KEDUSHA?" [an echo]
	R:	8–	"*TASHMISHEY MITZVA*" [an utterance difficult to classify]
	S:	9–	*THINGS THAT HAVE BEEN* [a cue, or a spontaneous remark]
	R:	10–	*THINGS THAT HAVE BEEN* USED FOR RELIGIOUS DUTIES.
	R:	11–	*TASHMISHEY KEDUSHA*
	R:	12–	Things that have been used—things that are sanctified.
	R:	13–	VE'ILU HEN . . . TSITSIT [and these are *tashmishey mitzva*: a Sukkah booth, a palm branch, a ram's horn, fringes].
	R:	14–	After their use. *This is a primary imperative: to* [be permitted to] throw out [*tashmishey mitzva*].
	R:	15–	Nonetheless, we customarily store these as well today
	R:	16–	VE'ILU HEN TASHMISHEY KEDUSHA [and these are *tashmishey kedusha*]
	R:	17–	whose primary imperative is that they be stored and not thrown away.
	R:	18–	DELUSKAMEY SEFARIM
	R:	19–	This is an "ark for books."

R: 20– TEFLIN . . . U'RETSUOTEYHEN [phylacteries, mezuzas, the case or coverlet of a Torah scroll, the phylactery bag and the straps of phylacteries].

R: 21– *U'RETZUOTEYHEN*. These are the "TASHMISHEY KEDUSHA" which one must store because they have become spoiled or for any other [like] reason.

II. A: 1– What is the meaning of "NIGNAZIN" [store], not to bury? To put in some place, eh, uhm—
—

III. S: 2– A storehouse.

      N: 3– This is "a storehouse."

IV. R: 1– Mr. Alexanderovich, it is necessary to look into [the commentary of] the Rambam and [there] we shall see difference and distinction between a Torah scroll and other TASHMISHEY KEDUSHA and if indeed the laws of printed books pertain at all in this matter, whether or not they are like the Torah scroll which has in it the Divine Name and which therefore must be stored. And indeed, the essential law pertaining to the Torah scroll requires it to be placed in a grave, next to a Jewish scholar in an earthenware jug. With God's help, I hope during the course of our class we shall get to the question of all matters recorded on a tape recorder, words of Torah or blessings spoken under the wedding canopy or matters such as these—what must be done with these tapes. Is it permissible to erase them?

From here the discussion continues apace as the men discuss the issues raised by the Rav in his explanation. Finally, cutting into the discussion and cutting off the digression, the Rav moves us back to a reading of the text with a remark that seems to be a natural extension of the conversation: "What you have said is of course taken up in the Tosafot where I see written as follows . . ."

Throughout this episode, or series of turns, there has been a variety of nonverbal moves carried on by the players, during which those who seem to be silent act out their involvement and comprehension of what is going on. Some are reactive moves. During the first turn—the Rav's recitation, translation and explanation—these are: brows knitted in obvious puzzlement following move 6 and several heads nodded in a sign of comprehension or agreement during the spoken moves 10 through 12. There are also the structuring moves accompanying the page announcement in move 3; here a number of men dramatically handle the large books, leaf through pages finding the proper one, and prominently move their fingers along the columns of the page until they have found the right place, and then draw the tomes toward themselves, adjusting them for comfort. One fellow hums, a traditional tuning up for the sing-song of recitation, and then mumbles "aha" in a stage whisper, indicating thereby that he has now got the correct spot. Others rush to find it and then lean over to their neighbors to publicly assist them in finding the correct line. All these moves carried on as byplays along with the Rav's recitation of text served to publicly align the participants to the central performance of *lernen*. As the Rav signals his degree of involvement with his recitations, translations, explanations, and discussion, so the others mark theirs with this series of nonverbal moves. Finally, having indicated that they are ready to begin their run of *lernen*, some students move on to the cuing and echoing that display a sustained engagement. Near the end of this extract, one man, Mr. Alexanderovich, finally asks the first question of the session, proving how animated he has become, how quickly he has gotten into the page.

If one analyzes the character of each of the spoken moves, it immediately becomes clear how complex and keyed the performance is and how swift the movement during these opening turns of *lernen*. To understand the game it will be useful to consider each of the moves in turn.

1. This first move of the first turn seems clearly a recitation of what is here being called the primary matter—the text. It is, however, at least to some extent, a keying as well. By beginning with these words and pausing after the second, the Rav has transformed two words on the page into, as it were, an opening gambit. He is not only reciting text here; he is also summoning our attention just as surely as if he had struck a gavel or called, "Ready, set, go!" This is so because—as these culturally competent participants know—the words "*tanu rabanan*" would never be used

in simple conversation. They must therefore signal the start of the formal study.

2. This is a translation but without doubt a keying of the opening words since he has taken the word *"rabanan,"* which means rabbis, and transformed it into "the wise" in which a comment upon the nature of the rabbis is clearly being made. It is a slight change but alters radically the definition of who has been cited. It thus also keys what is to come. The clear inference to be made is that what will follow is the product of wisdom and not simply authority.

3. This is essentially a structuring move, taken out of turn but clearly in the character of a byplay. The Rav has made clear that the study has begun; now, with one another's help, the rest of the players get ready. For the speaker who obviously knows the place and is prepared to go, the utterance provides a convenient display of erudition and engagement in what is to follow.

4. Here recitation continues. Its cadences, however, indicate that two topics are being discussed. A drop in register after the recitation, "NIZRAKIN," the disposition of *tashmishey mitzva,* and a consequent rise for "TASHMISHEY KEDUSHA" provides both an interpretation which indicates the bifocal nature of the statement and a key which sets the questions to follow in move 6.

5. This byplay and involvement display has already been considered.

6. The rhetorical questions reframe the recitation in move 4. They indicate the problematic nature of the statement. What may have seemed to be a straightforward judicial assertion in the text turns out upon explanation—the core character of this move—to be a pretext for taxonomic excursions into Jewish ritual life. The stammer-like repetition in the opening of this move comes about in part because a major shift in key has occurred. It is as if the speaker had to break his recitation in order to reframe its content.

7. Here is an echo, animating the speakers while displaying their involvement.[34] With their echo at this pivotal juncture, the moment that the central concern of the text is first expressed, they indicate their involvement in the game. It is as if they knew that now is an important time to indicate engagement. Alexanderovitch and Schmeltzer (A & S) seem to be racing each other to demonstrate their being in play.

8. Here is the first of several ambiguous moves. Looking up from his book, the Rav seems to be answering his question. Yet

his words are, as moves 9 and 10 will make even clearer, part of the opening words of the recitation of the Rashi commentary written in the text. Thus move 8 may be either explanation (an answer) or recitation. In fact it is both and hence the complexity of the game.

As is often the case (see the discussion of prefiguration in the previous chapter), the lerners try to frame their text with their own remarks so that what they need to say is what the text has written. What is written becomes animated, keyed into dialogue rather than being left as document. The Rav plays it perfectly; he "reads" text while looking his students in the eye. To respond to his face-to-face interaction one must move along the line of his locution to the page.

9. Here is a possible cue to the reading of Rashi, whose commentary begins with these apparently spontaneous words. It also serves to reframe move 8 so that what may have appeared as an ad hoc explanation turns into a recitation of text. Shmeltzer has caught on to what the Rav was doing in the previous move, and by reading the Rashi he demonstrates that he is keyed to the occasion, likewise able to make the right moves. The student displays his awareness of what is going on, competence in the *lernen* game and involvement. It is the performance of one player that structures and elicits the performance of the other. Together they define the situation and ultimately themselves. The game has begun in earnest.

10. There is an ambiguity here which emerges from the previous move. Has the Rav been cued into a recitation in place of his independent explanation or did he all along mean to recite Rashi? It is the Rav's move now that has turned what might have been Shmeltzer's spontaneous remark into a cue. But it was the latter that may have turned the Rav's explanation into an echo.

These are not simply hair-splitting points. They touch upon fundamental issues of interactional drama, namely, who is the initiator of an interaction and who the respondent, who directs the performance. These are questions both of role, who is doing what, and frame, what exactly is being done. They refer too to issues of activity and passivity in the drama. Finally, since turn-taking is often a matter of initiative, move-making may determine the extent to which one gets a turn to play. To decipher this pattern of interaction, moreover, is to understand the character of the social organization of the gathering—and the ways in which that organization either remains stable or undergoes change. In *lernen* as interaction, taking turns and making specific moves is the heart of the drama.

11. This move continues the ambiguity of the last three. Again the Rav might be reciting text. Does Rashi go on to provide an exegesis for this second concept as he did for the first? A look into the text indicates that he does not. But the Tosafists in the other margin do. Perhaps then the Rav is about to recite their commentary. The line between recitation and explanation has become sufficiently blurred in the swift movement from one to another and by virtue of the fact that the experienced playing of the performers has confounded the distinctions between these two.

12. Only here is it clear that we have moved into the realm of extemporaneous explanation. In this move the Rav makes a freely spoken gloss; but at the same time he bases it on the Tosafist commentary. He thus becomes the bridge between recitation and explanation. Through his moves, the Rav establishes a situational role. He meshes his activity with the text and comes to represent, if not altogether embody, *lernen*. Those others who can likewise deftly move from recitation to explanation can share in this quality.

13. Here is a recitational move which is, like the previous one, a vehicle for structuring what will follow. It summons us back to text and in a sense keys the previous questions and answers so that they are seen as prologues to further reading.

14. This is a move which begins as gloss but then passes into the ambiguous domain in which explication gives way to discussion. Explaining that the issue that links all the items mentioned in the text is that they are all *tashmishey mitzva* and therefore permitted for disposal, the Rav at the same time sets the stage for a discussion of a point of law in move 15. The discussion there reframes the explanation in this move so as to make it seem a preface.

There is a sense in which the brief remark "after their use" seems to be written in the text. Spoken in tones and rhythm which suggest continuity with the preceding recitation, these words aurally bridge gloss with Talmud. Anyone not following the text carefully might not even catch this new move. To fail to be aware of it is, however, to remain unaware of the elements of instruction embedded in the turn. A good player will try to avoid this and remain keyed to exactly what is going on. Hence the near obsession of keeping one's finger pointing to the words read in the text (something which in the public reading of the Torah scroll comes close to being a ritual during which an ornamental pointer shaped like a finger stays on the words read by the cantor).

15. This is a discussion move. It shreds all that has been recited and explained from the text since it indicates that in fact contemporary practice is different.

While it may appear somewhat forced to label such a brief comment a discussion, one must realize that in a way discussion moves are cumulative and intermittent. They not only key material beforehand, they also set up what will happen later in the interaction. Thus, the discussion begun with move 15 will be followed up later in turns 2, 3, and 4 as well as in subsequent ones beyond those chronicled in this extract. They will in fact key the entire drama into a pretext for the discussion of contemporary norms and practices. As seen in the previous chapters on social and cultural drama, discussion may be perceived as the ultimate keys to understanding what is going on during *lernen*. As one participant once put it to me while explaining what it is he thinks is really happening in the circle: "We use the *gemore* as a chance to discuss things that are important to us and the Jewish people. That's really what *lernen*'s about."

16. Here again is a recitation move. Again, it has summoning authority which aborts the previous discussion, implying the importance of reading further.

17. This is an explanatory move, a gloss to the recited material in the previous move. As a reaction, it transforms the preceding material into a stimulus for this move rather than leaving it as a simple, intransitive recitation. It turns what appears as a single move into an adjacency pair, a couplet. Thus blurring the distinction between moves, this sort of action forces a player to be highly attentive if he is to be informed about exactly what is pure text and what explanation, what is sacred pronouncement and what its distillation. This is no small matter for those who consider the actual words in their texts to be divine declarations.

18. Here is a recitation.

19. Since the opening words, "tanu rabanan," there have been no uttered translations. This is accounted for at least in part by the fact that the language of the text in the interim has been sufficiently close to the participants' vernacular Hebrew as to obviate the need for translation. Like the last words translated, how-

ever, "*deluskamey*" is in Aramaic and hence could conceivably require translation. It can also call for explanation as a glance into the book at Rashi's commentary on the term reveals. Hence, to indicate that his remarks are not recitation, the Rav prefaces his translation with "this is," framing his translation as a quasi-explanation, almost a gloss. He also breaks the tempo so that there will be no mistaking this move. "This is" is not the sort of phrase that normally appears in Talmud. Hearing it, the informed—even if not completely synchronized with the Rav—will catch the gist of the move.

Unlike the case earlier in moves 9 and 10, here, therefore, the group does not use this as an opportunity to segue into a recitation of the Rashi, to embed that commentary in theirs. They indicate thereby their competence as players. This move is far less ambiguous than those earlier ones. The "this is" has a disambiguating effect. A similar use of "these are" follows in move 21.

20. Here again is a recitation.

21. The opening word in this move is ambiguous. As a repetition of the last word of the previous recitation, it sounds like an echo. It cannot, however, be termed an echo in interactional terms since it is not the result of one person's reacting to another but rather comes from one speaker—the Rav—continuing from one type of an utterance to another. Yet the question remains as to whether it continues the recitation of the previous move or begins the explanation which constitutes the essence of this one. Here again is an illustration of the fluidity of moves between text and commentary that makes the process of *lernen* so difficult for frame analysis. The words of Talmud and the speech of its students overlap, leaving the boundaries not always definite. The use of the framing words "these are," however, clearly establishes the move into explanation.

With this explanation, the Rav has reached the end of the passage in the text, something obvious for anyone who knows or has been following along in the Talmud. As if to underscore this boundary, he drops his voice and makes a slight pause. It is sufficient to mark the end of this turn at talking. If no one else were to speak now, the Rav would take another turn. However, the expectations of active involvement inherent in the *lernen* game make it likely that someone else will take at least a brief turn, that another performance will occur. This time that someone is Alexanderovich, one of the students who demonstrates his involvement with a question.

With Alexanderovich's turn, the drama takes an extended turn toward discussion. Ultimately, this discussion will lead to a digression (not fully transcripted in this extract), which goes as far as an extended consideration of whether or not recording tapes, such as those used by this researcher to construct this transcript, constitute *tashmishey mitzva* or *tashmishey kedusha*. In the end, however, that issue will be set aside with a segue by the Rav back to the text in which he makes the entire discussion seem like a pretext for a consideration of the Tosafist commentary on the page. His proficiency in playing the *lernen* game will make it seem that our every move in what sounded like a spontaneous line of talk was leading to further *lernen* in the text.

The group's familiarity with the way the game must be played, its adherence to tacit norms about where initiatives may be taken and where interruptions must cease, is of course also important for the game's success. In the end, no one will voice a doubt that all we had been doing ineluctably led up to a reading of the Tosafot. Among the ideologically committed people of the book, this loyalty to the page is a sustaining fiction of the game. Accordingly, the recitation is once again taken up, the men once again nod their heads in agreement, as if silently affirming the necessity and naturalness of this return to the beginning of the cycle, a new recitation.

Throughout this brief episode and others like it, the performers' attention and involvement is held tightly by the game, which with its many moves and turn-taking sweeps them up. No one dares tune out for too long or often for fear that he will lose his place, both in the text and the group, by having missed too many moves and end up speaking out of turn, or even out of frame. Action moves quickly. The player who falls behind or out of the interaction finds himself ultimately falling out of the circle and the world it describes. Precisely that tension endows the interaction with its abiding sense of drama.

While contemporary Talmud study circles are in the main nominally open to all those who want to join, there are ways of excluding newcomers. One of these is by indicating to them that they are incapable of making the appropriate moves during the interaction. This may be accomplished in a variety of ways. During the game, questions or comments which are inappropriate can be ignored or responded to in ways that make both the speaker and his remark appear absurd or wrongheaded. The person who, for example, asks to have the "obvious" explained may be met by signs of exasperation or outright scorn. Consider the following case.

During the course of *lernen* in Smotra, the term *"goofah"* came up in the Talmud. A word used to indicate that after a textual digression the substantive topic is being returned to, it is one of the staples of *lernen* language. Nevertheless, one man asked for a translation. Learning the meaning, he tried to compensate for his display of ignorance by commenting reflectively, "That's a strange *lashon* [terminology]." Inserting the superposed term *"lashon,"* another staple of the language of *lernen*, the man apparently tried to indicate his insider status, offsetting the negative self-presentation engendered by the earlier wrong move. But this only compounded his error.

"It's only strange for someone who doesn't *lern* a lot," the Rav, speaking for the group, answered to the amusement of the others who perhaps sought by their laughter to distance themselves from the gaffe.

Blushing, the inquirer knew he would have to make several right moves in the future to avoid the stigma of becoming defined a poor player. As if to make certain he got the message, the Rav and several of the students asked him several times during the rest of the *shiur* when other common terms come up, "Also a strange *lashon?*"

To thus exclude wrong movers is to tacitly warn others about the importance of making right moves. The tensions of proper playing, the need to display the appropriate kinds of curiosity and understanding, buttressed by the desire to remain implicated in the collective life of the circle, keep the interest and involvement in the interactional drama high.[35]

To be sure, the motives underlying the players' willingness to remain thus committed to the game are complex and come not only from the playing itself. They derive as well from the religious sentiments that may have stimulated the initial involvement, the sense of fellowship which commits the participants to one another and their common task, an interest in the material studied because of felt ties to the culture from which it emerges or because of its inherent intellectual appeal. Social dramas, as we have seen, overlay the *lernen* at times; and these too hold the participants' attention. Nevertheless, whatever other motives are at work during *lernen*, the character of interaction is such that it can, by itself, command, commit, and sustain the players' involvement.

RULES OF IRRELEVANCE AND TRANSFORMATION: ASKING QUESTIONS

The limits of what may be properly included and what should be disattended or ruled irrelevant within the interactional drama of *lernen* constitutes one of the latent yet constant concerns of the performers. Another is the continued capacity to transform what might otherwise be considered irrelevant into something in harmony with their *lernen*. In the course of their becoming experienced members of a circle, players normally assimilate the tacit rules governing inclusion, exclusion, and transformation. Gradually they learn to key their interest, experience, and abilities so that they appear game-relevant. Life is made, as it were, into a pretext for *lernen*, which in turn is seen as completing that life— a point made in the previous chapter.

Occasionally there are errors and someone does or says something out of place or rather out of key. He thereby demonstrates that he is not quite "with it," not totally an insider, or at least not completely competent in the game of *lernen*. These errors vary for spectacle and game. Thus what might be appropriate as part of the spectacle, for example, exchanging money to repay a debt or talking about the difficulty of getting a good used car, would be irrelevant to the *lernen* game. Conversely, the debate and controversy that might stimulate the players in the course of their talmudic review might seem forced, counterfeit, and out of place during the liminal openings and closings of the spectacle when people are normally engaged in behavior more emphatically sociable. This is not to preclude overlap, particularly at closing time, when participants carried away by the subject of their study continue their *lernen* past the end of formal study. In most cases, however, the beginning and end of the *shiur* is not identical with the beginning and end of the gathering, the spectacle.

Similarly, the actual content of the spectacle or game may vary from group to group so that what would be appropriate to each for one circle might be out of order in another. A group of men emphasizing their contemporaneity might, for example, allow for greater digression to discussions of current events during the

game than their more traditional counterparts for whom the text
is sacred and not to be mixed with the mundane present. For the
latter, current events, if considered at all, are talked about only
when the books are closed. The rules may thus be understood as
emerging from the character of the circle.

Commonly within the domain of a particular circle and the
framework of its *lernen* game, one move seems from the players'
perspective to lead inexorably to another, giving the practiced
insider a feeling of the inevitability of action. Questions appear
to be asked just when expected; pauses seem to become impreg-
nated with meaning at the proper time and in the right way;
digressions seem to stimulate drama and group involvement just
when needed; displays like cuing, echoing, or citations of parallel
texts occur as if on schedule. In short, wrong moves stand out,
while right ones seem to follow a taken-for-granted pattern. When
a person finds himself in a circle where he can make the right
moves, recognizes the wrong ones, and can become involved as
do the other insiders, he gains a feeling of being in tune with the
proceedings, of being in the right place and group.

Perhaps nowhere is this made clearer than in the asking of
questions. As already noted several times, questions asked during
lernen, fulfilling various functions in various sorts of drama, are
the blood and tissue of the activity. Just as they are inherent to
the dynamics of the Talmud, which is after all an abbreviated
record of rabbinic questions and answers, so do they drive the
lernen. Each performer must know what sort of a question is
relevant or appropriate, when to ask, and how much of an answer
to expect as well as how much to be satisfied with when he
receives it. Thus, for example, in the Kahal Reyim circle where
the emphasis was on covering a great many pages of Talmud in
a short period of time, where the text is chanted through in short
order with cryptic Yiddish translations and glosses, questions
were at most aimed to clarify rather than to explore. During a
discussion of the various sacrifices brought to the altar at the Holy
Temple, the men might ask why one sacrifice preceded another
or whether the high priest sprinkled its blood with an overhand
motion or simply by flicking his wrist. In Smotra, on the other
hand, where the group appeared more interested in cultural performances and making the connection between text and Jewish
life, where the reading was slow and measured, men would sometimes ask clarifying questions but were far more likely to ask

exploratory ones. During a similar review of the sacrifices, they might ask what the connection between a sacrifice and the social status of the person bringing the sacrifice was: Did all people bring exactly the same sorts of lambs, or was there an effort then as now to outdo one's peers in the gifts brought to the Temple? To ask a Smotra question at Kahal Reyim or to ask only Kahal Reyim questions in Smotra would be wrong. It would undermine the order of the interactional drama. And it would—if repeated— lead to the speaker's experiencing a kind of alienation from the action.

One man who joined the Smotra circle for a while and discovered that he was—in a Kahal Reyim style—more interested in making progress through the pages than exploring what *he* considered to be tangential matters left the circle. He later explained that the Smotra group asked too many *"klotz kashes,"* a Yiddish expression for wrongheaded questions. For him the moves he wanted to make were inappropriate to the circle he was in, and so he moved to another group. Hence it appears that some part of the sense of one's belonging to a circle lies beyond the Talmud itself or even in being Jewish and arises rather from the social circumstances of those engaging in *lernen*.

THE SOCIAL ORDER OF QUESTIONING

Through questioning, rules of irrelevance and transformation are evolved and established in every circle. They guide and frame the action. Within the *shiur*, they discipline feelings and guide behavior. They include some speakers and exclude others. They also, however, allow for distinctions within the circle. People type themselves according to the type of questions they ask. Thus the Rav and the top students ask "top" questions, those which prefigure the text or are literate and erudite. On the other hand, the *"klotz"* asks wrongheaded or *"klotz kashes,"* questions which betray his ignorance and distance from the world of *lernen*.

Between these extremes are a variety of types, which although not describing a perfectly ordinal scale clearly characterize the speaker as something less than a top-student but something more than a *klotz*. In one circle, for example, was the man whose questions characterized him as "riddler." His inquiries were always the sort no one could precisely answer and which therefore required him to provide—with a flourish—his own solution in which could always be found some gem of folk wisdom or esoteric knowledge. In another class, one man presented himself as the inquirer who always managed to find a flaw in the Talmud's or Rav's logic. Inevitably these "discoveries" were shown by the Rav or other students to be fallacies. Such was the regularity of Reb Naftali's fallacies that he became typed accordingly. Likewise one could discover the puns in Reb Reuven's questions and answers, the narratives embedded in Reb Uriel's always long inquiries, the grammatical points raised regularly by Reb Jonah, and so on.

There is a second observation to be made about the sociological side of questioning. Not only do inquiries type the inquirer and characterize the circle in which they are common, they also delineate a group pecking order. That is, not everyone can expect his questions to be responded to in the same way. The Rav's questions, like most of his game-oriented remarks, must always be taken seriously and answered. Only he himself or the text with someone else citing it can provide or at least ratify an answer to them. The case of the puzzling redundancy reviewed in the chapter on social drama may be cited as an example. Since, moreover, he often asks the Talmud's own questions (i.e., the "best" ones), he thereby assures in great measure his authority and ascendancy among other "people of the book."

The Rav alone can limit the line of questioning. His pauses are the tacitly legitimate prerequisites to interruption, and his recitations bracket those breaks. If he finds a question or other remark inappropriate, he can ignore it and thus keep up the pace of the proceedings; or he can answer it quickly or offhandedly so that it hardly breaks the action. When a series of digressive questions has been going on for what he senses to be too long, a simple "*shoyn*" (enough) from him can end them.

The top-student, by virtue of his capacity to ask rabbinic/talmudic questions and make similar comments, ones informed by *lernen* experience and scholarship, may expect to have his questions answered either by the Rav or rhetorically by himself with the former's ratification. If others try to answer him, he may commonly display his disdain for their solutions by a continued exhibition of puzzlement until the Rav has satisfied him. This jockeying for top spot may often make not only for high drama in the framework of interaction but, as in other games, evolve into a social drama.

For example, at Kahal Reyim, two men, Reb Yitzhak and Reb Mendel, carried on an unproclaimed competition for the top-student spot. Yitzhak would always try to challenge the general reading of the text, drawing from his apparently strong talmudic background in order to ask complex questions. Mendel, a ceaseless echoer and cuer, would always try to display the fact that he was right with or slightly ahead of the Rav's reading. When Yitzhak's question would demand a subsequent explanatory move, Mendel's response would instead lead to nearly immediate further recitation. That is, what Yitzhak saw as puzzling, Mendel would present as obvious. Occasionally these roles would be reversed.

The competition between the two often accounted for tension in the interaction. One did not really need to understand the substance of their disagreement to sense the formal action of moves and countermoves. One man's voice would be inflected in question, the other would sound assured. Sometimes these brief duels erupted into a full-fledged social drama in which the Rav would mediate to bring about a balance of sorts. Here the substance of the argument had to be casuistically reinterpreted so that the conflict would be explained away. It always was, for the men were as tied to one another as to the book they studied. Even the apparently unresolvable contradictions would disappear in a mumble of recitations or a shrug of shoulders. Much as a friendly card game can become a contest for stakes much higher than the actual game, so an interactional drama can become enveloped in another drama, social, cultural, or (as shall be later shown) linguistic.

The pecking order beneath Rav and top-student is far less precise. Nevertheless, the more simpleminded one's questions, the less talmudic and erudite their character, the lower the speaker finds himself in the circle's game hierarchy. And the lower one is, the more others are tacitly permitted to answer his questions— and the more he must be willing to accept those answers. If he refuses, the group and Rav will more and more ignore his subsequent questions and remarks. One must know one's place. Thus, for example, at Kahal Reyim where my weaknesses both in Yiddish and Talmud—to say nothing of my youth, the absence of a beard and earlocks—made me low man in the order, my rarely asked but most pedestrian questions could be answered even by Reb Zanvil, the man sitting next to me who dozed during most of the *shiur*.

"*Klotz kashes*" of course can be answered by anyone too. In these, however, there is a risk not only for the inquirer but also the respondent. By dignifying and thereby legitimating a wrong-headed inquiry with too serious an answer, one risks sharing in the stigma of wrongheadedness. Thus these are generally avoided or else handled with the distance of humor and sarcasm, as indicated in the earlier example.

At the very bottom of the order are those who fail to ask questions at all or sit in vacant silence. The latter quiet is one unpunctuated by any speaking. It disqualifies one for even the role of auditor and rather marks one as outsider. Indeed, reluctant newcomers are commonly silent in this way. If they continue to fail to find a way of taking a spoken turn, ultimately they may drop out of the circle. This was in fact the case in several of the circles I joined. To be sure, an experienced *lerner* who wants to "check out" a circle without committing himself to it will in this way fail to take turns or make spoken moves. This makes a subsequent dropping out easier. It is, after all, with questions and answers, cues and echoes that one enters the game.

PACING

During *lernen* it is sometimes the case that the pacing of the *shiur* prevents the inclusion of those who cannot keep up with the action. Moving rapidly through a recitation or an explanation, skipping translations, carrying on telegraphic or erudite discussion, players indicate both their experience and capacity for playing the game. A skilled *lerner* can animate matters almost as quickly as they are raised. He is never at a loss for words, can give an answer, repeat an argument, or else time a question so that he avoids having to explain or account for something he has not fully comprehended. He knows how to demonstrate involvement even if he has tuned out for a while. He knows when he can slow things down or when to sit silent so that progress through the page can be made. If he cannot do this, he will drop out of the interaction and be left behind.

This sort of pacing may, however, in extreme cases lead to an *interaction consciousness*, a felt need to display proper involvement which focuses a player's attention on the presentation of self to the exclusion of everything else. In my own case this began to occur at Kahal Reyim. Around me the men were racing through pages upon pages of complex text. They described and discussed, in what was to me a cryptic Yiddish, an order of Temple sacrifices that I could hardly decipher. While they elliptically debated the order of the priest's sprinkling of blood on the four corners of the altar, I remained ignorant of which sacrifices were being discussed or what exactly a priest was supposed to do. That is, while they engaged in brief but dense dramas, I was lost. Yet if I was to remain at all a part of the game, I had to show some involvement. Echoing was not easy, for I was not always sure where a statement ended and what was significant enough to echo. Cuing was obviously a hopeless possibility. Questions were unthinkable unless I was willing to display how out of place I was. And the chanted Yiddish made it more difficult for me to even keep track of the recitations.

Nevertheless I tried. I asked questions, often inappropriate. I miscued, laughed at the wrong times, and so on. For a time my interaction consciousness sustained my involvement. Although I understood very little, I felt engaged in the setting because my mind was on playing at the game. But interaction consciousness alone cannot sustain one in a game when a basic knowledge of the moves is missing. One can play *at* a game for only a limited time. Finally one must genuinely play it. Without a substantive competence, I could not keep up the pace. More and more I found myself drifting "away," preoccupied with thoughts altogether irrelevant to the *lernen*. Finally I found myself nodding off in sleep and awakening with a sense of disorientation and disenchantment. Lost in the class, I had also lost the charm of the drama. Gradually I became more and more silent and at last found my departure from the circle inevitable.[36]

For a little longer, I continued to attend the *lernen* at Kahal Reyim, no longer really an active part of the *shiur*. Increasingly, I was ignored by the other players—although always treated with warmth during the preliminaries before class and the moments after closing. The pace, however, was too much; in time I dropped out of the game.

INVOLVEMENT AND DISPLAY

At the heart of interaction stands the matter of involvement. Perhaps the single most important obligation upon participants, involvement is not, however, all of a kind. Rather it may be divided into two general types: deliberate and spontaneous. *Deliberate involvement* may be understood as a premeditated, designed, self-conscious set of actions in which a participant, having learned what part of himself is relevant to a particular activity, manipulates himself so as to become committed to engaging in it. On the other hand, *spontaneous involvement* is meant to describe the kind of engagement in action during which one is caught up, carried away, and un-self-consciously engrossed in what he is doing. Thus involved, he not only finds it psychologically unnecessary to dwell on anything else but also impossible to refrain from being so caught up.[37] If deliberate involvement allows for a degree of affective distance by the participant, spontaneous involvement distinctly does not; in it, doing is being.

During a face-to-face encounter such as occurs during *lernen*, a participant's display of involvement in the game, the official focus of attention, "tells others what he is and what his intentions are, adding to the security of the others in his presence."[38] Where the involvement is obviously spontaneous this "often brings the sharers into some kind of exclusive solidarity and permits them to express relatedness, psychic closeness, and mutual respect."[39] During *lernen*, this results in each person thus involved feeling a sense of obligation to the others likewise involved and a sense of loyalty to the situation. He becomes affectively committed to the interaction and dares not allow his attention to flicker. Coupled with the imperatives of Judaism which mandate his enthusiastic involvement in Torah study and the social expectations that he will be loyal to the learning fellowship in which he is a member, the pressures for active involvement are extraordinary. Thus even where spontaneous involvement is not possible, deliberate involvement is—and the latter will be made to appear as the spontaneous.

Shared involvement confirms and ensures the reality of the world in which the participants are implicated; seeing that everyone seems to perceive and experience the proceedings in more or less the same way, the *lerners* see little or no room for doubt about what is happening. Finally, in face-to-face encounters like *lernen*, the fact that generally persons will feel an imperative to remain involved guarantees that the action will be steadily sustained in spite of an individual's occasional dropping out. Thus a *shiur* in which the level of involvement is appropriately high more easily allows for dozing by one or two people or for other mental emigrations from the action. One, however, where this is not the case demands no transparent displays of dropping out. Thus one understands why the noisiest (i.e., most engaging) classes were precisely the ones in which some participants would allow themselves to drop off while the quiet ones often left everyone struggling to stay awake.

On the other hand, too intense a level of involvement can create a tension too great to be borne by those who have come for *lernen*, a "friendly game," and not for *limud*, the serious vocation of scholarly study.

The crucial obligations implicit in the game of *lernen*, the precise nature of the animations, can perhaps best be understood through an adaptation and application to the matter of involvement of four concepts normally associated with discussions of role behavior. These are: *commitment, attachment, embracement*, and *distance*.

An individual may be said to be "committed" to a particular line of involvement when, because of the interdependent character of interaction, his doing one thing irrevocably conditions preceding and succeeding actions, forcing him to behave in very specific ways. Typically, in a focused interaction, particularly one like *lernen*, individuals will become committed to involvement in one way or another. This is what was meant earlier when the moves in the course of *lernen* were said to seem to lead inexorably from and to one another.

One may be considered "attached" to a particular line of involvement when doing feels as if it expresses one's sense of self. That is, if a person feels a loyalty to the encounter and a consequent self-identification with his performance of the activities which align him with the action, he may be said to be attached to his involvement. Clearly the emphasis here is on affective ties. Normally, persons are expected to become attached to the involvements to which they are committed, but this is by no means always the case.

A person who is *both* committed and attached to a particular line of involvement may be said to be "embraced" by it. The man who becomes spontaneously involved in the recitation of Talmud, a process which once begun must necessarily be continued, who sings or otherwise animatedly reads the words before him on the page as if they were coming out of his own consciousness and intelligence, may be said to be embraced by his involvement in *lernen*. To become embraced by an involvement is to disappear completely into it, to be fully seen in its terms, "and to confirm expressively one's acceptance" of the legitimacy and attraction of it.[40]

Finally, "distance" from involvement occurs when one is *in* the interactional play but not fully part *of* it. This is the opposite of embracement; the performer does not deny his commitment to a line of involvement nor even publicly question its legitimacy, he simply feels unattached to it. That is, he considers other actions more affectively important to him than what the situation has locked him into doing.

Because, as I have already suggested, embracement in involvement (most commonly advanced when a person is carried away by actions and events) is the norm, particularly in the game of *lernen*, participants in the *shiur* are sometimes forced to feign it when they are not genuinely caught up by the proceedings. Put differently, when they cannot bring themselves to play the game of *lernen* wholeheartedly, the performers must play *at* it. The latter is simply a managed impression, a display of the former.

"Displays," a term taken from ethology, are typified, sometimes formalized, performances during which an actor deliberately produces "a readily readable expression of his situation."[41] Through them he signals the position he seems prepared to take in what is about to happen or is already ongoing in the social situation. Engaging in a display allows one to avoid the embracement of spontaneous involvement while at the same time reap some of its social psychological benefits.

To be sure, within the context of interaction, a display may require as much attention as real play if the performer is to sustain himself and the fiction of his spontaneous involvement. Playing it as if one were embraced by his performance denies one the possibility of complete distance. This is clearly seen in the case of *lernen*. Connected as it is to religious, cultural, and social imperatives, the performance of *lernen*, as already noted, must at the very least appear to be engaging. When an individual finds himself committed to it but affectively distant—detached—from its substance and spirit, he is likely to contrive the appearance of being really involved.

At times the exigencies of successfully managing an impression of involvement among one's familiars is enough to spontaneously engage the actor. Rewordings of explanations, cuings, echoings, inquiries, solicited responses and reactions, animated recitations, and gestural displays like the sway, page-stare, and nearly obsessive efforts to keep the place with one's fingers, which begin as shows, have a way of sweeping up their performers. Certainly this was the case with me. Beginning with a research plan that would have me simply display involvement while in fact concentrating my energies and attention on ethnography and social anthropological observations, I found quite quickly that I was becoming drawn into the world of *lernen* more and more as a full-fledged participant. Only where my background weaknesses prevented me from making the right moves—as in the aforementioned case of Kahal Reyim—did I manage to maintain distance for a while. Here, however, as already noted, display became increasingly impossible, and so as a result of my growing distance I fell out of the interaction altogether in the end—all of which suggests that in the world of study circles there is a whole range of situations, from the necessarily engaging to the entirely undemanding.

It is worth recalling here the traditional rabbinic attitude toward Jewish observance in general and the process of *lernen* in particular (an attitude incidentally expressed in the Talmud). Recognizing that attachment is not always found among those who are situationally or culturally committed to be Jews, the rabbis called for the imposition of commitments. Asking the Jew to place himself in situations where he would become committed to an involvement in Jewish life and observance, they reasoned, "What is begun *not* for its own sake may in the end be done for its own sake" (B.T. *Pesakhim* 50b). In other words, they recognized that the distinction between deliberate displays of spontaneous involvement and the genuine article has a tendency to become blurred, and what may begin as a self-conscious manipulation of self or playing *at lernen* can evolve into a full-blown playing *of* it with the actor taken in by his own performance. Commitment would lead to attachment and thus embracement. In the study circle, moreover, operating among one's familiars, those who can easily recognize the slight deceptions that might elsewhere pass unnoticed, those familiar too with the games of *lernen*, one must be so attentive to detail in carrying off a display that it is even more likely that one becomes caught up in the playing. The harder I tried to perfect my displays of *lernen*, the more I found myself carried away by them.

In part as well this occurs because in the immediacy of face-to-face interaction one must often forego the time necessary for premeditated displays. Instead a performer must often give an instantaneous show of his involvement. For this reason, if for no other, *lernen* has tacitly been allowed to evolve its formalized moves which display involvement. These, already listed several times in these pages, are however so close to what characterizes spontaneous involvement that they may lead to it. Thus, for example, when a player cues for display purposes, he discovers that this requires a relatively intense level of engagement in study. A display does not only signal involvement, it fosters it.[42]

To be sure, displays of spontaneous involvement and even genuine embracement by a performance during the interactional drama of *lernen* does not necessarily imply that the player has acquired either a talmudic understanding or even penetrated the meaning and significance of Jewish culture. Sensitive to this possibility, experienced *lerners* often point out that persons may animatedly engage in the game for years without ever really assimilating much in the way of content. Such players learn how to make the right moves without ever really perceiving the overarching purpose of the game. Describing just this sort of a player, Rav Horowitz of Beit Rachel characterized him as "one who had spent so much time *lernen*, he never found an opportunity to know." From this the Rav concluded, to the agreement of a number of his students, "To *lern gemore* is easy; to know it is far more difficult."

There is perhaps some exaggeration here. As I have already suggested, no person can consistently make the right moves, whether spontaneously or deliberately, without some competence in Talmud and an intellectual contact with the substance of the text. Moreover, even as a game, *lernen* is sufficiently complex so as to exclude total incompetents. There are of course those who fail completely to play the game properly, who sit in empty silence or make inane remarks, who fail to sustain themselves in the situation while they also threaten thereby to break the flow of interaction. These are persons who appear at a *shiur* once or twice and then stop coming, finding there is nothing that can sweep them up or into the action and through it the fellowship of *lerners*. Nevertheless, the game dimension of *lernen* makes it possible that some people will *lern* for years, remain fascinated with the process, but never approach anything close to becoming Talmudic scholars.[43]

What about distance? Are there situations in which it is appropriate for the *lerner* to disengage himself from a concern with the Talmud? If he does so, what does this mean both to him and the circle of his fellows? Can he remain within the boundaries of the group while simultaneously denying his attachment to the activity that manifestly accounts for its gathering?

To answer these questions it is necessary first to elaborate the process of distancing in general and its particular form during *lernen*. The wedge an individual drives between his doing and his being is commonly expressed over the back channels of interaction, the result of messages given off rather than those communicated generally. He feels forced to express this distance when he finds himself obliged to engage in activity that he considers "unsuitable for him, activity that cannot be easily seen as consonant with what he brings to his roles and takes away from them."[44]

While committed to *lernen* by virtue of his membership in the circle and attendance at the *shiur*, the distancing *lerner* will somehow indicate that he is not completely attached to what he is doing. The *lerner* who drums his fingers impatiently, dozes off in the middle of a *shiur*, ostentatiously and frequently checks his watch for the time, or carries on a series of side involvements like chatting with a fellow student, paring his fingernails or reading something irrelevant to the ongoing activity makes clear his distance from it. Similarly, a person who playfully guys his action and treats what he is doing or others around him are doing with unseriousness, joking about talmudic reasoning or satirizing its contents or exhibiting impatience with the discussions of its students, displays a distance from the interaction. Such a person reveals feelings of disenchantment, alienated from the magic of the circle and the book.

One of the most obvious circumstances of such disengagement occurs when a person seeks to drop out of the study of Talmud and the circle doing it. In a limited sense this occurs at the end of many classes. The terminal squirms, the flagging of attention, the yawns, the repeated looks at watches are all ways in which members indicate that for them the game is just about over. A well-tuned teacher tries to close before these signs appear. Failing that and sensing the growing alienation from the action among the others, he will follow the cues of his fellows and call for adjournment. While he may occasionally try to squeeze in a little more time, he will commonly preface this effort with the indication that he is just about to end.

"Just one more line," "We're going to end in a minute," "Let's just finish the Rashi" are common expressions that signal that the teacher is aware that the others are ready to close the book. The Rav's countersignals are his way of displaying a sort of formal control over the action. Nevertheless, the remaining moments become transitional—periods during which the players are still playing the game but at the same time no longer openly displaying embracement by it. Not infrequently, students will sit through the final moments with their books already closed; sometimes they will even begin putting on their coats or they will stand up. Distancing is thus the procedure by which players move away from what they are still doing but what they soon plan to end. The presumption here is that, because these men are pursuing *lernen* as a part-time activity, they may appropriately indicate their readiness to disengage at times, particularly when they are about to pass over into their dominant out-of-class lives.

Of course the person who aims to disengage altogether from the *lernen* and the circle may likewise begin his emigration with distance. Someone who has wandered into a class perhaps by accident[45] or out of mistaken judgment and once there decides this is not where he would like to be but nevertheless feels he cannot simply cut and run may display distance as a prelude to his leave-taking. One instance of such distancing occurred in the case of a man who for a time joined the Mekadshey Torah circle at the urging of his friend. He never penetrated the boundary of the circle, sat generally in vacant silence, and often exhibited signs of distraction. When he stopped attending meetings of the fellowship, it came as no surprise; and unlike the regulars who upon their absence are remarked upon, this player disappeared without a trace.

As shall be clearer after a discussion of the role that religion and fellowship play in *lernen*, the nature of study circles commonly militates against distancing of this sort. Even when the text fails to hold a player's attention, his religious inclinations and the obligations flowing from them hold him to it. These persuasions view Talmud as quintessential holy writ, divinely inspired Torah. Disenchantment with it is to undermine those doctrinal commitments. However semantically opaque the Talmud may seem, the religious feelings that tie one to the book demand that it be perceived or at least be treated as if it were spiritually engaging.

Failing this there are always the demands of fellowship. Loyalty to the circle encourages and sustains at the very least displays of involvement. To display distance from what embraces one's fellows is after all to express distance from them.

I don't always feel like *lernen*," one informant explained to me. "Sometimes the *gemore* is too complicated or confusing. Sometimes it's raining or I'm tired and would rather stay home, but I know I have to go for the *mitzva*, to keep my *lernen* constant. And besides, the other fellows are counting on me to come—so I do, and I make every effort to get involved."

Those who have firmly established a public face of attachment to *lernen* and a commitment to the study circle may be tacitly allowed occasional displays of distance. A momentary lapse, an off-night, a brief shift away are all prerogatives of the confirmed insider. The contingent and temporary character of such inner emigrations from the activity at hand is apparent when one observes the steps taken when a player seems to have dropped away for too long or displayed too much distance. The Rav may begin to ask him questions, the answers to which will draw the student back to a heightened degree of attention or at the very least encourage displays of involvement. I soon learned, for example, that if I wanted to carry on my sociological observations of the preceedings unimpeded, I would have to at least signal my participant status. A well-timed question or answer relevant to the *lernen*, a cue or an echo were the requisite moves that would allow me to carry on.

Not only the Rav but fellow *lerners* as well reach out to their distant colleague. A common device used here is cuing. The involved student will turn to his distracted fellow and point out the place in the text for him, as if shaking him out of his reveries and back into involvement. As he physically turns to him and stretches out his finger on the page, he figuratively embraces him in what the group is doing.

He may also ask the disengaged player for an explanation of something the Rav or the Talmud has expressed, thereby drawing the fellow back into the paramount reality of the *shiur*. The involvement of one man becomes the grounds for the involvement of the other.

These sorts of efforts at embracement do not, however, occur all the time. Clearly at the end of the class they are less likely than during the middle of it. They are also less likely when the player only partially distances himself. To understand *partial distancing*, examination of a particular incident will be helpful.

The scene takes place around Rav Rotenbush's table in his Jerusalem apartment. Their books open before them, the young men are led by their teacher through a complex talmudic discussion of the ancient and for them archaic rites of Temple sacrifices. Unlike their more traditional counterparts at Kahal Reyim who nightly reenter the world of sacrifices with all the ease and familiarity of Temple priests, these contemporizers find such discussions *"shver"* (hard)—hard to visualize, hard to accept, hard to understand, and perhaps even hard to take seriously. Playing them out in discussion is particularly difficult. Nevertheless, for reasons already noted, these modern Orthodox *lerners* make the obligatory moves and countermoves so as not to become alienated from the interaction, the text, and one another. Committed to the idea of *lernen* as well as to the other *lerners*, they keep up a show even when they are having a hard time with the script of the central performance. They cue, echo, ask, and answer questions and thus make their way down the page and through the hour.

The Rav asks a continuing set of questions to which the students offer individual and choric responses. These lead them to articulate in their own words precisely what the Talmud is saying. The performance, at least on the surface, begins to take on the style and character of a cultural drama. Likewise, the responses of the students, stimulated by interactional imperatives, appear to signal their embracement by the ethos and sensibility of the text and the Rav who evokes it.

"Kakh omeret ha-gemara," thus saith the Talmud, the Rav replies, punctuating almost every remark the students make.

While these players might be quite at ease about sustaining the flow of interaction, they are not uniformly comfortable about participating in the cultural drama which it generates. The latter forces them to take personally and seriously the world of sacrifices, a domain largely dissonant with the modern world they normally inhabit and which even in the enchantment of the circle they choose not to abandon completely.

"You had a Passover sacrifice," the Rav explains in answer to one of the obligatory requests for explanation, countermoves to his recitation. "It was lost—ran off before it was slaughtered. A month later you find it, after the Passover has past. What do you do with it?"

"*You* had," "*you* find," "*you* do"—the listener is being asked to perceive himself as sacrificer. This is a position the traditioning *lerner* would willingly and could easily fulfill. But like most of his modernist confederates, this listener balks at becoming so personally embraced by it.

"What do you mean, it disappeared for a month?" he asks in a tone of incredulity. The speaker refuses to be completely drawn into the text's world.

Another man follows up with a joke that likewise implies distance: "Disappeared? It was called away for reserve army duty."

The striking remark, the tone of incredulity, the humor all tacitly describe a sense distance. But it is not a complete distance for the men keep on answering questions, echoing, cuing, and the like. What they are moving away from is not so much the interaction but rather its cultural implications. They indicate that while they may not take the entire content of the text seriously and are unprepared to absorb completely the cultural implications, they are nevertheless ready to remain interactionally in play.

For the Rav, however, such partial distancing is unacceptable within the boundaries of the game. For him cultural and interactional dramas run concurrently; for him there should be no talk that is not aimed at elaborating the text and its meaning. Like all cultural guides, he is embraced by his sense of mission.

"Pay attention, pay attention, pay attention," he calls, continuing his personalized and panchronistic explanations as if in defiance and challenge to the displays of distance around him.

He goes on: "So now what do you do? You take this Passover sacrifice and you want to slaughter it—but not for some other purpose."

Turning particularly to the two students who led the group in laughter and drew themselves away from the implications of the text, he asks the first, "And what kind of sacrifice is it that you want to bring?"

"*Shlomim*" (The peace offering), the student replies, drawn back to a full involvement (or at least its display) in the central performance of *lernen*.

"And why?" the Rav now turns to the second. Again he elicits an engaged answer. And now everyone seems again to have taken on a serious attitude toward the *lernen* and plays with the demeanor of the fully involved.

To be sure, in this the Rav seems at least on the surface to act like any pedagogue trying to keep his audience interested and involved. But, precisely because he is more than teacher, because he is a cultural guide—a Rav—he is able as well to draw upon his students' inherent willingness as cultural insiders to be drawn back from their distance. Their general attachment to the ways of the Talmud and its circle give the Rav who stands at its symbolic center a magnetism beyond that of any normal teacher and even beyond that with which his personality is endowed. During the *shiur*, "this exceptional increase of force is something very real; it comes to him from the very group which he addresses."[46] As he asks questions and receives answers, "the sentiments provoked by his words come back to him, but enlarged and amplified, and to this degree they strengthen his own sentiment."[47] That sentiment in turn arouses the involvement of the circle even more. He is, after all, for the most part calling the distant back to where they feel they ought to be, to a kind of engagement they consider ideal within the framework of their lives as Jews. So now his gestures show a certain domination, which is magnified during the game, and his words gain a grandiloquence and authority greater than before. The insider who has momentarily dropped away from a wholehearted embracement of the game can be called back—if not to the game then to the culture of *lernen*—with a simple "pay attention" from the Rav. For the confirmed *lerner*, this call from the Rav is the call of his cultural conscience. The Rav's "authority comes out of the projection—and introjection— of ideals."[48] It is answered by the faithful with sincere efforts at involvement in the activity at hand.

There are two kinds of interactional euphoria. The first occurs when what the social situation forces a person to attend to and involve himself in coincides with his own individual inclinations, when personally generated spontaneous involvement coincides with obligatory ones; when what a person is situationally committed to is also what he wants to do.[49] Such a meeting of ego and the world constructed by others yields a feeling of one sort of interactional euphoria.

A second type occurs when what the social situation forces one to attend to and become involved in is what his conscience and sense of peoplehood tells him is right. When these culturally generated imperatives of involvement, these loyalties, coincide with what a person is situationally committed to by the occasion and interaction, when he is forced to animate his cultural being, this too yields a sense of euphoria. In this feeling there resonates a sense of moral confidence, rectitude, and interior peace—the opposite of the feeling of transgression. The Rav's call to "pay attention" and his listeners' compliance provide the basis for this second sort of euphoria—the sure knowledge that one is in tune with and not transgressing a moral ideal.

If as well the players become personally engaged and spontaneously caught up in the action in which they feel a moral as well as situational obligation to be involved, they are likely to feel both sorts of euphoria and thus experience a sense of utter well-being. The possibility of those feelings constitutes one of the fundamental attractions that the interaction of *lernen* has for those who engage in it and the reason they learn rapidly how to make the right moves. Where else could they find so relatively simple a vehicle for feeling so good about themselves?[50]

CONCLUSION

I began this chapter by suggesting that the essence of interactional drama is the animation by which a person shows off who he is and what he is doing—dramatically depicts himself in public action with others. I have ended by suggesting that the distinction between the interaction and the freight it carries is not always clear in the actual experience of the *shiur*. The person who is interactionally in tune with those among whom he finds or counts himself, who makes the right *lernen* moves ultimately finds himself drawn toward a moral harmony with the Talmud. A successful performance in one domain elicits its counterpart in another. The emergent feelings of confidence and propriety encourage and sustain continued *lernen*.

If it is true that the interactional drama of *lernen* carries meanings that go beyond the moves made, it is likewise true—as already hinted—that the actual words spoken and cadences sounded carry additional meaning. That is precisely what makes the talk of *lernen* so appealing and engaging for insiders. In the next chapter, I shall try to describe and discuss the significance of those words and sounds.

5
WORD PLAY AND THE LANGUAGE OF "LERNEN"

The word's power does not consist in its explicit content—if, generally speaking, there is such a thing—but in the diversion that is involved in it.

CHAIM NACHMAN BIALIK, "Revealment and Concealment in Language"

Among Jews in general and more especially among those disposed to *lernen*, the significance of words cannot be minimized. For them, "language is not a reflection of life, but the mirror itself," refracting the character and content of matters Jewish.[1] Indeed, there are occasions when the mirror seems to be the life itself: when to be Jewish is to sound and talk like a Jew. Never is this more the case than during *lernen*. If, as earlier suggested, doing is being, then during *lernen*, saying is doing. People come to the study circle to speak in ways which are specific to the occasion. To understand the appeal and meaning of such word play, however, one has first to know something of the place of words and language in Jewish tradition.

In that tradition, thoughts are seldom left unspoken; they must be expressed. "Words in the heart are not words," the Talmud warns (B.T. *Kedushin* 49b). Devotion alone is not enough; prayers must be spoken, and lips must move. Good wishes are meaningless until a benediction is recited. Evil thoughts and intentions do not count or take effect unless a curse is harangued. Folk wisdom remains sterile unless it is repeated, and homilies must be publicly declaimed. Finally, and from the point of view of culture, perhaps more important, Torah is not simply a document—"the Jews knew that even when books are burned it is only the parchment that goes up in smoke, the letters remain intact."[2] While a Torah scroll or other holy book may burn, it can still be preserved by study and vocal review. That is how its letters are kept intact. The People of the Book are in fact the keepers and speakers of its words.

The book or written word may thus be considered as a kind of script for a play, the words the voice of a culture and a people. For the Jews, the Torah can transform its people only insofar as they repeat its words, chant in its cadences, think along its syntactic lines, and thus make them their own. And because a word, however powerful, seeks completion in a flow of words, recitation leads to explanation and discussion. For some, the child or the simpleminded, "the centuries-old method is followed of endlessly repeating the incomprehensible Hebrew words, memorizing each letter, each word, the meaning of each word and of the sentence."[3] For others, the words and sounds are intellectually assimilated and then elaborated. Indeed, "the highest form of literary creativity is the *commentary*," and no creativity is greater than that accomplished with words.[4]

Among Jews, words are a "medium of high virtuosity."[5] They must be used carefully. To say the right words in the right way is not, however, given to everyone. The *tam* (simpleton) and the *golem* or *shoyte* (dummy) say too little. The *yente*, on the other hand, talking endlessly, says too much. The *am-ha-arets* (boor) and the *shlemiel* (dolt) say the wrong things, while the scholar or *talmid khokhm* is one who manages to say the proper things in just the right way. He can produce the *"gut vort"* (good word) that instructs while it displays his wisdom and reveals the genius of the sages and the Torah upon which they comment. The *tzaddik* or righteous person is one who is expected to have a kind word for everyone.

Words are also "a highly potent weapon."[6] Perhaps the greatest violence one Jew may commit against another is in an improper use of words. According to Jewish law, embarrassing another is tantamount to murdering him while false testimony is a cardinal sin. Insults are often most severe when a simple cadence is reversed from its normal pattern. And perhaps no more potent Jewish weapon for aggression exists than silence.[7] To cease to speak to another or actively ignore his words is in effect to place him in *kherem*, the excommunication that is a symbolic death.

When, however, Jewish life is most intense—as in the case of cultural performances like *lernen*—talk is too. During these occasions, debate and conversation, a feature of all vital Jewish encounters, vitalizes one's ties with his fellow Jews and their ways of life. At such times, "it is not unusual, in effect, to see two or more individuals talking at one and the same time."[8] Any *shiur* lacking such an expressive exchange of words is dull and lifeless. And as the *lernen* loses its vitality, so too do the words and world of the Talmud.

As jumbled as the talk during *lernen* may sometimes sound, it is, as should by now be clear, regulated by a series of constraints: social, cultural, and interactional. Until now these have been examined without looking precisely at the choice of words and the specifics of cadence. Yet it is exactly in those words and sounds that the way of the Talmud intersects with the particular ways of its *lerners*. Accordingly, it is to this linguistic and cultural crossroads that our attention must now turn. Here, in microcosm, will be found not only the words of their mouths but also the meditations of their hearts, what is on their minds and in their collective conscience and consciousness. When we hear the play of their words, we also hear how their words play upon them.

To understand both the intensity and constraints of this play, three theoretical assumptions will be helpful. The first is that human culture and language are in an inherent dialectical relationship with each other: "Men invent a language and then find that its logic imposes itself upon them."[9] Second—and this is particularly true for *lernen*—religious outlook is woven into that relationship between speakers and their words. Thus, according to Max Weinreich, "variations in religion may be said to occasion some separateness in culture which, in turn, leaves its mark in the form of language differences."[10] *Lerners* with varying religious viewpoints will speak and sound differently from one another during the *shiur*. Similarly, the talk and cadences of *lernen* will vary from circle to circle according to the general religious outlook for each fellowship.

A third assumption pertains to the self of the individual participant in the circle. It maintains that there is "a functional relationship between the structure of the self and the structure of spoken interaction."[11] That is, talking and being are inextricably interwoven, and who we are or at least believe ourselves to be at any given moment will play a significant role in determining what we say and the way we say it.

TALMUD AND ORAL TRADITION

The crossroads of *lernen* and language, where saying, doing, and being mingle with one another, stands at the end of a long road of oral tradition. That road begins, shrouded in myth and religion, at Sinai where the Torah is believed to have been orally given by God to the Jewish people through their teacher, their Rav Moses. It winds through Jewish history and widens as it passes through the academies of Jewish learning in Babylonia. Here, the oral laws, not incorporated in the Bible but already formulated as Mishna around 200 C.E., became debated and elaborated between the third and sixth centuries. Those debates and discussions—divided generally and discretely into *halakha* (law) and *aggadetta* (lore)—became the *gemore*, literally the completion of the Talmud.

Abbreviated and stylized, those grand discourses became the core of talmudic or rabbinic exegesis and the heart of Jewish study. The language of the rabbis—Hebrew, Aramaic, loan words from

Greek, Persian, and other indigenous tongues—became immortalized in the written text of the Talmud. "The use of the vernacular in study . . . had come into being at the time of the formation of the Talmud in the Babylonian and Palestinian yeshivas.[12] This pattern was historically maintained. Accordingly, the nearly mandatory commentaries of Rashi, the eminent French-Jewish exegete, and the Tosafists, his kin and disciples, which were added between the eleventh and fourteenth centuries, while primarily in the Hebrew-Aramaic of the text also contain here and there elements of the vernacular of the day. This is true for other commentaries too. Thus words in Old French and Old Italian as well as some German, Spanish, and Arabic along with their Jewish dialectic correlates made their way into the Talmud.

During the Middle Ages, Yiddish gradually became the accepted language of Talmudic discussion and legal disputation among the Ashkenazim, Jews of Central and Western Europe whose descendants constitute the majority of those who pursue *lernen* as an avocation. While traditional Hebrew or *Loshn Koydesh* (literally, "holy tongue"), "the oldest linguistic garb of Jewishness," remained strongly represented and the largely Aramaic text continued to lie at the heart of all recitation, increasingly these two were followed with Yiddish translation (*"taytsh"*) explanations and discussions. Yiddish became the linguistic framework within which *lernen* was most at home.[13] For centuries, *taytsh*, a form of Yiddish which is heavily superposed with idioms from sacred literature and with scriptural Hebrew (*Loshn Koydesh*), remained the primary language of talmudic review and discussion. Its syntax and cadences along with much of its vocabulary became in great measure indistinguishable from *gemore-loshn*[14] (language that is peppered with talmudic terminology) and *gemore-nign* (speech that sounds like talmudic recitation or chant). Although the twentieth century, a period of increasing Jewish cosmopolitanism has seen an increase in the use of the vernacular among *lerners* (English in America and modern Hebrew in Israel—to mention the two primary speech communities from which students of Talmud come now), Yiddish has, as I shall demonstrate in this chapter, left its mark on *lernen*.[15]

Those Jews of Europe who in the early years of the emancipation and Jewish enlightenment sought or learned to speak the non-Jewish languages of the area (primarily German, French, Polish, and Russian) were also the ones most likely to cease *lernen* as part of their disengagement from most active involvement with religious or parochial matters. Accordingly, these languages generally did not become integrated into the study process except in the form of loan words which made their way into Yiddish. While the use of European languages seemed to symbolize (if not always effect) a break with the culture of Judaism during those early years of the nineteenth and twentieth centuries, by the interwar period the growing propensity of large numbers of European Jews—particularly those in the cities and in trade—to speak in the indigenous vernaculars had a growing effect on *lernen*. Even yeshivas were required, at the very least, to teach their students the local language. Gradually, therefore, even those who still maintained affective and instrumental ties to the culture of religious Judaism and *lernen* began to speak in the "foreign" tongues.[16]

This process was by no means uncontroversial nor did it occur in all Jewish communities simultaneously. Thus while, for example, German Jews led the way to incorporating German language (and hence its culture) into Jewish text and study, traditionalists to the East in Hungary and Russia resisted. Accordingly, Rabbi Abraham Sofer (1816–71),[17] for example, warned his German contemporary, Jacob Ettlinger, to minimize his use of German in Jewish study, and the prominent yeshiva in Volozhin, Russia, closed its doors twice rather than allow its students to be taught the Russian which the local authorities mandated. Nevertheless, despite such efforts, "foreign" languages entered Jewish life in general and *lernen* in particular.

Nowhere has this process been clearer than in the contemporary situation of modern Orthodox Jewry in America and Israel. These cosmopolitan parochials who seek to be neither remote from nor untouched by modern society while remaining steadfast in their ties to tradition and the Orthodox Jewish community speak in their indigenous vernaculars, English and modern Hebrew, while still maintaining an interest in and commitment to *lernen*. Accordingly, in America and Israel, the vernacular of the significant numbers of these Jews involved in Talmud study has begun to play a larger linguistic and cultural role in the life of the *lernen*.[18] The precise nature of this role will be examined in detail below.

For now, it may simply be said that both the history of the Talmud's evolution and its study manifests a kind of "supplementary syncretism" wherein prior linguistic elements have been incorporated into whatever has been the current mode.[19] The effect, however, has been dialectical: both prior as well as contemporary linguistic elements are modified in the process.

Generally, syncretism of this sort is fostered by the process of translation, which has become a part of *lernen*. Translation, it will be recalled, is more than the simple replacement of one word or phrase in one language for its equivalent in another. It requires a penetration of the original "verbal envelope" of a message and a repacking of it in terms that make sense in another communication system, another community of speakers.[20] This may call not only for a *semantic extension of meaning* wherein new interpretations are added to the original meaning of a word or phrase, but also *cultural transformation* wherein an idea meaningful in one culture and expressed through its language and in its cadences is supplanted by a similar but not identical idea in another culture because the latter has no exact lexical or intonational parallel to the former. In the case of *lernen* this has sometimes meant recasting ideas from a previous Jewish culture into terms meaningful in the present (this is the linguistic element of contemporization and traditioning). It has also sometimes required extending and transforming "meaning related to Jewishness to another related to the world in general."[21]

In many ways Yiddish with its polyglottal transformations became the ideal vehicle for this sort of translation. With its Hebrew alphabet but German, Slavic, French, and later English vocabulary elements integrated with biblical and talmudic language, Yiddish reached into most Jewish speech communities and seemed able to reflect and inject Jewishness (Yiddishkayt) into life, into the non-Jewish world, while drawing from that world into the domain of the Jewish.

Hebrew, the special language of many contemporary Jews, might be expected to have many of the same qualities. To some extent it does; and in many settings, especially where it is considered a truer expression than the local vernacular of things Jewish, it has replaced Yiddish as the primary language of talmudic translation. A closer examination of Hebrew, however, reveals at least two types: *Ivrit* or modern Hebrew, and *Loshn Koydesh*, the holy language steeped in and associated with sacred literature. *Ivrit* displays many of the secular and non-Jewish characteristics of other modern languages (just as modern Israel is similar to other contemporary nation-states). As such it is flexible and capable of semantically handling even the most secular and modern matters. *Loshn Koydesh* on the other hand, is filled with *gemore-loshn*, the unchanging language of talmudic idiom, and freighted with scriptural quotation. Along with Yiddish *taytsh*, whose accents and inflections it shares, it has become generally associated with tradition and semantic stability. Unlike *Ivrit* which with its closed sibilants and accents on the ultimate syllable is Sephardic in pronunciation, *Loshn Koydesh* has open sibilants and accents the penultimate syllable according to the Ashkenazic pattern of speech. Thus the Ashkenazic sound has come to be associated with *Loshn Koydesh* and its traditionalism. The Sephardic sound has come, alternatively, to symbolize the opposite. Accordingly, speakers who wish to signal their association with tradition and holiness will often revert to an Ashkenazic pronunciation—even if they commonly speak Sephardic Hebrew outside of class. Indeed, even Sephardic Jews have taken up this practice although it is ethnically foreign to them. When *lernen* they sometimes sound like Ashkenazim. It is as if they implicitly sense the symbolic significance of their usage.

Similarly and by association, as other vernaculars take on the accents, syntax, and cadences of *Loshn Koydesh* and its Yiddish correlate, they may also acquire a quality of cosanctity.[22] Hence, English that sounds like Yiddish and that is dosed heavily with *gemore-loshn* and *gemore-nign* becomes for the traditionally Orthodox a superior argot for *lernen*.

On the other hand, Hebrew speakers who wish to signal their contemporaneity stay with *Ivrit* and its Sephardic accents and cadences. Similarly, modernist speakers of other vernaculars will switch back to those vernaculars as much as possible after their recitation of the text in order to signal their own attachment to the world outside as well as the relevance of their holy books to it. Yet it is precisely this association with the non-Jewish that has led many traditional Orthodox Jews to eschew the use of any modern language (including *Ivrit*) in favor of *Loshn Koydesh* and Yiddish during the study of the sacred canon. This shall be demonstrated ethnographically a little later on.

THE CIRCLE AND SOUND

Applying these linguistic distinctions to the settings and people I observed, one might suggest that each circle has its own par-

ticular blend of sound and language. Taking as a range of possibilities the five primary settings of my observations, I shall
simply describe in general terms the particular aural character of
each.

Kahal Reyim was a circle marked by an almost exclusive use
of Yiddish, *gemore-loshn* and *gemore-nign*. Occasionally, paren-
thetical sorts of remarks were spoken in *Ivrit*. Little explicit translation was offered since the men seemed to have what they
considered a sufficient understanding immediately upon having
recited the text. Their knowledge of where to pause, what was
question and what answer in the text, and what was the beginning
and end of an argument was all communicated in the cadences
of their recitation. Such explanations and discussions as there
were were carried on telegraphically, almost mimicking the style
of the Talmud itself. They were microdialogues, embedded in the
recitation. In a rhythmic rise-fall and in the vocabulary of the
Talmud, mixed with the expressions of Yiddish, the men spoke
their way through their class. It was a sound that they often
carried over into their lives outside of class, but never in such a
highly stylized way as in it. Here, after all, was the source of the
sound that they had injected into their everyday speech.

The sound at Beit Rachel was one which, while resonating
gemore-loshn and *gemore-nign*, made at least equal use of the *Ivrit*
vernacular, with its staccato rhythms and low-to-high cadences
that are so different from the rise-fall, Ashkenazic sound of Yiddish and *gemore-nign*. Often recitations and some translations re-
verted to chant. When discussion—almost always carried on in
Ivrit—occasionally lagged, chant and *gemore-loshn* would increase.
When the Talmud became less a matter of intellectual inquiry, less
a pretext for social crisis or interactional games and more a matter
of ritual repetition, the patterned and ritualistic phrases and cadences were heard. Here there would be little translation. Whenever, on the other hand, translation increased in complexity,
where transition into the page was difficult, where more rather
than fewer words were necessary for communicating the meaning
of a phrase, talmudic idiom and chant disappeared and vernacular
enveloped all speech. It was as if the presence of *gemore-loshn* and
gemore-nign signaled the capacity of the participants to pass easily
into the world of the Talmud, while their absence meant the opposite.

Mekadshey Torah's circle as well as those at Rav Rotenbush's house and in Smotra displayed this tendency even more. Here there was very little *gemore-loshn* and *gemore-nign* to be heard. Instead there was a great deal of explanation and discussion, always in the vernacular. On occasion, the final word of a reci-tation of a Rashi commentary which was being reviewed in an obligatory manner, after the discussion was completed and the text penetrated, would be chanted—a kind of reminder and sym-bolic expression of the ritual and traditional side of *lernen* and a sign that we had successfully entered the world of the Talmud.

So each group had its own sound. The more they chanted, the less they discussed, the more easily they seemed to make the transition into the pages and ways of the Talmud. But no group remained completely outside those pages just as no group re-mained purely in the vernacular. All switched and all moved between the language of the text, Yiddish, and their vernacular.

The Smotra group—perhaps the most cosmopolitan of all those observed and the one I shall focus on most in this chapter—once reviewed a section of the Talmud that describes a man who, while passing through a marketplace, finds a *get*, a bill of divorcement. The bill lists as correspondents a man and a woman with names identical to those of his and his wife. On impulse, he decides to make use of the document for himself—in contravention of the law which requires such a document to be expressly written for those planning divorce. Framing this episode, the Rav expressed it in terms which both stressed its contemporary possibilities while resonating its Jewish character. The means he used to signal these two elements were language or code switching and ca-dence.

Beginning by placing the event in a contemporary setting, he explained: "A man is walking along Thirteenth Avenue in Boro Park, and there lying in an ashcan he finds a *get*."

The sentence starts in the relative monotone of English; but as it nears the code switch and the Hebrew word "*get*" in the embed-ded quotation, it begins to take on the characteristic rise-fall con-tour of Yiddish.[23] The Rav continued: "And he thinks to himself, 'Hey, here's a *get* with my name and Janey's! Why don't I use it?!'"

The metatextual remark, while spoken mostly in English, echoes the Yiddish inflections that seem appropriate to someone walking down a street in the Jewish neighborhood of Boro Park and concerned with the matters associated with the Jewish divorce. The switch to the word *"get,"* moreover, comes from *gemore-loshn*. The text, in this elaborated expressive repetition is thus being made to sound as if it resonates both the cultural milieu of present-day Jewry and traditional concerns.

To return to the general issue of switching, it is apparent from this example and others like it that, at least within the boundaries of the *shiur*, the participants must be considered multilinguals. Given the choice of any language, all members of the Smotra circle would in the course of a normal conversation use English. In the Talmud *shiur*, however, linguistic exclusivity is out of place, if for no other reason than that the text must be recited and then explained in language less archaic. Accordingly, one might say that during *lernen*, as the moves change from recitation to translation, explanation, and discussion—so may cadence and language. One might, however, also suggest that language and cadence vary along with content.[24]

The languages in contact during *lernen*, those used alternately by the same persons, are essentially Hebrew, Aramaic, Yiddish, and English.[25] Each, as we shall see, is appropriate for various sorts of texts and discussions. In addition to the alternations among these various languages, there are also phonemic, syntactic, and intonational interferences. In the course of a typical Smotra class, the language may become so fraught with switching as to suggest an argot all its own.

The notion of a group developing its own special language is one that Arnold Van Gennep long ago pointed to when he asserted the principle: "The linguistic situation of each language will depend upon the social situation of the group which speaks it."[26] He went on to suggest that the more the group is "organized around a special sacred activity, the more its special language is so organized as well, to the point of sometimes being a veritable argot outside of general usage."[27] The sacred and religious character of Talmud study would perfectly fit this description, and the special sound and language of *lernen*, its chant, vocabulary, and syntactic structures, should therefore come as no surprise.

The argot—*gemore-loshn*, *gemore-nign*, and code switching—serves in some measure as an exclusionary device which helps guarantee that the circle will remain relatively unbroken, homogeneous, and at least linguistically protected against the intrusion of heterogeneous elements (sounds and speakers). Indeed, the surest way for an outsider to signal his presence is through his inability to display proper usage or to switch language and tone along with the others.

As shall become increasingly apparent, the Smotra sound of *lernen*, with its syntactic, intonational, and linguistic combinations is culturally emblematic of modern Orthodoxy. It reveals the compromise character of their existence in ways that their speech outside of class, their dress, occupation, education, and place of residence do not display nearly as clearly. That all of this revelation is done in the fellowship and intimacy of the circle, in the absence of outsiders, is characteristic of modern Orthodox Jews who generally choose to express their Orthodoxy or at least cultural dualism in private. Like other moderns, they have largely relegated parochial matters and religious orthodoxies to the nonpublic domain where they can be separated from the public cosmopolitan face.[28] So sounding Jewish, expressing oneself in the inflections of a Talmud scholar or one modeled after him, is something to be done within the sanctuary and isolation of the study circle— at least in American modern Orthodox communities like Smotra.[29]

The switching in Smotra becomes so frequent at times as to be taken for granted. It and becomes subconscious both to the interlocutors, senders, and receivers of communication, and the audience, those others present who are not the primary addressees but who nonetheless follow the talk. So much so is this the case that, for example, during one *shiur*, the Rav—as he frequently does—stopped in mid-sentence and asked one of his students, "How ya' doin'? By the way, do you understand Yiddish?" only to receive the reply, "Fine, I thought you were speaking English."

In the past as now, students were not always proficient in the language of the text, and hence they translated it. They quoted it in the original always, regardless of the language of their discourse.

The character of the occasion, with its alternating recitations and translations, undoubtedly became associated with multilingualism. Hence leaving or entering the situation often became habitually marked in changing syntax, vocabulary, and cadences. People actually began to speak differently the minute they opened their volumes of study.

The rhetorical purposes of switching are epitomized in the speech of the Rav who, by his nuanced switching, instructs and also aurally distinguishes himself from the unlearned who cannot speak as he does. No one else knows as well how or when to make a switch, what words may be properly spoken in the vernacular and which must be repeated in the language of the Talmud, Yiddish or Hebrew. Indeed, the Rav's phrases, vocabulary, and cadences often serve as a model for others in the circle who would emulate his obvious proficiency in *lernen*. His speech is a kind of treasury from which the others may draw their wealth of words and sounds. He sets the linguistic standards, which the members of the circle echo and prefigure.

Dorothy Henderson, in her sociological examination of language, perhaps sums up the entire matter best: "It is clearly the case that all cultures or subcultures are realized through communications from which contain their own unique, imaginative and aesthetic possibilities."[30] This linguistic distinctiveness creates complex problems for translators and especially for amateur metaphrasts like most Talmud students who, during their *lernen*, must switch from one language or code and cadence to another or several others.

LANGUAGE CHOICE AND CODE SWITCHING

At the same time, however, these very problems of language choice, use, and code switching may serve as a rich source of sociological and psychological information about the speaker and the linguistic community with whom he seems to identify by virtue of his speech. All communities, after all, provide their members with a set of linguistic resources, a lexical and intonational repertoire (which an outsider may discover over time as he is exposed to speakers from that group). Moreover, "language is both the foundation and instrumentality of the social construction of reality."[31] Hence the choices a speaker makes in any given speech situation reveal a great deal not only about him, his loyalties, and his identifications but also about his social constructions of reality, the way he conceives of the world he inhabits. These choices, made from the range of open alternatives, can be used as a behavioral index of his group preferences.[32]

What is true for the individual likewise may be applied to the group. When a collection of people speak along the same lines, develop certain idioms and a particular linguistic style, make similar language choices and switches, these may be used as an index of collective identity and cultural loyalty. As already suggested in the opening sentence of this chapter, the patterns of speech appropriate for any given group may be considered the mirror of its collective existence.

Not only does speech reveal group preference and reference, it also discloses the speaker's state of mind and his command of "all the relevant contextual information, linguistic and nonlinguistic, that the language user needs when carrying on communicative activity."[33] Indeed a person's talk over an extended period betrays his inner conflicts and ambivalences as much as anything else.[34] It is "a record of the means by which that person tries to achieve, maintain, relieve or avoid certain intrapsychic states through the verbal management of his relations with his social environment."[35] Again, what may be said of the individual also may be said of the group. Its talk as well reveals its intrapsychic character and cultural locus. In sum, "it is not so much the facts of life as such that affect language as the amount of psychic energy vested in them; in other words, what shapes language is not the occupation of its speakers but the preoccupation of their minds."[36] And thus what is expressed in speech are these very preoccupations.

There are, to be sure, a variety of preoccupations that absorb the people I have observed *lernen* and that are at least partially revealed in speech. Since my interest is not so much in individual personalities but rather in social and cultural types, I will not focus here on those preoccupations which are personal, anchored in the psyche and biography of any particular person. These are only significant for this discussion insofar as they represent common preoccupations within the circle. Among the latter there are several, including those I have already mentioned in the previous chapters. Perhaps the most ubiquitous is the preoccupation with identity and cultural dualism. The modern Orthodox Jewish problem of proceeding simultaneously in the direction of the cosmopolitan, secular world while trying also to follow the pathways of tradition, staying within the boundaries of the *halakha* and in the ways of the Talmud, seemed to resonate in countless speech situations. With their words and sounds, participants displayed their movement in one or another direction—or even in both simultaneously. This point will be elaborated later.

As the artist becomes swept up in his artistic creation, as a people becomes mesmerized and exalted by its own ceremonies and rituals, so too can an individual or group become fascinated

with its speech. Coming from the social and psychic involvement
and energy that goes into choosing and expressing words and
communicating meaning, this fascination is at the heart of the
play with words that may enrapture *lerners*. The speakers may
not be fully cognizant of what it is they enjoy about their talk or
even its full meaning—"which of us knows all the words of the
language he speaks and entire signification of each?" as Durkheim
aptly put it—but they are no less engrossed by the business of
talking. Given this caveat, attention may now be turned back to
the question of language choice use and switching.

For all the circumstances of switching, in the final analysis one
must conclude, as did Uriel Weinreich, that "there are no strictly
linguistic motivations in language shifts."[37] Rather, the roots of
switching—as I have begun to suggest—may be discovered
through a sociology and psychology of the *lerners* and their circles.
A speaker may wish to appear as a member of a local, parochial
community on certain occasions, speak from within the bounded
pages of the Talmud and its implicit world. On other occasions,
he may wish to jump off the page, to identify with the cosmopolitan values of other worlds he inhabits. While it is not the only
way, the medium of language and intonational switching in great
measure help him mark these moves. So recitations and translations may sound like chants, heavily punctuated with talmudic
terms and Yiddish expressions, while explanations, discussions,
and digressions may take on the sound of the vernacular and
with it signal an outside involvement. Even where certain spheres
of activity are dominated by one language rather than another,
the socially and psychologically motivated switcher may nonetheless use the language and cadences of his choice to thus indirectly make a statement about himself, his loyalties, and his
identity. For example, he may choose to phrase an ancient talmudic tale in English or modern Hebrew, using the syntax and
cadence of these languages in order to stress the tale's contemporary relevance as well as his ability to perceive matters in modern terms. Or, vice versa, he may phrase a contemporary matter
in *gemore-loshn* using the distinctive rise-fall intonations of *gemore-
nign*, thereby asserting the matter's traditional Jewish character
and his capacity to perceive even the modern in the framework
of traditional *lernen*.

In order to understand the particularities of code switching and
the nature of word play during *lernen*, one needs to remember

that a "speaker in any language community who enters diverse social situations normally has a repertoire of speech alternatives which shift with the situation."[38] Where the speaker is multilingual, and especially where the situation allows (e.g., where there are other multilinguals present with whom he can speak a variety of languages), this repetoire is accordingly enlarged. Given such an array of choice, each language is in a sense in competition with the others—and its being chosen represents an implicit victory for the community in which that language is dominant.

Specifically in the cases of the languages in use during *lernen*, one might suggest that the use of *gemore-loshn* and Yiddish—languages formed in and generated by the Jewish community—represents a victory by that speech community. Contradistinctively, the use of English (along with its syntax and cadence) represents a victory for the English-speaking community—in the case of Smotra. Or, the use of modern Hebrew, with its Sephardic pronunciation, may represent a victory for secular Israel.

Further, speech that is a combination of all the languages represents a stalemate or cultural compromise. The speaker using a language mix indirectly identifies himself with both communities. He also signals that he is, at least during the time of his compromise verbal construction, not completely embraced by any single speech community. To discover the precise mechanics and nuance of this compromise, however, one needs to look more closely at the process of switching, at the actual word play—word play that turns out to be in fact a world play.

Certain code variations in the Talmud class can be easily explained. These are what J. J. Gumperz calls "superposed varieties of speech," such as occupational argots and language indigenous to a particular activity.[39] The *lernen* reveals many such expressions which come from the text. Here I may quote from my previous work on this subject:

The Talmud in its text makes use of shorthand terms for various of its conceptualizations. Such terms act as representations of complex Judaic legal arguments. When translated literally, they make little or no sense, since they are usually composed of key words of the argument. Although these words could be translated into English abstractions, to do so would destroy their codical and referent qualities. Moreover, such efforts are intellectually gratuitous, since they often ob-

literate important nuances of meaning in the interests of coin-
ing some pithy neologism. Accordingly, such terms remain
untranslated. For example, in the sentence *"Hasholayach es ha
kayn* is the principle working here," the first words refer to
a legal principle which mandates one to chase away a mother
bird from a nest before taking away her eggs. The words
themselves make little sense if literally translated. However,
they act as simple referents to the complex argument of which
they are the opening words. In much the same way as a
pope's encyclical may be referred to by its opening words,
so certain legal and talmudic principles become epigram-
matized.[40]

In addition to such mandatory code variations, there are
switches that come from the interspersing of explanation and
discussion with textual cantillation. Strictly speaking, such recitation constitutes switching, although the switch is determined
by very formal rules governing it. Before launching and explanation, for example, one reads until the end of an idea. Unfamiliar
words, however, may be translated in a bracketed fashion in the
midst of such a recitation. Still, as has been already noted and as
the examples will later make clear, recitation may become expressive repetition and thereby integrated into the explanation
and discussion of the text. Where a speaker expresses himself in
gemore-loshn, with its heavy use of quotation, one may assume
that at least to some degree he is willing to identify himself with
or through the text and its viewpoint.

TOPIC SWITCHING

Topic switches, as already noted, constitute another ground for
code variation. "The implication of topical regulation of language
choice is that certain topics are somehow handled better in one
language than in another in particular multilingual contexts . . .."[41]
Thus some multilingual speakers may acquire the habit of speaking about a particular topic in a particular language partially because that is the language in which they were trained to deal with
this topic, partially because they and their interlocutors may *"lack
the specialized terms* for satisfying discussion" of a particular topic
in another language, partially because that other language itself
may lack as exact or many terms for handling the topic as those
possessed by the language normally associated with the topic,

and partially because it is "considered strange or inappropriate" to talk about certain topics in a "foreign" language.[42]

Each of these possibilities comes into play during *lernen*. The trained Talmud student who has spent time in the traditional yeshiva where study is carried on in the traditional languages of the Jewish world—*Loshn Koydesh* and Yiddish—accordingly may feel compelled to continue his avocational *lernen* in the same way. Likewise, participants who have reviewed Talmud with such a yeshiva student may take on his patterns of speech during *lernen*, even when they are on their own. The technical grounds for switching have already been noted with regard to superposed terminology. Finally, there is a sense in which the traditional concepts of Talmud, the expressions of its often archaic reasoning or convoluted logic sound strange when translated into contemporary language and sound. In *gemore-loshn* and Yiddish, however, they sound perfectly appropriate and correct. What the modern student might never be able to bring himself to say in contemporary English or Hebrew for it would undermine the way he has learned to think in those languages, he can far more easily express in the channels of traditional Jewish communication. Examples will follow.

Normally, speakers indicate that they know they have made a topic shift, changed the manifest content or referent of their speech. When only one language is in use such shifts are marked by what Goffman calls "weak bridges," expressions like "oh, by the way.[43] Uriel Weinreich notes as well the marking accomplished "by special voice modifications (slight pause, change in tempo, and the like) in speech."[44] In multilingual situations, all these markings may obtain, but in addition there is the assertive and unmistakable sign of the different language in use.

An illustration from Smotra will be helpful here. The following interchange occurred during a one-minute digression from the text. The stimulus for the digression had been a phrase in the text in which the Emperor Vespasian is quoted as asking the great Jewish sage Rabbi Yokhanan ben Zakkai, who had just come out of the besieged Jerusalem to ask for mercy, why he had not come earlier. The phrasing of Vespasian's question as articulated by the Talmud is: "*Ad ho idno amay lo osis le gaboy?*"[45]

The digression begins. It aims to bring to life the emotional quality of Vespasian's remark, but it draws from a particularly

Jewish experience. The Rav does most of the talking, but Henry, one of the participants, signals his involvement with a verbal cue.

R: Amongst hasidim it's supposedly Reb Aron Karliner, one of *gdoley khasidus*, one of the giants of our hasidic world, who used to on *Rosh Hashono* [pause] go before the *omed*. And the story comes back that one year [pause] as he approached the *omed* [pause] to say *"hamelekh"* [pause] he went into a faint [pause] and he actually fainted [pause], and it took quite a to-do to revive him [pause], and when they revived him, he was speechless [pause]. And the whole *besmedresh* [house of study (and prayer)], and the whole spirit of the holiday [long pause]—"What's with the rebee? What happened? *Hamelekh?*"

  He says he approached there *lifney melekh malkhey hamlokhim, ot zokh zikh dermant di gemore: "eey malko ano," oyb ikh bin take Got, ikh bin di melekh malkhey hamlokhim* [before the King of all Kings, he reminded himself of the Talmud: "if I am a King," if I am indeed God, I am the King of all kings] *ad——*

H: Why did you not come be——

R: *"Ad ho idno amay lo osis le gaboy?" Vus varts di a gans yor?* Why didn't you come before now?

There are various sorts of code variations here, including loan words and superposed varieties of speech, particularly those which name what Max Weinreich called "concepts of concrete Jewishness": *omed* (lectern), *besmedresh* (house of study).[46] There are also referential terms deriving from liturgy: *hamelekh* (the king), the opening word of the morning prayers on a holy day and one with which the cantor formally begins the service. Additionally, there are special and traditional names of God which are commonly not translated: *melekh malkhey hamlokhim* (the King of all kings).

By far the most significant language switch occurs, however, when the topic shifts back from a simple description of the Reb Aron Karliner episode to a gloss and explanation of the original Talmud text. Here, in its expressive repetition, the text is bracketed with Yiddish, Hebrew, English, interfered versions of each, and finally a reversion into the text. And when one of the members of the circle, Henry, tries to translate the quotation, to prevent the spoken return to the Talmud as it were, the Rav cuts him off with words recited first in the original Aramaic (*Ad ho idno amay lo osis le gaboy?*), followed by a Yiddish gloss (*Vus varts di a gans yor?* [Why have you been waiting an entire year?]). Only after these are matters closed with an English restatement of meaning.

While Henry has tried to skip the shift back to the text and rather seeks to keep the entire discussion in English, the Rav chooses to emphasize the Jewish character of the episode and topic. He lingers in *gemore-loshn* and *taytsh*. The Aramaic, Hebrew, and Yiddish—the *gemore-loshn*—the easy reference to concepts of concrete Jewishness all emphasize solidarity with the text and its Jewish people. The English, on the other hand, takes the story into the domain of the modern American English speaker. Left there it is not nearly as charged with either talmudic or Jewish significance. It is as if the Rav were finally overcome by the Jewishness of his story and could no longer bear to listen to himself communicate its message in words other than those associated with the Jewish universe. The English from Henry, however, reminds him where he is and to whom he speaks—modern Orthodox Jews of Smotra. Following a bold last cry in Jewish speech, he finally closes in English.

The episode nicely illustrates some of the character of word play during *lernen*. The switching from one domain to another and the implications which it carries take up the attention of the *lerners*. They can find out who they are, challenge one another's perceptions of that identity and loyalty, all through the process of word use. Other illustrations will underscore this point.

In a sense, the language shifting here is a means of bracketing the Jewishly oriented activity. Not only are matters integrated into an English-speaking situation, but one might argue that English speakers are forced to leave that linguistic world and dip into *gemore-loshn* in order to keep up with what is going on. The speech of the Rav represents an instance of "embedding," a process in which the speech of another is reported in its original form and where reporting is done by means of "expressive repetition," repeating those words in a manner in which they were presumably spoken. Reb Aron Karliner could not have spoken in English. His speech came out of a Yiddish-speaking world. Likewise, when the Rav here repeats Reb Aron's repetition of the Talmud, he too speaks in the Yiddish of that far more Jewishly oriented world. He moves, as it were, back into it, and we hear him take Reb

Aron's words and make them come to life. We become the hasidim who stood around him and heard his explanation.

To be sure, it is hardly likely that Vespasian, whose words Reb Aron is quoting and which through him Rav Gafny, our teacher, is reporting, sounded like a hasidic rabbi, using Yiddish inflection or even Aramaic language. Indeed, in reporting the emperor's words, the Talmud itself has likely translated and transformed them so as to make them in greater harmony with its own style and hence the Jewish domain. The Rav's expressive repetition here is thus a transformation of a transformation. He has re-keyed the Talmud so that it comes out of the more recent Jewish experience of Reb Aron Karliner. It is as if he had to make the Talmud's statement even more Jewish by embedding it in the world of Eastern European hasidic life, bracketing it with Yiddish, *gemore-loshn*, and the mantle of a hasidic tale. In doing this, the Rav demonstrates the extent to which the phrases of the Talmud can be associated with Jewish experience. It is, if you will, a cultural performance carried out through the medium of language use. Leaving behind the English-speaking world—if only for part of a sentence—he can in the course of a simple locutionary shift enter and echo the Jewish one. It is a marvelous performance and very much at the heart of the word play that fascinates *lerners*.*

In this example, one last note is in order. I remarked earlier that this speech contained language interference. In the intonational contour (which I have not here precisely described; I will focus on this more specifically later), there can be no doubt about interference since the English which normally does not have a rise-fall cadence characteristic of Yiddish is here made to undulate in just that way.[47] The syncretistic combination of English language and Yiddish cadence is, one might suggest, an example of cultural compromise and characteristic of modern Orthodox Jews, like those of Smotra, who want to be part of at least two worlds at once.

There are also Yiddish syntactical structures, the most obvious of these being: "And the story comes back that one year," a construction much more at home in Yiddish than in English. The

*This is not to say the speaker is aware of all he has done. All he may know is that it feels right to use the words and sound the way he does. He may say that he enjoys or feels most comfortable talking this way. What I am trying to suggest is why he needs to speak this way, even if he may not fully be aware of the need.

interference results in a kind of English one is most likely to hear spoken among those who *lern*.

Finally, there is English morphological structure. The Yiddish word *rebe*, the title of a hasidic leader, has become "rebee," a sound morphologically as appropriate to English as, say, "cabbie." Here too is an example of language created, as it were, by the modern Orthodox Jewish speaker.

WORLD VIEW AND WORD PLAY

These examples raise some important questions. If indeed code variation and interference signal the particular cultural dualism and compromise characteristic of the contemporary Orthodox, why do modern Orthodox Jews not always speak in this polyglottal way? One might answer simply that in great measure they do. The syntax, cadence, and morphology of their speech is filled with interferences from the various languages of their lives. They sound a bit like chronic immigrants. Indeed, one might suggest that through a process of cultural exosmosis, the American Jews, and most particularly the New York variety with its heavy concentration of the Orthodox—many of whom talk this way—have infused American, and especially New York, English with some of the vocabulary, syntax, cadence, and morphology of their multilingualism.[48] How far is Brooklynese from *lernen* language?

Beyond this sort of simplistic answer one must note that language choice and switching are also grounded in situational factors; that is, not only topic change accounts for shift, but situational change does so also. A situational shift occurs "when within the same setting the participants' definition of the social event changes [and] this change [is] signalled among others by linguistic clues."[49]

In the case of the Talmud class, situational factors may account for switching. We have seen already how, in spite of Henry's effort to stay in English, the situation of *lernen* forced him to acquiesce to the Rav's switch. One might generally suggest that the situation of *lernen* fosters and demands specific sorts of speaking. Those who speak an otherwise faultless English or, in the Israeli cases, perfect modern Hebrew, find themselves sounding like polyglots during *lernen*. Not only do they switch into and out of the language of text, but they also resonate the Yiddish and tone of the yeshivas of Eastern Europe where, in recent historic memory, the Talmud was a complete way of life. Those who fail to handle the switching during *lernen* are either neophytes, outsiders, or rebels. For the rest, the situation demands it.

There is a qualification that must be made here. Alternative definitions of the situation may occur within the same setting. *Lernen* may be different things for different people. It may be a chance to absorb information housed in the text. It may be a religious experience, a form of worship.[50] It may be seen as an opportunity for anthropological research. Each of these varying definitions of the situation may manifest itself in linguistic terms. Thus the person looking only to understand the facts of the Talmud will speak in the language he best comprehends, to the exclusion of all others. The worshipper will use as much holy tongue as possible to allow him to resonate liturgical sounds in his *lernen*. The anthropologist will perhaps speak in ways that at once signal his sympathy for those he observes but also his distance from them—mispronouncing Hebrew words which he nonetheless struggles to use, or else self-consciously enunciating them. For those who come only for fellowship, this definition of the situation may be displayed by a willingness to shift language in ways that are most flexible. One speaks as much like everyone else as possible so as to be close with them; talk like others and you appear to be one of them.

Although among Jews who sought to become acculturated to American life and society, English became the "prestige language" and preferred, and in the Israeli case those who sought to complete the "ingathering of the exiles" sought to speak a Sephardic and modern Hebrew, Orthodox Jews, as already noted, generally held onto Yiddish and Ashkenazic *Loshn Koydesh* as an antidote to the threat of what Irving Howe has called "religio-ethnic abandonment."[51] That holding action eventually evolved into synthetic forms—interlanguage—under the tremendous acculturative pressures of modern American life as well as the cosmopolitan influences in modern Israeli society. Through the schools, in the streets, and at work Jews learned to speak English, and through it some of the ways of America. Similarly, Israel insisted on the use of modern Hebrew as a means of enculturating the diverse ethnic immigrants that built its population and mandated it in the schools, on the streets, and in the workplaces. The refusal of the isolationist Orthodox, whether in Boro Park, New York, or Mea Shearim, Jerusalem, to speak anything other than a yeshiva-like

Yiddish is, in effect, a signal of their contra-acculturative ideology. The men at Kahal Reyim with their Yiddish *lernen* represent a segment of that population.

Modern Orthodox Jews, the participants in some of the other circles herein described, generally find a greater comfort in the interlanguage their more traditional brethren eschew. But the choice is not always simple. They are after all both modern (cosmopolitan) and Orthodox (parochial). In the former incarnation, they may feel moved to speak in the best vernacular of the day; in the latter, they are more comfortable speaking in parochial tongues. The controlling factor here is "the socio-psychological sense of *reference group membership*."[52] Language will reflect the group with whom the speaker feels associated. Where the association and sense of reference changes over time and in various situations, so too will language choice and use.

In public, outside the Talmud study circle, away from the synagogue and the wholly Jewish domain, the modern Orthodox Jew may seek to identify himself with the cosmopolitan world, accomplishing this aim at least in part through his speech. On the other hand, in the private world of his parochial Jewish community, he may "employ dialect . . . to signal his Jewishness to other Jews," or his Orthodoxy to other Orthodox.[53] That is, he is public about his Jewishness in a private domain and private about it in a public one.

When these worlds intersect, when a group of Jews wishes to assert some modicum of parochial solidarity at the same time they wish to demonstrate a cosmopolitan orientation, a belongingness to other worlds beyond the Jewish one, they may—in the sphere of language—turn to a highly nuanced form of interlanguage. Often among Jews this takes the form of using intonational signals that point one way and lexical ones that point another. The Jew who recites traditional Talmud in the English monotone or who speaks American English in the inflections and cadences of Yiddish and *gemore-nign* are but the most prominent examples.

The intersection of the cosmopolitan and parochial—Orthodox Jews in the modern world or moderns in the precincts of traditional Orthodoxy—may occur purely in the mind of the speaker who refers his behavior to a group other than the one in which he may at any given moment find himself. Thus, for example, sitting in a modern university, perhaps the paradigm of contemporary heterodoxy, an American professor may turn to another like him and linguistically display a cultural duality by inserting a talmudic expression into an otherwise totally English conversation. "Maybe you think the faculty committee will approve the new courses? *Aderaba* [on the contrary], they are dead set against it."

The syntax, the statement turned into a question is characteristic of Yiddish, and the term *"aderaba,"* drawn from the Talmud and here embedded into an English locution, recalls the speakers' parochial ties. Perhaps the notion that the faculty committee stands opposed to the speakers' expectations calls out this reminder of other loyalties; maybe there are other reasons. Nevertheless, the language choice and use is significant.

Similarly, during immersion in the parochial domain of the Talmud study circle, a *lerner* may recall that he also inhabits another secular world, beyond the boundaries of the parochial one in which he temporarily exists. He may show this by making repeated efforts to translate and express talmudic matters in contemporary language and terminology. This he does even as the linguistic nexus with Judaism is assiduously maintained through recitation, intonation, and topic.[54] An example is in order; again, I draw from Smotra, a cosmopolitan-parochial crossroads.

Much is going on in the following two-and-a-quarter-minute speech event. I wish, however, to focus upon the effort to maintain ties with both the Jewish and English-speaking societies—an effort resonant in the word play. This remains the social and psychological motive—whether conscious or not—that seems to explain a great deal of the language choice.

The selection quoted within this extract comes from a section of the Talmud which is *aggadetta* (lore), describing an encounter between Abba Sikra and Yokhanan ben Zakkai. The Talmud is concerned with the confrontation for it represents a kind of watershed in Jewish history—a moment when those who sought to move the people toward an identification with scholarship (the followers of Yokhanan ben Zakkai) came into conflict with those who aimed for political autonomy in Israel (the followers of Abba Sikra). The former group went on to Yavneh, a city on the shores of the Mediterranean, where they founded a yeshiva and began the era of Jewish history that picked up the pieces after the fall of Jerusalem and the subsequent diaspora. The latter fought for and lost Jerusalem, Massada, and political control over the land

of Israel. If Abba Sikra represented the group that identified Jewish existence with the land, Yokhanan ben Zakkai stood for the
People of the Book, those who saw Jewish life inherent in the
study of Jewish sources in sacred literature.

The Rav begins with an identification of the characters involved
in this talmudic narrative:*

	R:	Abba Sikra who was head, one of the heads of the *biryoni*, the *biryoni* were a group of fanatics or— —
	S:	Zealots
5	R:	——people, zealots who refused to take leader-ship, a peaceful resolve on the basis of the spiritual leaders of Israel. Instead they decided, and they forced the issue, to bring about a war between the besiegers as against the inhabitants of the holy
10		land, of *Yerushalayim* [Jerusalem], by burning down all the storehouses of food and forcing the siege to reach the point that the people can't hold out and they have to go to battle.
		In any case, one of their leaders was Abba Sikra.
15		And Abba Sikra turns out to be no less than a nephew of Reb Yokhanan ben Zakkai.
		Hertzokh ayn, haynt az men hert a mol a rebe hot epes a mishpokhe vos er iz nisht azoy hoo-ha-ha *makht men* shh! *Bald zogt men do* [Listen to this, today
20		when one hears of a rabbi who has something of a family which is not so hoo-ha-ha one says shh! Presently it says here]; "Abba Sikra *reysh biryoni*," the whole *tsore-makher e' geveyn* a nephew, a son of a daughter [sic] [pause]
25	H:	Yeah, but he wasn't a, he wasn't a [pause] a gangs-ter, he was a . . .
	R:	On this point he was willing to listen to Yokhanan ben Zakkai. But basically, if somebody becomes a general amongst vagabonds, amongst brigands,
30		eh, he must have earned his title and such.
	H:	He wasn't even a vagabond amongst, amongst brigands. He was a leader of the——
	R:	——"*Biryoni*."

*Line numbers (marked in the left-hand margin) are used to facilitate the location
of words and phrases referred to in my subsequent discussion of this episode.

	H:	Of the——
35	R:	*Shteyt dokh, "Reysh biryoni hava"* [But it says, "He was the head of the *biryoni*"].
	H:	Meyer Kahane. Something like Meyer Kahane, *nu* not necessarily the, the *loshn* brigands [pause]. He was a, he was a nationalist, eh——
40	R:	The *khazal gebn zogn* [rabbis say this] *dis az zey hobn ongebrengen dem khurbn* [that they brought on the destruction]——
	H:	That's right, no question about it.
	R:	Alright, *shoyn.*
45	H:	But it's not necessarily that he was a, he was a robber or stealing money.
	R:	*Ober dos vort* [But this word] *"biryoni"* iz/is a very negative term.
	H:	[softly] Yah.
50	R:	*"Biryoni."*
	H:	He wasn't——
	S:	——a *bulgan* [ruffian]——
	H:	——stealing money.
	R:	What? [to S]
55	S:	A *bulgan.*
	R:	I like your word better.
	H:	He wasn't robbing money; he wasn't stealing money [pause].
	R:	Na, no. No!
60	H:	He was a——
	R:	No, they had their ideologists——
	H:	——a nationalist, eh [pause].
	R:	But they would not take spiritual guidance, *nu?*
	H:	That's right; that's right.
65	M:	That wasn't his real name anyway.
	R:	What, "Abba Sikra"?
	M:	No, his name over here was [pause] "Ben Batya."
	S:	That's his last name.
	R:	*M'vet nisht onheybn lernen haynt mit, mit eym, mit*
70		*dem* [we won't start *lernen* today with, with him, with this], with all this historical and literary criticism. [pause] *Shoyn.*
	H:	[chuckles]
	R:	*Lomer shoyn onfengen lernen epes* [Let's begin *lernen*
75		something].

Perhaps the most striking feature of this interchange is the code variation during which the Rav speaks a mix of English, Yiddish, and their combinations along with some textual quotation, while Henry, Sidney, and Mark speak predominantly in English but make clear in their responses that they have fully followed the Rav from language to language.

Generally, one might describe the entire discussion as an effort to contemporize as well as translate the Talmud, to make it sensible and alive to moderns. Those speaking in English, Henry primarily, are trying to portray Abba Sikra and the *biryoni* in terms intelligible to contemporary Americans—a group with whom they choose to associate themselves linguistically—while the Rav continually tries to draw the focus back to the Talmud and its particularistic concerns.

But why should it be of such concern to Henry, Sidney, and Mark as well as the others who make up an interested audience to understand and translate the term *"bironyi"* in contemporary terms? One might suggest the motive lies in the fact that to some extent the modernist who associates himself with the contemporary world feels—as I have argued repeatedly—a compelling need to transform and comprehend the various layers of his experience in its terms. Linguistically this need can demonstrate itself in the desire to translate literally and figuratively into the contemporary vernacular as much as possible what goes on during *lernen*. Word play becomes world play. To fail to make the transformation is perhaps to signal the division between the world of the Talmud and that of contemporary life, a division which is anathema to the modern Orthodox who wish to assume continuity. On the other hand, to succeed in identifying *"biryoni"* in present-day terms is to once again give evidence of the ceaseless relevance of the Talmud and, by association, Jewish tradition.[55] It is to take the otherwise archaic tale of the fall of Jerusalem with its legendary characters and understand it in contemporary terms, literally and therefore *also* symbolically.

While it is Henry who leads the contemporization efforts here, even the Rav in his initial translation of *"biryoni"* made some moves in this direction. His effort was, however, far more tentative. Choosing uncommon, if not archaic, words ("vagabonds," "brigands"), he does not smoothly make the transition from the parochial language of the Talmud to English, leaving the task to be completed by others, those more comfortable in choosing the right English words. Moreover, to underscore his downplaying of English and all it portends, he reverts frequently to the languages of Jewishness, Yiddish, and the textual quotations of *gemore-loshn*. In so doing he acts in line with his situational role, protector of the tradition (and traditional language) and defender of the parochial (through his emphasis on the text). He is Rav.

Repeatedly the Rav tries to cut off moves into contemporaneity and its linguistic reflection, English. To English remarks he responds in Yiddish or with talmudic quotation (lines 33, 35, 40, 41, 44, 47, 50, 69, 74), as if refusing to ratify and give in to the American identity of his interlocutors. In addition, twice—at what he considers opportune moments for closure—he tries to end the digression with *"shoyn,"* a Yiddishism meaning "already," but which has become a common lexical marker among Yiddish speakers in general and talmudists in particular for framing and closing conversation.* *"Shoyn"* often serves as a bridge to something else: another conversation, a change in action, closure. Finally, following his last *"shoyn"* he remarks in close to proper Yiddish, *"Lomer shoyn onfengen lernen epes"* (Let us begin already to *lern* something). Speaking in Yiddish constitutes a linguistic emphasis on the need to return the group from its digression into contemporary concerns to the traditional words and concerns of the Talmud page.

Lest one suppose that the Rav represents a pristine example of the parochial, one ought to note that his speech is heavily marked with—indeed predominantly—English. To be sure, it is not an English that could pass easily as representative of American vernacular. Rather it is a kind of Jewish-American, modern Orthodox interlanguage.

Even his Yiddish displays English interference. Perhaps the most blatant example is in the use of the expression *"tsore-makher"* (line 23), which he uses as an epithet to characterize Abba Sikra. The Rav has undoubtedly meant to call Abba Sikra a "troublemaker," an epithet coming from contemporary American English. Rather than using the actual Yiddish word for troublemaker, which is, according to the authoritative Weinreich dictionary, *"shterer,* he has translated literally from English by combining the word *tsore* (trouble) with *makher* (maker) in a structure rooted in American speech.

*Its English (or rather Yinglish) incarnation is in the locution "enough already!"

Beyond this example of a calque, there are other illustrations of English (and, by association, American cultural) interference in the Rav's speech. A morphological interference occurs (line 40) in the word *"dis,"* which more properly should be the word *"dos."* *"Dos"* is Yiddish for "this." "Dis" thus seems to be a compromise form. Or, again (lines 47–48) one discovers a sentence which is part Yiddish and part English. The bridge between these two parts is a quotation from the text, *"biryoni,"* and the word "is" which may be either English or the Yiddish *"iz,"* both of which mean the same thing. The morphological ambiguity is ideal here for the speaker since it serves easily and usefully to connect a sentence (and idea) which begins in a linguistically (and hence culturally) parochial realm—spoken about and to a strictly speaking Jewish audience—but ends by being put into contemporary American terms.

Finally, although this is strictly speaking more a matter of speech content than form, even in his Yiddish remark (lines 17–19), the Rav is making something of an effort to contemporize—"today when one hears . . ." However, by considering the Talmud in the context of contemporary *Jewish* life—what happens *today* in a rabbi's family—the speaker is in effect keeping matters parochial. This is a kind of specialized contemporization, a way of showing how Jews have changed. Since the Rav is talking about matters he considers only relevant to parochials, albeit contemporary ones, he speaks in a Jewish language.

One also must not assume that Henry, as quoted in this digression, represents a pure expression of the cosmopolitan modern. Not only does he respond to the Yiddish (proving the extent of his linguistic intersubjectivity), but his English is likewise heavy with Jewish influences. First is his accent, which although not indicated in the transcript resonates the sounds of Eastern and Central Europe that have in America become associated with immigrant Jewish speech. Second, there are cadences, also not noted in the transcript but present in the speech, which follow the rise-fall of the Yiddish speaker. Finally, there is the lexical parochialism which appears in (line 38) the phrase, "the *loshn* brigands." This insertion of the Yiddish *"loshn"* (language or words) serves as a linguistic marker of Henry's insider status among those who speak the language of *lernen*. It is a small touch, but in the play of words singularly revealing of the speaker's willingness to be associated with the ways of the circle. Although he speaks in

English about matters an English speaker might otherwise comprehend, he is still Jewish enough to throw in a word, whether
conscious or not is irrelevant here, which will mark him as parochial insider.

In all of this code variation and interference is a sense in which
each foray into one world—be it the parochial or the cosmopolitan—seems to bring about a pulling back to the other. Yet the
swings from one domain to the other continue. Interference in
language resonates a cultural interference within the lives of the
modern Orthodox speakers. All of the preceding suggests the
intimate connections between world view and word play. In a
sense, language choice, shift, and use objectivates world view as
it expresses it.

In Smotra, the Rav, when he forgets for a moment whom he
is among and lets himself express his Jewish orientations and
sentiments, plays his words Jewishly. At Kahal Reyim, where the
lerners come from a world anchored in tradition and organized
almost totally around Jewish ritual, where the daily repetition of
a page of Talmud is an expression of that tradition, a completion
of the evening prayers, one likewise discovers speech and sound
that are undeniably Jewish. Even their Yiddish is a highly stylized
form of *gemore-loshn*, Talmud language, which draws much of its
vocabulary from the text, its morphology from Yiddish, its syntax
from both, and unites all with a single strand of sound called
gemore-nign.

On the other hand, those who tend toward cosmopolitan contemporaneity, who in America which to refract modern American
values and world view and in Israel its secular counterpart, can
be expected to distance themselves from this parochial speech
and sound. This is accomplished in the former case by a heavy
emphasis on translation, mispronunciation of key expressions in
the text, and a use of cadences much closer to the sound of the
vernacular than to *gemore-nign*. In Israel, this means not only
cadences associated with modern Hebrew, which in most cases
are distinctly un-Yiddish, but also a reading of the text as if it
were morphologically closer to the vernacular than to the ancient
Aramaic. In its most extreme incarnation—say, in the study of
Talmud at the university—the speech of the class would be indistinguishable from speech during any other course. In America
it would be speaking about matters in the Talmud as if it were all

in English, while in Israel it would be spoken as if it were written in *Ivrit*.

There are limits. *Lernen*, as the Yiddish etymology of term itself suggests, is not something that can be completely transformed into the vernacular without losing its essential character. It remains embedded in traditional Jewish life. Thus, even in Smotra, the most modern of the circles examined in this book, there is a periodic return to the languages and cadences of Jewish life; a link of oral, semantic, and aural touching of base with tradition.

INTONATION

Throughout the discussion thus far, in previous chapters, and especially in the last few pages, the matter of intonation has been raised as an important component of the drama of *lernen* and in particular of world play. This matter needs further elucidation and consideration, something that will require at first a bit of recapitulation.

To begin with, in order to understand the importance of intonation in *lernen*, one must recall that the Talmud—including most of its important commentaries—is essentially a cryptic compilation of the notes of rabbinic debates on topics of orally transmitted law and lore. It is unpunctuated and devoid of vocalization so that even the basic exercise of reading it properly requires an expertise beyond that available to the unschooled. In part as a result of this fact, a method of cantillating the text developed. This cantillation, or *gemore-nign* as it came to be called in Yiddish, served syntactic and interpretive functions. Cadence helped one disambiguate the text. It provided "a shade of meaning added to or superimposed upon . . . intrinsic lexical meaning," allowed one to distinguish between primary and subordinate clauses or ideas, rhetorical questions and real ones, one topic and another, speech and reported speech, sarcasm and seriousness, and so on.[56] Still today, "melodic variety is used for the phrasing of the Aramaic text which, as it stands, is compressed to the point of obscurity."[57] It also still serves to restore blood and tissue to the bare bones of the printed text. There is something of a parallel to all this in the biblical text. The Torah scroll, in which the Five Books of Moses are handwritten on parchment and from which they are publicly and ritually read, also lacks punctuation or vocalization. To disambiguate this text, a series of notes for cantillation have evolved. Far more specific melodically than the chant lines of *gemore-nign*, these notes for reading (which in their melody differ between Ashkenazim and Sephardim as well as among the various ethnic groups within these larger categories) allow the cantor to associate a specific sound with each word and let him know when sentences begin and end. Other rhetoric and semantic overtones of these notes have, however, long since atrophied. Once standardized, these notes lost the capacity to resonate emotional and semantic meaning for those generations beyond the ones who first instituted them. *Gemore-nign*, less specific and perhaps accordingly more flexible, retained its capacity to dis-ambiguate as well as to semantically vitalize the text. A loss for ritual was a gain for meaning. The flexibility of *gemore-nign* may be a product of the Talmud's association with oral tradition. The Bible, on the other hand, remains the core of written law and thus relatively more distant from matters of intonation.

The study of Talmud became increasingly accessible to larger numbers of Jews during the great cultural flowering of Jewish life in Central and Eastern Europe. Along with it came an increasing familiarity with the prestige of *gemore-nign*. In the process, the "chant figures, or analogs of these figures, deprived of their sing-ing voice quality, [were] easily transposed . . . from the reading of the Talmud to oral discussions about it, and thence to ordinary conversation."[58] Gradually, the entire community of Ashkenazic Jewry seemed to adopt talmudic cadence as a feature of speech. Different from the intonational contours of European languages and American English, it became the under and overtone of Yid-dish and through it of the Jewish people of the West.[59]

Basically, the intonational pattern consists of the "rise of the pitch from a low point to a peak, followed by a distinct fall . . ."[60] More precisely, a level intonation is used for an unmarked tran-sition, a partial rise signifies a marked transition and the rise-fall cadence indicates a dramatized transition. In *lernen*, this last sound plays an especially large part since it serves to indicate the remark that is unexpected but nevertheless instructive. It is the cadence of the rhetorical and rather incredulous question which not only appears in the Talmud but which has become closely associated with Yiddish in particular and Jewish inflection in gen-eral.

Ironically, the very cadences which for the traditional Jewish community had been a mark of one's high status as a scholar became a stigma in the era of emancipation and acculturation. The Jew who did not wish to stand out among the other nations had, among other things, to learn to control his intonation. In America, where the rise-fall contour is rarely a part of normal speech, this Jewish inflection was particularly noticeable. Compared to Yiddish and *gemore-nign*, the sound of English seems rather monotonic (reflecting perhaps the regularity of a Protestant heritage rather than the cataclysm of a Jewish one with its many rises and falls). And although it is undoubtedly true, as Pike notes, that "no language uses a pure monotone," to the traditional *lerner* English seemed to approach that.[61]

In Israel much the same occurred. The conscious effort to speak a Hebrew that sounded more like other middle-eastern languages led to a Sephardic pronunciation over the Yiddishist Ashkenazic one. This was the secular Zionist version of a new Jewish tongue, a language devoid of the parochialisms associated with *gemore-nign*.*

Cadence is one of the aspects of a language most resistant to change. Long after the Jews learned new languages and began on the path to acculturation, which their emancipation had seemed to put within their reach, they remained imprisoned within the intonational contours of their past.[62] They carried their sounds into their speech in America and Israel as they had in the various provinces of Europe. In time, however, the vernaculars have begun to work their influence even on talmudic discourse, making it relatively "less sing-song in nature."[63] It became possible to recite and discuss Talmud in a sound that was attuned to the culture of the place in which one found himself: Americans in American English, Britishers in their own form of English, Israelis in modern Hebrew, and so on. In this way, Talmud no longer needed to sound so foreign; it could almost fit aurally into the contemporary world. This is of no small consequence to those who sought modernity and cosmopolitan identities (or at least new civil ones which from the parochial perspective of the ghetto

---

*To be sure, the choice of Hebrew as the language of Israel was by no means stimulated by an effort to cut ties to the tradition. On the contrary, it was a getting back to deeper roots. Nor was the decision favoring the Sephardic morphology purely a matter of avoiding Ashkenazic parochialisms—but this element remained. Over time, the Ashkenazic/Yiddish sound became associated more and more with the world of Orthodoxy and tradition.

Jew was tantamount to cosmopolitanism—being an American was somehow more universal than being a Jew).

To Orthodox Jews, champions of the tradition, Jewishness was, however, not a stigma. Accordingly, for them the singsong sound of *gemore-nign* retained its association with high social status and prestige even in the face of the acculturative pressures in Europe, America, and modern Israel. Long after the most marked inflections of Yiddish had disappeared from the speech of most American Jews and modern Israelis, the Orthodox generally still talked in cadences which resonated traditional *gemore-nign*. Their exposure to Jewish learning, their tradition of *lernen*, and even more important their continued reverence for it served to support a speech contour clearly at odds with the sound of contemporary America, Israel, or anywhere. What for moderns was an intonational prison had for the Orthodox all the comfort of a home. It was "*heimisch*" (homey) to talk this way, to sound so Jewish. Among one's fellow Jews this was the way to talk and sound. Even today those who stress separation from the American or modern Israeli milieux—various hasidic sects, for example—may be recognized by the singsong Yiddish character of their speech. And in the boundaries of the study circle, the most Jewish of enclaves, this same sound frequently surfaces, underscoring the intimacy and sense of fellowship within the group.

When some Orthodox Jews began the cautious move toward modernity and the world outside the Jewish one, they, like their non-Orthodox modernist counterparts, began to change their language. New vocabulary, in morphology, syntax, and cadence became the order of the day. Yet unlike so many Jews who in great measure accepted acculturation as a paramount goal and the contemporary world as the temporal center of the universe and therefore hoped to mute their separate identity as Jews, modern Orthodox people wished at once to become part of the modern civil society while still remaining true and anchored to their past. Rather than viewing tradition and parochialism as anachronisms, these Jews adopted an attitude that could best be described as panchromistic. They wanted to be cosmopolitan and civil parochials who would include past and present, Jewish and civil into a single life space.

In the sphere of language this meant a kind of tacit championing of interlanguage. More to the point here, it meant—among other things—retaining the cadences of *gemore-nign* while speaking the

vocabulary of the contemporary vernacular.[64] In Hebrew nothing
more clearly illustrates this than the sound of *lernen* at a place like
Beit Rachel, where chant occasionally makes its way into the discussions which are carried on in the Sephardic vernacular. In
English, Smotra best exemplifies this for it is here, during the
lernen, that the participants play with their words so that they
end up "speaking English as if it were Yiddish," a lexical, syntactic, and intonational reflection of the interphase between
America and the way of the Talmud. A closer look is in order.
Again, for simplicity's sake, I will use Smotra where the language
is largely English—or rather the Yiddish-interfered-form of it that
I shall call "Yinglish."[65]

The section of text around which the following discussion revolves deals with an incident during which the rabbis of the Talmud upbraid the sage Yokhanan ben Zakkai for having failed to
ask the emperor Vespasian to save Jerusalem but instead to have
requested simply the preservation of the small city of Yavneh and
its scholars. It is, to be sure, a singular episode in Jewish history
for, as I have noted earlier, it symbolizes the decision of Yokhanan
ben Zakkai and his fellow scholars to give up being a Temple cult
in favor of becoming interpreters of sacred literature and laws.
This being an interior matter, of special concern to the Jews, the
Rav, as it were, begins the discussion, which has begun as an
explanation of the talmudic text, by speaking in *gemore-loshn*. He
explains the gist of the Talmud's questions.[66]

        2   2 2 3 2   2   2 2 2 2 2 2 2
Fregt di gemore [the Talmud asks]: And *Reb Yokhanan ben Zakkai*

      2   3   3 4 4 4 4 4 2
hot nisht gevist vegn di zakhn?! [Reb Yokhanan ben Zakkai did
not know about these things?!]

      2 3 4 3   2 2   2   2 2 2   2
"Vehu sovar [and he thought]," *ober* [but] Reb Yokhanan ben

    2 2   3-2   3 2 2 2 3-2 2 4 2   3 2   2   2
Zakkai thought: *"Dilmo kuley hay lo ovid"*; Listen, there are

    4 2 2   2   2   2 4-2   3-2 3-2 2   2   2   2
limits to what you can ask. He felt there are things he can

    2 2 3 2   2   2   2 4-2
get away with and things he can't.

What stands out intonationally in this extract—reverberating as it does the sound of traditional European yeshivas which for generations were associated by many with the authentic voice of Judaism—is the preponderance of rise-fall contours which are normally associated with Yiddish occurring here in the English. While much of the English is spoken in a slightly up-pitched monotone (2) characteristic of American speech, there are notable exceptions:

3-2   3 2   4 2   4-2 3-2 3-2   2 3   2   4 2
thought, listen, limits, ask, felt, there, away with, can't.

These contours are what give the English its particularly Jewish sound, a sound one discovers to predominate in the Yiddish and talmudic quotation which makes up the rest of the utterance.

The rise-fall and the partial rise (to pitch 2) that occurs in the English has the effect of integrating what is in fact a metatextual remark with the text. Thus, beginning with the words, *"vehu sovar,"* the precise meaning of the text is: "And he [Yokhanan ben Zakkai] thought that perhaps he would not have been able to gain so much." The subsequent English remark, beginning with "listen," assumes one to have comprehended the preceding and, instead of translating it, dramatically elaborates it using language that speaks to the contemporary American. Yet while the language is distinctly American, the intonation is unmistakably talmudic, so much so that the English *sounds* as if it is simply a continuation of the text, a part of it.

When one speaks English in a cadence that is Jewish in its genesis, one thereby at least partially leaves the domain of the English-speaking world. The same might be said of the modern Hebrew speaker who suddenly reverts not only to *gemore-nign* but also to Ashkenazic chant. He too abandons the world of his modern secular civil tongue, the *lingua franca* of a modern secular state, and orally takes on the parochial sound of the traditional yeshiva. Such departures cannot be assumed to be accidental. Rather one must suppose that the speaker has been swept up by the world of the Talmud and its special sound, and this involvement is reflected in his word play. At times the reflection is lexical, at times syntactic or morphological, and at times intonational. Whatever the sign, the fact remains that language use cannot help but demonstrate social and cultural identification.

Surely, one might ask, it is equally conceivable that the sound of English would dominate the sound of Talmud or that, likewise, study of sacred texts would be spoken in Israel in ways no different from any other conversation. That is precisely what happens among those who study in a primarily nonparochial atmosphere. Thus, for example, at the Jerusalem Social Club, a civic institution open to the public and sponsoring a variety of social activities including dances, lectures, yoga as well as Talmud study, the class given by Rav Auerbach was carried on in a language and sound that hardly distinguished it from general Hebrew conversation. Similarly, in the university—that paradigm of nonparochialism and universality—where Talmud may be studied, like any other subject in the curriculum, by Jews and non-Jews alike, the rise-fall *gemore-nign* so noticeable in the extract cited here is absent. Instead, one hears a Talmud that sounds like English. In sound this latter type of review is more "study" than it is *"lernen"*; that is, it is so removed from its parochial Jewish incarnation that it no longer makes sense to even refer to it with a Jewish name. Indeed, a person who has learned (rather than *lerned*) his Talmud in the university setting rather than in the parochial *besmedresh* reveals his background and the social location it implies both by the intonation and language choice of his speech. The former sound like American English speakers (or modern Israelis) while those who have done their *lernen* in parochial domains and remain there in spirit sing the words.*

By choosing to sing both English (or whatever the local vernacular is) and text, the speaker implicitly identifies himself with the generations of those who have religiously cantillated *gemore*, for whom it has been a sacred duty. The signal, although neither formal nor explicit, is never misunderstood.

Finally, intonation has a semantic expressiveness. That is, insofar as the speakers and listeners are a part of the Jewish world from which the cadences and stresses that make up the intonational contour of *lernen* come, they can somehow understand the meaning of what has been said even if they do not altogether comprehend the words. It is sometimes the case that *lerners*, upon

*Dr. Shlomo Noble, the noted linguist, tells the story of his first day of Talmud study under the late Professor Harry Wolfson at Harvard. Noble had just asked a question using *gemore-nign*. Using the same cadences, Wolfson replied, "Mr. Noble, this is not a yeshiva; this is Harvard University." Noble learned where he was and never again made the same intonational mistake.

hearing the Rav or fellow student recite a piece of the text, find that they are not able to translate word for word what they have heard. An expressive intonation, however, allows them to know immediately if what has been recited is question or answer, a new idea or a reiteration of an already stated one, sarcasm or assertion, and so on. This is simply because the intonation is more than simply a lamination attached to the meaning of the words; it may instead carry the meaning. To be able to "read" the cadences, something only the insider, the one attuned to the sounds of *gemore-nign*, can do, is crucial for those who would remain a part of the study circle and the group it encloses.

Until now, I have focused primarily on the psychological disposition, sociocultural identification, and symbolic meaning of word choice and sound. These matters are a large part of the subtext, the deep structure, of *lernen* word play—particularly among the modern Orthodox Jews who make up the largest single population represented in the circles I have observed. Long after most Jews abandoned the characteristic patois that was neither quite the vernacular nor wholly Yiddish, at least within the context of the Talmud study circle (in microcosm, the parochial community), modern Orthodox Jews—those living with determination on the crossroads of several worlds—still retain remnants of it. The reasons are only in part technical and linguistic; they are as well social and psychological. Talmud study, as has already been suggested, is more than simply an intellectual or ritual exercise. It is a celebration of culture and communion during which students become "inhabitants of a partly shared social world, established and continuously modified by their acts of communication."[67]

When the others with whom one is talking share the same ethos and state of mind, when their preoccupations are similar, the interplay of words cannot help but intensify that preoccupation and at times make it manifest. For modern Orthodox Jews this means that the dualism of their existence displays itself in their conversation among themselves. It is there whenever these Jews are together in a homey (*heimisch*) intimacy, seen mostly boldly in the *lernen* fellowship. As such it serves not only to make these people as a distinct group, as all argots do, but also provides a linguistic basis for their solidarity. As with all other ludic behavior, togetherness at once makes word play possible while the play in turn solidifies the sense of unity.

In the outside world, the civil society (be it American, Israeli, or other) where parochial ties must be gainsaid, this argot may disappear—except among those who are aggressively contra-acculturative, the Hasidim, for example. But in the intimate Jewish environment—the home, study circle, or synagogue—the special sound and language reappear and resound.

THE BEST WORDS IN THE BEST ORDER

In addition to the particular social and psychological reasons seeming to underlie much of the talk I have observed and thus far described, there seems to be something else. Perhaps it might be called the "poetry of *lernen*." As in poetry, the words associated with *lernen* have the power to transform the speakers and listeners, to sweep them away from their normal way of speaking into another realm of syntax, semantics, and sound. The apparent ease with which many players inject the words and cadences of the Talmud into their speech, and vice versa, moreover suggests a willingness to be thus transformed. Repeating the lines of the text in recitations and quotations, cues and echoes, questions and answers, glosses and extended remarks, pouring their voices into the rising and falling cadences associated with the traditional People of the Book, the *lerners* often give themselves up to the charm of the special language of *lernen* as one might give himself over to poetry, subject to the truly magical power of words.

Speaking a special blend of the vernacular text, Yiddish and Hebrew, convoluting syntax, switching from *gemore-nign* to normal speech, the members of the study circle create a unique aural and oral atmosphere associated with *lernen*. Those who speak in this way belong to the activity; those who do not cannot share in the spoken magic of the occasion. And, without a sense of this magic, they lose a special relation to the ages of sages who expressed themselves thus and to all those who continue that special oral tradition. This is perhaps what Malinowski meant when he asserted "the power of words in establishing human relation," and what Merleau-Ponty hinted at when he described "language as the reverberation of my relations . . . with others."[68]

When a person enters the circle and opens his mouth his fellows know immediately from whence he cometh and whither he goeth, with whom he has studied and with whom he would study and identify himself. His cadences, syntax, and vocabulary (and, in

Israel, his accent) mark him as surely as the content of words or
the nature of his questions. The speaker who, for example, ex-
amines the talmudic argument defining the proper testimony for
bearing witness to the signing of a bill of divorcement and remarks
in his best American English: "If I can infer from the language
used here that the Talmud means to imply that someone witnessed the signing and sealing of the bill, I will have found a
perfect analogy with an earlier statement of this principle"—such
a speaker has chosen to express himself in standard prose and
in the sounds of his civil existence. In this he may have—to borrow
from Coleridge—put his words in their best order.

This speaker, however, has not expressed in the most "poetic"
language of *lernen*. To do so he should have chanted something
like: "If from here I *lern* out the *loshn* of '*befonay nekhtav u befonay
nekhtam,*' I will have a perfect *hekesh* with what we *opshlogged*
before." This curious sounding locution—curious only to the *non-
lerner*, of course—represents the argot so at home in the study
circle. Here it expresses the *best* words in the best order. Of those
who speak this way, one might say—much as one could describe
the speech of ecstatics—"They fall under the influence of the
emotional value of the sounds, rhythms, melodies, rhymes, al-
literations," indeed, the Jewish character of their word play.[69]

CONCLUSION

There is no simple way to close this chapter on the sound and
language of *lernen*, no simple way to articulate and summarize
the experience herein described and analyzed. To be sensed it
must be heard and watched; it must be enacted. When observer
becomes participant and shares the transforming experience of
the word play with others, an insight is gained that cannot be
fully described or discussed here. The experience of the sound
and play is indeed worth thousands of words of description. In
that experience, created through linguistic manipulation and the
social and psychological tendencies of the speaker, language and
lernen meet. Afterward, the words and sounds with which the
lerners have played, through which they have acted out their
talmudic review, remain as echoes in one's mind.

6
FELLOWSHIP

*If it has any value at all the fellowship must be regarded as a tentative
. . . step towards meaningful and creative use of that interim between
birth and death that each man knows as life.*

JACOB NEUSNER in *Fellowship in Judaism*

Throughout many of the preceding pages, the idea of fellowship has been suggested as inherent to the process of *lernen*. As Jacob Neusner, in the preface to his guide for those who would study on their own, puts it: "You do not 'read' the Talmud, you 'learn' it, preferably with a *haver* or fellow student, and always with a rabbi."[1] Rabbi and *haver* were always considered similar: "Provide yourself with a *rav,* acquire for yourself a *haver,*" as Yehoshua ben Perakhya puts it in the Talmud (*Avot* 1:6). The *haverim* (fellows) with whom one joins in the recitation, translation, explanation, and discussion of the text and its commentaries form the basis of the *havura* or *khavruse*[2] as it is commonly known, the fellowship.

In the discussion of the various dramatic aspects of *lernen*, I have tried to demonstrate that it is the group that carries out and appreciates the cultural performances. Indeed the entire play of *lernen* is only meaningful within the *khavruse*. Outside of it, the drama and importance of the activity disappears. What is engaging and exciting within the group is to the outsider trivial and arcane. Who, besides an insider, cares if the Rav cannot explain a piece of Talmud or if commentators and student interpretations appear to be in conflict with one another?

Among the fellows, however, such breaches are social crises during which intellectual or moral leadership falters and social order is disturbed—but *only* among the fellows is this the case.

Precisely because fellowship is so much a part of *lernen*, therefore, it deserves more than passing reference. Instead, the social threads of the study circle must be examined directly. Only thus can these People of the Book and the world of the Talmud be fully apprehended.

While the *khavruse* may begin as a fellowship, it often evolves into more. At various times and under certain circumstances, it is, also, a community, a circle of friends tied together by sentiment and morals, and a brotherhood or quasi-kin group. And sometimes it is all of these in combination. To understand what is meant by this, certain relatively simple definitions are in order.

Borrowing again from Neusner, one may sharpen the concept of fellowship "as a relationship among individuals characterized by both reciprocity and profound concern for one another and dedication to a goal held in common."[3] Synergistically, that common goal in turn necessarily generates increased reciprocal sentiments and stronger mutual concern. Simply put, people get together ostensibly to *lern*, but their common activity makes them care more about getting together and about one another than they did at the beginning. Nevertheless, friendship is not guaranteed within a fellowship for the latter, "unlike a clique, does not depend on congeniality, nor does it regard love as sufficient."[4] In sum, "fellowship engages isolated individuals in common enterprise, thereby creating between them common bonds, providing for them common experience, uniting them for reasons [sometimes] quite external to the structure of their own personalities."[5]

To be sure, as Emile Durkheim long ago noted, the recurrence of union has its own dynamics: "It is impossible for men to live together, associating in industry, without acquiring a sentiment of the whole, preoccupying themselves with its interest, and taking account of it in their conduct."[6] The spontaneous element of this sentiment, which Victor Turner has labeled "communitas" and Herman Schmalenbach calls "communion," is the pure expression of camaraderie and sociability. These feelings, however, tend to be fleeting and require "fairly intense mutual involvement and emotional ecstasy."[7] To foster these while stabilizing the spontaneous outbursts of collective enthusiasm, the fellows encourage an ethos of loyalty. Loyalty in turn leads to a sense of "community," a taken-for-granted "order of social coherence" that comes to feel for insiders like "an organic and natural coalescence."[8] Thus does "communitas" or "communion" become "converted into institutionalized structure, or become routinized, often as ritual."[9]

The community offers the framework in which feelings of closeness can be expected to be expressed. But even in their absence, the community insures group ties. Even when people do not feel a particular closeness to particular others, they feel an attachment or loyalty to the whole, the community.

"It's not always so important what we *lern*," as one of the men of Mekadshey Torah put it once, "but it's important that we get together regularly, share company, and feel we belong together."

This is no small matter to many of the insiders. Those who participate in the life of the study circle feel as if they have no choice but to be close to one another, as if they are one family. Not only do they maintain a fellowship, friendship, loyalty, sense of community and intimacy, in the final analysis they also feel united by a common life force.

In all of this there is a Jewish element emerging from the assumption that all these ties begin from within the Jewish cosmos. Whatever else ultimately serves to tie the people together as a result of their common actions, they are ab initio bonded through their sense of Jewishness and what they believe it demands of them as Jews. That collective tie is acted out when "a small number of people come together regularly for specific, Jewish purposes."[10] In the present case,[11] these purposes are the study of Torah in general and oral law or Talmud in particular. And the participant, the *haver*, from the beginning connoted one "who is an associate in a common sacred task," tied to his fellows by some sort of "charm, knot or spell."[12]

ORIGINS OF JEWISH FELLOWSHIP

What began among the ancient Pharisees of Jerusalem as a kind of religious commune (called a *havura*), fundamentally organized for maintaining among the select a strict observance of the laws of ritual cleanliness and Temple offerings, by the first century evolved into a group organized around Jewish study. This common interest in study yielded more than an educated elite. "It created a community, bringing student and teacher together; sitting, travelling by the way, the sages speculated together on momentous matters," and in the process created a bulwark against the potential anomie of exile, cultural change, and religious disintegration.[13] That bulwark, supported by common religious commitment, was the scholars' social commitment to one another. According to the Talmud, a Jew owed greater respect and loyalty to his Rav than to his parents. Indeed, as one reads the Talmud, which recalls this world of scholars, one is struck by the sense of kinship that disciples felt and expressed toward one another and their teachers: "Give me a *khavruse* or give me death," as one of the sages of the Talmud put it (B.T. *Taanit* 23a).* Even disputants on matters of law usually demonstrated an ultimate sense of com-

*For the American reader these words cannot help but recall Patrick Henry's famous challenge during his speech before the Virginia Convention of 1775 when he asserted, "Give me liberty or give me death." If these two statements are taken to be symbolic or at least indicative of a cultural ethos, then one might conclude that, where Americans consider liberty to be more important than an individual's life, traditional Jews, for whom life is with people, regard fellowship to be as paramount.

munion with one another, a willingness to live together in spite of differences of legal interpretation.*

The members of these ancient fellowships transformed themselves within the boundaries of the *khavruse*. Not only did they concern themselves primarily with matters of Torah (or, more precisely, they saw all of life through the prism of Torah so that even mundane experience became sanctified and mythologized so as to seem to impart an understanding of Scripture), they also seemed to sense that only in that domain did their true selves reside. Thus, even the names by which they sought to be known in their time and for posterity were those acquired through their relationship to the fellowship and the academy in which it met. Not only was the leader known as "Rabban," but others took on special names as well.[14] From the beginnings of the recorded history of these fellowships, new identities and their associated cosmologies became an appendage of belonging. Rabban Yokhanan ben Zakkai, among the first to reorient Jewish fellowship from a total concern with ritual cleanliness and Temple sacrifice to one focused around study, demanded that his students take on new names (*Avot d'Rabbi Natan* 14).

Although not completely documented, the beginnings of the *havura* as a concept in Jewish life antedates the formation of study fellowships. The earliest *havurot* were apparently organized as burial societies and were perhaps modeled after similar societies in Greco-Roman civilization.[15] Syncretistically, the Jewish fellowships took on these burial functions. Each group laid its own to rest.[16] In the first century, following the model set by the aforementioned Yokhanan ben Zakkai, these cults evolved into study groups as well. What may have begun as a secondary function—scholarship perhaps being a prerequisite for being a member of the holy burial society or a Pharisee—became in time a primary one.

The first documented reports of joint study are from the Jerusalem of the fifteenth century. However, as Shochet points out, "It is plausible that this practice was in existence there beforehand."[17] Jews from Italy subsequently reported on this practice of communal study that they had seen during their travels to

---

*The same sort of tolerance among those who engage in legal disputes in the present day is no longer a given in Jewish life. To be sure, the Talmud is telegraphic, and the animosities and grudges engendered in disputes of the past may simply have been lost in the transcription and redaction of the Talmud.

Jerusalem and Damascus. The fact that they found it necessary to add this point in their letters may suggest that the practice had not yet become established in Italy. Nevertheless, by the first half of the sixteenth century the example of Jerusalem was being taken up in Italy. Around the same time, one discovers it to be a feature of Jewish life in places as diverse as Yemen, Spain, and Central Europe. By the last half of the sixteenth century the notion of group study seems fairly well established in Europe. Shochet links this to the famous European rabbi and leader, the Maharal of Prague who, he claims, assembled fellowships "which daily concerned themselves with a chapter from the Mishna without fail," an innovation that "spread to other communities both near and far."[18]

The special advantages of group study were several. First, and most obviously, the presence of others would assist the individual student in making his way through the complexities of Jewish texts: "I have learned much from my teachers but even more from my *haverim*," as the talmudist Rabbi Hanina puts it (B.T. *Taanit* 7a). Second, there was an institutional quality about anchoring study in a group experience, something which guaranteed the steadfastness of learning: "Even if one person was missing, the process of study would nevertheless be constant and permanent."[19] The fellowship linked men to one another and to the tradition of Torah study.

From early on there were varying curricula among the various groups. For the most scholarly and erudite, the entire Talmud served as the focus of study. For the less scholarly, only the Mishna, that portion of the book which lacked the complex debates and legalistic formulations of the *gemore*, was the subject of review. Below those in the Mishna fellowship were the men who limited themselves to reviewing "En Yaakov," a compendium of legends and tales culled from the Talmud but lacking the difficult legal disputations, the *halakhic* sections. Next came those who would review the Bible, rereading verses of the weekly portion of Scripture that was read in the synagogue on the Sabbath. Finally, those with least education who were nevertheless dedicated to the idea of group study organized fellowships for the recitation of Psalms. These fellows were not so much analyzers of poetry as they were men who sought to extend their prayers and enhance their spirit through the chanted, collective repetition of holy verse.

What all the groups had in common was the sense of fellowship.
That is, they shared bonds that had as their manifest raison d'être
some form of *lernen* but which in fact went far beyond this cir-
cumscribed task.

For a time, these fellowships—particularly the ones dedicated
to Talmud study, the *"Khevre SHaS"*[20]—limited themselves to
those who came from an elite scholarly stratum. Indeed, there
were rabbis, like the famous eighteenth-century Ashkenazic
leader Yaakov Emden, who opposed anyone outside the rabbin-
ical ranks joining a Talmud study circle. He argued that were
these groups to become open to all, the humble and unschooled
would be joining the elite ranks of talmudists and thereby free
themselves from the authority of scholars: "For he [the un-
schooled], will say, am I not myself a *talmid khakham* [scholar] and
concern myself with Torah and join a class in *gemore* each day?"[21]

Ultimately, however, the fellowships became open "not only
to the learned by profession, but also to men of the humblest
callings in life . . . Jews who, during the day, were hard pressed
in their pursuit of a living, and yet in the evening went to the
"Beth Hamidrash" [House of study] where they spent a happy
hour that helped them to forget the misery of their material lot."[22]
There were efforts to divide the humble and the educated into
different sorts of fellowships of learning, as already noted. The
chaos of pogrom and persecution, poverty and social ferment that
affected European Jewry, however, finally disturbed these status
balances. More and more, the number of those dedicated to *lernen*
dwindled and fellowships opened themselves to any and all who
were interested. Finally, even the highly elite *Khevre SHaS* became
open to the interested who might nonetheless be unschooled and
intellectually unprepared for the complex hermeneutics of tal-
mudism.

One might argue that the upheavals of the European holocaust
and the mass expulsion of Jews from Arab lands following the
birth of the modern state of Israel were the final dislocations that
opened the circles of study to all Jews. Exclusion by non-Jewish
society led to tolerance in the supremely Jewish one of the *khavruse*.

By the time this last change occurred, the study of Talmud had
already become divided into those who pursued it vocationally
in the yeshivas, as a way of life, and, on the other hand, those
who pursued Jewish study during leisure hours, "to lift oneself

out of the everyday world and to forget for a moment the lowliness and hardship of normal life."[23]

For the latter, *lernen* was escape to a world concerned with matters distant from the hard realities of diaspora existence. The fellowship, moreover, represented a defense against the wandering and exclusion that the Jew increasingly had forced upon him. Indeed, wherever the Jews went, they would seem to organize learning fellowships. There are reports, records of material studied, rulebooks of such *khavruses* from all over the European continent, the Netherlands Antilles, Yemen, Britain, Ireland, the Americas, and wherever else a significant Jewish population existed.[24]

The fellowship often became more important than the study which served as its initial stimulus. As an association, it sometimes collected dues "in money, in kind, or in personal service, and gave in return the associative, ceremonial and intercessional benefits of which the individual Jew stood in need, mentally and emotionally."[25]

As already noted, a paramount activity of the early fellowships was the burial of the dead among its members. But there were other rules and expectations that served to reinforce fellowship by demanding members share several common attributes. That they would be men was taken for granted. (Women, excluded from Torah study generally and talmudic review in particular, could enjoy none of its fellowship.)[26] In addition, all the men had to be Sabbath observers, that is, Orthodox in their Judaism. Most circles aimed at reviewing at least one page daily. Accordingly, regular attendance by everyone was required. No particular families or individuals were expected to take over exclusive leadership of the group, either by always having the class meet in their houses or by always leading the recitation. The group would attend certain community and culturally significant events together. In Belfast, for example, the fellowship was expected to spend the vigil night of Shevuot, the holy day on which the Jewish people celebrate their receipt of the Torah, in joint study. In some places—Zhagory, Russia, for example—the group was expected to worship together regularly. In Grodno, elaborate organized conversations were held before and after formal study sessions— ostensibly to keep them from distracting the formal study. Yet they also reinforced feelings of fellowship. In Kovno similar gettogethers took place. And in all groups, the death of a member or someone in his family meant that the others in his *khavruse* would join in the mourning and help complete the quorum (*minyan*) to enable the survivors to recite the mandatory "*Kaddish*" memorial. Of these men, one could surely say, in the words traditionally recited and reaffirmed in the synagogue on the occasion of blessing each new month: "*haverim kol Yisrael*" (all the people of Israel are knit in fellowship).

THE CONTEMPORARY OBSERVANCE OF FELLOWSHIP

Against this history of fellowship, it is not surprising to find evidence of such bonding, communion, and sense of friendship and kinship among the contemporary study circles I observed and joined. Of the six groups I have considered in these pages—Smotra, Kahal Reyim, Beit Rachel, Mekadshey Torah, the group at Rav Rotenbush's house, and those meeting in the Jerusalem Social Club—all but the last displayed a closeness that went beyond their common interest in regularly reviewing Talmud. Later I will offer an explanation for the failure of fellowship at the Social Club; for now, let us examine more closely the social character of each of the other circles.

The bonds tying those in Smotra were interwoven with the general condition of its members living in an Orthodox community on the suburban "frontier." That is, the fellows of this circle also were co-worshippers who lived in the same geographic area, within walking distance of one another and their synagogue. They sent their children to the same school, shared many of the same socioeconomic characteristics, educational background, and world view. The study circle was thus not so much at the source of their fellowship as an intensified expression of it. Those who attended regularly were drawn to the circle as much by the drama of what went on there and the religious imperatives (of which more in the next chapter) that support *lernen* as they were by a special sense of fellowship with one another. And yet, beyond the ties that the men shared with others in the Smotra Orthodox community, they seemed to share something special with one another. Toward the Rav they felt or at least displayed a special closeness, and whenever there was a Smotra Jewish community event the members of the circle would gravitate toward one another, forming a small knot in the larger fabric of Smotra society. Reflecting on his experiences in this study circle, Rav Gafny once described it as "some of the best evenings I've experienced in Smotra, trying to *lern a blatt* [page] *gemore*, but more sensing a camaraderie with some bright, good friends."

When one man left the group to move to Israel, he wrote back to the others through the Rav, and his letters were read aloud before or after meetings. During these liminal periods, the beginnings and endings of class, there always seemed some business that members of the circle had to transact with one another. That is, they found additional ties to one another and used the occasion of their meeting to reaffirm and strengthen those ties. One man, for example, inscribed the *ketuba* (wedding document) of another's daughter. Another few began a common basketball game for a time. Still others would ride together to and from class meetings, spending almost as much time in preliminary and postliminal conversation as they did in study.[27]

Unlike the men in Smotra who have a variety of communal links beyond their *khavruse* that tie them to one another, the members of the Jerusalem study circles began and continued, in many instances, to establish mutual bonds of fellowship as a direct consequence of their joint *lernen*. As already noted, the dense and varied Jewish character of this holy city made synagogue and neighborhood less significant factors in fellowship and allowed study circles to emerge with a greater social and cultural importance. In this, Jerusalem is closer to the traditional Jewish milieux in which *havurot* first developed. In Europe where there were a great many Jews crowded together in a small area, the *lernen* fellowship served as a kind of community within a community, a kind of kin or primary group in which one shared the most intimate of ties. The same was true in the Jerusalem I observed.

More and more as I reflected on the special feelings of genuine belonging that the study circle engendered in me and in other insiders, I came to realize that what drew me out in the evenings when I was tired, when the rain would make me want to stay home, when my wife and children sought my company, or when I simply wanted to relax in front of the television or with a good book was the sense of fellowship and community which I shared with others in my circles. Like the bowler who goes bowling often more to be with the gang than to knock down pins, the card player who joins three others for a rubber of bridge not so much to play cards as to be with friends, or the person who goes to the pub to throw darts and drink beer but is really there to be with the boys, I was drawn out of the house to *lern* often because I knew I was expected and when I failed to come, or another insider was missing, that absence was felt.[28]

For a time, when I was ill with the flu and missed four weeks of class, I found my return marked with special signs of my belonging. The men at Beit Rachel, after greeting me like the prodigal son, blessed me with the benediction of renewal (*shehekhiyanu*). Indeed, for a while they debated whether or not they were required to recite the benediction which celebrates the resurrection of the dead. "No," explained the Rav, that was only when someone returned after having been gone for a year or more.

At Mekadshey Torah, the Rav publicly announced my return at the beginning of class and everyone stopped the action to ask after my welfare—although to be sure they had kept up on the progress of my flu throughout the weeks I was away by means of calls and gossip. Similar greetings were tendered at Rav Rotenbush's house with the additional apology from the Rav for not having visited me while I lay in my sickbed. And at Kahal Reyim I was greeted with the announcement that while I was away the group had celebrated a *siyum*, the completion of a tractate of the Talmud. They had, I was informed, waited several days before completing the volume in the hope that I would return and could share the event with them. Telling me this of course served to inform me of the extent to which I had penetrated the circle and was missed.[29]

By no means was my experience unique. When other members of the group were away, no one failed to notice their absence sometime during the evening. Visits to a sick member were common and expected, as were celebrations of his return. The circle was not to be lightly broken.

Deaths were responded to in the same way. During the course of my involvement in these groups, one of the members of the Beit Rachel circle, Schneider, died. He had been sick for about five months beforehand, during which time the members of the circle individually visited him. For those five months, our classes would often be preceded by informal exchanges about Schneider's condition. Surrounded by mystery, his disease seemed to be consuming him, and it worried us. We talked about his spirits, the regimen he had been pursuing to get better, and about what we could as a group do for him. One man proposed that we meet in Schneider's house for a *shiur* on occasion.

"He would like that, I think," said another who was among his closest friends in the circle.

"No, perhaps it would tire him out too much," the Rav supposed. We accepted that judgment.

So it went, week after week, until the man died. His funeral was of course attended by members of the group; and the seven-day period of mourning celebrated by his family saw members of the *khavruse* at the prayer services each day. Even afterward he was talked about, his presence recalled and his seat left vacant. Neither sickness nor death easily breaks the circle; the group will be the final judge of who has joined and who has left.

Just as one sensed the bonds of fellowship when insiders left, either by sickness or death, so too one could sense them when newcomers joined. In all study circles, the stranger is soon asked to comment on matters before the group. Often this responsibility is left in the Rav's hands since it is he who can most easily elicit answers in response to questions he puts to the newcomer. These are not meant to embarrass the neophyte and often take the rather open form of: "Are you following the argument?" or "Did you understand that point?"

Often the first-time visitor to a circle remains rather passive, tentative in his commitment to the group and its activities. Occasionally, if he comes early or stays late after the formal end of the *lernen*, others may ask him where he is from, what he does, and other general questions that both indicate that they have been aware of his presence and wish to socially locate him. Of course, as he takes an active part in the class, when he speaks, many of these questions—which normally begin after the second visit for by then the stranger has demonstrated more than an incidental interest in the goings-on—become moot for, as I have already pointed out, the way one plays with words, interacts, and generally performs during a *shiur* is often sufficiently revealing and serves to answer initial questions others might have about him. In such cases, direct answers to subsequent inquiries are often responded with "I thought so," indicating perhaps that the inquiries were being made more out of a sense of social etiquette, as evidence of interest in and awareness of the newcomer's presence, than out of genuine curiosity.

What is crucial to note here is the fact that *lernen* fellowships abhor a social and communal vacuum. To study with another you must know something about him and have some means of forming a moral and social bond with him. Strangers become new-comers; the missing are not easily let go, and those present must always be engaged.

"Where were you?" someone at Mekadshey Torah asked Beryl, a member of short standing who had already missed a class.

"You know that we want you to come *lern* with us; we are all one family," added another.

"Any friend of Eliezer's [a member of long standing] is to be welcomed here," noted a third.

ALLEGIANCE AND LOYALTY

Implicit in these last few observations about the *khavruse* is its capacity to elicit allegiance from its members both to one another as individuals and to the group as a whole. Their studying together is simply a vehicle for this, or more precisely a metaphor for it. As the men must be loyal to the Torah, and as they hold allegiance to its ways, its laws and world view, so too they come to feel close to one another. They study together and through it learn to be together. This allegiance and loyalty revealed itself in a variety of comments, in reactions to the missing and the gone—as just noted—and in the regularity of men's attendance at the *shiur*. There are, however, two instances, beyond those already cited, when I became acutely aware of this attachment.

For anyone who has regularly attended study circles like those I have been describing, it is not unusual to find one or two members who nod off in sleep during the course of the class. In some groups the same person will fall asleep each time; in others, the people may vary. One might interpret such sleepiness as a simple consequence of the convergence between the natural fatigue that people feel in the evenings and after-hours of a workday, as they digest their suppers perhaps or cool down from the pace of their labors, and the boredom that may set in during the review of a difficult and sometimes inpenetrable text like the Talmud. Add to that the sing-song of *gemore-nign* and the intimate security or homeyness of the *khavruse* and sleep seems rather more expectable than attentiveness.

Nevertheless most participants do not fall asleep, for reasons of drama perhaps or out of loyalty to their fellows and teacher. It may even be that they stay awake out of a belief that God is watching and will not countenance anything less than devoted attention to his sacred and holy books. To be sure, some stay awake because they are busy reciting and talking, and others are engaged actively in the mental acrobatics of talmudic logic. Still, there are those who sleep, sleep, sleep.

So if they sleep, why do they bother to come at all? One reason, as I will suggest in the next chapter, is out of a sense of religious obligation and loyalty to the dictum that demands a steadfast effort to study or at least be among those who study Torah. But others surely come out of a loyalty and allegiance to the group. Lest one doubt this, one need simply watch the response of the others to the absence of the "sleepers." Reb Nehemia, a regular sleeper in the Beit Rachel circle, had missed a few classes. When he returned, he was greeted with all of the warmth and attention that other less somnolent members received. To be sure, his snoring during class often required extraordinary efforts at disattention from his fellows. Occasionally, some sitting near him would nudge him softly to stop the snore. Nehemia would awaken, place his finger on the appropriate spot in the text, perhaps ask a question or echo a remark, and then inevitably his head would begin to nod, his jaw become slack, and his eyelids close.

Like him there were others: Richie in Smotra, who would come and doze; Reb Zanvil in Kahal Reyim who, tightly wedged between me and another student sitting on our bench, would rest his eyes in such a way that one was never sure whether or not he was reading the page or dreaming. All of these men, however, came because the group expected them and because, along with their other reasons for attending, this was important to them.

If loyalty and allegiance are simply implied in the regular attendance of those who dozed their way through class, they were made explicit in the following incident that took place at Mekadshey Torah. As a functionary in the Israeli Ministry of Religion and a parish rabbi assigned to his district through the office of the Jerusalem chief rabbinate, Rav Rotenbush was in the course of his duties often required to attend civic gatherings where he would be called upon to offer invocations, benedictions, or capsulized classes in Torah. Sometimes he was asked simply to honor an occasion with his presence. With his reputation as a scholar and his amiable personality, his stately bearing, neat frock coat, homburg and dashing red beard, Rav Rotenbush looked every bit the "Rav," one who—according to the whispered evaluation of many—was destined for an even higher position in the Israeli rabbinate.

Assigned the responsibility of serving the religious needs of his district, he was busy much of the day leading Talmud classes in various synagogues or study halls. Indeed, so much did Rav Rotenbush appear to be consumed by his vocation that one might not always be certain whether or not his participation in a study circle was stimulated by professional, civic, religious, or personal motives.

For the group which met weekly in his house, among whom were included two of his brothers-in-law, a neighbor, and friends, this was not really in doubt. The ambience of the setting, the informality of the Rav—he took off his jacket, loosened his tie, and joked liberally with all of us—the occasional involvement by other members of his family all served to heighten the sense of avuncularity which permeated the fellowship. This left little doubt that here the Rav was fully attached and committed to the circle, his allegiance beyond question.

The case of Mekadshey Torah was not as clear. A small synagogue in his district, this place was within his "circuit," and he would visit on a Sabbath morning at least once a month or come when some member asked him to honor a special occasion. Thus, it might appear that his involvement in that study circle was likewise a commitment engendered by his professional obligations and not one of personal loyalties. If so, there would be a formal sort of fellowship that tied him to the others, but no genuine communion or sense of community.

To be sure, the group here was relatively small—twenty men on a full night, but sometimes as few as thirteen on others. As such, one might guess that only a sense of communion propelled him toward them for they were not large enough to merit official concern by the chief rabbinate. This is, however, no evidence since study circles are almost always small by nature, and the expectation is that the district rabbi will serve all groups which call upon his services—regardless of size.

Yet if there were any doubts about the Rav's commitment and attachment to the circle these were dispelled one night. Called away to a meeting with the mayor and various dignitaries of the state, the Rav found himself with official duties scheduled on the same night as his class at Mekadshey Torah. He had, however, sent word to the group that he would nonetheless appear in class.

The men assembled at their regular hour of eight-fifteen in the evening and waited. In deference to the Rav, no one began the actual study, and the period of waiting was extended easily with conversation and sociability. This was a time for the men to exercise the ties they felt toward one another. They reviewed events of their personal lives, talked about matters of joint concern (politics, economics, and religion), and generally settled in as they always did before class to a comfortable relationship with one another. Having thus warmed up[30] to one another and the idea of common activity, they watched the minutes tick away from the hour or so they normally devoted to study. No one, however, left. All felt a loyalty to one another, to the occasion, and to the Rav whose arrival had been assured. And the Rav returned that trust.

Rushing in breathlessly about thirty-five minutes late, he sat down and commented: "Gentlemen, I was called, as you all know, to a meeting with the mayor and some government officials. It was a big affair, many important people. But I knew you would be waiting for me, and I was waiting to come to you. So I warned the mayor that I could stay for only a short time because I had another obligation which could not be unfulfilled. So when I had said my few words, I slipped off the stage and, with a driver waiting for me, I rushed over to you.

"You know, my friends, that this class is very important to me. Here you are, after a long workday, and yet you come to study Torah purely out of love. It is a marvelous thing and must be requited. So I have made a promise to myself that I shall always try to be with you where I feel I truly belong. There may be other more august gatherings that I am forced to attend; and there are other classes that I am teaching, but this one is one I look forward to especially. It is an obligation I feel personally and an occasion that I try—as you all know—never to miss."

To be sure, in this speech Rav Rotenbush had perhaps been a bit overdramatic. Still, as he spoke, one could sense that the men were disposed to believe him; and, whether or not he was simply managing an impression of closeness to them, he had articulated a feeling that all wanted to believe in, including the speaker himself. There would be other like occasions when the Rav or someone else would echo these sentiments of communion and loyalty, but never, after this, was the allegiance of the members to one another and the fellowship ever in the slightest question.

TIE-SIGNS

In his essays on relations in public, Erving Goffman[31] defines a phenomenon he calls the "tie-sign." He explains: that "when those with an anchored relation come into unobstructed range for effecting social contact, the fact that theirs is not an anonymous relation is made evident. . . . All such evidence about relationships, that is, about ties between persons, whether involving objects, acts, expressions, and only excluding the literal aspects of explicit documentary statements, I shall call 'tie-signs.' "

During *lernen*, members of the fellowship express a variety of tie-signs. Indeed, every circle had a special set of these. They not only demonstrate evidence of ties of fellowship but act to reaffirm them as well.

I have already explained that the opening, warm-up periods were filled with this sort of expression. No group—except the one at the Jerusalem Social Club—sat in silence before the formal study began. Rather the men exchanged news, gossip, ideas, and in general created an atmosphere of community and closeness. Indeed, one might even go so far as to say that, for some of the participants, the actual period of study was simply a pretext for the getting together before and after class. They came out of their homes not expressly to review the Talmud—although that was the source of legitimacy for their assembly. They came rather to be with their friends.

Even during the actual study, however, the men had ways to display tie-signs to one another. At Kahal Reyim this consisted of a stylized and extended handing around of snuff (what the men called "*shmek tabak*") during the early moments of recitation. Only after my repeated appearances had demonstrated my allegiance to the circle did I begin to be offered my daily pinch. Reb Shmerl, who usually provided the snuff, handed the tin first to the Rav and then it was passed around from man to man. The sweet aroma filled our nostrils; and as each man experienced this sensation in common with his fellows, one got a sense that they became ready to *lern* together in fellowship. If Shmerl was missing, Reb Borukh would proffer his own snuff and begin this interpersonal ritual of tie-signing. And if both were gone or one was late in arriving, someone else would produce a tin, for each man carried his own and stood ready to offer it all around. So important a tie-sign was this distribution and acceptance of snuff at Kahal Reyim that one day, somewhat to my surprise, I found myself entering a tobacco shop and purchasing a small tin for myself, which I ever after carried in my pocket, ready to offer some to my fellows in the circle.

At Beit Rachel cigarettes served much the same function. While most of the smokers had their own packs, the norm of circle behavior apparently required the giving of one's own to another. Even those who were nonsmokers sometimes reminded the smokers to pull out their packs. And everyone stood ready to provide the Rav with the first cigarette (which he would hold in his hand unlit until sometime in the course of the class he would have it lit for him by one of the students).[32] The handing around of the cigarettes and later their lighting (or the passing of fire, as some of the men referred to this practice) was a Beit Rachel form of tie-signing.

At Mekadshey Torah, the distribution of tea and cookies fulfilled many of the needs of tie-signing. In part this group ritual provided Reb Mendele, an elderly man who did not normally join in the actual study (his Hebrew was weak since he was a new immigrant) but spent most of the time preparing the refreshments and then cleaning up the plates and glasses, with a manifest reason for attending the *shiur*. Yet it also served as a means of tying the men to one another. As they passed around the cookies, the sugar, the stirring spoon, as they deferred to one another by passing around the first glasses served, as they alerted Mendele who should get an extra cup or who should be served next, whose tea should be strong and who liked lemon in it, they indicated their ties to one another. So Alexanderovich would always pass his tea to Marcus, or Sadek would inevitably see to it that Schwarcz got the sugar first and so on. Each was at once both host and guest as they expressed these communal, friendly ties to one another. And the Rav always got the glass with the tea bag in it, since, out of respect and affection, he was offered the strongest tea. When Reb Mendele was absent someone else would serve the goodies; never would the ritual be missed.

At Rav Rotenbush's house a similar thing happened. Here it was Turkish coffee that replaced the tea, but everything else seemed to be the same. Again one of the members was responsible for bringing the drinks from the kitchen after they were prepared. When once the Rav's wife (who during most of the classes re-treated to a bedroom and out of the way) offered to prepare the coffee, she was jokingly told that in this case she was not mistress of her own kitchen and could not take the task away from the men. They and they alone were, as it were, tying themselves to one another—and anyone who could not share in the fellowship of *lernen*, as she could not, could not likewise share in the ritual of coffee preparation.

When for two weeks the fellow who regularly prepared the coffee did not come to class and no one stood up to prepare the drinks in his place, the Rav reprimanded us all for not seeing to it that this informal routine had been carried out.

"It's not right to skip this. No, *khevre*, this is not to be missed," he exclaimed when he noticed that the hour for *lernen* had passed and still no coffee had been served.

Here, as in other classes, prestation—the process of gift giving, receiving, and repaying—was an inherent and undeniable element of the *lernen*, not to be overlooked. One had to give and take snuff; distribute, light, and smoke one another's cigarettes; pass around tea and cookies or Turkish coffee; exchange news, gossip, jokes or ideas if one was to properly indicate fellowship. In each case, "to refuse to give . . . like refusing to accept . . . is a refusal of friendship and intercourse."[33]

All this became even clearer when on occasion someone refused to participate in this tie-signing. When, for example, a newcomer to Rav Rotenbush's house refused coffee, in spite of the importuning of the other fellows, one got a sense that he was holding himself distant from the *group*. Indeed, the man who refused soon ceased coming to the circle. And when I once turned down the drink, I soon felt that I had implicitly turned my back on the fellowship.

"You have to drink. It's part of the *shiur*," I was later told. "Are you alright?" someone asked, as if refusal could only be accounted for by illness.

Perhaps the most remarkable illustration of the extent and sweep of tie-signing was made apparent to me not at one of my regular circles but at one which I attended for only a short time. This was a circle of elderly men who each night gathered in one of the many rooms of a synagogue with as many services as there were rooms. Here, between the afternoon *mincha* prayers and the evening *ma'ariv* ones, these twelve or fifteen men would under the leadership of one of them review En Yaakov, the narrative portions of the Talmud. I had wandered in one evening suspecting that I might find some *lernen* here and hoping that by coming to a new setting I might succeed in noticing something new.

As I walked through the door, several faces turned toward me, and with gazes fixed on me as I made my way to a seat around the table informed me silently that I was a stranger penetrating a circle with regular insiders. Still, room was made for me on the bench, and when I sat down I was handed a large volume and shown the place. After *ma'ariv*, which everyone joined at the conclusion of the study period, I was greeted by the Rav who invited me to come again to the *shiur*.

The next night, arriving a bit earlier and in time for the afternoon prayers, I was able to watch the entire gathering. It was at this time that I discovered another kind of tie-sign.

Among these old men were one or two who, as it turned out, were mendicants—"schnorrers," in the parlance of the Jewish community.[34] At the beginning of each class, apparently, one of them would make his way around the circle, collecting his fixed alms from each man. To be sure, the association of charity with *lernen* is firmly rooted in Jewish mystical tradition. Here the belief sometimes held is that, when confronted with a particularly opaque text, one simply gives charity and in reward the meaning of the difficult passage of Torah will be revealed to the benefactor.[35] This, however, did not seem to be the underlying reason for the gift of alms in this case. Rather, by passing forward their donations to the schnorrer who was also a fellow of the *khavruse*, each man signified his tie to the fellowship through him. As other groups might signal their joint ties and the start of proceedings by passing around snuff or tea, here the same end was accomplished by everyone giving alms. Insiders knew that this was the transition between prayer and *lernen*, the reminder of their responsibility toward one another.

I, alas, did not know this, nor did I, like the regulars, have a kind of common sense or recipe knowledge of what to do and how to act when I was touched by the schnorrer for funds. Instead I responded to his request as I had learned to do with so many of the other beggars who made their way into the many synagogues I had attended: I gave him a few coins. No sooner had I done this than he began to scream and berate me for my niggardliness. This was something that had never happened to me before, nor was it the normal sort of response from a synagogue mendicant, who commonly takes whatever is given in silence.

What had of course happened was that I had treated this man like a common beggar and not one who shared in the fellowship that I had presumed to join. Put another way, my inappropriate donation was a refusal to express the proper ties to him and thus to the group. So he did not berate me directly but rather screamed at the Rav and to the others, asking how *they* could allow him to be treated in this way, how *they* could accept such an affront to him.

"This is a *bizayon* [shame]," he repeated again and again in Yiddish.

Moving to return my coins to me, he was stopped by the Rav and one of the other students who seemed to be embarrassed by this outburst. They did not disagree with his judgment, perhaps, but simply with the means of redress he had chosen.

"Not now," said the Rav.

"Sit down," said several of the others, while some men simply motioned to him to be seated and to calm down.

Reacting to the situation, I took out a bill and handed it to the man next to me who passed it forward to the mendicant.

"You see?" the Rav now asked him. "Ask his forgiveness; you embarrassed him."

"You see he has given you the proper amount, so be quiet," said another.

"Let's get on with *lernen*," the man next to me remarked.

But the poor man would not be calmed; he waved the note at me, making signs that he would return it. He was not willing to accept my money now, to become thus tied to me. By refusing my donation he would keep me on the outside. The group would not, however, allow this and again signaled him to be seated. For them the mistake had been rectified and the *shiur* was now ready to begin. The decision of whether or not to accept the money and through it the legitimacy of my presence was not the poor man's alone to make.

Of all the tie-signs I witnessed during the several years of my observations, however, none was more striking and stylized than one I saw at a *shiur* I attended in which the participants were all members of the Bratslav sect of hasidim. This group, unlike other hasidim, has no living "rebbe" or charismatic leader. When their rebbe, Nachman, died in 1810, they, unlike other hasidim, did not crown another with his authority.[36] Instead they maintained that Reb Nachman was still their spiritual leader and could guide them by means of the epistles and lessons which he left behind in a written record and which had been collected in several volumes entitled *Likutey MoHaRan* (The gleanings from Reb Nachman), and *Sippurey Ma'asiyot* (Tales). These they considered part of Jewish sacred literature in which could be discovered answers for all questions of all times. Like Torah, the writings of Reb Nachman were to be reviewed and studied.

One might suppose that the absence of a living rebbe instilled among Bratslaver hasidim a more intensive group consciousness than that normally associated with hasidic life. Somewhat like orphaned sons, the followers of Reb Nachman might have been drawn closer by their common situation as survivors. Without launching into a kind of psychohistorical analysis of this sect and similarly considering others, it is hard to determine if such is the case. Nevertheless, simple observation reveals among the Bratslavers a plethora of activities that stress group ties. One of these I discovered was associated with *lernen*.

Like other Orthodox Jews, these hasidim customarily sat down to *lern* together between the afternoon and evening prayers. In their one-room synagogue, which served as both house of prayer and study, the volumes of *Likutey MoHaRan* were more prominently displayed than the Talmud. While there were only two sets of the Talmud, there were nearly a dozen of *Likutey MoHaRan*, and these appeared far more worn and used. This was no surprise since the Bratslavers reviewed the writings of Reb Nachman faithfully each evening.

After the *mincha* prayers, those who were not members of Bratslav but who had nonetheless joined in worship in the synagogue left. One or two of the non-hasidim might sit in isolated corners of the room reviewing some large tome on their own. The Bratslavers, however, sat down at the old table in the southwest corner of the room and opened up their *Likutey MoHaRan*. As in a Talmud class, one man would recite the text and translate or comment upon it while the others followed along in their books or asked questions, echoed, cued, made comments, and so on. As with Talmud study, there were digressions stimulated both by the text and by explications of it. Since much of the substance of the writing is metaphor, homily, and ethics, there is a great deal of room for discussion. The conversation ranged from simple reminiscences about life in Warsaw to the more ethereal discussions of theodicy and response to the holocaust. Charity was passed

around to the mendicants who periodically came into the room
but who were not members of the study circle. Yet it was only at
the end that I saw the elaborate tie-sign that so captured the
imagination.

Reaching the end of the chapter of study for the evening, the
leader closed his book. The others followed his example. Then
he stood up and left the table; the others again followed. Forming
a circle in front of their study table, the men then clasped hands
and began to dance and sing. Slowly at first, with a regular
rhythm, they gradually increased their tempo and moved more
and more quickly. It was, I thought, a metaphor as well as a literal
expression of the circle of belief, fellowship, and study in which
they were tied. And although I had sat in on the class, I felt no
claim to the dancing circle. I stood outside of it because I was
outside. Had I wanted to join in the dance, I could have—for on
another occasion I did. But on that first night, before I had penetrated the moral consciousness of their circle, before I felt a closeness or sense of fellowship with them that would enable me to
see things as they did, I felt incapable of breaking into the circle
of dance. I could not signify a tie that did not yet fully exist.

MORAL FELLOWSHIP

The example of the Bratslaver hasidim points to the moral dimension of fellowship. Here one finds the source of feelings of
well-being that members enjoy as a result of their belonging to
a *khavruse*. These must now be more closely examined.

As a major proposition of his sociology, Durkheim once suggested that: "the domain of the moral begins where the domain
of the social begins."[37] That is, the constraints of group existence
serve as the framework for defining morality. To join in a fellowship is to be limited by the mores and taken-for-granted sense of
reality that dominates the group. Not only behavior but also beliefs, thoughts, and opinions are affected since "moral relations
are relations between consciousnesses."[38]

When the fellowship is organized around the study of Talmud,
an additional set of moral constraints enter into the mix. These
are the world view and ethos of the text and the culture it represents. Thus participation in a *khavruse* may bring about a transformation of individual consciousness. The insider to the circle
may suspend his own individual conceptions of the world—at

least within the framework of the *shiur*—and see things instead through the prism of the group and text. He merges his lonely individual identity with those of his fellow Jews—both those in the study circle and those in the pages of the Talmud. In return, however, he experiences a sense of belonging and moral rectitude.

The attraction such an experience has for the individual, especially for the modern cosmopolitan who often suffers from the anomie of enforced flexibility and moral relativism, is its capacity to help him overcome feelings of existential isolation that have become so much a part of contemporary existence. After all, again to cite Durkheim, "Man is more vulnerable to self-destruction the more he is detached from any collectivity, that is to say, the more self-centered his life."[39] In the *khavruse* and during the *shiur*, there are, however, no rewards for individualism and self-centeredness. Rather, here one can escape feelings of isolation and share instead familiarity, fellowship, and community.*

Throughout much of Jewish history, the study fellowship provided this sort of moral security. In the face of persecution and derision, in the midst of pogrom and holocaust, the *khavruse* offered the Jew "shelter from the storm outside, warmth and love instead of rejection and hostility, simultaneously strengthening self-esteem."[40] Then, as now, while the Jew might have to discipline himself in order to join a *lernen* fellowship, and despite its tensions, the circle "gave in return the associative, ceremonial and intercessional benefits of which the individual Jew stood in need, mentally and emotionally."[41]

It has been this social and psychological security, out of which grows a feeling of well-being that the fully committed insider

---

*Although not referring to a study circle, Sigmund Freud, in a letter to members of his B'nai B'rith lodge, a fellowship of Jews suggested historically by the example of the study circle, poignantly describes these feelings in his own case:

 . . . the disclosure of my unpopular discoveries led to my losing most of my personal relationships at that time [of my being invited to join the lodge]; I felt as though outlawed, shunned by all. This isolation aroused in me the longing for a circle of excellent men with high ideals who would accept me in friendship despite my temerity. Your Lodge was described to me as the place where I could find such men.

 That you are Jews could only be welcome to me, for I was myself a Jew . . . [and] there remained enough to make the attraction of Judaism and the Jews irresistible, many dark emotional powers all the stronger the less they could be expressed in words, as well as the clear consciousness of an inner identity, the familiarity of the same psychological structure.

[From a letter of May 6, 1926, to the members of the Lodge]

comes away with from his time in the circle, that has made participants willing to suspend their divergent personal views of the
world in favor of moral unity—if only for the period of the *lernen*.
In order to share in the feelings of moral fellowship, I found
myself during the *shiur* tacitly accepting premises—that women,
for example, are in the same legal status as slaves and cattle, or
that it is important to know the precise order of the priestly sacrifices at the Holy Temple in Jerusalem, or that divine voices can
be heard descending from heaven in order to engage in talmudic
disputation—which were at odds with my contemporary ideals
and emotionally distant from my modern consciousness. Nor was
I alone in this.

To be sure, as I have already explained, members do at times
engage in contemporization, rationally reinterpreting the seem-
ingly archaic so as to make it appear in harmony with contemporary ideals and consciousness. But this can only be done with
the tacit approval of the entire fellowship. One does not contemporize among traditioners, those for whom the past is sacred and
untouchable—anymore than one depends on the ways of the past
to satisfy the radical contemporizer. What is crucial is that one be
willing and able to bend one's consciousness to the collective
perspective. That viewpoint is the one normally expressed by and
through the Rav who perhaps more than anyone else embodies
the fellowship and expresses its conception. Were he to strike out
on his own, he like any other participant would find himself
outside the circle. For the Rav that would mean losing his students.

Debates and controversies of course break out on occasion.
These have already been described as forming the basis of social
drama. It will be recalled that the norm is that such crises are
resolved, leaving intact the fellowship and position of the Rav at
its head. There are few if any individual victories won at the
expense of the group (or the text). Anyone looking to score points
that way wins a Pyrrhic rather than a moral victory, for what he
finds is that for him the *khavruse* is no longer a comfortable or
secure place. Accordingly, insiders "forget" the values and beliefs
that run counter to the *lernen* fellowship; and they learn to swallow
personal prerogative and pride in order to maintain moral ties.

STUDY EMBEDDED IN SOCIABILITY

In all that I have written thus far about fellowship and the study circle, the communal feelings engendered seem embedded within *lernen*, a kind of social deep structure. There are, however, circumstances when the reverse becomes true: *lernen* becomes embedded within a social or communal occasion. Here the Torah-*lernen* remains in a kind of "hiding" under the guise of ordinary conversation and intercourse.[42] Among these are the times when the members of the *khavruse* meet together as a group but not for the express purposes of *lernen*. The gathering may in a sense be considered an embodiment of the sense of community and mutual obligation that has grown out of the *lernen*. Some illustrations will perhaps be useful here. I offer three.

The first concerns the men of the Beit Rachel circle. One evening in January, Rav Horowitz concluded the *shiur* with the announcement that his daughter had that week given birth to a son. As is the custom among Orthodox Jews, such an event is marked on the first Friday evening of the child's life with a get-together called a *"shalom zakhor,"* literally "peace to the male child."

For the *shalom zakhor*, relatives and parents traditionally gather in the home of the parents (or grandparents) of the child in order to congratulate them and to witness the recitation of various prayers and psalms for the welfare of the mother and child. The party is meant also as a consolation since, according to various folk beliefs, the newborn has forgotten the Torah which he was taught in heaven before his birth and therefore must learn it all over again. The origins of the ceremony are found in the Talmud (B.T. *Niddah* 31b) where the expression is found: "If a boy is born, peace comes to the world."

Accordingly, the Rav invited us all to join him and his family for this celebration. Similar announcements were made in his synagogue and at the other places where the Horowitz family was known. As I walked out of the class I turned to one of my fellow students and asked him if he intended to go.

"Of course, we always go to things like this," he told me.

Several of the men agreed to meet on the corner near the Rav's house on that Friday night. The top student, Zusya, set a meeting time of seven-thirty, which, although several of the others thought it too early, nevertheless became the time we met. The desire to enter together, to come as a group, overcame any misgivings we might have about the proper time to come. (It later turned out that Zusya had pushed the group to go at this time so that he would be able to leave the Horowitz's house in time to make a Friday evening *shiur* he normally attended in a nearby synagogue. Looking for a way to fulfill his obligations to two *khavruses* at once, he settled on an early arrival and departure time.)

On Friday evening, when I joined the few men assembled on the corner, I found that one who had agreed to join us had not yet arrived. The group waited for him, in spite of the fact that the Rav's house was just a few paces away. There was of course nothing to stop any of us from separating ourselves from the group and making our own way to the gathering—nothing except an unspoken sense that we were a unit and needed to arrive together.

In a short time the straggler arrived and we all walked the short path leading to the Rav's house.

Once inside we were greeted by the Rav who introduced us to the members of his family: "These are the men who *lern* with me at Beit Rachel."

As individuals, most of the men were known to the family. Clearly our individual identities, while important perhaps in other situations, were here, however, to be submerged in our identities as members of the *khavruse*.

We had indeed arrived early. The Horowitz family, not yet finished with the meal, was still sitting at the Sabbath dinner table. Quickly, however, the table was cleared of the dinner dishes and the grace was recited. We sat quietly on a nearby couch and chairs while the transformation of the setting took place. The women ran into the kitchen and the younger men and daughters brought out the bowls of food for the celebration. The lentils and chickpeas, traditional folk symbols of birth and death, came first. Next came the fruits, drinks, and cakes that had been prepared in advance.

While this was being done, the Rav continued to introduce us to his family. Now, however, he focused on each of us individually. But these singular identities were not anchored in our lives outside the *khavruse*. Rather, each of us was characterized by our special role in it: Zusya was the one with "the good head for *gemore*," Moshe was a "*masmid*" (diligent student), Reuven was the one who always asked the good questions, I was the one who recorded everything on my tape machine, and so on. These individual characterizations served to underscore our being in the fellowship since they only made sense against that social background.

With the table now reset, we were asked to come forward and sit around it. More and more people began coming. Several of those who entered commented to the effect that "the men from the Rav's *shiur*" were present. To the community at large this too was our identity. That is, while each of the men had personal acquaintances and ties in the neighborhood, these were overlooked when we were thus arranged together. Under the present circumstances, we seemed to carry around with us the membrane of our *lernen* fellowship.

As will be considered in greater detail in the next chapter, all Jewish gatherings that have some religious significance are appropriate opportunities for the study of Torah. Certainly the *shalom zakhor* was no exception. In this case, however, this imperative was supported as well by the nature of the ties among the men of the *khavruse* and Rav Horowitz—*lernen* was what symbolized those ties. Thus it seemed quite "natural" that, after the initial conversational interchanges had been completed, the Rav would pull from his shelf some sacred volume from which a few words of Torah could be recited, explained, and discussed.

While the tea was being served, the Rav suggested: "*T'hilim* and tea," [the onomatopaeia works in Hebrew too] go well together," and then he opened his Psalter (*T'hilim*).

"Only when they're both warm," added his father who, as patriarch, sat at the head of the table.

This metaphor and homily segued us easily into a more serious discussion. Turning instead to the portion of the Bible text which would be read the next day in the synagogue, the Rav recited several verses and proceeded to discuss them. The lesson was brief, focusing on the idea that the Torah was something that one generation had to hand over to the next rather than something that could be passively inherited. It was a point that fit neatly to the occasion and to our relationship with one another and the Rav. We were, after all, actively inheriting the cultural and sacred testament of our forebears every time we studied together; and this was something worth remembering on the occasion of the birth of a new male, one who presumably would one day too *lern* in this way.

With the symbolic *lernen* over, we exchanged a few more pleas-
antries, nibbled a few more chick-peas, and toasted the new child.
Then, at the whispered urging of Zusya who suggested we leave
and make room for others who were continuing to come, we left.

As we made our way up the street and away from the Horowitz house, I reflected on my feelings. Although most of the
time had been spent in sociability, the *lernen,* brief and embedded
as it was in the social occasion—and the people with whom I
spent the time—called out the same feelings as those I experienced
whenever I left my regular *shiur* at Beit Rachel.

A few steps in front of me, Zusya and Meir were walking
toward their Friday night class in the Ohel Torah synagogue.

"I think you're going to fall asleep there tonight," I heard Meir
say to his friend.

"Well, anyway, I'm going for the company," Zusya answered.
Fellowship was not to be gainsaid even if one was made tired by
a few drinks at a *shalom zakhor.*

A second illustration of *lernen* embedded in a social occasion
occurred at Rav Rotenbush's house. As the Hanukkah season
approached, the Rav announced to the men at Mekadshey Torah
that, as was his custom, he would not meet with the class during
the week of the holiday but instead wanted the group to join him
and his family for a party celebrating Hanukkah. Most of the men,
and especially those who attended the circle regularly, came. This
evening the emphasis was on sociability. The Rav watched to see
that all his guests were trying all the different cakes and foods
his wife had set before us. Unlike the *shiur* when only men came
together, on this night some of the men brought along their wives.
The conversation was similar to what we normally carried on
before and after the formal study: gossip, jokes, politics, and
stories about the workplace were the order of the evening.

Here, as had been the case at Rav Horowitz's *shalom zakhor,*
lernen found its way into this sociable atmosphere. Here, as in the
first example, the *lernen* was more symbolic than substantive. One
or two men began asking the Rav questions about Hanukkah,
inquiries they had likely made for years in the past but which
traditionally came to mind during this season and which were
then asked with all the freshness and gusto of a first time.[43] In
answering and discussing these inquiries, moreover, the men
provided a ritual expression of Torah. They turned the table, as

it were, from one oriented purely to eating and assembly to one over which sacred matters had been discussed.*

A third such occasion on which one could observe study embedded in sociability occurred at the close of one of the classes at Mekadshey Torah. The *gabbai*—the man responsible for the organization of activities in the synagogue, and one of the leading students in the group—announced that Reb Uriel, one of the regular fellows, was mourning for his father who had died earlier in the week. The announcement that one of our own had suffered this loss was sufficient to assemble us for a visit to the nearby home for a condolence call. Walking behind the Rav and *gabbai* the fifteen or so men marched down the street and into a small alley at the end of which stood the dead man's house. We wound our way up the narrow stairs that led to the second floor where the bereaved family sat on the mandatory low seats for the traditional seven-day mourning period. In we walked, a phalanx of the faithful. Each of us greeted Uriel and his family with a silent nod and found places along the walls of the small room.

"These are the men of Uriel's *shiur*," I heard one of the sons whisper in explanation to his brothers and uncles. The women were all in another room.

Seeming to speak for all of us, the Rav solemnly cited the Talmud and its commentary on the importance of comforting the bereaved; the rest of us sat in silence. The *lernen* fit in smoothly with the rest of the discussion, not only because the Rav was doing most of the talking but because in a sense all the conversation had a symbolic character to it. Everything seemed prefigured, including our conduct.

A few words were spoken about the steadfastness of the dead man's faith and his regular attendance in the synagogue as well as his dedication to his family. He had been a local grocer, and this too was mentioned as we went through what seemed like an obligatory and almost ritualized recounting of the religious and communal aspects of his existence. Suddenly the Rav stood up, shook several hands and intoned the customary parting phrase

*The idea that a table can thus be transformed is embedded in the ritual status of tables among observant Jews. According to the law, a table is considered an "altar," and accordingly must be treated with circumspection and respect. Though not a sacred item, it does have the capacity to be thus transformed. Indeed the table is a long time symbol for Torah study, as demonstrated by its inclusion in the titles of a number of commentaries on Scripture and Jewish law.

when leaving the house of a mourner: "May you be consoled among all the mourners in Zion and Jerusalem." As if on cue, the rest of the *khavruse* stood and did likewise. No one left before the Rav, nor did anyone stay longer than he did. Similarly, no one in the group had elected to pay this call on his own. Rather the entire activity was carried out as an extension of our fellowship. Leaving the house, we walked the two blocks back to the synagogue. On the way, no one moved to leave the group. There seemed to be a tacit understanding that we would remain together until we returned to our geographic and social point of origin.

By no means were these three situations unique. Rather, they are representative of the fellowship that finds ways of surrounding the individual members of the study circle even when study becomes incidental to a gathering. Like members of other groups ostensibly anchored to a particular activity—from bowling and cardplaying to theatergoing and literary review—the insiders discover, either explicitly or by way of experience, that their group can transcend that particular activity and find ways to tie itself to other matters. Once people learn this, they become both committed and attached—embraced—by their fellowship. There is nothing that can more certainly insure that a person will continue to participate in the circle of *lernen* than to have him participate in some other group occupation. That is why all *khavruses* have always found ways to institutionalize such occasions of extended fellowship into their existence—from the *siyum* to the holiday gathering, from the celebrations of birth to the assemblies of mourning.

THE ABSENCE OF FELLOWSHIP:
THE CASE OF THE JERUSALEM SOCIAL CLUB

Sometimes the best way to understand the importance of a particular element in the whole is to examine a situation in which this element is missing in order to see how the whole is affected. In the observation of real life human behavior, this kind of manipulation is seldom if ever possible. Occasionally, however, serendipity offers a chance for such observations. In the case of my field work this happened.

One of the settings in which I carried on my systematic observation and recording was the Jerusalem Social Club. Here a whole array of courses and activities were open to the community. Included among the courses in Hebrew language, art, tennis, bridge, literature, and poetry was a course in Talmud. Like the other courses, this one met once a week and had to be paid for by those who enrolled. To be sure, the charge was small since the club was subsidized by the government, as were many other civic facilities. Nevertheless, the fee added an impersonal element to the classes, one that proved crucial in the case of the Talmud session.

Placed in competition with the other courses on the curriculum, the Talmud class did not draw great numbers of students. When I joined I found four people other than myself enrolled in Rav Auerbach's course. We did not know one another, nor did anyone seem to have any special ties to the teacher. The only source of bonding among us was our presumed interest in studying Talmud.

A second difference between this group and the others I had joined elsewhere was the fact that throughout its duration it included both men and women. This mixing of the sexes also seemed to inhibit the establishment of a sense of fellowship. To be sure, it is possible for men and women to join together in communion. Among Orthodox Jews, however, a tradition that discourages the mixing of sexes during religious activity (included in which is the study of Torah) is deeply ingrained in their consciousness. This has been especially true for the study of Talmud, which is still endowed with a certain residual high status—a status not open to women. These factors created a sense of unease in the integrated situation of the club—at least for those whose consciousness resonated with those traditions.

Finally, the behavior of Rav Auerbach, the teacher, also served to discourage the establishment of anything beyond a most rudimentary sense of fellowship. He would enter the room, move immediately to a desk in the front, open his book and take out a roster on which the names of those registered for the course appeared. After some few minutes had passed during which all of us would sit in silence, staring at our open books, he would call off the names.

Missing here was any of the opening banter and sociability that characterized the other groups I attended. Only when the class was actually underway would there be any communication among the students, and then always through the person of the Rav. He might, for example, be asked a question to which he would offer an answer, which in turn stimulated a comment from another student who was in effect reacting to the earlier questions. Or sometimes one student would ask a question that another would answer, often phrasing the answer as a question that the Rav would have to ratify.

There was some cuing and echoing, but for the most part we sat silently as the Rav took us through the page and through his ubiquitous notes on the tractate. There were few if any noticeable displays of social drama, no clear moments of high tension or crisis. Rather, there was a kind of emotional and social distance that everyone seemed to maintain throughout the hour or so that we met.

Meeting in the club setting brought with it certain other ramifications. This setting carried neither the veneer of sanctity that the *besmedresh* housed in the synagogue had nor the intimacy that meetings in someone's home implied. Rather, the Jerusalem Social Club was a public and civic place, a setting for the anonymous individual. Indeed, there was a certain irony in the title "Social Club" since it was a club for the marginal and unaffiliated, the solitary. Anyone else would probably have joined a more traditional circle. But rather than succeeding in helping the individual who entered it to overcome his loneliness, it seemed at times to assimilate this loneliness and then reflect it back onto the group.

Even after several weeks of meetings, the people would leave the class in silence. Once out of the room, there was little more than a "good evening" spoken. Those who walked in the same direction away from the building walked alone. No one ever offered another a ride home, nor did anyone seem interested in the lives of his fellows. Such ties as existed were purely focused around the narrow task of studying the Talmud.

One should not be surprised to learn, therefore, in light of everything I have suggested in this chapter, that the people meeting in the club gradually stopped coming to the class. The number of attendees fluctuated a bit, sometimes rising to six and other times falling to two (myself and another student) and the Rav. Finally, the course simply ended. Scheduled again by the administration of the club who felt an obligation to offer something in the way of "sacred study," the course never really managed to become anything like a genuine study circle.

Lacking a sense of fellowship, the people could simply not sustain the experience of *lernen*. They could likewise not develop the dramatic quotient of their encounter. As for religious imperatives, these too could not be fulfilled easily in the club setting and in mixed company. That left only the interest in Talmud, apparently an insufficient basis for *lernen*. When I came one evening and found only Rav Auerbach and myself, and when I could not tell him where the others might be nor did he have any ideas about their whereabouts, I knew that my observations here were for all intents and purposes complete.

CONCLUSION

When considering the institution of the Talmud study circle, one must of course examine the manifest content of *lernen:* recitation and exegesis. One looks too at the implications of this activity—what I have here generally termed the "drama" of *lernen*. But one must explore as well in the interstices, niches, intervals, and peripheries of the action to discover the web of human relationship that binds together much of what occurs. Here one sees how profoundly social *lernen* is. Without the fellowship, the pages of Talmud—regardless of their inherent worth—cannot be brought to life. Without the *haver* with whom one joins to play out the dialogues, debates, and narratives of the text, the Talmud rests in silence, and Judaism and Jewish feeling remain unexpressed. And yet, once the group of *lerners* comes into being, it has the capacity to go beyond the boundaries of its specific tasks. The relationship is a synergistic one. Without the Talmud as an object of study, no *khavruse* could come into being; and without the *khavruse*, the Talmud often gathers dust lying on a shelf. Together, they create something precious and meaningful for all concerned.

But what brings the two together? What presses people into a search for a *haver* or a group with whom to *lern?* Loneliness alone is not enough, for this would as much send a person to playing cards as to *lernen* Talmud. There must be something special.

That something is, in a word, "religion." The religious Jew, Orthodox in his orientation, feels a historical and personal religious obligation to *lern Torah*. Out of this felt need he seeks out others who are likewise moved. Once having found them and begun the process, however, he soon finds himself swept away by far more than matters of religion. We have already seen what these other matters are. What remains now is to look at the original spark—the religious feeling that leads one to the circle and the book.

7
THE RELIGION OF "LERNEN"

The religion of Israel is supremely the religion of the Book.
MIRCEA ELIADE, *A History of Religious Ideas*, vol. 1

Rabbi Meir says: He who has in his city a study house and does not frequent it has no share in the world to come.
Avot d'Rabbi Natan 36

As scriptural verses and rabbinic homilies make clear, "The study of Torah excels all" (B.T. *Shabbat* 127a). It is not simply an intellectual matter but even more a core element of religious life. Throughout their history, the people of Israel have become identified with their books, which they have "reinterpreted, corrected, and redacted in the course of several centuries and in different milieus."[1]

That history begins in an almost legendary primordial past during which a mass of former slaves evolved into a nation and a religious community. Pivotal in the founding myth was the revelation at Sinai where, according to believers, the Torah—the corpus of Jewish law and lore—was received and Judaism as a collective experience began.

From thence onward, the veneration and study of that Torah was perceived as fundamental to Jewish religious, cultural, and national survival. As the nomadic wanderers, after forty years in the wilderness, prepared to enter their "promised Land," their leader Joshua, in words that would be repeated for generations afterward, was admonished to observe and review the sacred Scriptures: "The Torah shall not depart from your mouth, but you must meditate therein day and night, that you might observe and do according to all that is written therein" (*Joshua* 1:5).

After the return from the Babylonian exile, Ezra, the priest and scribe who played a major role in the rebuilding of the destroyed first Temple and the reinstitution of its sacrificial rites, nevertheless once again reminded the people of the place of Torah in their religious life. He therefore instituted the public recitation and instruction of the Five Books of Moses. The merger of study and worship would, he apparently believed, serve vitally in the spiritual and national rebuilding of the Jewish people.

Generations later, following the final Roman conquest of Judea, when the Jews were about to begin a diaspora that would last nearly two millenia, Yokhanan ben Zakkai would likewise remind his followers, in words that have since become immortalized in the Talmud, that Jewish study was at the core of their existence: "If you have reviewed much Torah, do not claim credit for yourself, because you were created for this purpose." As I have noted previously, this emphasis on the Book as the lone remaining structure of Judaism took on a special poignancy and importance during the early years of exile when the memory of other fallen structures was still fresh in the national memory. Unlike the Temple and the Holy City, Torah was not something which could be overrun by infidels, burned, or destroyed once it had become a part of Jewish consciousness and religious existence.

Among those whose scholarship and debate fill the Talmud and who serve as the source of millenial Jewish wisdom, this idea became a religious ideal. There could be no end to study, they asserted, just as there could be no end to worship: "Study the Torah again and again, for everything is contained in it; constantly examine it, grow old and gray over it, and swerve not from it, for there is nothing more excellent than it" (*Avot* 5:22). As prayers and sacrifices once served to sanctify self and community, so now could Jewish study: "Anyone who occupies himself with Torah is exempt from offering sacrifices or sin-offerings" (B.T. *Menakhot* 110a). Indeed, according to the talmudic interpretation of the law, anyone sincerely engaged in Torah study was to be simultaneously exempt from all other religious obligations: "Whoever occupies himself with the study of Torah for its own sake merits many things; nay more, the whole world is worthwhile for his sake" (*Avot* 6:1).

The person who immersed himself in the review of the Book shared in its majesty and divine authority: "Anyone who occupies himself with the study of Torah shall be exalted" (Avot 6:2). Rabbis and scholars took social positions of authority once held exclusively by priests. "He that does not make it a habit to attend upon scholars has no share in the world to come," says the revered Rabbi Akiva (*Avot d'Rabbi Natan* 36). Scholarship, unlike priesthood, however, was an achieved rather than an ascribed status. Priests were only those descended from a priestly family; anyone could aspire to be a Torah scholar—anyone ready to pursue Jewish study relentlessly.

"From the day that the Holy Temple was destroyed, the Holy One, blessed be He, dwelt only within the structure of the *halakha*," the talmudist Rabbi Hiya bar Ami suggested. The implication was clear. In the structure of *halakha*, the Jewish law, the rabbis were in charge.

The dislocations that the Temple's destruction and ensuing diaspora brought about could not help but change social and religious order. When the Temple was traded for *halakha* (Jewish law), priests became rabbis and worship became study.

Following along in this new tradition, Jews increasingly located their religious life in the house of study:

"I pray only in the place where I study," the scholar Abaye is quoted as asserting in the opening pages of the Babylonian Talmud.

Many Jews began to do likewise. The synagogue, *Bes Knesses* (literally, house of assembly) became not only or even primarily *Bes Tefila* (house of prayer) but *Bes Medresh* (house of study.) Today, among those for whom the ways of the Talmud remain authoritative, it is simply called "shul," a word etymologically closer to "school" than to "synagogue." Indeed, by now worship and Jewish study have become so intertwined that it is often hard to think of one without the other. The Jewish liturgy is heavily laden with quotations from Scripture and Talmud. Among the first words recited in the daily prayer book are those which bless God for having given the Jews the Torah and assert its dominance in Jewish life. Most services held in the synagogue contain a formal recitation or chanting of some Scripture, meant as a source of religious instruction and inspiration. Over the years, sermons have become a common feature of Sabbath services. These too are opportunities to teach Torah either by means of homily or textual analysis (a favorite device is often to quote a verse or two from Talmud and then explore its meaning).

On the other hand, when the manifest activity is Jewish study, prayer becomes added as well. Not only is it common to assemble for a *minyan* before or after a session of study, but also each extended period of Jewish study, if attended by a least ten adult males (a *minyan*), is followed by the recitation of a *kaddish*.

This last practice is one that is particular to the kind of *lernen* I have been describing throughout. That is, one would not expect the class in Talmud carried on at a university or even in a yeshiva where it is a part of the regular curriculum to be punctuated with a prayer. Indeed, at the class held in the Jerusalem Social Club, a class modeled more after the sort given as part of a curriculum and less as an extension of fellowship and religious obligation, no such prayers were recited. At all the other circles—Smotra, Mekadshey Torah, Rav Rotenbush's house, Beit Rachel, and Kahal Reyim—the last words spoken in the period of formal study were those of the kaddish.

The association of study with religion is, to be sure, not limited to Orthodox Jews. "The respect for learning was ingrained in the Jewish people as a religious . . . imperative" throughout their history, and it "remains a central value of Jewish . . . life today, even when apparent religious underpinnings have disappeared."[2] Indeed, by now "the idea that learning is a form of worship" has become a firmly established principle in the civil religion of those areas of the Western world where Jewish culture has made an impact.[3] Yet, strictly speaking, learning and *lernen* are not identical. The former, as I have previously noted, is an essentially intellectual activity while the latter is at its core a matter of religion, culture, and tradition.

REPETITION

Throughout these pages I have tried to suggest the intrinsically religious character of *lernen*. Although this is not the place to recapitulate all those references, a few major points are worth recalling at least briefly. Perhaps foremost among them is the imperative that requires members of the study circle to review and re-cite familiar talmudic texts. This sort of repetition which is foreign to "learning" and its search after novelty and intellectual development is essential to *lernen*. There are, as I have noted before, people who try to learn Jewish sacred texts rather than *lern* them. These are persons who are, however, more at home studying in the university than in the *khavruse*.

Repetition is of course also essential to religion, in which the great experiences of the past must always be repeated and thereby revitalized. Just as the religious person's life consists of "the ceaseless repetition of gestures initiated by others," so the *lerner's* life consists of an unending reiteration of the ideas generated by others.[4] Just as the traditional worshipper seeks to use the established liturgy as a receptacle for all of his spiritual feelings, so analogously does the *lerner* try to utilize the constructions of the sacred texts and holy rabbis as a framework and guide for his own thinking. As the Talmud itself puts it: "Anyone who says anything that he did not hear from his Rav causes the Divine Presence to depart from Israel" (B.T. *Berachot* 27b). Maimonides in his authoritative listing of the code of Jewish law, the Mishna Torah, is even more precise on this point, arguing that even if one has a new idea or better interpretation of the Torah "he does not say it before someone greater than him in wisdom," that is, his Rav. The implication is unmistakable: calm repetition is preferable in *lernen* to critical innovation.

Consider an example from life in the circle at Kahál Reyim. During a review of a section of the Talmud dealing with the sacrificial rites at the Temple, one of the members of the circle, Reb Lippe, asked a question he seemed to believe would help the group and him better understand the text. Puzzling through his remark, the Rav and several of the others finally decided that his question was not well taken.

"So what have you added?"

"What are you mixing something *new* in for?"

"This has nothing to do with what we are dealing with here."

And then, underscoring the authority of the Talmud and our collective need to be guided by its ways of thinking, the Rav concluded: "But the *gemore* asks a better question."

Listening as he read further and elaborated the line of talmudic reasoning, the men all nodded in agreement. This was indeed a "better question," one that accordingly we all should have asked. The Talmud itself contained the right words and ideas—not Reb Lippe.

"*Yo', a gite kashe*" (Yup, a good question), Reb Lippe agreed. Releasing himself from the restraint of his own curiosity and the need to add "something *new*," he took on the question that had been asked for generations at this point of the page in the Talmud with an adopted enthusiasm—indeed, with a great sense of attachment. The interests of the Book above all others had to be repeated, appreciated, and reassimilated.

The forces which impelled Reb Lippe to take on the Talmud's question in place of his own, as I have tried to demonstrate throughout these pages, are complex. Behind his decision may lie group pressure, the accepted authority of the Rav's interpretations, cultural traditions, or even the tacit rules of play that apply to *lernen*. Yet there is as well a religious belief in the ascendancy of the Book over all independent thinking, which stimulated the enthusiastic, perhaps overplayed, response cry: "*Yo', a gite kashe*."[5]

From here on Reb Lippe would reread the Talmud "once more with feeling"—not his own feelings but those of his forebears and religious superiors. Their questions would become his. That was what, in the words of one man at Kahel Reyim, was meant by "*lernen* in the spirit of the *gemore*."

HOLY ACTIVITY

While not all the men approach *lernen* from a predominantly religious perspective—I have already suggested that for some it is
drama, play, fellowship, or social interaction—those who do tend
to look upon the review of Talmud as a sort of holy activity, akin
to worship or other service to their God. Consider the following:

Often in order to end their preliminary banter, the men at Mekadshey Torah would call out: *"K'vod ha-rav, ovar zman; oleynu lilmod"* (Your honor, the Rav, time has passed; it is incumbent upon
us to study [Torah]).

This summons is not simply a call to begin; it rather intimates
a sense of religious duty. To say "it is incumbent upon us to
study" is to remind all those listening that they share an obligation, which they must fulfill regardless of their individual desires. The obligation to which the speaker refers is framed in the
language of prayer. The phrase *"oleynu lilmod"* (it is incumbent
upon us to study) echoes similar phrases from the liturgy such
as *"oleynu lishabeakh"* (it is incumbent upon us to praise God).

"Kayn, az natkhil, be-ezrat hashem" (Yes, then we shall begin,
with the help of God).

A response that invokes "the help of God" must be distinguished from the attitude the modern brings to his learning. For
the latter, efforts made toward understanding are generated from
within the individual himself. He learns out of a self-interest and
sees himself dependent only upon his training and his own innate
intellectual capacities. He is genuinely a free thinker. But the
person who applies himself to *lernen* does so because he feels the
duty to do so has been laid upon him by some superior force
whose help he must call upon when beginning. He is not at all
free but rather overwhelmed by a feeling of dependence, by his
"own nothingness in contrast to that which is supreme above all
creatures."[6] He has help from those sages who have gone before
(who likewise open their own commentaries with an invocation
of divine guidance and acknowledgement of their dependence
upon *their* teachers). Only the religious person, the one who per-
ceives his *lernen* as fundamentally holy activity, would begin his
study in this way.

Indeed, Jewish law clearly considers the study of Torah as holy
activity and demands that it, like other religiously significant acts,
be preceded with a benediction. There is even a rabbinic debate

as to whether or not meditation about matters of Torah, silent *lernen* as it were, requires similar circumspection and blessing. Most striking in its treatment of *lernen* as holy activity, as something different from other study, is a commentary by the twentieth-century rabbinic giant, the Hofetz Hayim (the nom de plume of Israel Meir Ha-Kohen, d. 1933) who in his exegesis of the codex of Jewish law, the *Mishna Brura* (1:47.A), writes:

> Our sages said that we lost our land [of Israel] because although [the people of] Israel occupied themselves with Torah, they did not occupy themselves thus for the purpose of *lernen* Torah but rather in the way that one learns other types of wisdom and therefore they did not recite the blessing of the Torah before their study. . . . Accordingly, one must be especially careful (to recite this blessing before study) and thereby give thanks that God chose us to study his Torah.

And what of the text? For the religious *lerner* it shares in the *mysterium tremendum*. To recite it is to resonate with the sounds of Sinai, mediated through the voices of the sages. It is the source of a religious experience, to be accomplished only in holy places. Thus, for example, a homiletic Midrash (legend) notes that, when one rabbi meeting another in the marketplace asked him to review some Torah with him there on the spot, he was told that *lernen* as holy activity was not appropriately carried on in such a mundane place:

"Go to the house of study[7] and there I will review it with you."

Only in the synagogue and the house of study is such holy activity properly taken up.

As the activity of studying the Books is holy, so too are they. Thus the actual volumes themselves are not to be taken to profane places, let alone studied there. One would not take them to the bathroom for reading, throw them to the ground to peruse them, or even sling them over one's shoulder while carrying them as one might other kinds of books. They are vessels that enable one to perform a religious act—they are not simply books. Accordingly, as well, the table on which they have been placed for the purpose of *lernen* takes on many of the attributes of their sanctity. Defined as akin to an altar, it must be treated with appropriate circumspection. So just as the *lerner* becomes a surrogate for the priest, so his study table becomes a replacement for the altar.

As holy activity, Jewish study need not always lead to intellectual comprehension. Consider the following assertion in the Talmud itself by one of its most prominent rabbis, Rabbah (B.T. *Avoda Zara* 19a):

> Rabbah said: "A man should always study Torah and (only) afterwards meditate upon it."
> And Rabbah said: "A man should always study—even though he forgets [what he has reviewed] and even though he knows not [i.e. fails to understand] what he says."

From this point of view, *lernen* is much closer to ritual than to intellectual activity. Its sound, format, the resulting communion with others and the implicit steadfast attachment to Judaism that it generates takes religious precedence over comprehension. To be sure, as I have already noted elsewhere, comprehension is hoped for—one does after all "meditate afterwards"—but it is not the sine qua non of *lernen* for the religious person.

The unknowable is no problem for the religious even though it is threatening for his contemporary counterpart who, while he may himself not know everything, firmly believes everything is knowable. The religious Jew begins his day with a liturgical repetition of a verse from Proverbs: "The beginning of wisdom is the fear and awe of God." He reflects this same attitude in his *lernen*. In an earlier chapter, I quoted the response of one of the students to a complex and puzzling piece of Talmud. "*Moiredik*," he said. At that time I translated this response cry as "formidable." The root of the word is, however, the same as for the word for fear and awe. When the modern responds to having puzzled through something with a sense of personal triumph, the religious *lerner* responds with a sense of humility and awe.

HOMILY AND SPIRITUAL INSTRUCTION

In the chapter dealing with cultural performance the matter of spiritual instruction was implicitly raised. There the focus was on the extent to which people can express the spiritual and cultural "truths" of Judaism during *lernen*. For the religious *lerner* such expression inherently becomes a kind of religious act. Consider the following conversation at Mekadshey Torah.

In the midst of a discussion of the efficacy of prayer, the Rav is reminded of a common question among the commentators.

"Everyone," he explains, referring to an "everyone" that includes only those seeking spiritual guidance in the ways of the Talmud. "Everyone asks why Noah [facing the possibility of a devastatingly destructive flood] did not pray to God to avert the flood.

"The answer is as follows: Because Noah knew that his prayers would not be accepted, he did not pray."

"But why did he have no hope?" asks a student, in an implicit call for religious instruction.

First he receives a simple answer, rooted in common sense knowledge. "He saw the people around him and don't you think he understood what manner of men they were?"

Next, however, the Rav goes on to give a homiletic explanation, one that will fire the religious spirit and give the spiritual seeker the response he needs. "This I saw in [the writings of] one of the giants of *Mussar* (homily). *You* must pray, for your own spiritual needs. It does not help? That should not stop you. Abraham did not stop praying for the people of Sodom.

"There is in the *gemore* something very interesting; this is something quite homiletic. It is written that three were in a situation of counsel: Balaam, Jethro, and Job. Balaam gave evil counsel and therefore was killed by the sword. Jethro was worthy because . . ."

"He withdrew after his advice had been given," Rafael, one of the students, fills in.

"And Job," the Rav continues, "who was silent was repaid with punishments. And afterward everyone asks why was Job so severely judged simply because he was silent. So it is explained thus: He was apparently asked once why he remained silent when Pharoh decreed a terrible fate for the Jewish people. He replied: 'What could I have done, what would have helped?' So accordingly, he received punishments—may God protect us all from the likes of these. And only then he cried out.

"So they said to him, 'What are you crying out now; it will not help. Why did you not call out earlier?' "

"Because, then, you were not personally in pain," answers one of the students, stepping psychologically into the homily. He now is teaching Job and himself—to say nothing of the rest of us—this old lesson.

Now the homily turns back to Noah—the exemplar of the righteous Gentile who has already been contrasted with Abraham the premier Jew.

"So likewise Noah was not in pain and therefore did not pray, didn't call out to God on behalf of those who were about to die in the flood. But Abraham did feel the pain of his fellows and did therefore call out a prayer. That is the difference between Noah and Abraham, between the righteous Gentile and the Jew."

The homily offers what might best be called "spiritual instruction." That is, the information it provides seeks primarily to enrich the religious spirit rather than add to rational intellect. Discovering thus what a Jew is supposed to feel in order to pray, the importance of a sense of common humanity, the members of the circle are essentially shown how to grow spiritually and not simply taught new "facts." For some, this sort of religious experience is precisely what draws them toward the *shiur*. They come to be uplifted by their Judaism even as they carry out their felt religious obligation to *lern*.

What has happened in this instance at Mekadshey Torah will happen there again and at other similar gatherings. Indeed, one might argue that the homily or sermon that has at this point in Jewish history made its way into the prayer service grows out of the experience of *lernen* in which it has always been embedded. The people who are spiritually invigorated by the words of their rabbi in the synagogue are in essence sharing in the age-old experiences of spiritual regeneration that were traditionally part of Jewish study.

It is this experience that remains accessible to even those who lack the background for full-blown cultural performance, the patience for social drama, the expertise for word play or interaction according to the rules, but who come with a simple desire to fill their religious needs.

PRACTICAL VERSUS PHILOSOPHIC KNOWLEDGE

One of the most common explanations offered to account for *lernen* has been that the participants do so in order to acquire a practical knowledge of the imperatives of Jewish law. One studies in order to know; and one needs to know in order to do.

To be sure, for many this may be a stimulus for starting or a way of explaining their behavior to the relatively uninformed. A closer look reveals the insufficiencies of this sort of explanation.

First, the Talmud is in fact not the best source for such knowledge, something better acquired through a reading of the various codifications of the law. Among the most commonly used and widely respected are the *Mishna Torah* of Maimonides and the *Mishna Brura* containing the work of Joseph Caro, the *Shulkhan Arukh* and of Moses Isserles, the *Mapa*, as well as commentaries by numerous later rabbinic exegetes. Yet even these texts require the working interpretations of a Rav who as a religious virtuoso can make his way through the complex legal paths that make up Jewish law. In fact, most Jews who wish to learn about matters of practical law often do so through the asking of questions outside the formal boundaries of a class or gain their knowledge informally by conforming to their local community standards. In this, the parochial community, often coinciding with the synagogue, most often serves to guide Jews.[8] Accordingly, if one asks, during the Talmud class, for the *"halakha le-ma'aseh"* (the practical law), the answer is often avoided.

"I'm not ready at this time to make a judgment of practical law," Rav Rotenbush, for example, would often reply to such questions.

If pressed for an answer, he like other *halakhic* experts would commonly respond in the most general terms. "Well, there are those who say," he might begin, providing one interpretation of the practical requirements of the law. "But then again there are others who argue differently," he might quickly add, leaving his questioner with too much information and grappling with no definitive answer.

These efforts to avoid getting committed to specific answers in the public forum are not unique to the Rav. Physicians and lawyers, for example, when lecturing before lay audiences are often asked questions that focus on particular ailments and remedies or specific legal problems. Rather than providing specific replies, these experts often respond in generalities during the public lecture. The doctors describe the etiology or most common therapies while the lawyers detail general legal principles. For more specific answers, the questioner is always directed to the office visit or private consultation. Here the expert can more easily tailor his answers, which might diverge or appear inconsistent with the ideal, as by nature particularities do. Similarly, the Rav relegates specific *halakhic* response to private consultations where he can presumably fit his answers to the situation and the needs of the inquirer.

Nevertheless, digressions of matters to practical *halakhic* knowledge with their search for technical mastery of the ritual demands of Judaism are frequent. People do want to learn what it is they must do in order to be nominally "good Jews." Yet these digressions, although frequent, remain brief; and those experienced in the ways of *lernen* get accustomed to having their specific inquiries deferred.

Instead, the person who wants to learn what he must do in order to be a "good Jew" is directed to a different kind of knowing. It is the sort of knowing which, in the words of Mircea Eliade, "can radically alter the structure of human existence."[9] This is a knowledge that rather than being practical or technical is anchored in faith and what is believed to be the revealed word of God. Abstract, philosophic, theoretical, and conceptual, it aims to inform the spirit while filling the deepest chambers of human thought.

Yet, just as Judaism places boundaries around human existence, so *lernen* restricts this philosophic knowledge. What belief in God engenders, the institution of religion controls. One must get beyond practical surface questions but still not delve too deeply. An example will be useful here. For it, I turn to an episode I recorded during my observations at Beit Rachel.

On this particular occasion, the general discussion taken up by the Talmud and the men of the circle dealt with the prohibitions of carrying objects from one domain to another on the Sabbath. This central restriction is considered at length in the text since the precise definitions of "domain" and "carrying" need to be worked out. In principle, such a topic offers plenty of opportunity for asking practical questions. After all, the matter of Sabbath observance is at the heart of the Jewish religious experience. "More than the Jews have kept the Sabbath," as the Hebrew poet Ahad Ha-Am once put it, "the Sabbath has kept the Jews."

Throughout the *lernen* practical inquiries are deflected and in their place the Rav raises matters of broader Jewish significance. The *shiur* becomes a means of revitalizing the religious consciousness of the *lerners*. The tacit assumption behind all seems to be that the genuinely religious man, the one with faith in God, will find a way to abide by any and all Sabbath restrictions.

"So, I'm not allowed to put the thing down?" Zusya asks, trying to determine specifically what completes the transgression of carrying on the Sabbath.

"This is what you just asked me before and I'm answering you again," the Rav replies. But instead of providing a technical answer he leads Zusya and the rest of the class into a dissertation on the supremacy of *halakha* over sense perception.

"We are not interested in looking at the object, to know if it is actually put down somewhere; but rather we are concerned with a *'halakhic* putting down,' to know if from the point of view of the law what has occurred constitutes a putting down," the Rav explains. That is, as Orthodox Jews, as religious followers of the way of the Talmud, our concern lies not with the sensual world but with the cosmos as defined by our acceptance of the structures of the law.

"Putting it down is prohibited. But I don't mean a putting down wherein I will *see* the object at rest; it is enough for me that the putting down is considered by the *halakha* to be a putting down."

"But in fact?" Zusya injects, still trying to find out the practical law.

Cutting him off, the Rav, attached to concepts rather than being bogged down in facts, goes on, "And this kind of 'putting down' can even be in the air."

Now of course this kind of abstract line of reasoning does not allow for any easy practical conclusions; it eschews them. One might argue that it leaves men like Zusya even more confused than ever about the technical demands of the law. At the same time, however, it impresses the men of the circle with the almost magical power of the law to transform reality, to shred sense perception and replace it with a sense that is filtered through a faith in the divine origins of that law. The entry into this new kind of knowing, away from matters of practical rules or even some sorts of common sense, cannot help but arouse in the men their philosophical inclinations.

In a mood of reflection his peers soon pick up, Shmuel, one of the students, comments: "Yes, even the stars while they move are at rest in the sky. So something *can* be both in the air and at rest at the same time."

"Yes, but Reb Shmuel," the Rav replies, noting the limits to such reflection, "if you say this then admit that after all the entire world hangs in space. There is no absolute putting down. There is no such thing as complete rest. Everything is circling around, moving. The world is in movement; we are in movement, the stars—all that we know is one great sphere that moves."

And then, pausing and waving his hand as if to dismiss all this philosophizing, the Rav concludes, "But this is astronomy and it has nothing to do with us." The flight into the stars is too extreme and so the teacher pulls himself and his class back to the world of the Talmud that holds him in the Jewish world. "If you want a good question, then you know that, for example, the *gemore* asks about a plate that is floating in the water with an object inside it—is this object at rest or in movement? But all this we shall review in good time."

Philosophic reflections must be grounded in the law, anchored in the Talmud's consideration of matter. But the mood of contemplation is not easily broken, and as the men struggle to continue in this new way of thinking, one of them suggests, "So we really have to know what the concept of being at rest is all about."

The men have now traversed the entire range of knowledge: from a beginning seeking after practical guidance to the last ruminations about the full meaning of rest and the absence of movement.

Now, just as at first he called the men away from their descent into praxis, the Rav now prevents them from floating away into the heights of theorizing. "Gentlemen, we are *forbidden* to pass over into the realm of extended and abstract philosophizing, asking questions like 'what is rest.' "

As he goes on to explain, if we try to define everything philosophically we shall end up being uncertain about everything. And for the religious, the realm of uncertainties is if not totally forbidden at least dangerous. Where dogma and law rule, the uncertain can never be completely at home and the philosopher is always suspect.

There are risks of course in thus restraining philosophic knowledge. The religious spirit they engender, the reflection out of which faith can be born, needs to be guided—not destroyed. A story will serve. Stories inform the spirit while anchoring attention and are therefore crucial for fostering yet controlling and shaping religious feelings.

"I once told you, perhaps, but at this opportunity I can tell you again," the Rav begins, hinting that we need this injection of narrative, a kind of religious refrain to our talk.

"There is a famous story from the Baal Shem Tov.* something he says about the *gemore*. The *gemore* says: 'There is no rock [*tsur*, in Hebrew] like our Lord.' This should be read, the *gemore* says, as: 'There is no artist [*tsayar*] like our Lord.'[10]

"Taking this point, the Baal Shem Tov explains matters in his own beautiful way. He tells of a famous artist who painted such wonderful pictures that they seemed to come alive. Once he painted a picture of a man standing with a basket of bread, and a bird actually came to eat the bread out of the basket.

"Now there was a king who heard about this picture and asked that it be brought to him. Seeing the birds come to the picture to eat the bread, he exclaimed: 'Throw out this painting; it is no good and the artist is no good either.'

"Now the people who were his subjects asked him, 'Our Lord, what is wrong with this picture? Look the birds even think the bread is real.'

"The king answered simply: 'If the painting were great, the birds would have been frightened away by the image of the man holding the bread basket. But if they approach the basket this must mean that they can see that the man is not real. And thus, this is not a perfect picture.'

"And still there was another picture, one that another painted of a lion. This one also was brought to the king. And when he saw it, he was afraid that the lion was real and would not believe that it was simply a painting. So he called upon some of his most faithful servants to approach and touch the picture so that he could be sure it was not real. The servants were found and warily they approached the picture until at last they touched it and all could see that the lion was not real.

"So the Baal Shem Tov explained that that picture was so lifelike that the visual sense could not be used to discern whether or not it was real. Only with the sense of touch could we learn that it was not real. But the Lord, blessed be He, is such an artist that even with the sense of touch we cannot discern that things are

*This is Israel ben Eliezer, the eighteenth-century founder of hasidism, the so-called Master of the Good Name, whose life is filled with miracle tales and adventures from which a wealth of homilies have since been drawn.

not real. We touch. We think there is something but it is not
something.

"And indeed I read recently in an article where a professor of
physics has explained that everything we touch is not what we
think it is but is made up of tiny particles we cannot even see—
atoms, molecules, that spin so fast that you think this is something
solid but in fact it is space. Everything is space and spinning. So
much so that if one took the Eiffel Tower and compacted it into
the actual material in it, there would be no more than there is in
a pack of matches!

"So he says, 'There is no artist like our Lord.' There is no Eiffel
Tower. You think you see it but it's all space and atoms. It's your
imagination.

"So too it is when we talk about an object put at rest. It is in
unceasing movement. But while all this is true, we are not interested in physics. For us the *halakha* is important and the *halakha*
concerns itself only with what our eyes can see."

At first glance, the Rav's narrative appears convoluted, a complex web of associations. Upon further consideration, however,
it reveals a kind of intuitive grasp of the needs of the occasion.
It begins by calling the group back to the world of the Talmud,
as a commentary on a talmudic text which in turn is a homily on
a Scriptural verse. Then, as a story, it captures the listeners' imagination and diverts their attention from excessive flights of philosophic fancy while they try to guess the point of each parable. In
the end there comes what until then remained implicit, in the
interstices of the narrative: a religious credo—an assertion of the
wonderful artistry of God which is both the point of the story and
the tacit conclusion of the religious experience of *lernen*.

Yet these are modern men who are being addressed, who perhaps have not spiritually purged themselves of their contemporary age of reason; and therefore the Rav contemporizes matters.
Drawing from an "article" by a "professor of physics," he restates
the idea of God's artistry in terms the contemporary might use,
hiding a religious message in the guise of scientism. But of course
citation of the article is not really a reference to the world of
modern science. Like the story of the painting of the lion, it leads
to the creedal call: "There is no artist like our Lord." Indeed the
phrase "so he says," which follows the reference to the 'scientific'
article, is sufficiently ambiguous so that we are not sure if the
"he" to whom the Rav refers is the Baal Shem Tov or the professor

of physics. And in truth, for the religious it is both. Professor and hasidic master both lead inevitably to faith.

With the belief in God asserted and reasserted, the Rav returns us to the institutional assumptions of *halakhic* Judaism, something which tempers the philosophic insights implicit in his story. Yet the explanation that "the halakha concerns itself only with what our eyes can see" does not really leave the listeners in the realm of practical knowledge. It leaves them once again in generalities, religiously revitalized and ready to *lern* further.

To say that the *lerners* sometimes come to the *shiur* to vitalize their religious inclinations is not to suggest that these efforts are always conscious. On the contrary, often the religious message makes its way into the *lernen* subliminally, carried between the lines of other sorts of conversation. It is not possible here to outline all the ways in which this can occur, but perhaps one example will demonstrate that indeed it does happen. Let us take what might seem the least likely vehicle for matters of religion: the joke.

Again I shall draw from Beit Rachel and an episode in which what appears to be simply an effort at humor turns out to be an expression of the ascendancy of the *halakha* and its divine power to transform reality. Coming at the conclusion of the same class I have just been describing, the episode in a sense recapitulates many of the principles of belief in the law which had been the concern during most of the hour.

"We have to know there are *halakhic* concepts," the Rav begins. We must in faith abandon sense perception and common reason in favor of the conceptions of Jewish law. That is the creedal opening to what follows.

"People tell a well-known joke, but it's not really a joke." A puzzle. How can a joke not be a joke? Only when what it has to say is serious. And what could be more serious than a matter of religious faith?

"There was a Jew who built a sukkah [a temporary dwelling]. But he didn't have sufficient materials with which to build his sukkah.[11] What did he do? One wall he made ten handbreadths long from the roof down, and the rest he left empty. And the *halakha* is that if he has ten handbreadths of wall from the roof it is considered to be a full-length wall, as if the wall went all the way down to the ground. A second wall he built up only ten handbreadths from the ground; and according to the *halakah*, if he has ten handbreadths from the ground it is a wall which rises all the way to the roof. A third wall he built, according to what is written in the *gemore*, with no gap greater than three handbreadths, which is considered by the *halakha* to be fully solid. And the fourth he left open as a doorway [which is likewise judged *halakhically* to have the status of a wall]. And thus he had his four walls.

"He then lay down to sleep inside this sukkah, took off his watch and put it beside his bed. When he arose he found that the watch was missing. He began to investigate. Heavenly Father, where did the thief enter? Here it is closed because of the principle that the wall comes down ten handbreadths. There it is closed because of the principle that the wall goes up ten handbreadths. Over there it is closed because the gaps are less than three handbreadths. And on the fourth side the doorway closes the wall. So from whence did he enter? He thought and thought until he concluded that the thief was no scholar, for he hadn't realized that the sukkah was completely closed!

"Now everyone laughs and says this is a wonderful joke. But the truth is, gentlemen, according to the *halakha* there are four walls. But what the law calls a wall is not identical with what is called a wall by a contractor! In the *halakha*, however, this is a wall. And we believe in this wall more surely than in any real wall. This is the *halakha* from Moshe [who received it from God] on Sinai."

In this last comment the Rav invokes the metahistorical memory of national revelation and reminds the men of the circle that for the believing Jew every jot and tittle of the *halakha* is rooted in a relationship with God and Jewish history. The laughter of the joke still reverberates in the little room behind the synagogue. These are not, however, laughs of derision or ridicule. In them rings the belief in the law which the men share with the character in the story. Strictly speaking, the men of faith, these People of the Book, are laughing at themselves for they too saw full walls in the sukkah. They saw those walls through the books they believe in.

"Why the Holy One, blessed be He, set matters as He did, we do not know," the Rav concludes. "But they are *halakha*."

And a belief in its legitimacy is tantamount to a belief in God's.

In the refreshment of spirit the joke provides is a religious vitality that mixes with it. In this the men of Beit Rachel have, one might suggest, experienced the religious imperative, expressed in the Talmud and Jewish tradition, to "rejoice with trembling." They laugh but in the heart of their mirth lie religious feelings. Even during joking, room is made for the expression of religious sensibilities.

THE RELIGIOUS IMPERATIVE

For the religious, the experience of *lernen* is both the fulfillment of the imperatives of faith and their source of support. It is in the nature of a supreme religious act. Nowhere perhaps is this more clearly seen than in the age-old tradition of the *tikkun*.

The concept of *tikkun* or restoration which has its roots in *Kabbalah* or Jewish mysticism is far too complex to be fully explained here. Suffice it to say that in essence it refers to the exercises—mental and spiritual—in which Jews may engage to restore themselves to the perfection with which they believe God meant to endow them. There are a variety of ways in which *tikkun* is carried out, but among the most important is the study of Torah. For the *kabbalist* mystics, the study often consisted of deciphering the hidden messages contained in the letters of the Scriptures, letters which once transformed into numerical equivalents could then be reformulated as hidden homilies and lessons.

For the ordinary Jew of Ashkenazic or Western origins, *tikkun* was something infrequently practiced. On one night of the year, however, the first night of the holy day of Shevuot, the festival devoted to a celebration of the Jewish receipt of the Torah on Sinai, *tikkun* in the form of an all-night study vigil became an accepted tradition. Among many, a set canon of selected passages from all Jewish religious classics was recited. This was a kind of *lernen* as worship in which the hum of men intoning the verses became indistinguishable from the drone of others singing through the liturgy. For others, *lernen* during that night became a kind of protracted *shiur* during which one Rav or several students led people through a variety of texts. What is crucial to realize, however, is that on Shevuot and during the *tikkun* any and all boundaries between *lernen* and worship or religious activity disappeared. What kept the men awake or at least seated around the table more than anything else was a belief that through their Jewish study they were serving God, repairing themselves spiritually, and celebrating the festival.

The culmination of that *lernen*, moreover, was not the gaining of insights or even the simple accumulation of knowledge but rather the joint prayer service held by the men who had been together throughout the night just as the sun rose over the horizon. In this the *lernen* became inextricably linked with the worship. The one activity could either be seen as the preparation for the other or its culmination. But in either case, one understood both study and prayer as part of the same experience. Both were generated by the religious imperative.

To be sure, some men came to spend the night in fellowship, for drama, for play, and so on. But as the hours ticked away and fatigue began to overcome even the most hardy, religion—the feeling that the fate of one's soul depends upon whether or not he makes the right interpretation of a sacred verse, or at least properly recites a passage of Torah—more than anything else held people around the table and over their books.

This imperative has of course been eroded, as has much of religion, by the tides of time and the wash of modernity. Accordingly, the *tikkun* of Shevuot night is no longer attended by the majority even among the Orthodox. Yet the survival of the practice of *lernen* all night, even if carried on by a precious few, is testament to the strong feelings that once supported it.

In his essays on *Jewish heritage*, Ludwig Lewisohn[12] perhaps captures best the extent to which the religious imperative toward *lernen* survives among the Jews. He repeats a story about a small group of Jewish survivors of the Nazi holocaust who in 1946 were making their way from Siberian exile westward to the Polish *shtetl* that had once been their home:

> The town was a mass of rubble. They did not find even graves. All their kith and kin had been burned alive in the crematoriums. The synagogue was in ruins. But a stair to the cellar had been saved. Descending that stair these Jews found a few Talmudic volumes, charred and water-soaked but still usable in part. And they procured them a few tallow-candles and sat down to read a page or two. There came one running then and cried: "Jews, do you forget that you are running for your lives? The Soviets are closing the frontiers. The American zone is still far off! Flee!" And one of the group waved the messenger aside: "*Shah!*" he said gravely [Be still]. *M'darf lernen!*" [One must learn].

It is a familiar theme among the Jewish people for whom "the house of study was not important because the world needed it, but, on the contrary, the world was important because houses of study existed in it."[13] Nearly two millenia earlier, confronted by the invading armies of Rome, the rabbis of Judea had been similarly engaged and engrossed. Their story, immortalized in the Haggadah, is recited each year at the Seder, itself an archtypical synthesis of worship, Jewish study, and national celebration. And, as we have seen, the imperative to *lern* is in certain precincts still felt today.

In the sacred volumes and holy folios, the religious Jew in search of his faith will find the vital ideas of his people. Here the faithful, perhaps more than anywhere else, find another world to live in—one that transcends place and history, where the beginning and end is rooted in belief and the path in between is no less than the only way imaginable for them, the *halakha*.

8
"SIYUM"

When something is not apprehended by the mind, only the imaginative faculty remains.

RABBI NACHMAN of Bratslav

Throughout the preceding pages I have considered *lernen* and those who engage in it from a variety of perspectives. Each chapter has tried to elaborate more or less a single line of vision and series of insights. While these may be combined by the reader in order to gain some sense of the whole, the effort to fill in the blood and tissue of the life of *lernen* is more properly the responsibility of the writer. Wherever possible I have tried to flesh out the meaning of my analysis with extended examples and vignettes from the real life of the circles I joined and observed. Now, at last, I would like to go further and provide a narrative account.

To be sure, a true sense of the life of *lernen* requires something more than even the most articulate of written records; it necessitates the actual experience. Nothing less can genuinely inform one of what it means to sit in the circle, hear the sounds of *lernen*, play by its rules, fall into the Talmud page and work one's way back out again, join in fellowship and become touched by the cultural sense of one's Jewishness and the religious spirit of one's Judaism. Still, with all its shortcomings, a narrative account is better than nothing. In what follows my earlier analyses will serve as the deep structure of what I describe. But even for those inclined to ignore my analysis, the following is meant to fire the imagination, give a sense of what goes on inside and what it is like to be there.

There is of course no perfect time to enter the circle, to experience every facet of its life and *lernen*; but some times are perhaps better than others. Among these is the *siyum*, the celebration that accompanies the group's completion of a tractate or volume of study. The *siyum* is the single most important festival of *lernen*, a commemoration of fellowship, an end and a new beginning, a nodal point in the cycle of *lernen*. One book is ended and another begun. It is a moment of effervescence during which the assembled find themselves aroused to an intensified communion, religiosity, and *lernen*. Everything they normally do they do with greater energy and devotion at the *siyum*. And added to all this social and psychological energy is a feast. It is an important meal, a happy one with the legal power to cancel less joyous events such as fasts and periods of Jewish national mourning. Like other feasts, it takes on certain characteristics of a religious ceremony and cultural performance, further intensifying the state of collective enthusiasm and effervescence.[1]

There were quite a number of such celebrations that I attended, benchmarks in the life of the circle. These occasions throbbed with life, and as I sat among the celebrants I often thought that this, more than anything else I witnessed, was what I wanted to replay. And so in these remaining pages I shall try to do so.

I have selected three typical occasions. One took place at Beit Rachel, another at Mekadshey Torah, and a third in Smotra. I shall recreate and try to communicate the character of each in its turn.

BEIT RACHEL

For several weeks in anticipation of their coming to the end of a volume of study, the men of the Beit Rachel circle had been planning a *siyum*. They controlled the pace of their *lernen* so that the conclusion of the tractate would come about on Rosh Hodesh, the beginning of the new month. Such a coincidence of end and beginning would, the men believed, endow the occasion with an extra dimension of religious significance. Holy days were especially auspicious times to complete a cycle of study and begin another. After all, at the beginning of the Jewish month the moon likewise ended one cycle and began another. On these days, therefore, the actions of men would most appropriately parallel the turning of the spheres and the patterns of nature. Carefully, during the last few weeks, the number of pages and lines had been calculated so that we would be certain to complete our volume precisely on time. If the *lernen* seemed to be proceeding too rapidly, someone would ask a digressive question or make a somewhat controversial remark that would grab attention and, in a kind of tacit agreement to slow our movement down the Talmud page, the entire group would launch a conversation perfectly timed to fill the evening. On other occasions, if we seemed to get too bogged down and increased recitation seemed called for, questions would be speedily answered or dismissed as too digressive. Sometimes they would simply be ignored as the review of the page moved forward almost mechanically.

Zusya, one of the organizers of the circle, took the lead in making preparations for the *siyum*. First, he collected the money from each of us in order to buy the refreshments. Later, he bought most of the food and, arriving earlier than usual on the *siyum* night, set the table with wines, herring, chick-peas, pickles, cakes, and cookies, which would be our treat upon completing the tractate.

On that evening there was an air of excitement in the little room behind the synagogue where our group met. As each man entered, he began to warm himself at the space heaters which melted away the raw January cold. The bare table around which we normally reviewed the holy pages of Talmud was covered tonight with a white tablecloth, upon which lay not only the large volumes of study which normally were there but also the sparkling drinks and food.

Zusya paced expectantly, puffing on a dangling cigarette and warmly greeting each man who entered. He acted tonight at once like a proud host and an anxious caterer as he pointed out the many dishes that had been prepared. Yoel, another member, brought in a bag of bananas that he placed in a dish. Moshe brought a bottle of slivovitz, the strong plum brandy that we would later use to toast one another to life and to continued *lernen*.

The Rav was late, and so we waited. "He's the *baal simkha*" (the celebrant), Mordecai explained, and so we had to wait for him.

We talked about a wide variety of things, sometimes in Hebrew and other times in Yiddish. But always we talked—almost as if silence was a sin. And as we talked I got a sense that we grew even closer than usual. The sound of our voices, the tempo of our banter rose and fell, sweeping over us like a tide coming in. At first it seemed distant, something one could stay clear of, but in time it reached everyone, and even Alex, the Dutchman who normally sat in near silence, began talking.

Each man who entered received a special greeting, as if we had not seen him for a long time. Several men were spontaneously assigned special identities appropriate to the occasion. Zusya became the *"baal akhsanya"* (innkeeper and caterer), Moshe the *"lamdan"* (scholar); I was the *"matmid"* (diligent student), and of course the Rav—for and with all of us—was the *"baal simkha"* (celebrant).

Amid the clatter of conversation—talk about the Soviet invasion of Afganistan, the price of hats, the effects of media attention on the Ayatollah Khomeini's power in Iran, the similarity between Russia and Nazi Germany, the growing weakness of America and the risks of nuclear war, the importance of *lernen*—Moshe began to sing. It began as one of those tunes that lack words but which are sung in a tempo and rhythm that make feet start to tap and fingers drum. A kind of subordinate accompaniment to our talk, it created an atmosphere in which even these serious political discussions took on the character of play and festivity. After all, how serious could matters be if we tolerated a happy melody as the background sound to our talk?

"Where is the Rav?" Mendel asked.

"Are you sure he's coming?"

"Of course, I spoke with him earlier at *ma'ariv* [the evening service]," Zusya explained, telling us all, incidentally, that he had been careful in this part of the preparation as well.

"But he's late," Shmuel noted.

"Look," Zusya said, "he knows that tonight we're not *lernen* so much—there are just a few lines left, so he's coming a little later."

"So, Yoel, where have you been all these weeks?" Mendel asked his friend and fellow student. One does not simply stop coming to class without giving a public accounting upon returning.

"Were you sick?"

"I was sick; I was resting."

"Alright, but you made it back for this special occasion—good. Now maybe you'll have a slivovitz and warm up a bit."

Moshe opened his Talmud. As if on cue, so too did Mordecai, Mendel, and Yoel. Their open books changed the character of the conversation. It was not the content of what the men were talking about that changed, but the open books seemed to frame it all and made every word spoken seem a part of the forthcoming study. As one man once explained, talk with the books closed is *hefker*, groundless and illegitimate. With them open, however, it becomes a part of the *lernen*.

Now, with the books open, the political conversation about Russia, Afghanistan, and America took a new turn.

"I always say," Yoel began, quoting Talmud, "'Who is wise? He who knows his place.' What does this mean?"

The men were all quiet now, listening to their fellows argue his point.

"If a man doesn't know the breadth of his possibilities, his potential, then he doesn't know his place; he's not wise. The same is true of a state. If the state doesn't understand its power, its possibilities and potential; if they don't know when to call in the army and when to stop talking or giving warnings, they lose everything. And that's what's happening today in America. They make sanctions; they stop sending wheat to the Russians. That's not wisdom."

"That's a nice homily, but are you prepared for a nuclear war, *'lehashmid, leharog ule'abed'* [to destroy, to kill and to annihilate] the whole world?" asks Zusya, quoting a phrase from the Purim Megilla we all know.

In the face of our open books, the conversation, concerned with profane, everyday news events, has begun to resonate with references to Torah. It's hard to say that the change is conscious, but it is perceptible.

And all the while Moshe is humming and singing.

"Did you understand this piece of Rashi?" Mendel asks Mordecai, pointing into his open book.

"Not completely. We'll ask the Rav when he comes in to go over it again."

And with that the Rav enters, and all the men half stand up in a display of respect. With a quick wave of his hand, he motions them to be seated.

"We were worried already," Mendel explains.

"About the food going to waste."

"No, no, no, heaven forbid."

"Well, I understand," the Rav answers, "that we shall review a bit and then we shall finish." He smiled broadly. "So let us begin with the last Mishna and review."

The same topics that in the preceding classes had taken up hours of debate and discussion now pass quickly.

Noticing the resplendent table for the first time, the Rav suggests in the midst of his opening recitation: "We should really take a picture of all this!"

"The last line, the other side of the page," Mendel whispers to Yoel who, having been away for several weeks, needs some help in finding the starting place. Everyone must have his place on the proper word. It is no formal rule, but we all know this is the very least expected of us.

Chanting and declaiming the words, the Rav makes it all sound like some grand proclamation that he is reading. His words and those of the text become intermingled so that book and teacher speak with a single voice and authority. The drama that is normally in his voice is exaggerated this evening. "How did they purify the Temple Court? First they immersed the vessels; and those vessels which could not be immersed—with regard to them, it was said to those who passed into the court: "Be careful not to touch the vessels!"

The students are quick to cue the Rav. They seem to be hurrying him through. But the Rav will not be hurried. His recitation is deliberate and calm. His translations come on cue. He asks the questions that remain implicit in the text and in answer to them notes: "We shall soon *lern* all this.

"For all the vessels in the Temple there were duplicates. And if the first became impure, the duplicates were brought out to be placed in use instead. And thus the Temple was never without its holy vessels."

For a moment, the food and drink on our table disappear from consciousness and instead we are thinking about the vessels of the Temple. One bottle of wine comes to signify one of these vessels while another is its duplicate. Playing with these articles, the Rav and students appear to visualize the Temple Court.

"All the vessels in the Temple were capable of immersion, except for the altar of gold and the altar of copper. These were considered connected to and a part of the ground."

"And ground?" Zusya cues.

"And ground cannot become impure, according to Rabbi Eliezer," the Rav continues reading from the Talmud.

"But the sages say," he goes on, citing the majority opinion in the Talmud, "because they are covered they do not become impure [and not because they are attached to the ground]."

Now he stops reading and launches a discussion. "But what have the sages really added? We shall have to *lern* further. For if they are indeed covered, they are made of metal—and metal can become impure. So why does the *gemore* say this? We'll see later on that the *gemore* will offer two explanations and that in fact our text here in the Mishna [we are now reading] is missing a word. There is a dissension: some say that the altars do become impure because they are covered with gold and copper while others say they do not because they are connected to the ground. But all this we shall *lern* a bit further on in the *gemore*."

The men begin to ask for clarifications. They want to be certain that they understand as much as possible in advance.

The Rashi commentary is next. It is recited quickly for it recaps precisely what the Rav has just told us and we have discussed. Still, we dare not skip this commentary—to overlook it would not only break the tradition of our review but also signify a laxity in our approach. This none of us is willing to do. As we would not skip even the most meaningless words of the liturgy, so we would not pass over reciting even the most repetitive of Rashi's commentaries.

The Rav goes on and on, reciting all we have already gone over during the last several classes. As he intones the words a few of the others begin to sway back and forth, much as they do while praying. He does too. The rhythm of his recitation, the tempo of his translations and glosses take on an imperative all their own. Only during a pause in his cantillation does anyone dare interrupt and ask a question.

Deliberately and inexorably, we approach the final lines of the text. In our right hands we all hold a heavy sheaf of pages, the symbol of the hours and days we have been together and turned those pages in this volume. In our left hand are but a few folios—the last steps of our journey through the book.

Scrupulously the men follow along with their fingers and eyes. Two fingers, the index and middle, keep the place. When we move our attention toward the margins and one of the commentaries, one finger stays in the middle, marking the core *gemore* text, and the other moves to the margin, marking the lines of commentary. And when we all look away from our books and talk to one another, both fingers hold the spot to which we must return when once again the Rav takes up his recitation.

"And the *gemore* goes on to say."

The book is speaking in the Rav's voice. Not simply a text to be read, it becomes words to be listened to and heard.

Gradually we all begin reciting those words along with the Rav, in strophic chorus. He asks questions, we read answers. We ask questions, he reads answers. His voice rises, ours falls. Ours rises, his falls.

The Talmud's discussion of the Temple and its vessels, the topic considered in these final lines, is filled with references to the miracles of God. Quoting the sage, Rabbi Joshua ben Levi, the Rav reads from the page before us:

"A great miracle was performed with the shewbread: as it was when placed on the table so it was when removed [a week later]—as it is written: 'to put hot bread in the day when it was taken away' [1 *Sam.* 21:7]. That is, the bread was as hot on the day it was removed as on the day it was placed from the oven on the table in the Temple."

In previous classes when this practice was discussed in detail, we all expressed our appreciation of this "miracle." Now once again the men marvel at the "miracle" in a kind of obligatory, even ritualistic expression of wonder.

"*Viter*," the Rav cues us to contain our discussions of the miracle and read on with him in the text.

We are ready for the quickened pace. One senses a growing impatience among those around the table. A finger that moves just slightly ahead of the recitation. A cover flapped or a plethora of cuing all indicate a readiness to get to the end and launch the festivities. While often ready to linger in their *lernen*, tonight the men's excitement about ending seems to bubble over, infecting even the Rav whose deliberate recitation and chanting becomes perceptibly faster. There are fewer pauses between one passage and another. Digressive questions seem by now all but gone from the proceedings, and the briefest of explanations suffices for even the most opaque passages in the Talmud.

And then, all of a sudden, just as we reach the last lines, the forward movement stops—almost as if we were ready to defiantly put off our completion and abandonment of the text. In part the Talmud itself is the cause of it all. In the text, somewhat distant from the topic of the Temple's vessels with which it was concerned until now, there appears a statement that celebrates *lernen* and scholarship.

With Moshe cuing him, the Rav recites: "Reb Abahu said in the name of Reb Eleazar, '*Talmidey khakhamim* [scholars] are not subject to the fires of hell.' "

Having completed a tractate of the Talmud, we cannot help but feel that perhaps we too may now count ourselves among the *talmidey khakhamim*. And if in fact we are among the scholars, this must be demonstrated. As if on cue, the next line of the Talmud draws a sudden outburst of questions and an extended discussion.

"As the fires of hell cannot subjugate the scholar so no fire can destroy the salamandra."

"And what is the 'salamandra'?" asks Mordecai.

"Oh, right away we shall see [the answer] in Rashi."

Reading from the commentary, the Rav explains that the salamandra is an animal created in a place where fire has been burning continuously for seven years.

"I never heard of such an animal," Mordecai objects while Shmuel whispers under his breath something that sounds like "preposterous."

"There are lots of things you never heard of," Zusya explains, taking up a kind of tacit defense of the text and its commentators.

"And the fire on the altar could not penetrate the gold and copper with which it was covered," the Rav continues, satisfied to let matters drop.

But the men hold on to the previous line in the text. Yoel's fingers do not move. He looks up: "Well, I never heard of it either."

"Anyone who *lerns gemore* knows of this creature," the Rav explains. Ignorance of the salamandra comes from too close an attachment to the real world while knowledge and experience comes from a pursuit of the ways of the Talmud, which clearly have an ontological superiority.

Pinchas, allying himself with that superior domain, reads from the Tosafist commentary: "The salamandra is like a mouse."

"Oh, so it *flees* from fire. That's what makes us think that it is born in it," Mordecai reasons aloud. No one seems to react to this reinterpretation. Instead, pursuing their own lines of *lernen*, some men are reading the Rashi commentary aloud; others have made their way to the other side of the page and review the Tosafot commentary. The Rav himself has taken another volume from the shelf and is looking up a cross-reference for the term, trying to demonstrate that anyone who knows his way through Talmud would have come across the salamandra elsewhere.

Mordecai, however, appears satisfied with himself, having reached an explanation with which he feels comfortable. "This salamandra," the Rav announces, reading from the second volume of Talmud, "is no common animal. It does not come from just any fire. You would not, for example, find it in an oven. No, no. It only comes to life as a result of a miraculous transformation of the fire."

This is apparently not the place or time for a theological debate about miracles. The men receive this declaration in silence. Having exercised themselves in a display of *lernen*—each man according to his needs and abilities—they go on to complete the tractate.

"The fires of hell cannot subjugate the sinner," the Rav reads aloud. "What does this mean? This speaks only of one who sins a little bit, like every Jew who makes a few sins. And why is this so? Because our Father Abraham redeemed us—all of us except those who marry Gentile women, for those men are among the uncircumcised."

The text is confusing in its syntax, language, and allegory. The look of puzzlement on the student faces which greet his looking up from the page moves the Rav to explain.

"In other words, all Jewish males are, after all, circumcised," he begins, taking for granted that in the world defined by Jewish law, the only one the Talmud, and we the students of it, can recognize, all Jewish men are indeed circumcised and share in the time-hallowed Covenant of Abraham. Those who are not inhabit other worlds.

"But if a Jew commits the heinous sin of marrying a Gentile woman," the Rav continues, raising his voice, "he becomes un-circumcised again. So you see everyone that is circumcised, Father Abraham—who sits at the gateway to hell—does not allow to be brought into that hell. He says: 'These are *my* people.'

"This is what the *gemore* tells us. Abraham our Father sits at the gateway to hell, and anyone who is about to be brought in there is first examined by him to see whether or not he is circum-cised. And if he is, he says, 'He's one of mine.' But one who has committed a sin such as this one——"

And now Shmuel cues the next obvious words: "——is no longer recognized as circumcised."

"This is only one opinion," Ezra whispers to Zusya, indicating his familiarity with the Talmud.

"You mean he actually loses his circumcision?" Mordecai asks skeptically.

"No, no, no. This is simply a concept. It is *as if* he were not circumcised," the Rav explains.

"But this is not the *halakha le-mayseh*, is it?" asks Shmuel, hoping for information regarding the "practical law" in such cases—as if there were anything "practical" about who does or does not get into hell.

"It depends," the Rav replies. Such quick judgments about the practical consequences of marrying out of the faith are not to be publicly made. The matter is far too charged with emotion. So without actually answering the question, the Rav goes on to finish the last few lines of the text.

"There is a fire from below and a fire from on high."

Again the men are excitedly swaying back and forth in obvious anticipation of the end. They once again cue or echo every other word the Rav recites.

"The fire from below is the fire of hell, but the fire from above is the fire of God; it is the fire of the burning bush, the fire which Moses saw in the wilderness. This is the fire; the same fire that did not consume the wood of the bush does not consume the altar. Which fire subjugates and destroys? The fire from below. But the fire from on high does not destroy, as it is written":

And the men all join in: "And the bush was not consumed."

With this we end the text and, without missing a beat, launch a chorus of recitations. The words come from the verses of conclusion that are always added upon ending a volume of study. Intoned like prayers, they express thanks to God for having enabled the completion of another tractate. A few words stand out clearly in the hum of recitation:

> May it be thy will Lord our God and God of our fathers that your Torah be our craft and occupation in this world and remain with us in the next.

The mumbling continues and again a few words stand out and receive a special emphasis:

> We thank you Lord our God and God of our fathers that you have placed our share among those who sit in the house of study and did not place us among those who sit on the corners and in the alleys. For we arise and they arise; we arise to busy ourselves with Torah, and they arise to be occupied with vanity. We toil and they toil; we toil and receive reward, and they toil and receive no reward. We run and they run; we run to everlasting life, and they run into a pit of destruction. . . .

The recitations continue, always drawing the line between two completely antithetical worlds, between the world of *lernen* and its profane counterpart. *Lernen* is not simply an avocation but rather an opportunity to become aligned with the forces of light, the sacred spheres and the favor of God.

Plainly moved by the words they have spoken and the experience of conclusion, the men stand up to recite the special *kaddish* or memorial prayer with which such occasions traditionally end. Suddenly, however, they realize they are only nine—one short of a *minyan*, without which no *kaddish* can be recited.

"If Reb Rafael had been here," says the Rav, noting that one of our regulars is missing, "we would have had the tenth man."

"Maybe Elijah, the prophet will join us," Zusya says, reminding us of the many folktales in which a mysterious tenth man appears only to turn out to be the immortal Elijah.

"Well, in case not, maybe we can catch someone passing by on the street," replies the Rav.

Moshe walks to the window and looks out. It is late by now and cold. The street is empty.

"Go outside and look. You can see the corner from there. Surely some Jew will come by and want to join us for this *simkha* [celebration]."

"Maybe we can count one of the scrolls of Torah as part of the *minyan*," Mordecai suggests, recalling yet another folk belief and tradition.

"Oh, now you're a *dayan*, Mordecai," says Zusya, laughing. The *dayan* or judge is commonly appointed only from among the ranks of the greatest scholars and rabbis. Mordecai laughs too. Perhaps he has gotten carried away with the sense of accomplishment that completing a volume of Talmud engenders.

"Look, with Moshe outside, we only have eight now."

"No, no. You needn't worry. We won't lose any of those we already have—not before the celebration. No one leaves before the celebration."

"In the yeshiva, they never had this problem. There were always enough people there to say the *kaddish*."

"Yes, but for them a *siyum* was a common occurrence. Hardly a month could go by without someone finishing a tractate."

"So in the yeshiva they must have been constantly celebrating."

"Look, when you *lern* all the time, *that* is a constant celebration!"

The books are now collected. Zusya piles them neatly on a corner of the table, and Ezra takes them and places them on the shelf.

A blast of cold air has come in from the open window where Shmuel is looking out after Moshe: "Oh, it's going to go down to zero tonight," he notes. It is a tacit admission that they are unlikely to find someone walking on such a night.

"No, no, don't worry. It'll be alright," Mordecai assures him, catching the drift of his meaning.

The Rav sits silently. With the formal part of the *lernen* over, he is now simply another man sitting around the table. This part of the proceedings offers an opportunity for the others to run things.

"Do you know of any group studying *kabbala* [mysticism]?" asks Shmuel, turning away from the window. "A friend of mine is looking to join such a circle."

"Oh yes, in Katamon, at Vingelberg's yeshiva," Yoel replies."

"Gentlemen, let us begin," the Rav announces suddenly, holding open a new book. The custom of the *siyum* always includes not only the formal conclusion of one volume of study but also the ritualized commencement of another. This *lernen* is however more symbol than substance since only the Rav holds a book. The others simply listen.

The tractate is one dealing with the laws of the Sabbath, a volume that the men have in advance agreed will be the next one they review in the months ahead.

"We shall only read the first sentence."

Zusya is busy opening jars and setting out toothpicks. Mordecai silently passes out forks. All the while the Rav recites and translates. But he makes no further moves to explain and discuss, noting, "The details we shall go over in our next class.

"Maybe I'll just add a word or two about what we have just reviewed in the volume we have concluded," the Rav continues after a moment's pause, as if stalling for time while Moshe is out looking for a tenth man. His monologue, filled with rhetorical questions and answers, simulates the dialogue of genuine *lernen*. "The *gemore* says that the fires of hell cannot subjugate *talmidey khakhamim*. Here we see something about the *talmid khakham* [scholar]. He is not just a person who has studied and then knows something. Rather a *talmid khakham* is transformed completely, and not just into a person who has knowledge. For the Talmud tells us that a *talmid khakham* has a body of fire—like the salamandra—and therefore the fires of hell cannot destroy him. Why 'a body of fire'? Because it is written [in Scripture]: 'All of my words are like fire.'

"But if it says 'all of my words are like fire,' how does this show that the body of the *talmid khakham* is 'of fire'? Ah, but a *talmid khakham*—that's the difference between all other wisdom and the wisdom of the Torah. All other wisdom transforms a person into a wise man. But the wisdom of the Torah transforms a person into becoming a part of the Torah itself. Now that he knows Torah, he and it are no longer two things, two separate entities. Rather, both of them are bodies of fire, different from all other wisdom. For the Torah is attached to the fire from on high of God, and the same fire lights up the *talmid khakham*. And if the man and the Torah are one then, as it is written in the *Zohar* [the source of most Jewish mystical tradition]: 'The Holy one blessed be He, the Torah and Israel are one.'

"The person involved in the study of the Torah is transformed. He makes himself into a Torah-true Jew, a spiritual man. And that is what attaches him to his God; and thus through the merits of *lernen*, no fires of hell can destroy or subjugate him."

"Wonderful. Amen," Zusya replies.

"*Yasher Koakh* [May your strength be increased]," adds Mordecai in a traditional blessing.

"A beautiful homily," Alex adds.

Seeing he has held the men's attention and still lacking a tenth man, the Rav continues. As long as the *lernen* goes on, it will be legally (*halakhically*) possible to recite a *kaddish* when a minyan is gathered.

"And there's one more thing I want to say. We have reviewed the tractate *Hagiga*. This volume begins with the idea that there is a special commandment 'to be seen.' Now what is this commandment? It requires a man to come to the Holy Temple three times a year 'to be seen' before God. There is no set measure of what a person must bring upon these occasions, but the Torah does say: "They shall not see my face empty-handed.'

"Why, in truth, did the Torah command us thus? It's simple. When a person knows that he must appear at the Holy Temple and is required to bring with him a sacrifice, then he prepares himself. He must think about it all beforehand. He does not just do it in an offhand manner—'I think I'll just drop in at the Temple.'

"No, he must enter into the Temple out of a sense of preparation. For days beforehand he must visit and examine the [animal which will be the] sacrifice, to see if it is without blemish. And so in all this time he is forced to think about what he is about to do.

"You are bringing a sacrifice? You are not coming into the Temple to say, 'Here I am, if you please!' No, you are coming with a sacrifice and you say, 'Here I am; I have come to be close to you, Master of the Universe.'*

"And when a person comes to be close, then 'being seen' brings him to such a height. In the beginning he comes to be seen, but in the end he is worthy enough to see. That is why we learned that a blind person is exempt from this commandment. For as the Lord must see him, so he too must be able to see the glory of the Lord at the Temple."

"He's coming, he's coming," Yoel calls out.

"Who?"

"Reb Moshe!"

The calm that reigned for a while during Rav's homilies is swept away by Yoel's announcement from his place at the window.

Trying still to maintain decorum, the Rav nevertheless continues: "So in the beginning, he came to be seen and in the end he gets to see."

Over and over he repeats this last point, and by the fourth time he has gotten several of the men to echo it like some refrain.

"That, gentlemen, is the special quality of the commandment to be seen."

With that, the door suddenly swings open and in walks Moshe leading a young boy of seventeen or eighteen who will make the *minyan*, who has "come to be seen" (and counted) and who will in the end "get to see" our celebration.

"Ah!" exclaimed the Rav, with a broad smile on his face that matched the expression of almost everyone else in the room. "We have a tradition from the Baal Shem[2]—where there are nine, he says, there will come a tenth. So I believed if I extend my words long enough, a Jew will in the meantime appear."

We all stood as the Rav began to deliberately and slowly chant the *Kaddish*. In a display of devotion and concentration, he closed his eyes and began to sway back and forth. There was no need for anyone to explain to the young man what was going on. The *yarmulke* on his head was enough to indicate to us that he knew the ways of tradition and must surely have realized what he had become part of in this room.

*There is a play on words here since in Hebrew the word for sacrifice (*korban*) is etymologically related to the words for "becoming close" (*lehitkarev*). The latter means, in addition, "to be sacrificed." The play on words is surely not lost upon these men for whom Hebrew is the language of everyday speech and to whom the notion of sacrifice and worship are not at all strange.

Here, from a corner or an alley, a young boy had come to join those who had just given thanks to their God for allowing them to sit around the *lernen* table. Here was the bringing to life of the aspirations of the prayer just recited. One could not help but feel moved.

With great ceremony, the Rav ended his prayers by picking up a piece of cake and intoning aloud the words of the common blessing over food.

"Amen, amen," everyone answered. And then each in his turn took some food or drink from the table and uttered his own words of blessing.

"*Nu, nu*, eat something, take a drink," the men called to the stranger.

"You see, we have finished a tractate," the Rav explained.

"Yes, so I understood."

"*L'chayim*" (To life), Yoel announced as he lifted his glass.

"*L'chayim tovim u-l'shalom*" (To good life and peace), he was answered.

"*Nu*, Reb Pinchas, eat a few chick-peas."

And now the Rav offered an extemporaneous benediction: "May we be worthy enough to be redeemed fully in the near future." No longer reviewing text or reciting homilies, he was now leading us in blessings. This one was the traditional call for a speedy return of the Messiah. The eating, which I had supposed would primary, was quickly giving way to an atmosphere of worship and hope. This was no simple collation but an occasion to express the lingering spiritual hopes of the Jewish people and to bless God. Now, perhaps more clearly than ever before, I could sense the connection between *lernen* and the cultural and religious existence of these Jews.

The remainder of the evening passed rather quickly, as if the call for redemption and the arrival of the Messiah had marked a climax. To be sure, there was a joint recitation of grace when everyone had eaten enough and some cleaning up of the many leftovers. But after the Rav's prayer, the focus had rapidly shifted toward the next class. Once again the group would commence the endless cycle of *lernen*, for the men had not joined the circle simply to review one tractate of the Talmud. They had joined to *lern*, and that was something that went on forever.

MEKADSHEY TORAH

As at Beit Rachel, so too at Mekadshey Torah the matter of the *siyum* had not been treated lightly. For weeks in advance preparations had been made and money had been collected to buy the food with which to celebrate the occasion. For this circle, this *siyum* had additional significance. After several years of *lernen* this would be their first conclusion ceremony, and they all worried over it, wanting it to turn out perfectly.

The wives would be invited—not to take part in the *lernen*, for this was not in the domain of their responsibilities. They would, however, prepare the food—a major feast was expected—and join in the actual celebration. Some men would even bring other relatives. I would invite my father who was visiting me at the time.

The occasion had all the drama of a school commencement. Save for the academic regalia and the marching, many of the other aspects of the occasion—the music, the speeches, the handing out of honors—all reminded me of graduations I had attended.

As the men entered, each one made note of the guests who were arriving.

"Look, Shmuel's father is here."

"And Mendel brought his son."

"My wife will be coming along a little later; I told her we would be *lernen* a little at first."

It is a time to exchange news and gossip, to catch up on what has been happening to everyone during the week.

"Shlomo, I see you had a day off from the bank today. What's the occasion?"

"My wife wasn't feeling too well so I stayed home to help with the children."

"Be'ezrat Hashem" (With God's help), the Rav remarks, overhearing this report, "she will feel better soon."

"I rushed here from the Knesset [Parliament]," Kalman announces. Everyone knew that he worked for the Ministry of Religion and had a job that often required him to spend time in the corridors of power. Now he reminded us all how important he was and yet how important we were as well. It was not for nothing that one rushed away from the Knesset. It was, after all, important that each member of the circle not arrive simply in time to take a bite to eat or a drop to drink, but he had to be present as well

for the actual recitation and explanation of the final lines. Wives
might skip this, for they were not principals in the celebration.
But men like Kalman would have to leave everything to be on
time.

"Well, you know the *Beit Knesset* [synagogue] is more important
than the Knesset," Shmeltzer joked, playing on the similarity
between the two words.

"Gentlemen," the Rav began, and everyone quieted down.
There was no mistaking this call to *lernen*.

"Let us just review a bit of what we have been studying the
last few times." Here as at Beit Rachel, *lernen* always begins with
a look back. *Lernen* is after all always "review." Either one reviews
what the circle itself has already studied, or one is reviewing what
the people of Israel, the cultural traditions, have already absorbed.
There is never anything completely new, but everything is a
"ceaseless repetition of gestures initiated by others."[3]

Completing his review in just a few sentences, the Rav announces: "Now let us read further in the *gemore*." Like the rest
of us, he knows that tonight the emphasis is on concluding.

The words of the text serve as a metaphor for our activity. They
celebrate *lernen*.

"Anyone who reads [the Torah] without a tune and studies
without singing—of him it is written: 'Wherefore I gave them also
statutes that were not good and judgments whereby they should
not live' [*Ezekiel* 20:25]."

With this—as if in response to what he has just read—the Rav
begins to chant his words in the rise-fall of *gemore-nign*. A few of
the men smile and begin to sway. Others echo his cadences or
mumble the words of the text.

The Rav continues reading: "Two scholars who dwell in one
city but do not study Jewish law together, of them likewise it is
written: 'Wherefore I gave them also statutes that were not good,
etc.' "

Again the men look at one another in satisfaction for *they* have
joined together to study, and their consciences may now be clear.

"And," the Rav goes on, "Rabbi Parnakh said in the name of
Rabbi Yokhanan: 'Anyone who grasps the Torah [scroll] naked
[i.e., with bare hands] will be buried naked.' The *gemore* asks, can
it really mean that he is buried naked? No, rather he is buried
'naked,' that is, stripped of good deeds. Can it mean that a person
who has throughout his life been scrupulous in observing all the

Torah's commandments but simply grasped a scroll of Torah without a handkerchief or cloth in hand is considered to be stripped of his good deeds? No, Abaye [the great rabbi] tells us. He is buried 'naked,' stripped of the observance of *that* commandment.

" 'Buried naked.' You know, gentlemen, this can be homiletically explained because people say that the Oral Law [the Talmud] is like a garment for the Written Law."

Even more than the actual words of the text, this homily touches the heart of our life. We have been clothing the Torah, as it were, with our efforts, efforts that will prevent us from being "buried naked."

Here, as at Beit Rachel, the invocation of eternal life through *lernen* resonates throughout the celebration. Death may end individual life but not the relationship to the Torah and the ways of its people. These are forever vitalized by life in the study circle.

The men listen in rapt silence to the promises of their Rav and their Book. The *siyum* reminds them not only that they have completed the tractate but that they have entered a sacred vocation, joined—at least symbolically—the community of Jewish scholars.

"When God gave the Jews the Torah," the Rav tells us, repeating a well-known legend which he now endows with an added significance, "he held a mountain over them and they said: 'We shall do and we shall listen.' We shall observe the commandments and we shall study the Torah. And had they not agreed to this, God would have buried them there, naked of the commandments, without the Torah. That is why we Jews have always known that without study we would be buried naked, stripped of everything. The Tosafot tell us all this, tell us that [true] study is only the study of the Oral Law, the *gemore*.

"There are even early scholars who suggest that the Oral Law preceded the Written Law, for how else could we have understood the Written Law?

"And where will we be buried if we are stripped of the Torah? There. . . ." The Rav points toward the window over his shoulder and through it to a distant place: "There, among the [Gentile] nations."

Only one line is left in the text, but the Rav, as did Rav Horowitz at Beit Rachel, has suddenly slowed down his rush toward the end. He extends his explanation, as if he were trying to see how long he could keep us engaged in this moment of high excitement

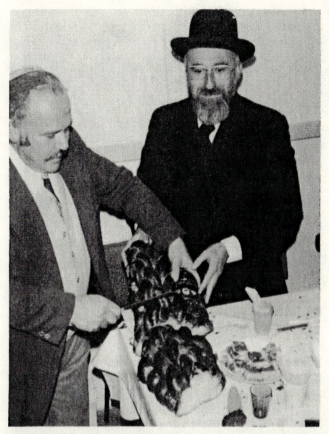

Breaking bread at the *siyum*. Showing off the bread at the beginning of the feast. (Photograph by S. Binstock)

The premier *siyum*. The last letters are written into the Torah scroll. The intensified communion is seen in the body contact among those present, the singing, the recitation of verses from the scroll, and the merrymaking. (Photography by S. Heilman)

The *siyum* table. (Photograph by S. Binstock)

The wives celebrate the *siyum* at their own table. (Photograph by S. Binstock)

The satisfied look of a man who has just returned from a *siyum*, sated with his *lernen*. (Photograph by S. Heilman)

and climax. No one interrupts any longer; no one cues him to read further. We sit still, listening as he spins a web of allegory and homily.

"The Torah is filled with mysteries," he explains. "Our understanding does not easily reach the level that the sages reached, and we cannot always fathom their reasons and explanations. This is especially true with the *agada* [legends]. The comprehension of *halakha* [law] is far easier; there is reason and logic. But the *agada* is difficult, mysterious.

"Yet they are all one in the Torah, and heaven forbid that one finds it difficult to believe in everything from this one 'Orchard.' He who does not believe is a heretic; he simply leaves the community of Israel. We have to know all this; otherwise we shall never comprehend the *gemore*."

Each morning in the first words of the daily prayers, each of these men of Mekadshey Torah repeats the words of the Proverbs: " 'The beginning of knowledge is the fear of God.' " And now that message is reechoed: the beginning of *lernen* is found in faith. To *lern* is not to pursue mere reason—that is too easy. It is to aim at mystery which reason leaves opaque but which belief clarifies. The men nod in agreement; they understand the limits of their understanding.

"Let us *lern* this last passage now," the Rav concludes.

The words pass quickly. Several of the wives who had not come earlier have started to come in. The sounds of the dishes and pots filled with the food for the celebration can be heard from the back. The smell of the stuffed cabbage is upon us. Along with everything else, it sets the juices of anticipation flowing once again.

The recitation of the prayers of conclusion jar everyone's reveries. At once we are back to the Book. In unison the words are recited, and then the intonation of the *Kaddish* by one of the men.

The celebration is elaborate. Everyone must share equally in it. We have been warned by Shmeltzer who has taken a large part in the preparations that everyone will be asked to offer a few words during the meal.

"Tonight the Rav can remain silent, and we shall do the talking," he explains. "First, however, we shall begin *Brakhot*." The new tractate, *Brakhot*, is distributed. Shlomo, one of the other students, has bought new books for each of us. The bindings are cracked open, and we listen as the Rav recites the first few lines of the volume.

Lines pass without even a single effort at translation or explanation. Apparently this is not the time to launch even a display of scholarship. The reading seeks instead to simply symbolize our commitment to keep on *lernen*. In one voice, the men intone the last two words of the first Mishna. Quickly, the books are put away and the celebration begins in earnest.

"All the ladies are invited to come sit at the big table where we shall drink a *l'chayim* and afterward we shall wash our hands," Shmeltzer, who has taken on the role of host, announces. This feast is a *seudat mitzva*, a commemoration of the fulfillment of a religious obligation. We shall wash our hands ritually, break bread, and finally say grace.

Spontaneously the men begin to sing and clap their hands. "Blessed is our Lord who created us in his honor, who distinguished us from among nations, and who gave us the true Torah." The words are familiar, recited in each day's morning prayers and twice on the Sabbath. As they are sung, drinks are passed around and bowls of fruit pass from hand to hand. At the head of the table sits the Rav, and next to him Shmeltzer. Rhythmically stroking his beard with one hand, the Rav keeps time to the singing by clapping the other against the table.

"May God bless you from Zion and see to the good of Jerusalem and may you see the sons of your sons, peace on Israel," the men sing.

"May he who makes peace on high bring peace to all of us and on all Israel."

"May the heavens rejoice and may the earth be glad, let the sea and all its fullness roar praise." The voices of the men fill the room with familiar lines from the Psalms.

Reb Meir, an old Sephardic Jew and one of the regular *lerners* among these Ashkenazim, sings loudest. The veins of his throat and temple bulge as he lifts his voice in song.

Over and over the verses are sung, one after another, as if the group can no longer tolerate even a moment's silence. The bottles on the table shake and the chick-peas roll around in their bowls. And still the men sing. As they have studied without end, so now they lift their voices in the songs that all of them have sung countless times before at other celebrations: weddings, bar mitzvas, and of course other *siyumim*.

"*Kvod ha-Rav*" (Your honor), Reb Meir begins, "with your permission I would like to say a few words, no not words but a special song. This is a song that we used to sing in Morocco where I grew up and which was especially reserved for the *siyum*."

"Please, please," Shmeltzer and Yonatan call out.

He begins to sing the "Song of Songs," the love song that tradition has it Solomon wrote and which the sages allowed into the canon only after they explained that it was really an allegory of God's love for the Jewish people. The melody is foreign to the Ashkenazim, sounding rather like a Moslem chant or song. And yet, in the spirit of fellowship, a few try to sing along, echoing a phrase here or there.

Meir leaves the text of the "Song of Songs" and adds verses from a host of scriptural sources. Like a melodic journey through the Torah, the song is impressive in its erudition and haunting in melody. And then it is over.

"Hurrah!"

"*Khazak u-barukh*" (Be mighty and blessed), Meir is wished in the traditional Sephardic expression of encouragement and praise.

Now it is Shmeltzer's turn: "Here in this place I always say that here there are no chairs but instead we sit on benches. *Mir zitsen oyf a bank*" (We sit on a bench), he adds in Yiddish.

"And why do we call this a 'bank?' [bench].* Because everyone puts into it his wealth. In a bank, everyone puts his money in with that of others. And everyone's money gets mixed together. So it is that way here too. Everyone gets mixed together with everyone else.

"Tonight we all feel a special sentiment, a common feeling. There are people here who remind me how it was when we started. There was an old man here, an invalid—God protect us from such things. . . ."

"May his memory be blessed," Meir adds, recalling the man and showing us by the way that he was there at the beginning as well.

"Yes, may his memory be blessed," Shmeltzer repeats and continues: "And anyone who passed by on the street, he would call in to make a *minyan*. And if they did not want to come in, he still forced them to. But thank God today, tonight, we have more than twice as many people. And we can always get together a *minyan*.

---

*Shmeltzer is playing with words here. The Yiddish word "bank" means bench. But in Hebrew, the language in which he is speaking, it also means bank. The double entendre is clear to his listeners, who like him are multilingual and fond—as are most *lerners*—of playing with words.

And here there is a warm feeling. You don't have to worry about taking off your coat in the morning or evening. The heat is always up in the winter, and no one would steal your coat. So you can feel doubly at ease. Our synagogue is like a home. May we go on from strength to strength."

Shmeltzer knows us all and he now demonstrates that familiarity by offering each man around the table a few words of praise.

"Oh, and we cannot forget the ladies," he adds, "who let their husbands out in the evenings to come to the *khavruse*. We have not spent the nights drinking or playing cards; we got together for *lernen*. And, thank God, we have arrived at this wonderful night."

"Amen," Naphtali whispers to Efraim who sits between us. "Enough already."

Naphtali will be next to speak and it is obvious that he is growing impatient with Shmeltzer's speech. But the floor is not easily given up tonight.

"I want to thank our comrade and teacher, the Rav, who has enabled us thus to serve the Lord. I don't want to thank him too much because I want him to continue with us. But let's be serious, gentlemen, he is like a brother and friend to us. May he be healthy and strong."

"How he goes on!" Naphtali repeats. Shmeltzer does not stop.

"Now, people come to the *shiur* and here they can undoubtedly relax more than at their jobs. The *lernen* surely is not taxing. And when they get home after the class, they return even more refreshed and relaxed. That is because here there are no worries. Here we sit and listen at the well-spring; we can serve God in joy and be with one another. 'Behold how good and how pleasant it is for brothers to sit in fellowship.' "

"Amen!"

"*Khazak u-barukh!*"

The men can barely contain themselves.

"And now, Mr. Aronovitch will say a few words," Shmeltzer adds.

An immigrant from America, Naphtali Aronovitch apologies for his poor Hebrew.

"So speak in English, we'll follow," Shmeltzer tells him.

But Aronovitch ignores this suggestion and goes on in the Hebrew that all those around the table share. He will in no way be made a stranger. His remarks are brief and pointed. And then he concludes: "We now have more people studying Torah in yeshivas than ever before in our history. The community is filled with groups and classes like this one. So I trust in consideration of this God will show his people mercy and send the Messiah to redeem us speedily and in our lifetime, amen."

And so it goes. Each man in his turn offering a few words of Torah. Some draw lessons from the portion of the week, which will be read from scrolls on the forthcoming Sabbath. Others cite lessons from the tractate we are to begin reviewing next time, or from the one just completed. One man has worked out a complex numerological *gematria** steeped in mysticism that culls the various numbers associated with the occasion to demonstrate that our *shiur* is the result of a convergence of mystical and divine forces.

The few outsiders among us, guests who have come to honor celebrant friends, are also asked to speak. While each man has his own way of putting things, the gist of all their remarks expresses an envy for those who have been "fortunate" enough to complete the tractate; they offer best wishes for continued study.

"Your joy is my joy," as one among them put it.

Almost everyone around the table has spoken. Only Reb Shimon, who sits on the Rav's left, remains. He begins: "I am not a man of words." The line is a famous one, spoken by Moses when God charged him to lead the Jewish people out of bondage. "I will just tell you a brief story. When I was a young boy growing up in Europe, *lernen* was probably the single most important thing my brothers and I were taught to do. It was not just an occupation; it was our way of life. It was more important than life. And when the Nazis came in—may their names be blotted out—and burned our synagogues and houses of study, they tried to destroy that life. And I remember when the Great Synagogue was set ablaze our rabbi ran into the flames to save a scroll of Torah, a piece of himself, and was burned along with it. May his memory be blessed.

*Gematria is the transformation of words into numbers. This is possible because in Hebrew each letter is equivalent to a number. Once a word has been translated into a numerical value, this sum can be redivided into different letters that are likewise arithmetically equivalent. In this way one word can be mystically linked to another.

"But now, my friends, we have succeeded in saving the Torah from the flames of Europe. We have given it life in our *lernen*. We have survived."

Now at last it is Rav Rotenbush's turn to speak again. Reb Shimon's brief but moving speech is a hard one to follow, but the need to offer some special words seem inexorable. "Gentlemen, you know, you are mine and I am yours and we are one together. You bring me to life after a hard day by letting me bring you to life in *lernen*. You represent not only the fulfillment of Torah study but its imperative. By your actions you not only obey the law to study, you reinforce its power and claim.

"In some matters I am not your teacher but your student. This is not what you think but it *is* what I think. If I come in in the evening after we have all had a hard day, a long day, and find you all concentrating on the *gemore*, immersed in the *shiur*, struggling with Rashi and the Tosafot, I learn from you how important the study of Torah is for people like yourselves.

"I come here in the evening, at the end of the day, yet here I experience a freshness and enthusiasm more properly part of the morning.

"And I want to thank the women who toiled so long and hard over this wonderful meal. I am sorry that my wife could not be here but she is quite strict in observing the law and is in the year of mourning after her mother and would not therefore attend [such a joyous occasion]. I told her that she was permitted to come, but she insisted it was not her custom.[4] Still, I am glad the rest of you ladies have come for you are certainly a part of this celebration. Your work and blessings give us strength to continue.

"On Simkhat Torah we dance and rejoice because we have finished the five books of the Torah.[5] But the *siyum* of learning a tractate is like the Simkhat Torah of the sages.

"It is written in our legends that when King Solomon completed building the Temple he likewise made a *siyum*, a feast.

"In Algeria, we learn there was a custom that on the day of a *siyum* one would not recite the *Tahanun*[6] in the synagogue. Clearly there is no greater joy than *lernen* and no time one experiences it more than at the *siyum*.

"Gentlemen, we live in a world where studying Torah and going to classes like this one is to sanctify life. We live in a world dedicated to action, a world in which one must really make an effort to be righteous and loyal to values of the Torah. And a person cannot easily overcome the obstacles to these efforts unless he has the light of *lernen* to guide his way.

"A man who sets himself a time to study Torah—he alone is the one who is building his home and life on the foundations of Torah. May our Lord bless us and enable us to open other tractates of Talmud, to study throughout our lives. May we never deny our wisdom, to become like animals dedicated only to our bodies. May we give our wisdom, our most precious possession, to the Torah and to *lernen*. This is what the Torah demands of us."

The room is silent.

"My dear friends, my brothers, as God has accomplished miracles for us in the past so may He continue to bring forth miracles in the future, as in the past so now today; amen and amen."

"Amen!"

"*Yasher Koakh!*"

"*Khazak u-barukh!*"

Another *kaddish* is recited. The men apparently judge these last words to count as sacred study, after which prayers are offered. The grace after meals is sung, and the men start to leave. Reluctantly they depart. So, as they stand, one last song is sung and a few men join in a small circle to dance, arms clasped in embrace around their fellows' shoulders. It has been a good *siyum*, the men agree.

"But I can't wait to start *lernen* again," someone adds as we pick up our books and leave for home.

SMOTRA

The *siyum* in Smotra was also a first for that group. After over five years of one-night-a-week *lernen*, the circle had finally reached the last few lines of their tractate by late summer. The actual celebration of conclusion had been held off until the fall when everyone would be back from vacation. The day selected was the one preceding Yom Kippur, the Day of Judgment and Atonement, the holiest of the Jewish year. It would, many of the group felt, be an appropriate way to begin the new year and to symbolize atonement. Concluding one tractate and beginning another was after all a supremely Jewish and religious act.

When the *khavruse* in Smotra had first been formed, it had met in various members' homes. This was ostensibly because the participants came from a variety of synagogues in the county and felt therefore that by meeting in homes they could guarantee the communal rather than the synagogal identity of the group. But for one thing, meeting in homes undermined the capacity of the circle to serve as a place of refuge from daily domestic struggle; and for another, with each succeeding meeting, the refreshments set out by the wives of the *lerners* became more and more elaborate until having the *shiur* in one's home became a burden. The implicit one-upmanship in trying to provide a more impressive collation, the necessity of baking and then washing dishes on a weeknight, proved more than many in the group seemed willing to bear. And so, following in a time-honored tradition, the men decided with the beginning of their second year of *lernen* to move the class to the Rav's synagogue, Knesset Jacob.

"The Rav is more comfortable there," one member suggested.

"This way the group is more accessible because outsiders will always know we meet in the same place," reasoned another.

With many of the wives breathing in relief, the group moved permanently to the library of the synagogue. Gone were the refreshments. But in their place came a kind of classless utopia, a relaxed clubhouse atmosphere in which coats were thrown across chairs and cigarettes smoked without fear of offending host or hostess. The library had once been the locker room and attached to the synagogue's gym. Although dedicated now to matters of the mind rather than the body, it still evoked the sense of ease of an all-male preserve, a place for the fellows to get together. Here the Rav, like a coach, remained in charge without having to defer to his host. Thus, the library at Knesset Jacob served the needs of the group quite well.

For the *siyum*, however, a decision was reached to go back to a home for one more time. A celebration such as this one required the special warmth that a home could give and the mandatory refreshment could, in the members' judgment, most easily be served there. The only question was, Whose house?

By the acknowledgement of most if not all the men, Hersh, a regular in the circle, had a wife whose baking skills were second to none. Her cakes and desserts, once the pride of Jewish Hungary, were now the talk of all Smotra. Her joy in watching people enjoy each cookie, cake, and pie she made seemed quite genuine. So when Hersh suggested that the *siyum* be held in his house, the offer was quickly accepted.

Calls went out to everyone who at one time or another during the last five years had participated in the *shiur* to come and join in the celebrations. Announcements were made in the various synagogues, and even the local paper in Smotra carried a short feature story about the occasion. By the night of the *siyum*, no one in the Smotra Orthodox community could claim to be unaware of what was happening at Hersh's house. The community calendar had been cleared for the occasion.

The atmosphere at Hersh's was electric with anticipation. As each man entered—some with wives and others alone—the noise level grew. Punctuated with the chimes of the door bell, the conversation reminded one a bit of the talk in a theater just before curtain time. Here too a drama would be played out this evening—and everyone assembled seemed to sense it.

At last the Rav walked in and sat down near the center of the table. Tonight he would not sit in shirt-sleeves but wore his jacket and tie, looking every bit the teacher and rabbi. For a while he also joined in the conversation and banter, sociable and friendly. In the end, however, it was he who would end it.

Turning to the two Markovitz brothers who were busy conversing, he remarked: "Look, it looks awfully good when brothers are talking to one another, but *lomer lernen a bissel*" (let's study a little). The call was a cue for all of us, we who were also like "brothers talking to one another," to turn our attention to the books before us. The Yiddish could not help but remind us that we were returning now to the totally Jewish world of Talmud and *lernen*, that at least for now we were the People of the Book.

Rav Gafny, like the others in his *khavruse*, was a modern man, a suburban American rabbi who, although Orthodox, had learned to temper his speech with the expressions more at home in contemporary America than in the precincts of tradition. Unlike Rav Horowitz or Rav Rotenbush, he did not begin by invoking the help of God as they had. Instead, in a much more subtle reference to divine assistance, he said: "Hopefully we're going to be *mesayem* [conclude] tonight the *mesekhta* [tractate]. We actually have some gaps here, but we're not going to go back. It's enough that I have spent time today *lernen* the *inyan* [subject]."

The men were used to the idea of the Rav's doing more preparation than they, and so this announcement raised no objections. They would be guided by him.

"We're going to *lern* the last *Mishna* and go through the *gemore.*"

"Are we going to start another *mesekhta* tonight?" Sid asked, wondering aloud if the cycle would begin and end at the same time.

"This is always done with Torah," the Rav answered matter-of-factly, but in truth no new beginning would be made this evening. The group, finishing a volume dealing with the laws of divorce, had elected to study *Kiddushin* next, the tractate detailing the sanctifications of marriage. They were eager to "get the other side of the story," as one of them put it. But there would be no meetings for several months after this *siyum*; as if having failed to start in right away, they would find difficulties in once again marshaling the necessary energy and inertia to embark on the way of Talmud. Perhaps this failure to start a new volume was symbolic. Indeed, a year later, this circle would become dormant. A new rabbi had come to Smotra, and Rav Gafny deferred to him. Many of the members of his circle gradually joined the new study group—but all of them missed their old *khavruse*. As of this writing, efforts are still being made to persuade Rav Gafny to revive the old circle. Tonight, however, everyone seemed at the peak of involvement in the world of the holy book.

A few men came late, after the Rav had begun to explain the Mishna. For each, he stopped and offered a few words of greeting. These were apparently not to be skipped.

"A man may not divorce his wife unless he discovers her to be unchaste," the Rav began, reviewing the opinion of the followers of the great rabbi Shammai. There was no response to this declaration from anyone in the room.

"*Bes Hillel,*" the followers of Hillel, Shammai's great disputant, the Rav continued, "on the other hand tell us that if she but oversalted his food or burned it, that is enough grounds for a divorce."

As if on cue, the door from the kitchen swung open and in walked Mrs. Hersh, her arms laden with a tray of cakes and cookies. The entire group broke into laughter—no grounds for divorce here. A bit confused by the scene into which she had walked unaware, Mrs. Hersh smiled the bland smile of the "perfect hostess" and returned to the kitchen for more food.

Undaunted by this break, the Rav continued with his recitation and explanation of the Talmud.

"Even if there's no fault with the woman but it's simply a matter of the husband's taste—that he found someone more pleasing or attractive—he can divorce her."

Silently the men listen to his exposition of the text with its various options for divorce. The Rav reframes his remarks.

"Look, till now we only talked about *how* divorce is accomplished. Now, on the last page of the *mesekhta*, we're going to talk about *why*." The comment suggests, in a sense, that all those who have been reviewing this volume for the last several years have been waiting for this final revelation. Now at last they would discover the answer that must have troubling them all along. To be sure, no one may have really been preoccupied with this issue, one that after all had been touched on in the course of the many discussions during *lernen*, but now we were all being told that we had been.

Apparently troubled by the text's constant references to the failings only of the wife, the Rav comments: "The Mishna says that she failed him, but whether or not he failed her—that the Mishna doesn't discuss."

Scanning the eyes in the room, as if to check whether or not the moderns in it have noticed this implicit deference to the rights of women, the Rav stops for a moment. He is met with silence. Continuing in a contemporary vein, he adds: "Look, the Mishna says that a man can divorce his wife if she oversalted or burned his food. It's but a euphemism, speaking of a woman who generally fails her husband. Either she messes him up professionally; she makes a wreck of him in *shul* [the synagogue] or in the yard or in the mountains or wherever."

Not altogether certain what will resonate meaningfully for his audience, he draws from the American Jewish world he knows. And then, to emphasize the Talmud's stake in that world, its capacity to speak to it, he adds: "And all this will be discussed further in the *gemore*. And I'll also make mention that this is touched upon in other sources."

Tonight, with the end of the volume in sight, however, little enthusiasm for researching these other sources is expressed— even on the Rav's part. When one or two questions are asked— almost like conditioned reflexes to *lernen*—the Rav replies: "We're one day away from Yom Kippur. We'll never finish the *mesekhta* if you keep asking questions."

There will be no second chance to finish. The day of judgment cometh, literally and symbolically.

When the motion forward is the most important one, even "good" questions must be set aside.

"*A gute kashe*" (A good question), the Rav replies to one man's inquiry. "We'll discuss this later. In the meantime, *lomer lernen*" (let's go on).

For those who have not engaged in *lernen* for a long time, tonight's program is a reeducation, a chance to recall and reexperience the limits this activity places upon curiosity and talk. Calm settles over the group. They follow in silence with their fingers and their eyes. Tonight, even more so than usual, the questions that count most, that receive immediate attention, are the ones the text itself asks.

"*Hertzokh ein, a moyredik kashe,*" listen to this, the Rav says in Yiddish, speaking to our hearts more than our minds, listen to this awesome question that the Talmud poses.

As if the group might have failed to understand the imperative nature of tonight's forward movement, the teacher finally remarks: "I must ask you not to stop me during this long Rashi that we're going to read now. It goes into the various meanings of the word '*kee*' in the *gemore*. We have to say this, but pay attention since I want to get through this so we can finally reach a *siyum*."

There are no translations and little or no explanation. The end draws into view. The last lines approach as our fingers slide steadily down the columns of the page.

Not everyone can sit in so disciplined a manner. After all, the occasion is a public one and some show must be put on.

"You know, over the years we have been *lernen*," Zlotnick, one of the loyal participants in the *khavruse*, begins a comment. The occasion is apparently too important for him to miss the opportunity of announcing, albeit indirectly, that he has participated from the beginning until now. Others likewise join in similar displays. One offers an inside joke; another cites a parallel to the current text from one of the early pages of the volume.

In each case the Rav, single-minded in his desire to reach the conclusion of the volume this evening, finds a way of cutting short the display and returning our collective attention to the text: "When we get through this *inyan* [topic], we'll have another perspective on the entire *mesekhta*. So gentlemen, I'm going to have to ask you to hold your questions and comments until the end. You'll see how beautiful the *gemore* is here."

Controversies lurk within the lines of the Talmud. These normally arouse debate and digression. Tonight, however, aesthetics count most, we must only see "how beautiful the *gemore* is here." The Rav will try to neutralize controversy, tempering the traditional view of the Talmud with contemporary ideas.

"The Talmud here is filled with a series of allegories," he notes, telling us that not everything we read need be understood at face value. A textual prohibition against men and women swimming together is not exactly what it seems: "By the way, I would assume—on the basis of Rashi and the other *meforshim* [commentators] here—that we're talking about nude bathing."

The people in the room who do engage in mixed bathing thus need not use the opportunity to challenge the norm of separate bathing.

"Not that I want to minimize that, according to the sages, any kind of mixed bathing is prohibited," the Rav continues, unwilling to abandon completely his role as defender of the tradition. "But this is not our subject here, so let's go on with the *gemore*."

The *siyum* is a time for unity, communion, and commensalism—not for controversy and legalistic debate.

At last the Rav has brought the group to the final lines of the page: "A man who sends his wife away arouses the antipathy of God."

"But he's not breaking the law!" one of the students interjects.

"Of course not," the Rav replies, "but we're not talking about matters of practical law now!"

As the *siyum* nears, the grand ethos of Jewish life looms larger while the details of Jewish praxis decrease in importance.

"The kind of *shiur* we have requires us to think a bit more profoundly," the Rav concludes. And now he launches a brief homily.

"This, my friends, is the eve of a holy day whose sanctity overwhelms us. On this day, when we who have spent—some of us many days and some of us fewer days—involved in *lernen*."

He switches to Yiddish and continues. "We should consider with respect the mother of our Jewish children, the woman of valor, the comrade. You know we talk so much about divorce and all this nonsense these days that we forget the greatest sanctity of life is the making of peace between a husband and wife. A man who goes to the synagogue on Yom Kippur must make his peace with his wife beforehand. God will only forgive him his sins if she has first done so."

Now turning back to the text, he continues: "In any event, let us end the *mesekhta*. Will you all please turn your attention to the end and let's say it together."

The Rav recites the lines, but at first no one accompanies him. He asks again for the others to join him in reading, and at last they begin to intone the formulaic words of closing. In chorus they recite the paragraph of prayer. After each stanza of prayer the Rav breaks in with a few words of explanation about the meaning of what has been said.

"These words mean that the *haverim* [fellows] should meet again and that we may always be able to continue our *lernen*."

The recitation continues and again the Rav interrupts: "The credit of our *lernen* should forever be with us. The time we have spent together and with the *mesekhta* should keep us from becoming strangers to one another or the House of Study."

The Kaddish is chanted, and everyone stands.

At long last the books are closed and the Rav summarizes for us what we shall begin to study next time. For tonight this will have to suffice in the way of new beginnings.

Again Mrs. Hersh has entered the room. A toast is drunk; cakes are handed out.

"Well, now that we have finally finished a *mesekhta*, at long last maybe the *Mashiakh* [Messiah] will come," someone can be heard saying amid the conversation and laughter.

EPILOGUE

There is the story of a learned man who came to visit a rebbe. The scholar was no longer a young man—he was close to thirty—but he had never before visited a rebbe.

"What have you done all your life?" the master asked him.

"I have gone through the whole of the Talmud three times," answered the learned man.

"Yes, but how much of the Talmud has gone through you?" the rebbe inquired.

"A Famous Hasidic Tale"

Closing a book such as this one, with its multiplicity of perspectives, is no easy matter. There is a temptation to sum up and to try for the comprehensive and totalistic explanation of *lernen* that I eschewed when starting out. I will resist it and allow each chapter to stand for itself and the whole to grow out of the parts.

That *lernen* is not learning, a merely intellectual activity, should by now be clear. That it does encourage mental exercise, symbolization, word play and cultural performance, interpretation, and reasoning should also be clear. That it is carried by drama, fellowship, and religion while reflecting and refracting Jewish culture and history is I hope by now obvious.

There will be those who will argue that I have missed something essential about Jewish study. They will say that my focus on Orthodox Jews has made me miss what other Jews find and express through their review of Talmud and other sacred texts. I think not. On the contrary, I would argue that Orthodox Jews are like other Jews—only more so. What is writ large in their experience of *lernen* is perhaps writ small (or, at least, differently) in the study of other Jews but is in many ways also there.

I began by asserting that this book would be about Orthodox Jews and especially those who could be literally and symbolically called the "People of the Book." I end by admitting that I believe this portrait to be at least in part about all Jews. People of the Book they are, and People of the Book they all remain. Chaim Nachman Bialik, the great literary voice of the Jewish people, whose writing in Yiddish and Hebrew captured much that was essential in their character, perhaps put it best in his poem, *"Im Yesh es Nafsnekha Lodass"* (1898). There he wrote:

> Should you wish to know the Source,
> From which your brothers drew . . . ,
> Their strength of soul . . . ,
> Their comfort, courage, patience, trust,
> And iron might to bear their hardships
> And suffer without end or measure?
>
> And should you wish to see the Fort
> Wherein your fathers refuge sought,
> And all their sacred treasures hid,
> The Refuge that has still preserved
> Your nation's soul intact and pure,

And when despised, and scorned, and scoffed,
Their faith they did not shame?

And should you wish to see and know
Their Mother, faithful, loving, kind,
Who . . . sheltered them and shielded them,
And lulled them on her lap to sleep?

If you, my brother, know not
This mother, spring, and lap, and fort,
Then enter now the House of God,
The House of Study, old and gray,
Throughout the scorching summer days,
Throughout the gloomy winter nights,
At morning, midday, or at eve . . .
And there you may still behold,
A Group of Jews—some young some old,
Upon the Talmud's folios bent.

And then your heart shall guess the truth,
That you have touched the sacred ground
Of a Great People's House of Life,
And that your eyes do gaze upon
The treasure of a nation's soul.

The places and people of which Bialik wrote still exist. I know, for I have seen and been among them.

NOTES

Chapter 1

1. In a kind of affirmation of this fact, the Voice of Israel, the official state radio of the Jewish state, begins its broadcasting day not with a recitation of Scripture but rather with a short class in Talmud.

2. I am indebted to Shlomo Deshen for most of what I shall say in this book about the avocational study practices of Sephardic Jews.

3. The concept of the anonymous *minyan* was first suggested to me in a paper by Aryei Fishman at the 1980 meetings of the Israel Sociological Society, in Jerusalem.

4. Samuel C. Heilman, *Synagogue Life: A Study in Symbolic Interaction* (Chicago: University of Chicago Press, 1976).

5. Although some women in Smotra would for several weeks join the Knesseth Jacob circle, few ever penetrated its membership, and all stopped coming after a while. While there exist fellowships of women—usually for the study of Bible or Codes—these are relatively rare. Traditionally, *lernen* has been an activity limited to males. To be sure, the increased literacy of women brought about by the now-generally-accepted practice of universal Jewish education has resulted in increasing numbers of women engaging in avocational study. Whether they will ultimately seek and achieve parity with men in the world of study circles, however, remains to be seen.

6. Emile Durkheim, *The Elementary Forms of the Religious Life*, trans. J. W. Swain (New York: Free Press, [1954] 1965), p. 483.

CHAPTER 2

1. Strictly speaking, in a staged drama the audience and actors do not usually overlap. However, as Erving Goffman has noted, in "real life" these two "parties are compressed" so that the actors at times also serve as audience (*The Presentation of Self in Everyday Life* [New York: Doubleday, 1959], p. xi).

2. Constantin Stanislavski, *An Actor's Handbook,* ed. and trans. E. R. Hapgood. (New York: Theatre Arts Books, 1963), pp. 25, 79, 124–25.

3. See Kenneth Burke, *Language as Symbolic Action* (Berkeley: University of California Press, 1968), pp. 445–51; Talcott Parsons, *The Structure of Social Action* (New York: McGraw-Hill, 1937), p. 44; and Goffman, *The Presentation of Self in Everyday Life,* pp. 10–46. Without the work of these authors, this string of terms cannot be properly understood. Since it is not my purpose here to launch into an analysis of the way in which each man's work dovetails with the others, I have simply combined their ways of characterizing drama in this sentence. The theoretically informed reader will, I trust, be willing to unravel my combination. The ethnography which follows should help.

4. Victor Turner, *The Forest of Symbols: Aspects of Ndembu Ritual* (Ithaca: Cornell University Press, 1967), p. 450.

5. Faubion Bowers, "Drama," *International Encyclopedia of Social Science,* vol. 4 (New York: Free Press, 1968), p. 256.

6. Victor Turner, *Dramas, Fields and Metaphors: Symbolic Action in Human Society* (Ithaca: Cornell University Press, 1974), pp. 33–43.

7. Ibid., p. 35.

8. Morris Adler, *The World of the Talmud* (Washington, D.C.: B'nai B'rith Hillel Foundations, 1959); also see Jacob Neusner, *Invitation to the Talmud.* (New York: Harper & Row, 1973).

9. I have taken some liberty with quotations here so as to make the superspecialized language of the class comprehensible to the English reader. Later, when the focus of consideration is upon the ethnography of speaking or word play, I will be scrupulous in quotation. Here and throughout this chapter, however, where the emphasis is on meaning rather than speaking, I shall translate what was said and read in such a way as to express the intended meaning of the remark. For a theoretical consideration of this sort of translation, see Eugene A. Nida, *Language Structure and Translation: Essays by Eugene A. Nida,* ed. A. S. Dill (Stanford: Stanford University Press, 1975).

10. Max Grunwald, "Das 'Lernen,' " in *Jahrbuch für Judische Volkskunde* (Berlin: Hanz Verlag, 1924–25), p. 103.

11. Goffman, *The Presentation of Self in Everyday Life,* p. 83.

12. Erving Goffman, *Interaction Ritual* (New York: Anchor, 1967), p. 10.

13. See ibid., p. 3.

14. See Samuel C. Heilman, *Synagogue Life: A Study in Symbolic Interaction* (Chicago: University of Chicago Press, 1976).

15. The idea of transparent intonation is suggested by its opposite, "opaque intonation," which Pittinger et al. define as an intonation that avoids or at least masks emotional overtones (R. C. Pittinger, C. F. Hockett, and J. J. Danehy, *The First Five Minutes: A Sample of Microscopic Interview Analysis* [New York: Paul Martineau, 1960]), p. 28.

16. See J. M. Cuddihy, "Sigmund Freud's Ordeal of Civility: Jewish Emancipation and Differentiated Modernity" (Ph.D. diss., Rutgers University, 1972), pp. 17 and 26; also see Sigmund Freud, *Jokes and Their Relation to the Unconscious,* trans. J. Strachey (New York: Norton, 1961), p. 81. Were the class to be made up completely of Sephardic Jews (although, as we noted, this is less likely since the tradition of Talmud study is not nearly as established a custom among them where the reading of the Zohar, an ancient mystical text, is more common), the use of

Yiddish would have none of these connotations. The Rav, however, knows to whom he speaks, and he reacts in ways that are meaningful to his circle.

17. Philip E. Slater, *Microcosm: Structural, Psychological and Religious Evolution in Groups* (New York: Wiley, 1966), pp. 2–3.

18. Turner, *Dramas, Fields and Metaphors*, p. 39.

19. Slater, *Microcosm;* also see Sigmund Freud, *Totem and Taboo*, trans. J. Strachey (London: Hogarth Press, [1953] 1974), p. 3.

20. Turner, *Dramas, Fields and Metaphors*, p. 35.

21. The principle of one person reacting for a whole group is well established in the literature of small-group interaction. For a case that is particularly trenchant and similar to the one here, see Robert F. Bales, "How People Interact in Conferences," in *Communication and Culture*, ed. A. G. Smith (New York: Holt, Rinehart & Winston, 1966), p. 101.

22. A "fractured utterance," as Pittinger, Hockett, and Danehy define it, is a remark which shows evidence of starting as one sort of utterance—e.g., a question or an objection—and ending as another—e.g., a rhetorical remark or an affirmation (Pittinger, Hockett, and Danehy, *The First Five Minutes*, p. 31). The ability to fracture one's utterances is an important tool in the dynamics of face-to-face relations for it allows for flexible responses to shifting social reality.

23. For an elaborate and definitive analysis of one-upmanship, see Stephen Potter's classic study of the same name (*One-Upmanship* [New York: Harper & Row, 1951]).

24. Turner, *Dramas, Fields and Metaphors*, p. 41; also see Victor Turner, *Schism and Continuity in an African Society* (Manchester: Manchester University Press, 1957), pp. 288–317.

25. Uriel Weinreich, "Notes on the Yiddish Rise-Fall Intonation Contour," in *For Roman Jakobson*, ed. M. Halle (The Hague: Mouton, 1956), pp. 639–40.

26. Stanislavski, *An Actor's Handbook*, p. 25.

27. Mircea Eliade, *Cosmos and History*, trans. W. Trask (New York: Harper & Row, 1959), p. 95.

28. Audrey I. Richards, *Chisungu: A Girl's Initiation Ceremony among the Bemba of Northern Rhodesia.* (London: Faber, 1956), pp. 117–18.

29. Pittinger, Hockett, and Danehy, *The First Five Minutes*, p. 70.

30. See Arnold Van Gennep, "Essai d'une theorie des langues speciales," trans. S. C. Heilman, *Revue des etudes ethnographiques et sociologiques* 1 (1908): 327–37.

31. Georg Simmel, *The Sociology of Georg Simmel*, trans. K. Wolff (Glencoe, Ill.: Free Press, 1950), pp. 154–55.

32. Turner, *Dramas, Fields and Metaphors*, p. 33.

33. Robert Nisbet, *Social Change and History* (London: Oxford University Press, 1969), p. 4.

34. Turner, *Dramas, Fields and Metaphors*, p. 30; also see Martin Foss, *Symbol and Metaphor in Human Experience* (Lincoln: University of Nebraska Press, [1949] 1964), p. 7.

CHAPTER 3

1. Clifford Geertz, *The Interpretation of Cultures* (New York: Basic Books, 1973).

2. Ibid., p. 449.

3. Ibid., p. 114.

4. Ibid., p. 113; cf. also M. Singer, "The Cultural Pattern of Indian Civilization," *Far Eastern Quarterly* 15 (1955): 23–26.

5. Mircea Eliade, *Cosmos and History*, trans. W. Trask (New York: Harper & Row, 1959), p. 70.

6. Geertz, *The Interpretation of Cultures*, p. 88.

7. I have used the terms "contemporization" and "traditioning" elsewhere in a slightly different and less developed way. My discussion here, however, supersedes the earlier one (see my article "Constructing Orthodoxy," in *In Gods We Trust: New Patterns of Religious Pluralism in America*, ed. Thomas Robbins and Dick Anthony [New Brunswick, N.J.: Transaction Books, 1980]), pp. 141–57.

8. Melville Herskovits, *Man and His Works* (New York: Knopf, 1949), p. 36.

9. Peter Berger and Thomas Luckmann, *The Social Construction of Reality* (Garden City, N.Y.: Doubleday, 1966), p. 163.

10. Jacob Katz, *Out of the Ghetto: The Social Background of Jewish Emancipation, 1770–1870* (Cambridge: Harvard University Press, 1973), p. 36.

11. In his book, *The Heretical Imperative* (Garden City, N.Y.: Anchor, 1979), Peter Berger refers to similar although more general concepts which roughly correspond to "contemporization" and "traditioning." He calls these, respectively, the "inductive" and "reductive" options. They seem to represent the "radical" forms of what I am here discussing (see also my article "Constructing Orthodoxy" [n. 7 above]).

12. Victor Turner, *The Forest of Symbols: Aspects of Ndembu Ritual* (Ithaca: Cornell University Press, 1967).

13. Geertz, *The Interpretation of Cultures*, p. 112.

14. Max Weinreich, *The History of the Yiddish Language*, trans. S. Noble and J. Fishman (Chicago: University of Chicago Press, 1980), p.44.

15. Ibid., p. 207.

16. Ibid.

17. Norman Lamm, "The Voice of Torah in the Battle of Ideas," *Jewish Life* (March/April 1967), p. 28.

18. Eliot Cohen, ed., *Commentary on the American Scene* (New York: Knopf, 1950), p. 254; italics in original.

19. M. Weinreich, *The History of the Yiddish Language*, pp. 214–15.

20. "Reb" is a Yiddish diminutive of "rabbi." It has come to mean something more than "mister" and less than "rabbi." It is a common title attached by *lerners* to one another. Commonly the more traditionally Orthodox use this term, while the more modern use first names or surnames alone, dropping the Yiddish "reb" being perhaps a bow to modernity.

There is another noteworthy point here. The title "reb" is a common appellation given the characters in the Talmud. Referring to one another as "Reb ——," the more traditional participants in a sense align themselves with or even transform themselves into peers of those in the text.

21. Uriel Weinreich, "Notes on the Yiddish Rise-Fall Intonation Contour," in *For Roman Jakobson*, ed. M. Halle (The Hague: Mouton, 1956), p. 639.

22. See ibid., pp. 634–35.

23. Ibid., p. 640.

24. M. Weinreich, *The History of the Yiddish Language*, p. 211.

25. The dialogue was spoken in the language of the Talmud and in Hebrew. Since my aim here is to illustrate the way content is used by the participants to

elaborate the text and also to give the English-speaking reader some notion of the dialogue, I have translated everything. The words of text are noted with quotation marks. The dash at the end of Zusya's remarks indicates that he has been interrupted by Moshe.

26. See H. Garfinkel, *Studies in Ethnomethodology* (Englewood Cliffs, N.J.: Prentice-Hall, 1967), pp. 24–75; and Erving Goffman, *Frame Analysis* (New York: Harper & Row, 1974).

27. A. A. Bellack, H. M. Kliebard, R. T. Hyman, and F. L. Smith, Jr., *The Language of the Classroom*. (New York: Columbia Teachers College Press, 1966), p. 4.

28. See Turner, *The Forest of Symbols: Aspects of Ndembu Ritual*, pp. 49–50.

29. Faubion Bowers, "Drama" *International Encyclopedia of Social Science*, vol. 4 (New York: Free Press, 1968), p. 256.

30. Ibid.

31. Constantin Stanislavski, *An Actor's Handbook*, ed. and trans. E. R. Hapgood (New York: Theatre Arts Books, 1963), p. 73.

32. See A. Schochet, "Chevrot Limud Be-Mayot Ha-Taz-Ha-Yach Be-Erets Yisrael, Be-Polin-Lita U-Be-Germanya" [Study groups in the seventeenth and eighteenth centuries in Israel, Lithuania-Poland, and Germany], in *Ha-Chinuch* (Kislev 1956–7).

33. See Jacob Neusner, *Fellowship in Judaism: The First Century and Today* (London: Valentine Mitchell, 1963), p. 46.

34. See Raymond Firth, *Symbols: Public and Private* (Ithaca: Cornell University Press, 1973), p. 176.

35. Max Gluckman, *Order and Rebellion in Tribal Africa* (London: Cohen & West, 1963).

36. See R. C. Pittinger, C. F. Hockett, and J. J. Danehy, *The First Five Minutes: A Sample of Microscopic Interview Analysis* (Ithaca, N.Y.: Paul Martineau, 1960).

37. Jacob Neusner, ed., *Contemporary Judaic Fellowship in Theory and in Practice.* (New York: Ktav, 1972), p. 71; see also Samuel C. Heilman, *Synagogue Life: A Study in Symbolic Interaction* (Chicago: University of Chicago Press, 1976), pp. 233–37.

38. Victor Turner, *Dramas, Fields and Metaphors: Symbolic Action in Human Society* (Ithaca: Cornell University Press, 1974), p. 273.

39. Ibid., p. 53.

40. Geertz, *The Interpretation of Cultures*, p. 90.

41. I am freely translating the quotation here since its content rather than its precise wording is the essential matter here.

42. Abraham Menes, "The Yeshivot in Eastern Europe," in *The Jewish People Past and Present*, vol. 2. (New York: Harstin Press, 1948), p. 109.

43. Turner, *The Forest of Symbols*, p. 50.

44. The prayer recited on the first day of each Jewish month and on holy days in the *amida*, the core of the daily liturgy. According to law, failure to recite this prayer requires one to repeat the entire *amida*.

45. These refer to various types of sacrifices which people were wont to offer in the days of the temple in Jerusalem.

46. Berger and Luckmann, *The Social Construction of Reality*, p. 23; Alfred Schutz, *Collected Papers*, vol. 1, trans. Maurice Natanson (The Hague: Martinus Nijhoff, 1964).

47. I have tried to provide the English reader with a nearly literal translation of the dialogue here. The unspoken but understood assumptions and background

knowledge have been bracketed. The need for these bracketed glosses in what even with them may still seem largely opaque surely underscores the extent to which the interlocutors share common, intersubjective grounds of discourse.

48. According to Jewish law all four-cornered garments must have ritually knotted fringes affixed at the corners. And if one owns no such garment, it must specifically be purchased and then worn.

49. Ruth M. Underhill, *Autobiography of a Papago Woman* (New York: Krause Reprint, 1936), p. 26.

50. Emile Durkheim, *The Elementary Forms of the Religious Life*, trans. J. W. Swain (New York: Free Press, [1954] 1965), p. 466.

51. Ibid., p. 467.

52. Orrin E. Klapp, *Symbolic Leaders* (Chicago: Aldine, 1964), p. 358.

53. To be sure, these questions assume the legitimacy of the present even as they seek meaning in the past. They have their counterparts in other essential questions which assume the legitimacy of the tradition even as they seek meaning in the affairs of the present, as we shall shortly see.

54. This kind of evaluative remark is common. Rav Gafny, leader of another circle, would often mark his discourses with comments like, "This is a marvelous example of the gemore's thinking," or "This shows the genius of Judaism," emphasizing the wider significance and moral aesthetics of the sacred literature.

55. See Martin Foss, *Symbol and Metaphor in Human Experience* (Lincoln: University of Nebraska Press, [1949] 1964), p. 129, where Foss defines this as the essence of drama.

56. Cynthia Ozick, "The Laughter of Akiva," *New Yorker*, November 10, 1980, p. 72.

57. Julius Guttmann, *Philosophies of Judaism*, trans. D. W. Silverman (New York: Holt, Rinehart & Winston, 1964), p. 153.

58. Ibid.

59. Ibid.

60. See Louis Finkelstein, "The Jewish Religion," and R. Gordis, "The Bible as a Cultural Monument," both in *The Jews: Their Religion and Culture*, ed. L. Finkelstein (New York: Harper & Row, 1955).

61. Mary Douglas, *Natural Symbols: Explorations in Cosmology* (New York: Pantheon, 1970), p. 37.

62. Sigmund Freud, "Further Recommendations in the Technique of Psychoanalysis: Recollection, Repetition and Working-through," trans. J. Riviere, in *Collected Papers* ([1914] 1959), 2:369.

63. Max Weber, *Theory of Social and Economic Organization* trans. T. Parsons (New York: Free Press, 1947), pt. 1, p. 114.

64. Geertz, *The Interpretation of Cultures*, p. 92.

65. Ibid., p. 140, 312.

CHAPTER 4

1. Victor Turner, *Dramas, Fields and Metaphors: Symbolic Action in Human Society* (Ithaca: Cornell University Press, 1974), p. 50.

2. Erving Goffman, *Encounters: Two Studies in the Sociology of Interaction* (Indianapolis: Bobbs-Merrill, 1961), p. 7.

3. James W. Fernandez, "Persuasions and Performances: Of the Beast in Everybody . . . and the Metaphors of Everyman," *Daedalus* (Winter 1972), p. 42.

4. See Erving Goffman, *Frame Analysis* (New York: Harper & Row, 1974), pp. 40–82.

5. Ibid., p. 508.

6. Ibid., p. 547.

7. Ibid., p. 558.

8. Ibid., p. 546.

9. A. G. Smith, ed., *Community and Culture* (New York: Holt, Rinehart & Winston, 1966), p. 94.

10. Don Handelman, "Components of Interaction in the Negotiation of a Definition of the Situation," in *Language and Man*, ed. W. C. McCormick and S. A. Wurm (The Hague: Mouton, 1976), p. 288.

11. K. L. Pike, *Language in Relation to a Unified Theory of the Structure of Human Behavior* (Glendale, Calif.: Summer Institute of Linguistics, 1955).

12. Erving Goffman, "Replies and Responses," *Language in Society* 5, no. 3 (December 1976): 308.

13. See Erving Goffman, *Frame Analysis* (New York: Harper & Row, 1974), pp. 247–300.

14. See Erving Goffman, *The Presentation of Self in Everyday Life* (New York: Doubleday, 1959), pp. 17–76.

15. Goffman, *Frame Analysis*, p. 346.

16. Robert F. Bales, "How People Interact in Conferences," in *Communication and Culture*, ed. A. G. Smith (New York: Holt, Rinehart & Winston, 1966), p. 101.

17. Goffman, *Frame Analysis*, p. 21.

18. Ibid., p. 21.

19. Ibid., pp. 43–44.

20. For this idea I am thankful to Professor Joseph Lowin.

21. See photograph of page of Babylonian Talmud in Chapter 1.

22. See A. A. Bellack, and H. M. Kliebard, R. T. Hyman, F. L. Smith, Jr., *The Language of the Classroom* (New York: Columbia Teachers College Press, 1966).

23. Ibid.

24. Strictly speaking, there is an element of translation implicit in an expressive recitation of the telegraphic text. Purists may correctly argue that the modifications of translation begin in the decision of how to vocalize and inflect the written words. The distinction between recitation and translation is emphasized here for heuristic purposes. It allows one to trace the process of the *lernen* interactions more easily.

25. Eugene A. Nida, *Language Structure and Translation: Essays by Eugene A. Nida*, ed. A. S. Dill (Stanford: Stanford University Press, 1975).

26. Goffman, *Frame Analysis*, p. 69.

27. Goffman, "Replies and Responses," pp. 270–71.

28. Ibid., p. 272.

29. See Goffman, *Frame Analysis*, p. 254.

30. In the *Makhzor Vitri*, a twelfth-century liturgical Jewish text composed in France, one finds: "And from the beginning they teach him to move his body in study" (p. 628, first edition of the Oxford manuscript).

31. David Efron, *Gesture and Environment* (New York: Kings Crown Press, 1941), p. 132.

32. There is a problem of orthography and notation here. The text is Aramaic and Hebrew; the rest of the speech is in Hebrew. Some of the speech requires

translation which I have put in brackets; some is translated by the speakers. What is boldface in brackets is my technical explanation of the *kind* of thing being said. This necessarily results in an additional keying beyond those already provided by the speakers. The problem is unavoidable for the nonliterate in Hebrew. Each move will be discussed in detail in the text. Turns at talk, of which there are four, are marked in the margins in roman numerals at the first move of each turn. Each spoken move in a turn will be individually numbered. Accompanying nonverbal moves will be described in a narrative form afterward.

33. Often called "back channel communications" (see Harvey Sacks, in Goffman, "Replies and Responses," p. 257).

34. These are incidentally not unlike the echoes one commonly hears in the American Negro church which seem to serve many of the same functions.

35. See Emile Durkheim, *Moral Education*, trans. E. K. Wilson and H. Schnurer (New York: Free Press, 1961).

36. To be sure, as a researcher swept up by another agenda, I could have stayed longer. My strategy from the start, however, had been to be both participant and observer. Only in this way would I get both an inside and outside view of the proceedings. With my genuine participant status evaporating as my game-generated role did, I no longer felt that I would learn all I could from the time spent in the circle, so I made the decision to move on to another.

37. See Goffman, *Encounters*, p. 38.

38. Ibid., p. 40.

39. Ibid.

40. Ibid., p. 106.

41. Goffman, "Replies and Responses," p. 1.

42. Goffman, *The Presentation of Self in Everyday Life*, pp. 17–22; see also Jerome R. Mintz, *Legends of Hasidim* (Chicago: University of Chicago Press, 1968), pp. 265–87, in which a hasid who acts as if he is a miracle rabbi convinces not only others but also himself that he is.

43. There is a parallel to this sort of behavior in what Orthodox Jews call "*davenen*." As I have argued elsewhere ("Prayer in the Orthodox Synagogue," *Contemporary Jewry* [Spring/Summer 1982], pp. 2–17), *davenen* is a typified display of prayer, something short of a holistic, spontaneous involvement in genuine worship. Anyone who learns how to make the right moves (the deliberate mumbling of liturgy, swaying in a show of rapture, sitting and standing at the appropriate times, etc.) can engage in *davenen*. Only a few, moved by genuine religious sensibility, can engage in *tefila*, spontaneous and holistic worship. Thus people may *daven* for a lifetime without ever having experienced the awe and engagement of *tefila*. The relationship between *lernen* and talmudic scholarship is more or less the same.

44. Goffman, *Frame Analysis*, p. 274.

45. The possibility of wandering into a class by accident is not as farfetched as it may seem. In synagogues like Kahal Reyim or Beit Rachel, where a number of rooms are often filled with small study circles, it is not inconceivable that a Jew may walk in off the street to collect alms, to warm up, to join a prayer service, and instead find himself caught in a *shiur*.

46. Emile Durkheim, *The Elementary Forms of the Religious Life*, trans. J. W. Swain (New York: Free Press, [1954] 1965).

47. Ibid.

48. Philip Rieff, "The Impossible Culture," in *The Soul of Man under Socialism*, by Oscar Wilde (New York: Harper & Row, 1970), p. xiii.

49. Goffman, *Encounters*, p. 41.

50. The experience of public prayer in the synagogue offers some of the same possibilities for the Orthodox and therefore holds many of the same attractions for them (see Samuel C. Heilman, *Synagogue Life* [Chicago: University of Chicago Press, 1976]). Bowling, when one is a member of a culturally significant bowling team, one whose successes and failures reflect the strengths or weaknesses of a local community, can offer a similar opportunity (see W. F. Whyte, *Street Corner Society* [Chicago: University of Chicago Press, 1951]).

CHAPTER 5

1. Max Weinreich, *This History of the Yiddish Language*, trans. S. Noble and J. Fishman (Chicago: University of Chicago Press, 1980), p. 5.

2. Ibid., p. 206.

3. Mark Zborowski, "The Place of Book Learning in Traditional Jewish Culture," in *Childhood in Contemporary Cultures*, ed. Margaret Mead and Martha Wolfenstein (Chicago: University of Chicago Press, 1965), p. 125.

4. M. Weinreich, *The History of the Yiddish Language*, p. 209.

5. Mark Zborowski and Elizabeth Herzog, *Life Is with People: The Jewish Little Town of Eastern Europe* (New York: International Universities Press, 1952), p. 149.

6. M. Weinreich, *The History of the Yiddish Language*, pp. 13, 416–17.

7. See Samuel C. Heilman, *Synagogue Life: A Study in Symbolic Interaction* (Chicago: University of Chicago Press, 1976), pp. 152–67, on the role of aggression in gossip, especially among Jews.

8. David Efron, *Gesture and Environment* (New York: Kings Crown Press, 1941), p. 66.

9. Peter Berger, "Identity as a Problem in the Sociology of Knowledge," in *The Sociology of Knowledge: A Reader*, ed. J. E. Curtis and J.W. Petras (New York: Praeger, 1970), p. 374.

10. M. Weinreich, *The History of the Yiddish Language*, p. 193.

11. Erving Goffman, *Interaction Ritual* (New York: Anchor, 1967), p. 36.

12. M. Weinreich, *The History of the Yiddish Language*, p. 255.

13. Ibid., pp. 195 and 255; for a full discussion of Yiddish in the framework of other Jewish languages, see pp. 45–174.

14. *Gemore-loshn* may be defined more precisely as a special type of *taytsh*. It draws its terms and idioms from Talmud primarily, whereas *taytsh* reflects the general sacred literature and culture of Yiddish.

15. See J. Fishman, *Yiddish in America* (Bloomington: Indiana University Press, 1965), p. 58.

16. See Abraham Sofer, ed., *Igrot Sofrim* (Vienna, 1928), pt. 3, pp. 6–8.

17. Ibid., pt. 2, p. 40.

18. Although I have not carried on systematic study of other locales, occasional fieldwork in Zurich and London has revealed that, in these places where modern Orthodox *lerners* are to be found, the vernaculars also enter the avocational Talmud study. That is, the principle of cultural integration through language is at work. There seems no reason to doubt that what I have found in America, Israel, England, and Switzerland also should not be the case among Belgian, Dutch, Argentinian, or other Jews who see themselves as members of two cultures

simultaneously. On this point more will be said later (see also J. Fishman, *Yiddish in America* [Bloomington: Indiana University Press, 1965], p. 59).

19. See H. G. Burger, "Syncretism: An Acculturative Accelerator," *Human Organization* 25 (1966): 103–15.

20. V. Vološinov, "Reported Speech," in *Readings in Russian Poetics: Formalist and Structuralist Views*, ed. L. Metejka and K. Pomorska (Cambridge: M.I.T. Press, 1971), p. 165.

21. M. Weinreich, *The History of the Yiddish Language*, p. 243.

22. Ibid., p. 124.

23. Uriel Weinreich, "Notes on the Yiddish Rise-Fall Intonation Contour," in *For Roman Jakobson*, ed. M. Halle (The Hague: Mouton, 1956), pp. 633–43.

24. Susan Ervin-Tripp, "An Analysis of the Interaction of Language, Topic and Listener," in *Readings in the Sociology of Language*, ed. J. A. Fishman (The Hague: Mouton, 1968), p. 198. Although Ervin-Tripp states this in the reverse, the correlation between content and language seems to be beyond debate.

25. See Uriel Weinreich, *Languages in Contact* (New York: Linguistic Circle of New York No. 1, 1953), p. 68.

26. Arnold Van Gennep, "Essai d'une theorie des langues speciales" in *Revue des etudes ethnographiques et sociologiques* 1 (1908): 328; my translation.

27. Ibid., p. 329.

28. See Peter Berger, *The Heretical Imperative* (Garden City, N.Y.: Anchor, 1979).

29. Smotra is by no means unique in this. For a similar case, see Heilman, *Synagogue Life*, pp. 221–52.

30. Dorothy Henderson, "Contextual Specificity, Discretion, and Cognitive Socialization: With Special Reference to Language," *Sociology* 4, no. 3 (1970): 331.

31. Berger, "Identity as a Problem in the Sociology of Knowledge," p. 376.

32. The obvious exceptions include the immigrant or neophyte speaker who involuntarily utilizes the old form of communication because he is incapable of carrying on in the new one that he would otherwise choose. The imposter who passes himself off as someone he is not by speaking in a way which will camouflage his true identity and loyalties might also be considered an exception. Since, however, we are all disposed to managing impressions, appearing differently to different audiences, the case of the imposter may be considered as simply an extreme variety of the normal case (see J. Fishman, "Who Speaks What Language to Whom and When," *La Linguistique* 2 [1965]: 67–88; S. D. Herman, "Criteria for Jewish Identity," in *World Jewry and the State of Israel*, ed. M. Davis [New York: Arno Press, 1977], p. 493).

33. V. Yngve, "On Getting a Word in Edgewise," *Papers from the Sixth Regional Meeting, Chicago Linguistic Society*, ed. M. A. Cambell et al. (Chicago: Dept. of Linguistics, University of Chicago, 1970).

34. Sigmund Freud, "The Loss of Reality: Neurosis and Psychosis," *Collected Papers*, vol. 2, trans. Joan Riviere (New York: Basic Books, [1924] 1959).

35. W. F. and J. V. Soskin, "The Study of Spontaneous Talk," in *The Stream of Behavior*, ed. R. G. Baker (New York: Appleton-Century-Crofts, 1963), p. 229.

36. M. Weinreich, *The History of the Yiddish Language*, p. 183.

37. Although language "shift" commonly refers to a community of speakers abandoning the use of one language and adopting another as a substitute whereas "switching" refers to alternation among codes during conversation, the principle cited above would seem to hold equally for language shift and switching: neither

can be purely explained without reference to social and psychological matters (Uriel Weinreich, "Influences of Yiddish on American English: Possibilities of a New Approach" [paper delivered at YIVO Conference, 1967], p. 1).

38. Ervin-Tripp, "An Analysis of the Interaction of Language, Topic, and Listener," p. 198.

39. Ibid., p. 197.

40. Heilman, *Synagogue Life*, p. 231.

41. J. Fishman, "Who Speaks What Language to Whom and When," p. 71.

42. Ibid.

43. Erving Goffman, "Replies and Responses," *Language in Society* 5, no. 3 (December 1976): 267.

44. U. Weinreich, *Languages in Contact*, p. 83.

45. To distinguish text from other words, I will surround all such excerpts with quotation marks. When foreign words or phrases are not followed in the utterance by literal translations or not translated in the ensuing discussion, I will provide such translation in brackets following the first appearance of the foreign material. All Hebrew pronunciation is, as spoken, in Ashkenazic accentuation.

46. M. Weinreich, *The History of the Yiddish Language*, p. 189.

47. See K. L. Pike, *The Intonation of American English* (Ann Arbor: University of Michigan Press, 1947); U. Weinreich, "Notes on the Rise-Fall Intonation Contour."

48. L. M. Feinsilver, "Yiddish and American English," *Chicago Jewish Forum* 14 (1956): 71–76.

49. J. Blom and J. J. Gumperz, "Social Meaning in Linguistic Structure: Code-Switching in Norway," in *Directions in Sociolinguistics*, ed. J. J. Gumperz and D. Hymes (New York: Holt, Rinehart & Winston, 1972), p. 424.

50. See Marver H. Bernstein, "Learning as Worship: A Jewish Perspective on Higher Education," in *Go and Study: Essays and Studies in Honor of Alfred Jospe*, ed. Raphael Jospe and S. Z. Fishman (Washington, D.C.: B'nai B'rith Hillel Foundations, 1980), pp. 15–28.

51. J. R. Rayfield, *The Languages of a Bilingual Community* (The Hague: Mouton, 1970); Irving Howe, *World of Our Fathers* (New York: Harcourt, Brace & Jovanovich, 1976).

52. J. Fishman, "Who Speaks What Language to Whom and When," p. 68.

53. A. A. Dubb, *Jewish South Africans: A Sociological View of the Johannesburg Community*, Occasional Paper No. 21 (Grahamstown, S.A.: Institute of Social and Economic Research, 1977), p. 56.

54. See, e.g., J. L. Moreau, *Language and Religious Language: A Study in the Dynamics of Translation* (Philadelphia: Westminster Press, 1961).

55. The notion of the relevance of Jewish texts to contemporary life goes back at least as far as Philo (ca. 20 B.C.E.–50 C.E.), the Alexandrian Jewish thinker who "developed to its acme the idea that whatever was noble in Greek thinking was to be discovered in the sacred scripture of Judaism" (ibid., p. 61).

56. Pike, *The Intonation of American English*, p. 21.

57. U. Weinreich, "Notes on the Yiddish Rise-Fall Intonation Contour," p. 639.

58. Ibid., p. 640.

59. See ibid.; also see M. A. K. Halliday, *Intonation and Grammar in British English* (The Hague: Mouton, 1967); and Pike, *The Intonation of American English*.

60. U. Weinreich, "Notes on the Yiddish Rise-Fall Intonation Contour," pp. 633–34.

61. Pike, *The Intonation of American English*, p. 20.

62. See Rayfield, *The Languages of a Bilingual Community*, p. 72.

63. U. Weinreich, "Notes on the Yiddish Rise-Fall Intonation Contour," p. 642.

64. The poetry of Chaim Nachman Bialik, meant to resonate with tradition even as it uses the vocabulary of modern Hebrew, is perhaps one of the best examples of this sort of interlanguage. Although Bialik was not strictly speaking a modern Orthodox Jew, his life with its Orthodox background and modernist foreground certainly approximates the modern Orthodox model. His poetry is meant to be read in the Ashkenazic accents of *Loshn Koydesh* and *gemore-nign*. Read in the Sephardic pronunciation and cadence of modern Hebrew it sounds all wrong, its meter confused.

65. Heilman, *Synagogue Life*, esp. pp. 229–32; see also H. Gans, "The 'Yinglish' Music of Mickey Katz," in *American Quarterly* 5 (1953): 213–18.

66. No universally agreed-upon notation for intonation has yet been established. Accordingly, I will use a combination of Kenneth Pike's numerical notation (lower numbers signify lower pitch, higher numbers high pitch) and Uriel Weinreich's punctuation (?!) for questions asked in a rise-fall cadence. I have also used a dash to note a glide when an intonational contour occurs in a single syllable. One last transcriptional point: non-English words are italicized. Of those, words quoted from the text are italicized and marked with quotation marks.

67. Ragnar Rommetveit, *On Message Structure: A Framework for the Study of Language and Communication* (New York: Wiley, 1974), p. 23.

68. B. Malinowski, *Coral Gardens and Their Magic*, vol. 2 (London: Allen & Unwin, 1935), p. 230; Maurice Merleau-Ponty, *The Prose of the World*, trans. J. O'Neil. (Evanston: Northwestern University Press, 1973), p. 20.

69. Karl Vossler, *The Spirit of Language in Civilization*, trans. O. Oeser (London: Routledge & Kegan Paul, [1932] 1951), p. 46.

CHAPTER 6

1. Jacob Neusner, *Invitation to the Talmud* (New York: Harper & Row, 1973), p. 11.

2. To be precise here, there are three indigenous terms for a Jewish fellowship. *Khavruse*, although assimilated by Yiddish, is originally an Aramaic term appearing in the Talmud. *Havura*, assimilated by Hebrew, also has talmudic roots. *Khevre* seems to be a shortened Yiddish form. For present purposes, these terms may be used interchangeably.

3. Neusner, *Invitation to the Talmud*, p. 67.

4. Ibid.

5. Jacob Neusner, *Fellowship in Judaism: The First Century and Today* (London: Valentine Mitchell, 1963), pp. 7–71.

6. Emile Durkheim, *The Division of Labor in Society*, trans. G. Simpson (Glencoe, Ill.: Free Press, 1949), p. 10.

7. Herman Schmalenbach, "The Sociological Category of Communion," in *Theories of Society*, ed. T. Parsons, E. Shils, K. Naegele, and J. Pitts (New York: Free Press, 1961), pp. 331–47; see also Victor Turner, *The Forest of Symbols: Aspects of Ndembu Ritual* (Ithaca: Cornell University Press, 1967).

8. Ibid., pp. 331–35.

9. Victor Turner, *Dramas, Fields and Metaphors: Symbolic Action in Human Society* (Ithaca: Cornell University Press, 1974), p. 248.

10. Jacob Neusner, ed., *Contemporary Judaic Fellowship in Theory and in Practice* (New York: KTAV, 1972), p. 67. There are other "Jewish purposes" that can bring about fellowship—worship, e.g.

11. For other cases, see Samuel C. Heilman, *Synagogue Life: A Study in Symbolic Interaction* (Chicago: University of Chicago Press, 1976); Bernard Riesman, *The Havurah: A Contemporary Jewish Experience* (New York: Union of American Hebrew Congregations, 1977).

12. Neusner, *Fellowship in Judaism*, pp. 11–12.

13. Ibid., pp. 43–44.

14. As noted earlier, the designation of participants in contemporary study circles as "reb" is a continuation of this tradition.

15. Fritz Baer, "Der Ursprung der Chewra," *Judische Wohlwartspflege und Sozialwissenschaft* 1 (1928): 241–47.

16. Salo Baron, *The Jewish Community*, vol. 1 (Philadelphia: Jewish Publication Society, 1942), p. 354; see also J. Shachter, *The Belfast Chevra-Gemorra* (London: Narod Press, 1945); and Isaac Levitats, *The Jewish Community in Russia, 1772–1844* (New York: Columbia University Press, 1943).

17. A. Schochet, "*Chevrot Limud Be-Mayot Ha-Taz–Ha-Yach Be-Erets Yisrael, Be-Polin-Lita, U-Be-Germanya*" [Study groups in the sixteenth through eighteenth centuries in Israel, Lithuania-Poland and Germany], in *Ha-Chinuch* (Kislev, 1956–57), p. 404.

18. Ibid., p. 406; see also Moses A. Shulvass, *The Jews in the World of the Renaissance: 14th and 15th Century*, trans. Elvin Kose (Leiden: E. J. Brill, 1973), pp. 267–80.

19. Schochet, "Chevrot Limud Be-Mayot Ha-Taz–Ha-Yach Be-Erets Yisrael, Be-Polin-Lita, U-Be-Germanya," p. 406.

20. "SHaS" is an acronym for the Talmud. It comes from the initials of the two Hebrew words, "*Shisha Sedarim*" (literally, "Six sections"), which denotes the six general topic areas into which the Talmud is divided.

21. Schochet, "Chevrot Limud Be-Mayot Ha-Taz–Ha-Yach Be-Erets Yisrael, Be-Polin-Lita, U-Be-Germanya," p. 414.

22. Shachter, *The Belfast Chevra-Gemorra*, p. 8.

23. Max Grunwald, "Das 'Lernen,' " in *Jahrbuch fur Judische Volkskunde*, ed. Max Grunwald (Berlin: Hanz Verlag, 1924–25), p. 100.

24. See, e.g., Louis Greenberg, *The Jews in Russia*, vol. 1 (New Haven: Yale University Press, 1944); Isaac S. Emmanuel and Suzanne A. Emmanuel, *History of the Jews of the Netherland Antilles*, vol. 1 (Cincinnati: American Jewish Archives, 1970); Simon M. Dubnow, *History of the Jews in Russia and Poland*, vol. 2, trans. I. Frielander (Philadelphia: Jewish Publication Society, 1918); Levitats, *The Jewish Community in Russia, 1772–1844*; A. Menes, "The Yeshivot in Eastern Europe," in *The Jewish People Past and Present*, vol. 2 (New York: Marstin Press, 1948); Shachter, *The Belfast Chevra-Gemorra*, and articles in *The Occident and American Jewish Advocate*, vol. 14 (1858).

25. Levitats, *The Jewish Community in Russia, 1772–1844*, p. 105.

26. The effects of contemporary feminism, while still weak among *lerners*, can be seen in the few women who join circles of men or start their own. It is still unusual, however, to find women in Talmud study circles (ibid.).

27. Heilman, *Synagogue Life*, provides a similar case study.

28. See W. F. Whyte, *Street Corner Society* (Chicago: University of Chicago Press, 1951), for a similar consideration of bowling.

29. This was before the disengagement from the group, which I have described in Chapter 4.

30. See Heilman, *Synagogue Life*, pp. 135 and 224–26, for a discussion of the notion of "warming up."

31. Erving Goffman, *Relations in Public: Micro Studies of the Public Order* (New York: Basic Books, 1971), p. 194.

32. Heilman, *Synagogue Life*, pp. 225–26, describes a similar use of cigarettes but considers them in different analytic context there.

33. Marcel Mauss, *The Gift*, trans. Ian Cunnison (New York: Norton, 1967), p. 11.

34. See Heilman, *Synagogue Life*, pp. 111–26, for an extended discussion of Jewish mendicants.

35. See Schochet, "*Chevrot Limud Be-Mayot Ha-Taz–Ha-Yach Be-Erets Yisrael, Be-Polin-Lita, U-Be-Germanya*," p. 406.

36. For a discussion of the reasons for this and a biography of Nachman of Bratslav, see A. Green, *Tormented Master* (University: University of Alabama Press, 1979), esp. pp. 264–91.

37. Emile Durkheim, *Moral Education*, trans. E. K. Wilson and H. Schnurer. (New York: Free Press, 1961), p. 60.

38. Ibid., p. 59.

39. Ibid., p. 68; see also Allen Wheelis, *The Quest for Identity* (New York: Norton, 1958), for a discussion of modern life and anomie.

40. L. Dawidowicz, *The War against the Jews 1933–1945* (New York: Bantam, 1975), p. 252.

41. Levitats, *The Jewish Community in Russia, 1772–1844*, p. 105.

42. For another example of this sort of camouflaged *lernen*, see Green, *Tormented Master*, p. 257; and Heilman, *Synagogue Life*, pp. 250–51.

43. The practice of asking old questions as if they were new is firmly established within Orthodox Judaism. This has already been seen in the earlier discussion of "prefiguration." It may also be seen in the traditional pre-Passover seminars when perennial questions of norm and practice are asked (by those who have celebrated the holy day all their lives) as if they were totally original.

CHAPTER 7

1. Mircea Eliade, *A History of Religious Ideas*, vol. 1, trans. W. Trask (Chicago: University of Chicago Press, 1978), p. 162.

2. Marver H. Bernstein, "Learning as Worship: A Jewish Perspective on Higher Education," in *Go and Study: Essays and Studies in Honor of Alfred Jospe*, ed. Raphael Jospe and S. Z. Fishman (Washington, D.C.: B'nai B'rith Hillel Foundations, 1980), p. 19.

3. Robert Maynard Hutchins, Commencement Address, University of Judaism, Los Angeles, June 24, 1965.

4. Mircea Eliade, *Cosmos and History*, trans. W. Trask (New York: Harper & Row 1959), p. 5.

5. For a full discussion of "response cries" and their role in anchoring and connecting conversation, see Erving Goffman, *Forms of Talk* (Philadelphia: University of Pennsylvania Press, 1981), pp. 78–122.

6. Rudolf Otto, *The Idea of the Holy*, trans. J. W. Harvey (New York: Oxford University Press, [1923] 1958), p. 10.

7. The Midrash itself (*Tanhuma Bekhukotai*) refers to the house of study as "Beit Ha-Talmud" rather than the more common *besmedresh*.

8. For a look at how this actually happens, look at my *Synagogue Life* (Chicago: University of Chicago Press, 1976), and especially at the chapter entitled "Gossip." The latter frequently serves to keep people informed about what is right and wrong among the members of the community.

9. Eliade, *A History of Religious Ideas*, p. 166.

10. A play on words that sound alike or have a number of letters in common but vastly different meanings is a frequent device used by the rabbis and exegetes as a source for homily. This kind of play is all part of the inherent fascination with words that makes its appearance throughout Jewish history and to which I have alluded in an earlier chapter.

11. Like many other articles of Jewish ritual life, the sukkah (a booth in which to dwell during the holy days of Sukkot when Jews ritually leave their homes and carry on life in the temporary dwellings that tradition has it they used during the period of the exodus) must be constructed in compliance with certain *halakhic* standards. These become the principles upon which this narrative, like the sukkah, is built.

12. Ludwig Lewisohn, *What Is This Jewish Heritage?* rev. ed. (New York: Schocken Books, 1964), p. 48.

13. Abraham Joshua Heschel, *The Earth Is the Lord's: The Inner World of the Jews of Eastern Europe* (New York: Harper & Row, [1950] 1966), p. 96.

CHAPTER 8

1. See Emile Durkheim, *The Elementary Forms of the Religious Life*, trans. J. W. Swain (New York: Free Press, [1954] 1965), pp. 425–28.

2. The Baal Shem Tov, Israel ben Eliezer, the founder of hasidism. Although the men of Beit Rachel are not hasidim, they like many other Jews are prepared to syncretistically accept folklore and folk religion from other quarters.

3. Mircea Eliade, *Cosmos and History*, trans. W. Trask (New York: Harper & Row, 1959), p. 5.

4. It is Jewish tradition to refrain from attending celebrations during the eleven months one is in mourning for a member of one's immediate family. There are a number of interpreters of the law, halakhic virtuosi, rabbis, who argue that a *siyum* is an exception to this. There are, however, others who do not exclude it.

5. This annual holy day marks the completion of the annual reading of the Torah scroll.

6. A prayer often associated with sadness and skipped in the daily liturgy on holy days and joyous occasions.

GLOSSARY

Although throughout the book I have been careful to define, at least at their initial appearance, every Hebrew or Yiddish term used, I am including a glossary of frequently used words for easy reference. While some words are either Hebrew or Yiddish, others, depending upon intonation and pronunciation, may be either. Some words are Aramaic, the language of the Talmud. All pronunciation is as suggested by spelling, the only exception being in the "ch" and "kh" sounds, which are guttural, as in the names "Khazars" and "Bach."

aderaba   (Aramaic) On the contrary. This phrase comes from the Babylonian Talmud.

ad ho idno amay lo osis le gaboy   (Aramaic) Why didn't you come before now?

aggada   (Hebrew) The corpus of Jewish lore.

aggadetta   (Aramaic) Lore.

a gute kashe   (Yiddish) A good question.

am-ha-arets   (Hebrew/Yiddish) Boor, illiterate, the Jewishly uninformed.

amida   (Hebrew) The core prayer of the Jewish service. Literally, "standing"; commonly refers to the silent prayer (composed of a series of benedictions, usually nineteen) which, recited without interruption, with feet touching at the instep, makes up the structural core of each prayer service.

313

az natkhil   (Hebrew) Then we shall begin.

baal akhsanya   (Hebrew) Innkeeper and caterer.

baal simkha   (Hebrew) Primary celebrant.

bald zogt men do   (Yiddish) Presently it says here.

be-ezrat hashem   (Hebrew) With the help of God.

befonay nekhtav u befonany nekhtam   (Hebrew) Before me it was written and before me it was signed. This is the formula of testimony to validate a bill of divorcement.

Beit Yosef   (Hebrew) A codex of Jewish law written by the medieval rabbi, Joseph Caro.

bes knesses   (Hebrew) Literally, house of assembly; the synagogue.

bes medresh   (Hebrew) Jewish study hall.

bes tefila   (Hebrew) House of prayer.

bizayon   (Hebrew) Shame.

blatt   (Yiddish) Page (of Talmud).

davenen   (Yiddish) Prayer.

dayan   (Hebrew/Yiddish) Judge.

deluskamey sefarim   (Aramaic) Ark for books.

devorim betalim   (Hebrew/Yiddish) Conversations perceived as profane or at least irrelevant to sanctified *lernen.*

divrey Torah   (Hebrew/Yiddish) Words of Torah, keys to comprehending the primary matter of the Talmud.

eey malko ano   (Aramaic) If I am a King.

En Yaakov   (Aramaic) A compendium of legends and tales culled from the Talmud but lacking the difficult legal disputations.

er ot dokh rekht   (Yiddish) He is after all correct.

farhern   (Yiddish) To aurally examine.

fregt di gemore   (Yiddish) The Talmud asks.

gabbai   (Hebrew) Officer in charge of organizing synagogue activities and disposing ritual tasks and honors.

gass ruakh   (Hebrew) Arrogant.

gdoley khasidus   (Hebrew) Giants of the hasidic world.

Gematria   (Hebrew) The Jewish mystical transformation of words into numbers.

gemore   (Aramaic/Yiddish) A portion of the Talmud, the so-called "completion" of the Mishna, as developed in the Jewish scholarly academies of Babylonia and Palestine (Israel). A record of oral debate and discussion among the sages that is neither concise nor systematic in its treatment of subjects. Sometimes used as a synonym for Talmud.

gemore-loshn (Yiddish) Language that is peppered with Talmudic terminology.

gemore-nign (Yiddish) Talmudic chant, a sing-song whose rising and falling cadences help disambiguate the text.

get (Hebrew) A bill of divorcement.

golem (Hebrew) Dummy.

goofah (Aramaic) A word used to indicate that after a textual digression the substantive topic is being returned to; it is one of the staples of *lernen* language.

Gra (Hebrew) Acronym for Elijah, the Gaon of Vilna (White Russia) and a major rabbinic leader of the eighteenth century.

gut vort (Yiddish) Good word, apt statement.

halakha (Hebrew) The corpus of Jewish law, literally "the way."

halakha le-ma'aseh (Hebrew) The practical law.

hamelekh (Hebrew) The king.

hasholayakh es ha kayn (Hebrew) A legal principle which mandates one to chase away a mother bird from a nest before taking away her eggs.

haver (Hebrew) Fellow (student).

haverim (Hebrew) Fellows.

haverim kol Yisrael (Hebrew) All the people of Israel are knit in fellowship.

havura (Hebrew) Fellowship (of students).

hefker (Hebrew/Yiddish) Ownerless, groundless, and illegitimate.

heimisch (Yiddish) Homey.

hertzokh ein, a moyredik kashe (Yiddish) Listen to this, this awesome question (the Talmud poses).

ikh halt as (Yiddish) I hold (maintain) that.

inyan (Hebrew) Subject or topic.

ish iti (Hebrew) "The man of the hour," designated man who would dispatch the scapegoat on Yom Kippur into the Judean wilderness where its end would come.

ivrit (Hebrew) Modern Hebrew.

iyun (Hebrew) The review and recitation of the Zohar and other mystical texts. It connotes a kind of meditation in which recitation of the sacred texts may be sufficient for the fulfillment of the imperative to study.

iz   (Yiddish) Is.

Kabbalah   (Hebrew) Jewish mysticism.

Kabbalists   (Hebrew) Mystics.

kaddish   (Hebrew/Aramaic) The Aramaic prayer of praise recited by a male relative in response to the death of a kinsman. It is recited during the morning, afternoon, and evening prayers throughout the first eleven months following bereavement and then afterward on the anniversary of the death. One can recite it only in the presence of ten or more males, all of whom must respond in formulaic language. The root of the word is the same as for the word *kadosh*, meaning "holy."

kakh omeret ha gemora   (Hebrew) Thus saith the Talmud.

kavannah   (Hebrew) Devotion, concentration, intensity, and determined intention. It is the subjective attitude which should properly accompany all conscious action, including, most especially, religious action.

kayn   (Hebrew) Yes.

kee   (Hebrew) Because.

ketuba   (Hebrew) Wedding document.

khavruse   (Yiddish) Fellowship of *lerners* or students.

khazak u baruch   (Hebrew) Be mighty and blessed.

kherem   (Hebrew) Excommunication.

khevre SHaS   (Yiddish) Fellowships dedicated to Talmud study.

klotz kashes   (Yiddish) Wrong-headed questions.

Knesset   (Hebrew) Parliament in Israel.

kotel   (Hebrew) The remaining Western Wall of the Holy Temple in Jerusalem.

k'vod ha-rav   (Hebrew) Your honor, the Rav.

lamdan   (Hebrew) Scholar.

L'chayim   (Hebrew) To life.

L'chayim tovim u-l'shalom   (Hebrew) To good life and peace.

lehashmid leharog, ule'abed   (Hebrew) To destroy, to kill, and to annihilate. This is a quotation from the book of Esther.

lehitkarev   (Hebrew) To bring close.

lernen   (Yiddish) The eternal review and ritualized study of sacred Jewish texts.

lifney melekh malkhey hamlokhim   (Hebrew) Before the King of all Kings.

Likutey MoHaRan (Hebrew) The gleanings from Reb Nachman of Bratslav, grandson of the Baal Shem Tov, founder of Hasidism; several volumes of his epistles and lessons.

lomer lernen a bisel (Yiddish) Let's study a little.

loshn (Hebrew) Terminology.

Loshn Koydesh (Yiddish) Holy tongue; traditional Hebrew.

Ma'ariv (Hebrew) Evening Prayers.

Magid Shiur (Hebrew/Yiddish) The narrator of the class.

Makhzor Vitri (Hebrew) A twelfth century liturgical Jewish text composed in France.

mama-loshn (Yiddish) Mother-tongue, Yiddish.

Mapa (Hebrew) The commentary of Moses Isserless on the codex "Beit Yosef" (see above).

matmid (Hebrew) Diligent student.

m'darf lernen (Yiddish) One must learn or study.

mefarshim (Hebrew) Jewish commentators of holy writ.

memra (Aramaic) Talmudic statement of an idea.

menorah (Hebrew) The candelabrum which was one of the most sacred objects at the Holy Temple in Jerusalem.

mesayem (Hebrew) Conclude.

mesekhta (Aramaic) Tractate of Talmud.

midrash (Hebrew) Jewish legend.

Mincha (Hebrew) Afternoon prayers.

minyan (Hebrew) Literally, "number"; commonly refers to the quorum of ten or more men necessary for the covening of communal prayer. It must consist of males over the age of thirteen. While others may participate in the service, only adult Jewish males are counted in the minyan.

mir zitsen oyf a bank (Yiddish) We sit on a bench.

Mishna Brura (Hebrew) One of the classic codices of Jewish law.

Mishna Torah (Hebrew) Repetition of the Law; this code written by Maimonides came to serve as the basis for many later compilations of Jewish law.

mitzva (Hebrew) Religious obligation, sometimes a synonym for "righteous act."

m'ken a zoy zugn und a zoy zugn (Yiddish) One can say thus and (one can say) otherwise.

moyredik (Yiddish) Formidable, awesome.

nignazin (Aramaic) Are stored.

nizrakin (Aramaic) Are thrown out.

nu   (Yiddish) So?

ober   (Yiddish) But.

oleynu lilmod   (Hebrew) It is incumbent upon us to study (Torah).

oleynu lishabeakh   (Hebrew) (From the liturgy) It is incumbent upon us to praise God.

omed   (Hebrew) Lectern.

ot a zoy, oh   (Yiddish) Oh that's it!

ot zokh zikh dermant di gemore   (Yiddish) He reminded himself of the Talmud.

ovar zman   (Hebrew) Time has passed.

oyb ikh bin take Got, ikh bin di malekh-malkhey hamlokhim   (Yiddish) If I am indeed God, I am the king of all kings.

Parashat Shekalim   (Hebrew) The Torah reading on one of the four special Sabbaths preceeding Passover (which) describes the annual Israelite contribution of a "shekel" from each household to the priestly treasure.

pilpul   (Hebrew) The talmudic, casuistic argument in which one tries to demonstrate that even opposites can be brought into harmony.

poshut pshat   (Yiddish) The simple interpretation of a text.

poskim   (Hebrew) Adjudicators of Jewish law.

rabotey   (Hebrew) Gentlemen.

Rambam   (Hebrew) Acronym for Moses Maimonides, twelfth-century Jewish exegete, philosopher, and codifier.

Rav   (Hebrew) Rabbi or leader of the class.

Reb   (Yiddish) Diminutive of "rabbi," which has come to mean something more than "mister" and less than "rabbi." It is a common title attached by *lerners* to one another.

rebe   (Yiddish) The title of a hasidic leader.

Roshey Yeshivot   (Hebrew) Principals of an academy of higher Jewish learning.

Rosh Hodesh   (Hebrew) The first day of the Jewish month.

schnorrers   (Hebrew) Mendicants.

Sephardic   (Hebrew) Jews of Mediterranean origin.

seudat mitzvah   (Hebrew) A meal commemorating the fulfillment of a religious obligation.

shah   (Yiddish) "Be still."

shalom zakhor (Hebrew) Literally, "peace to the male child," a get-together on the first Friday evening of the (male) child's life in order to congratulate the parents (or grandparents) of the child and to witness the recitation of various prayers and psalms for the welfare of the mother and child.

SHaS (Hebrew) An acronym for the Talmud. It comes from the initials of the two Hebrew words, "Shisha Sedarim" (literally, the "Six sections), which denotes the six general topic areas into which the Talmud is divided.

shehekhiyanu (Hebrew) Benediction of renewal.

shekel (Hebrew) A unit of currency.

Shevuot (Hebrew) The holy day on which the Jewish people celebrate their receipt of the Torah.

Shisha Sedarim (Hebrew) "Six sections"; the six general topic areas into which the Talmud is divided.

shiur (Hebrew/Yiddish) (Talmud) class.

shlemiel (Yiddish) Dolt.

shlomim (Hebrew) The peace offering, a sacrifice at the Holy Temple.

shmek tabak (Yiddish) Snuff.

shmoosn (Yiddish) The easy conversation in which what is said is less important than the fact that one person speaks and another listens and both are not alone.

shofar (Hebrew) Ram's horn, blown on the Jewish New Year and at other momentous Jewish occasions.

shoyn (Yiddish) Enough.

shoyte (Yiddish) Dummy.

shtender (Yiddish) Lectern under which is often stored a small library of Jewish texts.

shtetl (Yiddish) Hamlet.

shtoltz (Yiddish) Haughty.

shul (Yiddish) The synagogue, the congregation, the synagogue building.

Shulkhan Arukh (Hebrew) The major codex of Jewish law. See "Beit Yosef" above.

shver (Yiddish) Difficult (to comprehend).

shvitzer (Yiddish) Show-off.

simkha (Yiddish) Joyous celebration.

Simkhat Torah (Hebrew) This yearly holy day marks the completion of the annual reading of the Torah scroll.

siyum   (Hebrew) The celebration of a completion of a volume of Jewish study.

sken dokh nisht zeyn   (Yiddish) It cannot be.

sugia   (Aramaic/Hebrew) Talmudic discussion unit.

Sukkah   (Hebrew) A booth in which to dwell during the holy days of Sukkot when Jews ritually leave their homes and carry on life in temporary dwellings that tradition has it they used during the period of the exodus.

Sukkot   (Hebrew) Festival during which observant Jews sit in temporary boothlike dwellings to commemorate the passage through the Sinai when they lived in such dwellings for forty years.

Takhanun   (Hebrew) A prayer often associated with sadness and skipped in the daily liturgy on holy days and joyous occasions.

talmid khokhm   (Hebrew/Yiddish) Jewish scholar.

tam   (Hebrew) Simpleton.

tanu Rabbanan   (Aramaic) The wise (our rabbis) have taught.

tashmishey kedusha   (Hebrew) Items themselves endowed with sanctity.

tashmishey mitzvah   (Hebrew) Implements used for the execution of religious duties.

taytsh   (Yiddish) Yiddish translations.

tefila   (Hebrew) Spontaneous and holistic prayer.

tefilin   (Hebrew) Phylacteries.

T'hilim   (Hebrew) Psalms.

tikkun   (Hebrew) Restoration or repair, usually referring to matters of the spirit.

Torah   (Hebrew) The corpus of Jewish law and lore.

tsayar   (Hebrew) Artist.

tsur   (Hebrew) Rock.

tzaddik   (Hebrew) Righteous person.

tzitzit   (Hebrew) Ritually tied fringes worn by observant Jewish males on four-cornered garments.

vehu sovar   (Aramaic) And he thought.

Ve'ilu hen   (Hebrew) And these are.

viter de gemore   (Yiddish) Onward, (in) the Talmud.

vort   (Yiddish) Literally, word; the Yiddish expression *"vort"* is often used to refer to a disquisition which has all the makings of a full-blown reinterpretation of a matter under discussion, a reframing as it were.

vus darft er zokh shver makhn   (Yiddish) Why does he make it difficult for himself?

vus ligt er tsu   (Yiddish) What has he added?

vus varts di a gans yor   (Yiddish) Why have you been waiting an entire year?

Yaleh ve yovo   (Hebrew) The prayer recited in the *Amida*, the core prayer of the daily liturgy, on the first day of each Jewish month and on holy days.

Yerushalayim   (Hebrew) Jerusalem.

Yiddishkayt   (Yiddish) Jewishness.

Yo, avadeh   (Yiddish) "Yeah, certainly."

Yoma   (Aramaic) The tractate dealing primarily with the myriad procedures surrounding the Day of Atonement (Yom Kippur) as it was celebrated in the days of the Holy Temple in Jerusalem.

Yom Kippur   (Hebrew) Day of Atonement.

BIBLIOGRAPHY

Adler, Morris. *The World of the Talmud*. Washington: B'nai B'rith Hillel Foundations, 1959.

Baer, Fritz. "Der Ursprung Der Chevra." *Judische Wohlwartsflege und Sozialwissenschaft* 1 (1928): 241–47.

Bales, Robert F. "How People Interact in Conferences." In *Communication and Culture*, edited by A. G. Smith. New York: Holt, Rinehart & Winston, 1966.

Baron, Salo. *The Jewish Community*. Vol. 1. Philadelphia: Jewish Publication Society, 1942.

Bateson, Mary C. "A Riddle of Two Worlds. An Interpretation of the Poetry of H. N. Bialik." *Daedalus* (Summer 1966), pp. 741–62.

Bellack, A. A.; and Kliebard, H. M.; Hyman, R. T.; Smith, F. L., Jr. *The Language of the Classroom*. New York: Columbia Teachers College Press, 1966.

Bellow, Saul. "Starting Out in Chicago." *American Scholar* (Winter 1974–75), pp. 71–77.

Berger, Peter. "Identity as a Problem in the Sociology of Knowledge." In *The Sociology of Knowledge: A Reader*, edited by J. E. Curtis and J. W. Petras. New York: Praeger, 1970.

———. *The Heretical Imperative*. Garden City, N.Y.: Anchor, 1979.

Berger, Peter, and Luckmann, Thomas. *The Social Construction of Reality*. Garden City, N.Y.: Doubleday, 1966.

Bernstein, Marver H. "Learning as Worship: A Jewish Perspective on Higher Education." In *Go and Study: Essays and Studies in*

Honor of Alfred Jospe, edited by Raphael Jospe and S. Z. Fishman. Washington, D.C.: B'nai B'rith Hillel Foundations, 1980.

"The Beth Hammidrash, New York." From *Occident and American Jewish Advocate*, vol. 14 (1858).

Blom, J., and Gumperz, J. J. "Social Meaning in Linguistic Structure: Code-Switching in Norway," In *Directions in Sociolinguistics*, edited by J. J. Gumperz and Dell Hymes. New York: Holt, Rinehart & Winston.

Bowers, Faubion, "Drama." *International Encyclopedia of Social Science*. Vol. 4. New York: Free Press, 1968.

Buñuel, Luis. *Three Screen Plays: Viridiana, The Exterminating Angel, Simon of the Desert*. New York: Orion Press, 1969.

Burger, H. G. "Syncretism: An Acculturative Accelerator." *Human Organization* 25 (1966): 103–15.

Burke, Kenneth. "Dramatism." In *Communication, Concepts and Perspective*, edited by Lee Thayer. Washington: Sparton Books, 1967.

———. "Interaction," "Dramatism." *International Encyclopedia of Social Science*. Vol. 8. New York: Free Press, 1968.

———. *Language as Symbolic Action*. Berkeley: University of California Press, 1968.

Clurman, Harold. "On Drama and Humanity." *New York Times*, October 10, 1980.

Cohen, Eliot, ed. *Commentary on the American Scene*. New York: Knopf, 1950.

Cuddihy, J. M. "Sigmund Freud's Ordeal of Civility: Jewish Emancipation and Differentiated Modernity." Ph.D. dissertation, Rutgers University, 1972.

Dawidowicz, Lucy. *The War against the Jews 1933–1945*. New York: Bantam Books, 1975.

Deutsch, R. D. "On the Isomorphic Structure of Endings." *Ethology and Sociobiology* 1, no. 7 (October 1979): 41–58.

Douglas, Mary. *Natural Symbols: Explorations in Cosmology*. New York: Pantheon, 1970.

Dubb, A. A. *Jewish South Africans: A Sociological View of the Johannesburg Community*. Occasional Paper no. 21 Grahamstown, S.A.: Institute of Social and Economic Research, 1977.

Dubnow, S. M. *History of the Jews in Russia and Poland*. Vol. 2. Translated by I. Friedlander. Philadelphia: Jewish Publication Society, 1918.

Durkheim, Emile. *The Division of Labor in Society.* Translated by G. Simpson. New York: Free Press, 1949.

———. *The Elementary Forms of the Religious Life.* Translated by J. W. Swain. New York: Free Press, [1954] 1965.

———. *Moral Education.* Translated by E. K. Wilson and H. Schnurer. New York: Free Press, 1961.

Efron, David. *Gesture and Environment.* New York: Kings Crown Press, 1941.

Elazar, Daniel J., and Monson, Rela Geffen. "The Synagogue Havurah: An Experiment in Restoring Adult Fellowing to the Jewish Community." *Jewish Journal of Sociology,* vol. 21, no. 1 (June 1979).

Eliade, Mircea. *Cosmos and History.* Translated by W. Trask. New York: Harper & Row, 1959.

———. *The Sacred and the Profane: The Nature of Religion.* New York: Harcourt & Brace, 1968.

———. *A History of Religious Ideas.* Vol. 1. Translated by W. Trask. Chicago: University of Chicago Press, 1978.

Eliot, T. S. *Notes toward the Definition of Culture.* New York: Harcourt & Brace, 1949.

Emmanuel, Isaac S., and Emmanuel, Suzanne A. *A History of the Jews of the Netherlands Antilles.* Vol. 1. Cincinnati: American Jewish Archives, 1970.

Ervin-Tripp, Susan. "An Analysis of the Interaction of Language, Topic and Listener." In *Readings in the Sociology of Language,* edited by J. A. Fishman. The Hague: Mouton, 1968.

Feinsilver, L. M. "Yiddish and American English." *Chicago Jewish Forum* 14 (1956): 71–76.

Fernandez, James W. "Persuasions and Performances: Of the Beast in Everybody . . . and the metapphors of Everyman." *Daedalus* (Winter 1972), pp. 39–60.

Finkelstein, Louis. "The Jewish Religion." In *The Jews: Their Religion and Culture,* edited by L. Finkelstein. New York: Harper & Row, 1955.

Firth, Raymond. *Symbols: Public and Private.* Ithaca: Cornell University Press, 1973.

Fishman, Aryei. "The Anonymous Minyan." Paper presented at the meetings of the Israel Sociological Society, Jerusalem, 1980.

Fishman, J. "Who speaks What Language to Whom and When." *La Linguistique* 2 (1965): 67–88.

————. *Yiddish in America*. Bloomington: Indiana University Press, 1965.

Foss, Martin. *Symbol and Metaphor in Human Experience*. Lincoln: University of Nebraska Press, [1949] 1964.

Freud, Sigmund. "Further Recommendations in the Technique of Psychoanalysis: Recollection, Repetition and Working-through." In *Collected Papers*. Vol. 2. Translated by Joan Riviere. New York: Basic Books, [1914] 1959.

————. "The Loss of Reality: Neurosis and Psychosis." In *Collected Papers*. Vol. 2. Translated by Joan Riviere. New York: Basic Books, [1924] 1959.

————. *Totem and Taboo*. Translated by J. Strachey. London: Hogarth Press, [1953] 1974.

————. *Jokes and Their Relation to the Unconscious*. Translated by J. Strachey. New York: Norton, 1961.

Gans, H. "The 'Yinglish' Music of Mickey Katz." *American Quarterly* 5 (1953): 213–18.

Garfinkel, H. *Studies in Ethnomethodology*. Englewood Cliffs, N.J.: Prentice-Hall, 1967.

Geertz, Clifford, *The Interpretation of Cultures*. New York: Basic Books, 1973.

Gluckman, Max. *Order and Rebellion in Tribal Africa*. London: Cohen & West, 1963.

Goffman, Erving. *The Presentation of Self in Everyday Life*. New York: Doubleday, 1959.

————. *Encounters: Two Studies in the Sociology of Interaction*. Indianapolis: Bobbs-Merrill, 1961.

————. "Alienation from Interaction." In *Communication and Culture*, edited by A. G. Smith. New York: Holt, Rinehart & Winston, 1966.

————. *Interaction Ritual*. New York: Anchor, 1967.

————. *Relations in Public: Micro Studies of the Public Order*. New York: Basic Books, 1971.

————. *Strategic Interaction*. Philadelphia: University of Pennsylvania Press, 1972.

————. *Frame Analysis*. New York: Harper & Row, 1974.

————. "Replies and Responses." *Language in Society* 5, no. 3 (December 1976): 257–313.

————. *Forms of Talk*. Philadelphia: University of Pennsylvania Press, 1981.

Goodblatt, David. "Abraham Weiss: The Search for Literary Forms." In *The Formation of the Babylonian Talmud*, edited by Jacob Neusner. Leiden: Brill, 1970.

Gordis, R. "The Bible as a Cultural Monument." In *The Jews: Their Religion and Culture*, edited by L. Finkelstein. New York: Harper & Row, 1955.

Green, Arthur. *Tormented Master.* University: University of Alabama Press, 1979.

Greenberg, Louis. *The Jews in Russia.* Vol. 1. New Haven: Yale University Press, 1944.

Grunwald, Max. "Das Lernen." In *Jahrbuch für Judische Volkskunde.* Berlin: Hanz Verlag, 1924/25.

Guttman, Julius. *Philosophies of Judaism.* Translated by D. W. Silverman. New York: Holt, Rinehart & Winston, 1964.

Halliday, M. A. K. *Intonation and Grammar in British English.* The Hague: Mouton, 1967.

Handelman, Don. "Components of Interaction in the Negotiation of a Definition of the Situation." In *Language and Man*, edited by W. C. McCormick and S. A. Wurm. The Hague: Mouton, 1976.

Hare, Paul A. "The Dimensions of Social Interaction." In *Communication and Culture*, edited by A. G. Smith. New York: Holt, Rinehart & Winston, 1966.

Hazan, Haim. "Continuity and Change in a Tea-Cup: On the Symbolic Nature of Tea-related Behavior among the Aged." Unpublished paper, n.d.

Heilman, Samuel C. *Synagogue Life: A Study in Symbolic Interaction.* Chicago: University of Chicago Press, 1976.

———. "Constructing Orthodoxy." In *In Gods We Trust: New Patterns of Religious Pluralism in America*, edited by Thomas Robbins and Dick Anthony. New Brunswick, N.J.: Transaction Books, 1980.

———. "Prayer in the Orthodox Synagogue." In *Contemporary Jewry* 6, no. 1 (Spring/Summer 1982): 2–17.

Henderson, Dorothy. "Contextual Specificity, Discretion, and Cognitive Socialization: With Special Reference to Language." *Sociology* 4, no. 3 (1970): 311–38.

Herman, S. D. "Criteria for Jewish Identity." In *World Jewry and the State of Israel*, edited by M. David. New York: Arno Press, 1977.

Herman, Simon D. "Explorations in the Social Psychology of Language Choice." *Human Relations* 14 (1961): 149–64.

Herskovits, Melville, *Man and His Works*. New York: Knopf, 1949.

Heschel, Abraham Joshua. *The Earth is the Lord's: The Inner World of the Jews of Eastern Europe*. New York: Harper & Row, [1950] 1966.

Howe, Irving. *World of Our Fathers*. New York: Harcourt, Brace & Jovanovich, 1976.

Hutchins, Robert Maynard. Commencement Address. University of Judaism, Los Angeles, June 24, 1965.

Hymes, Dell. "The Grounding of Performance and Text in a Narrative View of Life." *Alcheringa* 4, no. 1 (1978): 137–40.

Kanter, Shamai. "Abraham Weiss: Source Criticism." In *The Formation of the Babylonian Talmud*, edited by Jacob Neusner. Leiden: Brill, 1970.

Katz, Jacob. *Out of the Ghetto: The Social Background of Jewish Emancipation, 1770–1870*. Cambridge: Harvard University Press, 1973.

Klapp, Orrin E. *Symbolic Leaders*. Chicago: Aldine, 1964.

Lamm, Norman. "The Voice of Torah in the Battle of Ideas." *Jewish Life* (March/April 1967), pp. 23–31.

Levitats, Isaac. *The Jewish Community in Russia 1772–1844*. New York: Columbia University Press, 1943.

Lewisohn, Ludwig. *What is This Jewish Heritage?* Rev. ed. New York: Schocken Books, 1964.

Malinowski, B. *Coral Gardens and Their Magic*. Vol. 2. London: Allen & Unwin, 1935.

Mauss, Marcel. *The Gift*. Translated by Ian Cunnison. New York: Norton, 1967.

Mayer, Egon. *From Suburb to Shtetl*. Philadelphia: Temple University Press, 1979.

Menes, Abraham. "The Yeshivot in Eastern Europe." *The Jewish People Past and Present*. Vol. 2. New York: Harstin Press, 1948.

Merleau-Ponty, Maurice. *The Prose of the World*. Translated by J. O'Neil. Evanston: Northwestern University Press, 1973.

Mintz, Jerome. *Legends of the Hasidim*. Chicago: University of Chicago Press, 1968.

Moreau, J. L. *Language and Religious Language: A Study in the Dynamics of Translation*. Philadelphia: Westminster Press, 1961.

Neusner, Jacob. *Fellowship in Judaism: The First Century and Today.* London: Valentine Mitchell, 1963.

———, ed. *Contemporary Judaic Fellowship in Theory and in Practice.* New York: Ktav, 1972.

———. *Invitation to the Talmud.* New York: Harper & Row, 1973.

Nida, Eugene A. *Language Structure and Translation: Essays by Eugene A. Nida.* Edited by A. S. Dill. Stanford: Stanford University Press, 1975.

Nisbet, Robert. *Social Change and History.* London: Oxford University Press, 1969.

Otto, Rudolph. *The Idea of the Holy.* Translated by J. W. Harvey. New York: Oxford Press, [1923] 1958.

Ozick, Cynthia. "The Laughter of Akiva." *New Yorker,* November 10, 1980, pp. 50–173.

Parsons, Talcott. *The Structure of Social Action.* New York: McGraw-Hill, 1937.

Pike, K. L. *The Intonation of American English.* Ann Arbor: University of Michigan Press, 1947.

———. *Language in Relation to a Unified Theory of the Structure of Human Behavior.* Glendale, Calif.: Summer Institute of Linguistics, 1955.

Pittinger, R. C.; Hockett, C. F.; Danehy, J. J. *The First Five Minutes: A Sample of Microscopic Interview Analysis.* New York: Paul Martineau, 1960.

Potok, Chaim. *The Chosen.* New York: Simon & Schuster, 1966.

———. *The Promise.* New York: Knopf, 1969.

Potter, Stephen. *One-Upmanship.* New York: Harper & Row, 1951.

Rayfield, J. R. *The Language sof a Bilingual Community.* The Hague: Mouton, 1970.

Reisman, Bernard. *The Havurah: A Contemporary Jewish Experience.* New York: Union of American Hebrew Congregations, 1977.

Reizler, Kurt. "Play and Seriousness." *Journal of Philosophy* 38 (1941): 505–17.

Richards, Audrey I. *Chisungu: A Girl's Initiation Ceremony among the Bemba of Northern Rhodesia.* London: Faber, 1956.

Rieff, Philip. "The Impossible Culture." In *The Soul of Man under Socialism,* by Oscar Wilde. New York: Harper & Row, 1970.

Rommetveit, Ragnar. *On Message Structure: A Framework for the Study of Language and Communication.* New York: Wiley, 1974.

Rubin, Israel. *Satmar: An Island in the City.* Chicago: Quadrangle Books, 1972.

Sapir, Edward. "Selected Writings of Edward Sapir." In *Language, Culture and Personality,* edited by David G. Mandelbaum. Berkeley: University of California Press, 1951.

Schegloff, Emanuel A. "Sequencing in Conversational Openings." In *Advances in the Sociology of Language* II, edited by J. A. Fishman. The Hague: Mouton, 1972. Originally in *American Anthropologist* (1968), pp. 1075–95.

Schmalenbach, Herman. "The Sociological Category of Communion." In *Theories of Society,* edited by T. Parsons, E. Shils, K. Naegele, and J. Pitts. New York: Free Press, 1961.

Schochet, A. "Chevrot Limud Be-Mayot Ha-Taz–Ha-Yach Be-Erets Yisrael, Be-Polin-Lita, U-Be-Germanya" [Study groups in the sixteenth through eighteenth centuries in Israel, Lithuania-Poland, and Germany]. In *Ha-Chinuch.* Kislev, 1956–57.

Schutz, Alfred. *Collected Papers.* Vol. 1. Translated by Maurice Natanson. The Hague: Martinus Nijhoff, 1964.

Schachter, J. *The Belfast Chevra-Gemorra.* London: Narod Press, 1945.

Shulvass, Moses A. *The Jews in the World of the Renaissance: 14th and 15th Century.* Translated by Elvin Kose. Leiden: E. J. Brill, 1973.

Simmel, Georg. *The Sociology of Georg Simmel.* Translated by K. Wolff. Chicago: Free Press, 1950.

Singer, M. "The Cultural Pattern of Indian Civilization." *Far Eastern Quarterly* 15 (1955): 23–26.

Slater, Philip E. *Microcosm: Structural, Psychological and Religious Evolution in Groups.* New York: Wiley, 1966.

Smith, A. G., ed. *Community and Culture.* New York: Holt, Rinehart & Winston, 1966.

Sofer, Abraham, ed. *Igrot Sofrim.* Vienna, 1928. Published in Hebrew.

Soskin, W. F., and Soskin, J. V. "The Study of Spontaneous Talk." In *The Stream of Behavior,* edited by R. G. Baker. New York: Appleton-Century-Crofts, 1963.

Stanislavski, Constantin. *An Actor's Handbook.* Edited and translated by E. R. Hapgood. New York: Theatre Arts Books, 1963.

Turner, Victor. *Schism and Continuity in an African Society.* Manchester: Manchester University Press, 1957.

————. *The Forest of Symbols: Aspects of Ndembu Ritual.* Ithaca: Cornell University Press, 1967.

————. *Dramas, Fields and Metaphors: Symbolic Action in Human Society.* Ithaca: Cornell University Press, 1974.

Underhill, Ruth M. *Autobiography of a Papago Woman.* New York: Krause Reprint, 1936.

Van Gennep, Arnold. "Essai d'une theorie des langues speciales," translated by S. C. Heilman. *Revue des etudes ethnographiques et sociologiques* 1 (1908): 327–37.

Vološinov, V. "Reported Speech." In *Readings in Russian Poetics: Formalist and Structuralist Views,* edited by L. Metejka and K. Pomorska. Cambridge: M.I.T. Press, 1971.

Vossler, Karl, *The Spirit of Language in Civilization.* Translated by O. Oeser. London: Routledge & Kegan Paul, [1932] 1951.

Weber, Max. *The Theory of Social and Economic Organization.* Translated by T. Parsons. Chicago: Free Press, 1947.

Weinreich, Max. *The History of the Yiddish Language.* Translated by S. Noble and J. Fishman. Chicago: University of Chicago Press, 1980.

Weinreich, Uriel. *Languages in Contact.* New York: Linguistic Circle of New York. No. 1, 1953.

————. "Notes on the Yiddish Rise-Fall Intonation Contour." In *For Roman Jakobson,* edited by M. Halle. The Hague: Mouton, 1956.

————. "Influences of Yiddish on American English: Possibilities of a new approach." Paper delivered at YIVO Conference, 1967.

Wheelis, Allen. *The Quest for Identity.* New York: Norton, 1958.

Whyte, W. F. *Street Corner Society.* Chicago: University of Chicago Press, 1951.

Yngve, V. "On Getting a Word in Edgewise." In *Papers from the Sixth Regional Meeting, Chicago Linguistic Society,* edited by M. A. Campbell et al. Chicago: Department of Linguistics, University of Chicago, 1970.

Zborowski, Mark. "The Place of Book-Learning in Traditional Jewish Culture." In *Childhood in Contemporary Cultures,* edited by Margaret Mead and Martha Wolfenstein. Chicago: University of Chicago Press, 1965.

Zborowski, Mark, and Herzog, Elizabeth. *Life Is with People: The Jewish Little Town of Eastern Europe.* New York: International Universities Press, 1952.

INDEX

Acculturation, 193–94; and contra-acculturation, 199
Alienation, 99–100, 102, 151, 154
Allegiance and loyalty, 36, 43, 146, 174, 179, 204. *See esp.* 214–18
Amplifying, 34, 43. *See esp.* 86–88, 109, 114, 156. *See also* Elaboration
Ashkenaz, 37, 69, 164, 167, 192, 193n, 196, 257, 308n64; role of *lerner* in Askenazic Jewry, 1, 3, 6; use of Yiddish in, 7–8, 37
Authority, 20, 22, 39, 41–43, 47; challenge to, 51–56, 120, 142, 156, 203, 265

Beit Rachel, 17, 18, 24, 67, 70, 73, 76, 80, 94, 98, 107, 115, 117, 150, 168, 195, 210, 212, 215, 219, 227, 228, 230, 241, 250, 255, 256, 262, 278, 279, 304n45, 311n2

Cadence, 31, 50, 51, 56, 62, 70, 125, 158. *See esp.* 161–63, 164, 167, 170–75, 180, 181, 183, 190–94, 196, 198–99, 308n64
Chant, 6, 41, 50, 52, 54, 62, 68–71, 125, 164, 168–69, 170, 174, 195, 196. *See also* Gemore-nign
Choric repetition, 74
Circle and sound, 167–72

Code switching, 169–76, 181, 190, 306n37
Collective sentiment, 87–88, 94, 97
Communion, 198, 204, 205–6, 210, 216, 217, 246, 261, 292
Communitas, 204
Contemporary life, 16–17, 19, 63, 64, 88–89; norms and practices of, 135, 187, 189, 194, 307n55
Contemporization, 62–66, 88–89, 92, 100, 107, 154, 187, 189, 226, 254, 300n7, 300n11
Cosmopolitanism, 169, 174, 183, 184, 190, 194; in modern Orthodox, 10
Cues and cuing, 6, 34, 52, 70, 74, 85. *See esp.* 86–88, 91, 98, 102, 104, 109, 114, 117, 120, 122, 123, 128, 153, 199, 234, 268, 271; as *lernen* move, 128, 131, 133, 140, 143, 144, 150, 154–55, 178
Cultural drama, 72, 154, 155. *See also* Cultural performance
Cultural expressions, 80–82
Cultural performance, 25, 51, 52, 61–110, 140, 143, 162, 180, 203, 246; siyum as, 261. *See also* cultural drama
Cultural ties, 94–97, 138
Cultural transformation, 166, 180

Devorim betalim, 118

333